"*Free Your Mind* by Ellen Bass and Kate Kaufman is one of the most important books compiled since the lesbian/gay/bisexual liberation movement started. This is a book that should be read and kept by every adult to give away to the young people they meet who are in the process of coming out. It is a book that should be in every school library to help young people who don't realize there are millions of fellow sojourners just like them."

—Rev. Troy Perry, Founder/Moderator, Universal Fellowship of Metropolitan Community Churches (MCC)

"This is the best single guide I have seen for gay youth. Truly readable, lively, and never stuffy, it covers every aspect of life—school, family, friends, romance, and sex. The style is conversational and filled with personal accounts and examples that bring reality to every topic. The counsel is sound and thoughtful. This book is long overdue and will become the basic 'first book' for young people."

—Mitzi Henderson, National President, Parents, Families, and Friends of Lesbians and Gays (PFLAG)

"Ellen Bass and Kate Kaufman have utilized their skills and experience as counselors, lecturers, and parents to provide an urgently needed resource for young people questioning their sexuality. I hope that *Free Your Mind* will soon be found in all libraries, high schools, and middle schools to help our young people cope with the difficult challenges of understanding their own sexual orientation."

—Melinda Paras, Executive Director, National Gay and Lesbian Task Force

"A wonderful resource for lesbian, gay, and bisexual youth. It will help many young people across the country understand that they are not alone. Unless we let lesbian and gay youth know they are valued, we will lose them to suicide, AIDS, or hidden unhappy lives."

—Frances Kunreuther, Executive Director, Hetrick-Martin Institute

"*Free Your Mind* is packed with personal vignettes, windows into the minds and hearts of real persons, teens and young adults confronting unwelcome personal realities or celebrating victories. . . . Most of those whose stories are in *Free Your Mind* have navigated successfully through stormy waters, and descriptions of experience as well as positive insights will touch a great many readers."

—Rev. Dean Hay, Coordinator, Presbyterians for Lesbian/Gay Con-

D0210579

"This book breaks new ground in the struggle to help young people survive in an anti-gay environment. *Free Your Mind* gives them practical tools for survival, and it encourages them to reach beyond mere survival to also create change and offer their greatest potential to their communities."

—Kevin Cathcart, Executive Director,
Lambda Legal Defense and Education Fund

"Gay, lesbian, and bisexual youth have grown up in a world where a lack of visibility and a general societal ignorance about who and what they were meant confusion, depression, victimization, even death. *Free Your Mind* contains the knowledge that is crucial for us all as we educate ourselves and others on how to change that world."

—William Waybourn, Managing Director,
Gay & Lesbian Alliance Against Defamation (GLADD)

free
your
mind

Also by Ellen Bass

The Courage to Heal: A Guide for Women Survivors
of Child Sexual Abuse
(with Laura Davis)

I Never Told Anyone: Writings by Women Survivors
of Child Sexual Abuse
(with Louise Thornton)

Beginning to Heal: A First Book for Survivors
of Child Sexual Abuse
(with Laura Davis)

Our Stunning Harvest (poetry)

For Earthly Survival (poetry)

I'm Not Your Laughing Daughter (poetry)

I Like You to Make Jokes with Me, But
I Don't Want You to Touch Me (for children)

free your mind

The Book for Gay,
Lesbian, and Bisexual Youth
—and Their Allies

Ellen Bass Coauthor of *The Courage to Heal*
and **Kate Kaufman**

HarperPerennial
A Division of HarperCollinsPublishers

Ellen Bass and Kate Kaufman offer lectures, seminars, and program consultation. For more information write:

Ellen Bass and Kate Kaufman
P.O. Box 994
Santa Cruz, CA 95061-0994

Grateful acknowledgment is made for permission to reprint portions of the following copyrighted material:

Rev. Dr. Professor John B. Cobb, Jr., *Is Homosexuality a Sin?* (Washington, D.C.: PFLAG) 1992.

Robert Francis, "Hallelujah: A Sestina," *The Orb Weaver* (Hanover, New Hampshire: Wesleyan University Press) 1960.

The excerpt from "On Children," by Kahlil Gibran, from *The Prophet* by Kahlil Gibran. Copyright 1923 by Kahlil Gibran and renewed 1951 by Administrators C.T.A. of Kahlil Gibran Estate and Mary G. Gibran. Reprinted by permission of Alfred A. Knopf, Inc.

Judy Grahn, *Another Mother Tongue* (Boston: Beacon Press) 1990.

"Shake Hands," by A. E. Housman from *The Collected Poems of A. E. Housman*. Copyright 1939, 1940 by Holt, Rinehart & Winston, Inc. Copyright © 1967 by Robert E. Symons. Reprinted by permission of Henry Holt and Co., Inc.

The lines from "(The Floating Poem, Unnumbered)" from "Twenty-One Love Poems," by Adrienne Rich are reprinted from *The Dream of a Common Language: Poems 1974–1977* by Adrienne Rich, by permission of the author and W. W. Norton & Co., Inc. Copyright © 1978 by W. W. Norton & Co., Inc.

Rainer Maria Rilke, *Letters to a Young Poet* (New York: Random House) 1984.

The lines from "Love," by May Sarton, are reprinted from *Halfway to Silence*, by May Sarton, by permission of W. W. Norton & Co., Inc. Copyright © 1980 by May Sarton.

Ntozake Shange, *for colored girls who have considered suicide/when the rainbow is enuf* (New York: Macmillan) 1976.

Marianne Williamson, *A Return to Love* (New York: HarperCollins) 1992.

FREE YOUR MIND. Copyright © 1996 by Ellen Bass and Kate Kaufman. All rights reserved. Printed in the United States of America. No part of this book may be used or reproduced in any manner whatsoever without written permission except in the case of brief quotations embodied in critical articles and reviews. For information address HarperCollins Publishers, Inc., 10 East 53rd Street, New York, NY 10022.

HarperCollins books may be purchased for educational, business, or sales promotional use. For information please write: Special Markets Department, HarperCollins Publishers, Inc., 10 East 53rd Street, New York, NY 10022.

FIRST EDITION

Library of Congress Cataloging-in-Publication Data

Bass, Ellen.
    Free your mind: the book for gay, lesbian, and bisexual youth—and their allies/by Ellen Bass and Kate Kaufman. — 1st ed.
        p.   cm.
    Includes index.
    ISBN 0-06-095104-4
    1. Gay youth—United States—Psychology. 2. Gay youth—United States—Social Conditions. 3. Lesbian Youth—United States—Psychology. 4. Lesbian Youth—United States—Social Conditions. 5. Coming out (Sexual orientation—United States. I. Kaufman, Kate. II. Title.
HQ76.2.U5B38   1996
305.23'5—dc20   96-4157

96 97 98 99 00 ❖/RRD 10 9 8 7 6 5 4 3 2

305.235
BAS
1996

contents

PART 3: FAMILY

PART 4: SCHOOL

acknowledgments

We are deeply grateful to the multitude of people who so generously shared their time, their stories, their talents, wisdom, and skills to bring this book into being. At the top of the list are the fabulous gay, lesbian, and bisexual youth whose honesty, courage, chutzpah, and determination have been an inspiration.

We'd like to thank:

Our original editor, Janet Goldstein, whose brilliant conceptualization shaped the formation of the book. And our present editor, Eric Steel, who has carried the book through with vision, distinction, and dedication, and Sarah Polen for conscientious attention.

Our agent, Charlotte Raymond, for her unflagging support and for helping us navigate unfamiliar terrain in what had to be the hottest summer in Massachusetts history.

In the category of people who helped more than can be imagined are Laura Davis and Chris Kryzan. Thank you Laura, for the inordinate time you gave to critiquing every blessed version of the manuscript and to Chris for reading the manuscript with particular insight, being interviewed twice, and providing essential resources.

For their perspective, encouragement, and criticism of the manuscript as a whole, Lucy Diggs, Jonathan Green, Sara Kershnar, Pam Mitchell, Sherri Paris, and Michael Stevens.

For their careful reading of portions of the manuscript: Kellie Allyn, Karyn Bristol, Jim Dickey, Denah Joseph, Rose Moonwater, Amy Pine, Megan L. Rudesill, Lynne Schaffer, Kristin Sharp, Eliza Linley, Robert Nation, Liz Ryan, Maryann Savage, Stone, and Darlene Wilcox.

For their contributions, information, expertise, support, and resources: Rick Aguirre of *InsideOUT*, Linda Alter, Terry Cavanaugh, Sarah Colby, Jim Dickey, Alyx Flatley, Kevin Jennings, Pat and Donna, Ida Kuluk, Arthur Lipkin, Audrey May of Meristem Bookstore, Shannon Minter, Suzanne Nicholas, Gary Pforzheimer, Mary Pforzheimer, Susan Rabinovitz, Avi Rose, Liz Ryan, Merrie Schaller, and Celia Schepps.

For transcribing almost a hundred and twenty long interviews, Susan Beck, Becky Luening, Sandralee Watters, and especially, Rose Moonwater.

For their fine photography, Joan Bobkoff and Cathy Cade. And the lesbian, gay, and bisexual youth—and their allies—who were photographed: K. Renee Albe, Kellie Allyn, Leonie Bavrera-Chin, Rachel Bills, John Bunch, Jaycee Crawford, Tommy Crawford, Quang Dang, Carolyn Derwing, Jim Dickey, Famy Diener, Armond Dorsey, Vanessa Dowling, Lisa Evert, Christine Fitzgerald, Alyx Flatley, Michael Galetto, Gary Harrold, Ben Hecht, Tracy Infante, Franklin King-Pierce, Carmen Klucsor, Ken Klucsor, Michelle Klucsor, Jim Kotaska, Yael Lachman, Pat Langlois, Richard Lidzbarski, Anne Lober, Jesus Martinez-Lopez, Rhondalyn Moran, Alicia Nickel, Daphne Oliver, Cori Oliveri, Susan Parrish, Alisa Peck, Chad K. Pifer, Barb Regan, Chad Sanger, Caroline Shipley, Stone, Kim Tiede, Penni Toledo, Laurie C. Van De Werfhorst, Carlos Vargas, and Michelle Vargas.

For sharing their experiences and wisdom, we thank: Rick Aguirre, Judy Allen, Brooks Anderson, Beth Anthony, Amy Armenia, Gail Atkins, Carroll Austin-Jewitt, Jerry Bang, Sharon Bishop, Frankie Bookey, Jack Bookey, Dan Brassil, Margaret Brown, Susan Butler, Cesar, Nancy Carrero, Heather Cassell, Vickie Clark, Ned Cost, Tommy Crawford, Denee Deckert, Quang Dang, Mike Durkin, Verna Eggleston, Ruth Eller, John Erwin, Al Ferreira, Dixie Fletcher, Craig Fox, Dorothy Garbutt, Tina Garrett, Kirsten Gerber, Laura Giges, Kathy Gill, Kevin Gogin, Jonathan Green, Chris Hannon, Stacey Harris, Jean Hart, Krisana Hodges, Carla Holt, Ed Holterhoff, Linda

Hooper, Andy Humm, Jon Imparato, Gail Jaffer, Jon Johnston, Nancy Kailing, Kaleo Kaluhiwa, Michael Kaplan, Jennifer Keesey, Sara Kershnar, Michelle Klucsor, Sam Kohn, Frances Kunreuther, David LaFontaine, Sandy Lane, Pat Langlois, Michael A. Latz, David Leonard, Joselin Leonard, Amy Lew, Richard Litvak, Brooke Lober, Frank Lonberg, Kate Lonberg-Lew, Anthony Lovari, Ruth Ellen Luehr, Renee McGaughy, Paula Marcus, Sandy Miller, Arwyn Moore, Richard John Nelson, Suzanne Nicholas, John Oleksy, Daisy Oliver, Daphne Oliver, Jimmy Oar, Luna Ortiz, Rachel Pfeffer, Ken Plate, Connie Pottle, April Quaker, Gary Remafedi, Hyde Revilla, Julio Rosa, Joe Salvemini, Ron Schmidt, Curt Shepard, Alice Sicular, George Sicular, Wiggsy Sivertsen, Chuck Smith, Corky Smith, Candace Steele, Charles Steele, Michael Stevens, David Stocks, Frances Stocks, Stone, Bunny Tarquinio, George Tarquinio, Rachel Timoner, Mary Tinucci, Leo Treadway, Judith Ulseth, Virginia Uribe, Michelle Vargas, Mary Voit, David Waterbury, Ruth Waterbury, Sylvia Weisenberg, Billie Weiser, Kay Williams, and Alessandra Zarate.

Thank you from Kate to:
My coauthor, Ellen, for being such a delight to collaborate with and for believing in me. My friends for cheering me on. My son, Guthrie Dolin, for his encouragement, advice, and unconditional love. My mother, Jinny Freidenberg, for her generous support. My brother, Bob Freidenberg, for shouldering extra responsibility when this book kept me too busy. Willie and Joey for providing such sweet comfort. Max for sharing his candy. And my partner, Kellie, for her contagious enthusiasm, nurturance, and enchanting love.

Thank you from Ellen to:
My coauthor, Kate, for your commitment and for your graciousness. My friends, for your generosity, community, and love. Amy Pine, for kindness and cappuccino. Lance Reiners, for beauty. And Irene van der Zande, for walks. My mother, Mildred Bass, for all the years of reassurance. My brother, Herb Bass, for never being too busy. My partner, Janet, for your tenderness and slipping in those good times. My daughter, Saraswati, for inspiring me again and again to try to make the world a better place. And my son, Max, for sheer joy.

◇   ◇   ◇   ◇   ◇   ◇   ◇   ◇   ◇   ◇

Our deepest fear is not that we are inadequate. Our deepest fear is that we are powerful beyond measure. It is our light, not our darkness, that most frightens us. We ask ourselves, who am I to be brilliant, gorgeous, talented and fabulous? Actually, who are you *not* to be? You are a child of God. Your playing small doesn't serve the world. There's nothing enlightened about shrinking so that other people won't feel insecure around you. We were born to make manifest the glory of God that is within us. It's not just in some of us; it's in everyone. And as we let our own light shine, we unconsciously give other people permission to do the same. As we are liberated from our own fear, our presence automatically liberates others.

—Marianne Williamson, from A Return to Love,
as quoted by Nelson Mandela in his inaugural speech
as President of South Africa, May 1994

introduction

> I've been active in lesbian and gay youth groups and we are
> not just suffering. We're challenging the boundaries. We're
> challenging the way relationships are viewed. We're chal-
> lenging the way that sexuality is being defined. We're not
> apologizing. We're not hiding. We know what we deserve.
> We're proud of who we are. We are groundbreakers.
>
> —*Doe, twenty-three-year-old lesbian*

"Free your mind—and the rest will follow." So go the words sung
by En Vogue about destroying stereotypes and overcoming prejudice. And indeed it is true. As we are able to recognize the beauty
and brilliance in each of us—including ourselves—it becomes possible for us to transform the world.

As gay, lesbian, and bisexual youth, you face formidable obstacles, but there are also exciting opportunities. Though you may be
grappling with the process of self-discovery—or rejection or harassment—the rewards are well worth the struggle. Few things in life

are more satisfying than the experience of being your whole self, simply and honestly, and feeling good about who you are. Whether you are terrified, optimistic, or both, the journey to wholeness and pride awaits you. Every day, more and more lesbian, gay, and bisexual youth are standing up, speaking out, and demanding both rights and recognition.

As you pick up this book, you may be on a college campus with other gay, lesbian, and bisexual youth. Or you may be isolated in a hostile high school. You might be in a family that accepts your sexual orientation. Or in a family that you dare not tell. You could be working in a cafe where you can be openly gay or in a job where you have to hide. You may be in a large urban area with many gay resources or in a rural community with no visible gay presence.

Wherever you are, the most important thing for you to know is that *you are not alone.* There are other gay, lesbian, and bisexual youth—lots of them—who are also moving along the spectrum of self-discovery, struggle, affirmation, and pride.

our rightful place in the world

Although it still exerts its ugly power, homophobia is old. All over the world, people are beginning to see that hatred and fear of people who are different from themselves are destructive to us all and instead are learning to welcome and celebrate our rich diversity. If this news has not yet reached your school, church, or town, it will. There's a whole new mentality being born.

Society has controlled us by teaching us to hate ourselves. The voices of homophobia can demoralize us so effectively that we don't need anything beyond their constant judgment to make us feel ashamed. But you don't have to buy it.

Through heroic acts of defiance, both in the delicate interior of the private mind and in the public world, gay and lesbian youth are casting off shame and the acceptance of second-class status and proclaiming their worth, their power, and their rightful place in the world.

it takes real courage

It takes real courage to explore your feelings and to acknowledge— even to yourself—your sexual orientation. We hope this book will be supportive to you. In it you'll find practical information, validation, reassurance, and some advice. Reading about the experiences of other gay, lesbian, and bisexual youth can give you more understanding of the process you're going through and some ideas about how to make it easier on yourself. And for those of you actively working to change the world, we hope it will give you inspiration.

Free Your Mind is divided into six parts that speak to the basic aspects of the lives of gay, lesbian, and bisexual youth: Self-Discovery, Friends and Lovers, Family, School, Spirituality, and Community. We have also included many suggestions for how to connect with other gay youth—and supportive adults—whether through books, mail, computer, phone, or in person. Feel free to read what you need—in any order. You can also give chapters to your parents, teachers, or religious leaders.

sharing their stories

In this book over fifty young people generously share their lives, their joy, their pain, their hopes and fears, their commitment, wisdom, and passion. They come from all across the country, from both urban and rural areas. They range in age from fifteen to their early twenties, and represent a wide variety of religions, races, cultures, ethnic backgrounds, and economic classes.

Mostly you'll meet them by their real names. A few are using pseudonyms. Invariably, *all* the young people wanted to use their real names, and those who couldn't wished it were safe to do so. This reflects a profound desire to be recognized in the world as one's true self.

We also interviewed many parents, siblings, teachers, religious leaders, counselors, and other adults who care about lesbian, gay, and bisexual young people. Over and over the youth and their allies expressed the hope that sharing their stories would help ease the path for other young people and their families. As Jonathan says, "If telling what I've gone through helps someone, then it makes it so much more OK that I had to go through it all."

the inadequacies of our language

We wish there were an all-inclusive word for "gay, lesbian, and bisexual" that everyone felt comfortable with. But unfortunately, there isn't.

Thus we wind up having community centers with names like the LGBTCC—Lesbian, Gay, Bisexual, and Transgendered Community Center.

Some people have reclaimed the word "queer," taking this epithet that's been used to demean and insult and transforming it into a source of pride. But for others, "queer" continues to be offensive. And "homosexual" feels too clinical here and has its own negative slant from the past.

Just as we have no all-purpose word for a domestic partner, or even for someone we're dating, there's no good, short name that includes us all. Therefore, we usually use the whole string—"gay, lesbian, and bisexual." And sometimes, for relief, we use just "gay" to mean everybody.

INFORMATION FOR PARENTS, EDUCATORS, CLERGY, COUNSELORS, AND OTHER ALLIES

Gay youth need recognition, understanding, and validation to succeed in a challenging and often inhospitable world. The statistics on the suffering of gay youth are staggering:

◇ As many as 30 to 40 percent of runaway and homeless youth are lesbian, gay, or bisexual.[1]

◇ Almost 60 percent of gay males and 30 percent of lesbians are verbally or physically attacked in junior high school, senior high school, or college.[2] And over a quarter of bisexual and gay male teenagers are forced to drop out of school because of this harassment.[3]

◇ Nearly 60 percent of gay and bisexual male teens have drug and alcohol problems,[4] and more than half of lesbian and gay youth report periods of extreme anxiety or depression.[5]

◇ Gay, lesbian, and bisexual youth are also at increased risk for suicide. In 1989, a study by the U.S. Department of Health and Human Services found that lesbian and gay youth are two to three times more likely to attempt suicide than other young people—and they may account for up to 30 percent of completed youth suicides. The report stated, "The root of the problem of gay youth suicide is a society that discriminates against and stigmatizes homosexuals while failing to recognize that a substantial number of its youth has a gay or lesbian orientation."[6]

Although these grim statistics are part of the picture, they're not the whole story. In spite of the treatment they have suffered and the obstacles they face, gay, lesbian, and bisexual youth are determined to create successful lives for themselves.

With enormous courage and vision, gay youth are at the forefront of an exciting movement working for respect for all people. They are making changes in their schools, churches, and communities, insisting that we all have the freedom to be who we are and to love who we love.

If you are reading this book, you are already an ally. You care about gay youth and want to learn how to be of help. We hope that *Free Your Mind* will provide the accurate information, guidance, and encouragement you need to support gay, lesbian, and bisexual youth.

[1]Michele D. Kipke, Susan O'Connor, Ray Palmer, and Richard G. MacKenzie, "Street Youth in Los Angeles," *Arch Pediatric Adolescent Medicine* (May 1995, vol. 149), pp. 513–519.

[2]Larry Gross and Steven K. Aurand, *Discrimination and Violence Against Lesbian Women and Gay Men in Philadelphia and the Commonwealth of Pennsylvania* (Philadelphia: Philadelphia Lesbian and Gay Task Force, 1992). Cited by Anthony R. D'Augelli and Lawrence J. Dark, "Lesbian, Gay, and Bisexual Youths," in Leonard D. Eron, Jaquelyn Gentry, and Peggy Schlegel, editors: *Reason to Hope: A Psychological Perspective on Violence and Youth* (Washington, D.C.: American Psychological Association, 1994), p. 179.

[3]Gary Remafedi, "Adolescent Homosexuality: Psychosocial and Medical Implications," *Pediatrics* 79 (March 1987). Cited by Rich C. Savin-Williams and Kenneth M. Cohen, "Psychosocial Outcomes of Verbal and Physical Abuse Among Lesbian, Gay, and Bisexual Youths," in Rich C. Savin-Williams and Kenneth M. Cohen, editors: *The Lives of Lesbians, Gays, and Bisexuals: Children to Adults* (Fort Worth: Harcourt Brace, 1996), p. 187.

[4]Remafedi, p. 189.

[5]Margaret Schneider, "Developing Services for Lesbian and Gay Adolescents," *Canadian Journal of Community Mental Health* (Spring 1991, vol. 10, no. 1) as cited by D'Augelli and Dark in *Reason to Hope,* p. 181.

[6]Paul Gibson, "Gay Male and Lesbian Youth Suicide," in *Report of the Secretary's Task Force on Youth Suicide,* Publication No. ADM 89–1623, vol. 3 (Washington, D.C.: U.S. Department of Health and Human Services, 1989), p. 110.

There are chapters here specifically for you—for parents, educators, clergy, counselors, and members of the community. We urge you to read not only the chapters addressed to you, but all the chapters for gay youth as well. The more you know about gay, lesbian, and bisexual young people, the more able you will be to offer meaningful support.

our hope

Our goal in writing *Free Your Mind* has been to contribute to making the world a safer, happier place for lesbian, gay, and bisexual youth and those who love them. We hope to help families come together in love and understanding, to affirm loving and respectful relationships, to lessen despair and isolation, to honor the fabulous youth who are leading this vital liberation movement, and to validate the worth of all young people, nurturing self-esteem, pride, and joy.

Cathy Cade © 1995

Cathy Cade © 1995

Joan Bobkoff © 1995

Joan Bobkoff © 1995

part 1

self-discovery

Joan Bobkoff © 1995

Cathy Cade © 1995

◇   ◇   ◇   ◇   ◇   ◇   ◇   ◇   ◇   ◇

1
we are everywhere

The only queer people are those who don't love anybody.

—*Rita Mae Brown*

> **Rita Mae Brown**
> (b. 1944) is a novelist whose first book, *Rubyfruit Jungle*, is undoubtedly the funniest, best-loved, and most delightful lesbian coming out story of the past two decades.
>
> *(Well-known gay, lesbian, and bisexual people will be highlighted with biographical notes throughout the book.)*

Gay, lesbian, and bisexual people truly are everywhere. They live in large urban areas and in rural communities. They come from every neighborhood. They are part of every kind of family. They are all races and come from all cultures. They work in every occupation. They have every kind of talent imaginable. And they are all ages.

There have always been youth who were lesbian, gay, or bisexual. What's different today is that many young people are able to recognize and name their feelings sooner. And an increasing number are joining the growing movement of gay youth who are demanding recognition as well as fair and equal treatment.

In the last few decades lesbian, bisexual, and gay people have worked for—and gained—significant progress toward equal rights in many areas of life. Openly gay and lesbian people have been elected to public office. Private corporations, as well as some cities, have extended equal benefits to gay and lesbian employees. Gay people are joyously celebrating their commitments to each other and raising families.

And gay youth are insisting that they be acknowledged and respected. They are creating successful lives filled with pride, friendship, love, and satisfaction.

who is gay?

There are all kinds of gay people. There are lesbian mothers, gay fathers, and bisexual grandparents. There are lesbian fire fighters, teachers, and waitresses. There are bisexual garbage collectors, lawyers, and librarians. There are gay poets, mail carriers, and stockbrokers. Gay men come from every race and ethnic group. Lesbians are found in every religion. Bisexuals are rich, poor, and from the middle class.

No one is sure what percentage of the population is gay or lesbian, and there is considerable ongoing debate. A number of studies have been done, with varying results.[1] Because of discrimination

[1]In 1948 the pioneering studies by Alfred Kinsey found that 13 percent of men had engaged mainly in same-sex behavior and 10 percent were almost exclusively homosexual. This study is the basis of the commonly held belief that one in every ten people is gay. In 1953 Kinsey found that up to 8 percent of women had mainly same-sex behavior. (Alfred Kinsey, Wardell B. Pomeroy, and Clyde E. Martin, *Sexual Behavior in the Human Male* [Philadelphia: W.B. Saunders, 1948] and Alfred Kinsey, Wardell B. Pomeroy, Clyde E. Martin, and Paul H. Gebhard, *Sexual Behavior in the Human Female* [Philadelphia: W.B. Saunders, 1953]). In 1993 the Batelle Human Affairs Research Center reported that 2 percent of sexually active American men had had same-sex experiences in the last ten years and that 1 percent reported being exclusively homosexual. (John

and fear, many gay people may not answer honestly when questioned about their attractions and sexual behavior, so it's hard to tell what the real percentages are. And ultimately, it doesn't really matter. What's important is that there are many lesbian, gay, and bisexual people—millions in the United States alone—and we have every reason to expect the same rights as everyone else. All people have the right to love whomever they choose and to have full, safe, and satisfying lives.

what does being gay, lesbian, or bisexual mean?

Being lesbian or gay means that a person's primary romantic, emotional, physical, and sexual attractions and connections are with someone of the same sex. Bisexual people have those attractions to both sexes. Being gay, lesbian, or bisexual is a label that identifies who we fall in love with.

Many young people question—or know—that they are lesbian or gay before they have any sexual experiences at all. Others may have had sexual experiences with the opposite sex but still feel that they are gay. Or they may have had sexual experiences with the same sex but still feel they are heterosexual.

There is an important difference between attraction and experience. You may have same-sex experiences for any number of reasons besides a genuine attraction—because you are curious, because it's convenient, or because you feel pressured. On the other hand, you might have sexual encounters with someone of the opposite sex for reasons other than your own desire—because you are trying to

Billy, Koray Tanfer, William Grady, and Daniel Klepinger, "The Sexual Behavior of Men in the United States," *Family Planning Perspectives* 25 [March/April 1993]:52-60). But the Harvard School of Public Health and the Center for Health Policy Studies in Washington published findings in 1994 stating that about 18 percent of both women and men have been *attracted* to or been sexual with someone of the same sex since age fifteen. From 2 to 4 percent of the women and 4 to 11 percent of the men reported homosexual behavior in the last five years. (Randell Sell, James Wells, and David Wypig, "The Prevalence of Homosexual Behavior and Attraction in the United States, the United Kingdom and France: Results of Population-Based Samples," *Archives of Sexual Behavior* [June 1995, vol. 24, no. 3], pp. 235-248).

fit in with society's expectations, because you are lonely, because you don't know how to say no, or because your "no" isn't heeded. Your sexual orientation is more about who you truly are drawn to than about what your experience has been.

If you are a young person questioning your sexual orientation, you may find it useful to ask yourself who your most deeply felt attractions are for. Who do you get crushes on most often? Who do you usually have romantic fantasies about? Who do you really wish you could spend the rest of your life with? Or just next weekend? The answers to these questions are often helpful in beginning to sort out your feelings.

the spectrum of sexuality

Although it's common to feel more strongly attracted to one sex or the other, many people feel at least some amount of attraction for both sexes. Alfred Kinsey, the famous researcher of sexual behavior, found that our attractions and our sexual behaviors are seldom absolute. While there are some people who have attractions and experiences *only* with the same or *only* with the opposite sex, most people fall in between the two extremes.

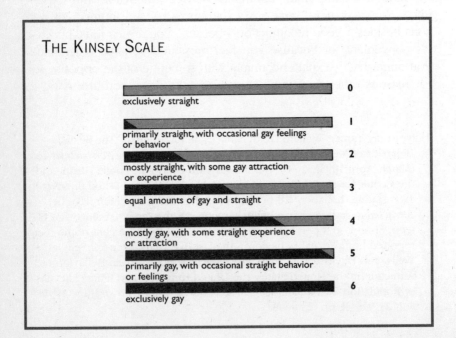

THE KINSEY SCALE

0 — exclusively straight

1 — primarily straight, with occasional gay feelings or behavior

2 — mostly straight, with some gay attraction or experience

3 — equal amounts of gay and straight

4 — mostly gay, with some straight experience or attraction

5 — primarily gay, with occasional straight behavior or feelings

6 — exclusively gay

We live in a society that is more comfortable when things are neatly defined—either gay or straight. But many people don't experience life quite that simply.

bisexual people

Bisexual people have the potential to feel sexually attracted to, and to fall in love with, someone of either sex. They are able to experience desire and intimacy with a special person, regardless of gender. Alessandra, who has had relationships with both men and women, explains her feelings:

> I like women because they are women and I like men because they are men. I used to think the feelings were the same, but they're not; not to me at least. The chemistry, the lovemaking, the communication is totally different. They're both wonderful and they're both part of me. I couldn't turn one set of feelings on and turn the other off. Both are always there.

Yet because society seems to like simple labels, bisexual people often experience pressure to fit into restrictive boxes. As Anni says:

> I find it real hard to describe myself as bisexual because the heterosexual community closes me out for having that gay part and the homosexual community closes me out for having that heterosexual part. I think it's almost harder to be bisexual than to be just gay or straight. I'm seventeen so I'm all over the place and I'm constantly changing, and if you don't like that, tough luck. I want to say I'm bisexual a lot. Instead people call me gay. I think a lot of bisexuals are hidden. They choose one world or the other to live in. I don't think it has to be that way.

Some bisexual people date both men and women. Others are in committed monogamous relationships. And sometimes bisexuality can be a transitional stage that people go through before they discover their gay—or straight—identity.

One bisexual, Susan, says, "People always ask me if I'm confused about who I like. I'm not at all confused. It feels perfectly natural to me to be attracted to both women and men. I think what those people are really saying is that my being bisexual confuses *them*."

Susan has coined her own word for people who define themselves as either gay or straight. She says they are "monosexual."

why are people gay?

Over the years there have been many theories about why some of the world's population is homosexual. Basically these theories fall into one of three possibilities: nature, nurture, or a combination of the two.

Nature, in this context, means you were born gay—it's your nature. Recently there seems to be evidence from scientific research to support this theory that homosexuality may be biologically determined.

Nurture refers to your life experience and how it has affected your development. In the past it was assumed that if you were gay, something damaging must have happened to make you that way. Now it's widely accepted that this is not true. Our experiences—both positive and negative—may play a part in determining our romantic and sexual attractions, but no one is gay or lesbian solely because of a harmful—or beneficial—experience.

While some people have favored the nature theory and some the nurture, others have proposed that a combination of both nature and nurture are involved in determining sexual orientation. At this point no one is totally sure, though scientists are continuing to study these questions.

Interestingly, although there is quite a lot of talk about why gay people are gay, no one has done much research on why straight people are straight. The reason for this, of course, is that much of our society still presumes that being heterosexual is "normal" and therefore needs no explanation, whereas being gay, lesbian, or bisexual is abnormal and so needs to be caused by *something*. In fact, homosexuality, bisexuality, and heterosexuality are *all* simply variations of human sexuality.

Understanding why people are gay may help some people accept gay, lesbian, and bisexual people. If that's so, then the information is certainly worthwhile. However, it is also possible that once scientists know why people are gay, that information could be used in discriminatory ways.

In the meantime, the question of why some people are lesbian, bisexual, and gay is less important than the fact that we *are* lesbian, bisexual, and gay. And that we—like all people—deserve to be treated with respect.

is it a choice?

The question as to whether being gay, lesbian, or bisexual is a choice is one that comes up over and over. Often there is an unspoken assumption that if there were any choice involved, then people would—or should—choose not to be gay. This attitude makes an exploration of the role of choice difficult.

We know that many gay and lesbian people have experienced absolutely no choice in their sexual orientation. From the time they were small children, and long before they had any words for homosexuality, they had feelings of attraction for people of their own sex. As Patrick relates:

> I was always a little bit different, even when I was very young. Now I'm sixteen and the feelings are still there. I think you don't choose to have these feelings, but you can choose to come out and affirm yourself being gay. That's where the choice part comes in for me. That's why I think there really shouldn't be discrimination, because all you're choosing is to affirm the fact that you're gay; it's not the fact that you've chosen to have those feelings.

In reality, people don't choose to be attracted to anyone. Straight people don't *decide* to be attracted to people of the other sex. They simply find that they have those feelings. And the same is true of gay people.

Choice may enter the picture, though, with bisexuality. Since bisexual people have the capacity to be attracted to someone of either gender, if they form a relationship with someone of their own sex, they are, in a sense, choosing. But they are not choosing to feel the attraction. They are simply choosing to follow their genuine feelings.

It's not sufficient to justify our lives based on the argument that we have no choice, because that is not the experience of all bisexual, lesbian, and gay people. Instead, we need to affirm everyone's right to be in whatever love relationship they find most healthy and fulfilling.

homophobia

We live in a society that is often prejudiced against gay, lesbian, and bisexual people. Gay people are subjected to discrimination, rejection, verbal assaults, and even physical violence. There are many negative stereotypes about gay people that fuel this homophobia. Because of these attitudes, many lesbian, gay, and bisexual people keep the truth of their sexual orientation hidden away—they stay in the closet, invisible.

There is a fantasy shared by many gay people about waking up one morning and finding that all lesbian, bisexual, and gay people have blue skin for a day. It would dramatically change the world if all people with same-sex feelings were visible to each other and to everyone else. Everyone would see *lots* of people that they know, respect, or love—people they never would have guessed were gay. Most people would find it hard to hold on to all their old negative stereotypes if they knew that all of these real people in their daily lives were gay.

Since most people are heterosexual, our society tends to assume everyone is—unless someone lets it be known otherwise. Revealing your sexual orientation—or coming out—isn't easy, because you often face some negative responses. But it's also hard to stay in the closet and hide your true self. Bisexuals, lesbians, and gay men make many difficult compromises along the way to try to be both true to themselves and to survive well in a sometimes unfriendly world.

◇ INTERNALIZED HOMOPHOBIA

It's virtually impossible to have grown up in a culture that generally has such vicious things to say about gay people and not come to believe those things about yourself. Because of this, even gay, lesbian, and bisexual people may think that there's something wrong with being gay. This internalized homophobia can leak out in both obvious and subtle ways. For example, one young lesbian thought that someone she had just met couldn't be a lesbian because she was "too pretty." And countless young people have feared that they couldn't have enduring relationships, raise children, or accomplish their goals. Even once you consciously begin to challenge those antigay beliefs, some still linger. But as you become more aware of the misinformation you've been taught, you will gradually unlearn these negative perceptions of yourself and the gay community.

people of color

Same-sex feelings have nothing to do with race, ethnicity, culture, or the color of someone's skin. However, the experience of being a gay person of color is often different from the experience of being a white gay person. As Mickie explains:

> I'm a woman, I'm a lesbian, I'm a Latina. I get trouble from everybody. I even get stuff from other Latina lesbians about betraying the culture because I date women outside my race. I don't think so! I'm just being who I am and loving who I love.
>
> All three things are linked together, making it harder for me to go through life. But they are also what I use to protect myself. They're like my guards, like bam, bam, bam, here, have this. Having these things to deal with has made me a stronger person—way more powerful and way more proud.

There are additional complexities when you belong to more than one group that faces prejudice and discrimination. Some people feel as if they became outsiders in their ethnic groups when they came out. Quang describes his pain about this conflict:

> I found strength being part of the Vietnamese-American community, and with my family, because we've had to struggle together about racism. And then having that community reject me as a gay man, and the rift with my parents, is really difficult. I think that's something people of color encounter a lot, the struggle against racism conflicting with the struggle against homophobia.

At times it can feel as if you don't fit with either the gay community or your ethnic community. As Yevette says:

> Sometimes I'll be in a gay group, but they're not racially sensitive. So that is uncomfortable. And it can be uncomfortable to be in an African-American group where they make rude

remarks about gay people. And I think, gosh, we're really all in this together. It's the same racism, sexism, homophobia, all the same thing.

Although being a person of color may make it harder to be gay in some ways, if you have had to face racism your whole life, you may have developed skills that will help you to deal with homophobia as well. As Quang explains, "I've found strength from one struggle and applied it to another."

Community is especially important if you are in a group targeted for prejudice. And if you are facing more than one oppression, it becomes even more vital. Yevette notes:

> There was a big transition for me when I started being around other Black gay women. They were so beautiful and wonderful. It helped me put the different parts of my life together and learn to fully love and accept myself.

TRANSSEXUAL PEOPLE

Transsexuals are people who, though they were born with the body of one sex, feel like they are really a person of the other sex. There is a common false belief that gay people want to be the opposite gender, but this is not true. Some gay and lesbian people have ideas about masculinity and femininity that challenge traditional gender roles, but this is different from feeling trapped in a body that is the wrong gender.

Cecile, a young man who attends high school in Texas, talks about his feelings.

> Starting in elementary school I believed I was a girl in a guy's body. I love being in drag; I love when guys treat me like a woman. It makes me feel good. I don't mind saying that I'm gay, but really I think I'm a woman trapped in a man's body. That's the way I see myself, and I know that I'm never going to change the person that I am. My brother, who accepts me, says he'll help me get treatments and surgery when I'm eighteen.

Transsexual people can be born in male bodies yet believe they are women or born in female bodies and believe they are men. In the last fifty years or so, hormone treatments and surgery have allowed people to change their bodies to match their internal experience.

There are also both straight and gay people who are transvestites—people who like to wear clothes associated with the other sex. People who cross-dress may be gay or straight, transsexual, or content with the gender they were born. The term "transgender" is commonly used to include both transsexuals and transvestites.

It is beyond the scope of this book to address fully the particular concerns of transsexual and transgender youth. For more information, see p. 370 of the Resources.

it's not a lifestyle, it's a life

You sometimes hear people refer to a "gay lifestyle." And well-meaning people talk about being gay, lesbian, or bisexual as a legitimate "alternative lifestyle." But although this is a common description, it is not accurate. Being lesbian, gay, or bisexual is not a lifestyle. Being gay is about who you feel romantic love for. It is a part of your being; it's who you *are* deep down. "Lifestyle" is about the style in which you live. As Carroll, the mother of a lesbian, says:

> There is no such thing as a gay lifestyle. My daughter has pets, she has laundry, she has litter. Come to my house. I've got pets, I have laundry, I have litter. Do I live a straight lifestyle?

Gay people have all different kinds of lifestyles. They may live in or out of the closet. They may care about earning big incomes or put a lot of value on living simply. They may be in committed relationships, raising children and driving a minivan, or they may be single, going to parties and driving a sports car. Lifestyle describes how you live, not who you are.

Al is a middle-aged high school teacher. He is out as a gay man in all parts of his life, including his profession. Here are his thoughts:

> The lifestyle thing is totally misleading to people. My lifestyle is that of an educator. I drive my partner crazy because even during the summer I look for materials to bring into my classroom.

My partner and I live in the suburbs. He's an office manager. When we come home from work most evenings, like a lot of Americans, we watch *Wheel of Fortune* and *Jeopardy* and are in bed by nine or nine-thirty. Fortunately both our families are affirming of us as a couple and we spend a lot of time with them. We haven't been in a nightclub in fifteen years. That's our lifestyle.

Although there is no single gay lifestyle, there *is* a gay community, which is made up of a diversity of subcultures. Though we have varied affinities according to class, race, gender, generation, and geographical region, the whole community shares an extensive history, a rich culture, and a common desire for full human rights.

it's not just a phase

For some young people their feelings of attraction to people of the same sex are a stage of their development that is not long lasting. However, to assume that same-sex attraction is a phase that will pass for *all* young people is a mistake. Yevette recalls:

I had a crush on my eleventh grade English teacher. I told her I loved her, and she said I would grow out of it, that it was normal for adolescent girls to have crushes on their teachers. If I ever see her again I'm going to tell her she was wrong. Now that I'm twenty-five, I think I can safely say that though I outgrew my crush on her, I sure haven't outgrown being gay.

If people discount your same-sex feelings by assuring you that it's a phase, you may feel uncomfortable, hurt, or angry. It's as though they are saying that your feelings aren't OK but you shouldn't worry because you'll get over them. It also implies that same-sex feelings are less meaningful or important than an attraction to the other sex. This is false and hurtful. Love between two men or two women is as intimate and profound as love between a man and a woman. Love is love.

Cathy Cade © 1995

Cathy Cade © 1995

2

coming into your own

And the day came when the risk it took to remain closed in a bud became more painful than the risk it took to blossom.

—Anaïs Nin

The age at which people first realize they have special feelings for someone of the same sex varies enormously. Some are sure of their sexual orientation at a very early age, like Matt, who says the feelings were always there, from as far back as he can remember:

Anaïs Nin (1903–1977) courageously explored her inner life as a woman and an artist in her six-volume *The Diary of Anaïs Nin*, where she wrote frankly of her sexuality, including bisexuality.

I've known really pretty much forever that I liked men, but I was not able to voice it. I remember when I was seven or eight wanting to touch my guy friends. I didn't know why, I just wanted to touch them.

Mickie, an eighteen-year-old lesbian, has this early recollection:

When I was very little I would kiss girls on TV—right on the screen. I would close my eyes and when I opened them, I would be kissing a chip commercial or the newsman.

And Nancy explains:

I was never confused. It was like I leaped out as a lesbian. A true lesbian adventurer, with my cape.

Many young people become aware of their same-sex attractions in adolescence, as they reach puberty and begin to have sexual feelings. Craig recalls his early teens:

In junior high—maybe ten years ago—I started having dreams about men. I remember imagining kissing one of my schoolmates. I remember really struggling with that image, and wanting to dismiss it.

Other young people don't start to think about being lesbian, gay, or bisexual until they leave home and go into the work world or to college. Doe remembers her first feelings for women:

The major changing point for me was in college, when I started to look at women and find them attractive and find them desirable. From that point on the rest just fell into place. I've always found women beautiful. My relationships with women have always been more fulfilling to me. I'd never been much interested in men, even though I'd dated them. So it was very easy for me to see myself with women. And then I just did. I was checking out all the babes in class.

responding to the feelings

When people grow up surrounded by healthy examples of being lesbian or gay, they are more likely to feel comfortable with their first feelings toward someone of their own sex. Stone grew up in a loving lesbian family:

> When I was thirteen and I first started feeling things for my friend, I was really excited. I used to go around on my bike humming "I'm in love with a wonderful girl" to my own made-up tune. I'd just hum. I was ecstatic. I was on top of the world—really, really thrilled. I wrote poetry. I'd dream about her and watch her walk around and watch her play soccer. She was so cute.

Unlike Stone, most of us still get very negative messages about being gay as we grow up, so it's unusual to feel happy about discovering that you are romantically attracted to someone of the same sex. As with any other important realization, most young people initially go through a period of denial and internal conflict before they accept themselves, come out to others, and, ultimately, celebrate who they are. For some people this process may take only months or just a couple of years. For others, it may continue even into adulthood.

The coming out process doesn't follow a direct path from the first to the last step. Nor do we complete a stage never to return to those feelings again. Very often we find ourselves spiraling back and forth as we find our way to fully loving who we are.

denial

Many people spend a long time trying to bury their same-sex feelings to fit into the straight norm. Michelle remembers falling in love with her friend at age thirteen:

> I knew that I loved her emotionally. But then I remember thinking one day I would be physically turned on if I kissed her. That's when I started going into denial. I was keeping a dream journal at the time, and I had a dream that we kissed. And I immediately stopped keeping my dream journal.

Matt had this reaction to his initial feelings:

> I thought I'll do anything for this not to be me. I decided I just won't have sex with men. I'll just have sex with women

and get married and live a normal life. That was my attitude for a long time. I didn't know anyone gay, not anyone. So I tried all this different stuff to make myself be straight, like going to dances with girls. But it really didn't work for me because it made me feel depressed.

recognizing that you're gay

The first step toward self-acceptance is to be honest with yourself. If you are gay, bisexual, or lesbian, it takes a lot of courage to admit it—even to yourself—because you know it's going to be hard to deal with a world that can be cruel to those perceived as different. But honesty, however difficult, is an essential step. It is only when you are real with yourself about what the feelings mean that you can begin to move forward on the journey toward affirming who you are. As Amy explained:

> I was eighteen years old and I was completely miserable. I realized that I didn't want to be in a heterosexual relationship at all. I said to myself, "I need to start over. What would I do if I lived in a perfect world? If I didn't care what my parents thought, what my friends thought, what everybody else in the world thought, who would I date?" I answered the question, "I would date women!" I still had negative images of lesbians, but that was the beginning of being open to the possibility.

When his classmates started calling him "faggot" and "fairy" in grade school, Chris tried to ignore his feelings and act straight, but it didn't last for long:

> I picked on other kids in the class for being faggots. I used my sexist brother-in-law as a role model and copied everything he did. I'm a damn good actor, I'll say. I had my sisters fooled, and I was accepted in class. I never stopped talking about hooters and chicks and babes. It got ridiculous.
> Then in junior high school I couldn't act like that any more. I was dating a girl and feeling so bored. The first time I had sex with her it made me sick. I literally threw up. I hated how I was acting like a sexist jerk, because I really

care about and respect women. So I stopped pretending and let myself feel my true feelings. I knew I was gay, even though I wished I wasn't.

Margaret describes how a conversation with a friend helped her find self-acceptance:

> About a year ago, a couple of friends were at my house. One of them, a guy, asked if he could speak to me privately. We went outside onto my porch and he said—it took him a while to say it because it was obviously very hard for him— "I'm bi." And the words "So am I" just popped out of my mouth.
>
> My heart raced every time I thought about it, but I knew it was true. And it was such a good feeling, such a relief to finally understand what had been going on with me for the last umpteen years.

Jonathan describes the moment when he admitted to himself that he was gay:

> In the ninth grade, major depression. I was still being tormented at school. And one day, my parents were gone and I was at home taking a shower. I was feeling really, really bad. So I'm standing in the shower and I remember saying to myself out loud, "You are gay." I heard myself say it and I absolutely bawled. I literally was crying so hard that I sat down in the shower and just had it out. These were the words I'd heard people say to me so many times, but saying it myself was a hundred times worse than them saying it. And I thought, "This is who you are and you're going to have to start accepting that."

GENDER ROLES

Most kids who grow up to be lesbian, gay, or bisexual seem no different from kids who grow up to be straight. Others, however, challenge expected gender roles at an early age. One mother of a gay son recalls that during the stage when other little boys were playing Batman and jumping off couches with towels tied

ALBUQUERQUE ACADEMY LIBRARY

around their necks, her son was gluing glitter to scraps of cloth and dancing around as a butterfly.

Although this boy grew up to be gay, not all young butterflies do. There are plenty of straight people who don't conform to rigid gender expectations. There are artistic, sensitive, tender gay *and* straight men. There are strong, aggressive, tough straight *and* lesbian women. You can't tell who's gay or straight just by appearance, personality, or behaviors.

It's also true that many young people feel different from others and it's not because they're gay. When you think about it, there are probably more of us who feel different than there are people who feel they fit in.

I KNEW I WAS DIFFERENT FROM AN EARLY AGE

In kindergarten we had a wonderful playhouse area with a little kitchen with a sink and a stove and all that. Well, I always acted out the female roles with the girls. I didn't want to play the daddy who went off to work. I would always want to be in the kitchen. So I knew there was something different even then.

—Jonathan

Even though I was a girl, I liked cars so much. I did have Barbie dolls, and I had the Barbie car. I grabbed the car and threw myself down the hill with the car, and the Barbies would be all bashed in and stuff. I cut my Barbies' hair and I dyed them all kinds of colors. I had chemistry sets, and I blew things up. I ate roaches and I ate flies. I was a complete boy.

—Mickie

I WASN'T SO DIFFERENT

When I was young I did regular guy things. I was big into the military and wanted to be in the army when I got older. I played with G.I. Joes. I had a huge collection. I liked setting them up with the good guys and bad guys getting ready to fight. I liked to leave the scenes all set up and I'd get upset because my big brothers would knock them down.

—Matt

No one had a clue I was going to turn out to be a lesbian. I loved dresses. I had this wonderful twirling dress with bands of color—red, yellow, and turquoise. I wore it almost every day one year in school. I begged for My Pretty Pony and Strawberry Shortcake dolls. I wore nail polish. You couldn't get more typical.

—Jessica

inner conflict

When lesbian, bisexual, and gay people begin to recognize their feelings they often experience a lot of inner conflict. It's natural to feel conflicting emotions given the world we live in—how could you not? Our society still teaches that having same-sex attractions is a negative thing. And yet that attraction is exactly what you may be feeling so deeply.

No one wants to be someone that other people hate. How much inner conflict you experience will depend on many things—the kind of family you have, your religious beliefs, and the nature of the community you live in. But although your circumstances may make it easier, it's never *easy*. Even with loving support, almost everyone goes through some inner conflict.

Chris remembers his early shame about his feelings:

I'd feel so guilty and dirty, like my mother could tell. She'd be looking at me as I was walking down the steps, and I'd want to just jump off the steps because I felt like I was so dirty and I was going to make my mother sad.

At age twenty-four, Arwyn still experiences real inner conflict:

Coming out, in terms of the external world, has been a breeze. My mother knows and my father knows and I haven't been thrown out of the house. I've never had a problem with discrimination. I've never had anyone call me an ugly name. I haven't been excommunicated from the church or anything like that. Internally is where all the turmoil is, to this day. I have a lot of problems in terms of dealing with negative stereotypes and feeling comfortable with myself. You know, if somebody came up to me and said, "I can give you this pill and you'll be straight," I would seriously consider taking the straight pill, because it's easier. It's as simple as that. It's just easier being straight. I feel hideous about that because not only am I saying I don't like who I am, but I don't like who my friends are. I don't really feel that way. It's just easier to get along being straight in a straight world.

For most people, inner conflict subsides over time. As you are able to dispel the negative stereotypes by getting to know real lesbian and gay people, you feel more comfortable being seen—and seeing yourself—as gay.

defining yourself

There is a lot of pressure in our society to define yourself as gay, lesbian, bisexual, or straight, but you don't need to give yourself a sexual orientation label right away. Some people feel these labels aren't useful for them, that they just box them into some arbitrary or limiting definition. As Rick says:

> I don't like labels. Even though I've thought of myself as gay for years, right now I'm feeling bi-curious. All my sexual experiences have been with guys, so I'm kind of curious about girls right now. That freaks some of my friends out, and others are like, "That's cool."

And Gillian advises:

> Try not to fit other people's images of what you should be. I think the most important thing is just to be who you are and not worry about what other people think. It's more stress than it's worth.

On the other hand, you may find it empowering to define your experience. Having a name for your feelings can help you become more settled inside yourself and more connected to others who have similar experiences.

Michelle describes how she feels sure that she is a lesbian:

> I had dated boys but I wasn't sexually or emotionally attracted to them. The reason I know I'm a lesbian is

because there was an emotional ingredient when I got involved with a woman that had been lacking in relationships with men. It wasn't just a pure lust experience for me. It was a love and a caring and an intellectual, physical, and spiritual connection.

Even after Matt knew he had feelings for boys, he tried acting straight for a while. Defining himself as gay was a way of being honest with himself:

> By seventh grade I had the words and I knew I was gay. It would have been easier to just pretend to have a girlfriend and all that sort of stuff, but it wasn't comfortable and it didn't feel right. I don't like lying. I pretended to be someone else for long enough. I don't want to do it anymore. I'd like to have some integrity.

what if i'm not sure

Many teenagers and young adults are questioning their sexual orientation and don't yet have a firm answer—or what they think is true may change. Stone initially defined herself as lesbian because she had fallen in love with a young woman:

> I had a few different relationships with women and then I fell in love with my best friend. There was only one problem—he was a guy. So, I sat there going, "I'm a lesbian and I'm in love with a guy—this is a problem." I thought about it and I tried to make myself fall out of love with him, but it didn't work. Then I had a friend who was very open about her bisexuality. And I was able to say to myself, "Gee, I guess I can figure out how I can be in love with a guy, after having been in love with a girl." It was confusing, but I felt OK once I had a name for it.

Arwyn, thinking about her own teen years, said:

> You're either in the hip crowd, or you're in the nerd crowd, or you're a jock, you're punk rock, or whatever. Teenagers always put themselves and other people in categories. And it's the same as far as sexuality goes.

Now that I'm twenty-three I think about what I would do if I had the chance to do it again. I would just go with whatever I was feeling at the time and not give myself a definition right away. Your friends of course are going to ask. There's going to be that constant "What are you, what are you?" Just say, "I don't know yet, I'm figuring it out."

Growth and change are a lifelong process, which is both rewarding and challenging. You don't have to have it all figured out already.

self-acceptance

It's a significant journey from inner conflict to self-acceptance. Self-acceptance is about feeling at peace with yourself and feeling comfortable with your sexual orientation. It usually starts tentatively and grows to be more wholehearted over time. Christopher feels really positive about himself now, after years of struggle:

Now that I'm a junior in college and head of the campus gay group, the best part of my life is a sense of inner peace, a sense of knowing that I'm not lying to myself and that I'm not lying to anyone else anymore. And if anyone else has a problem with my being gay, then that's their problem and not mine.

Occasionally, self-acceptance is there all along. Dan is the youngest of five children, four of whom are gay. Although he remembers praying that one of his brothers would be straight to make it easier on his mother, his own feelings about being gay were positive from the beginning:

I was eleven and I was walking to school. It was cold, a winter day, and I remember just thinking to myself, *you're gay.* It was something that I had always known, but finally putting it into words, it became real. And I was happy. It just gave me a sense of wholeness. I kind of smiled and I just kept walking. I was really bouncy.

Whether the journey takes a long time or is relatively short, many gay youth come to the place where they can affirm their sexual orientation absolutely. As Mickie proclaims:

I would never, ever change it, because for once in my life,
there's one thing that I've done right. I'm honest about who
I am. And I'm going to die saying I did this right.

Feeling glad that you are lesbian, gay, or bisexual doesn't mean
that all of a sudden you don't have any problems. The nature of life
is that there are always new challenges to be faced. But once you
really feel good about your sexual orientation, the hardest part of
this particular chapter of your life is behind you. And you are a
wiser, stronger person from your experience. As Devan said, "It was
either be strong or be destroyed—and nothing can destroy me."

coming out

Telling others, or coming out, is an important part of this journey.
It's hard to feel fully good about yourself if you have an important
secret that you can't tell anyone. That kind of hiding can reinforce
the belief that there is something shameful or faulty about you.
There is nothing wrong with you because you're gay. You are just
the way you were meant to be. There is something wrong with a
world that makes you feel ashamed or afraid because you are lesbian, bisexual, or gay. Sharing the truth about yourself in a safe and
supportive place is a big step toward feeling better about yourself.
(For more on coming out, see "How to Tell If Someone Is a Good
Person to Talk To" on p. 36, as well as the sections on coming out
in "Friends" and "Coming Out to Your Family.")

For Better or For Worse © Lynn Johnston Prod., Inc. Reprinted with permission of UNIVERSAL
PRESS SYNDICATE. All rights reserved.

THE BEST THINGS ABOUT BEING LESBIAN, GAY, OR BISEXUAL

For me being gay has not been an issue of just being gay, it's been more of an issue of being able to be myself. It's about being able to expose who I am and realize that if someone rejects me it doesn't mean I'm a bad person—not worth anything. It just means maybe they're an idiot; or they just don't like me.

—Patrick

The most rewarding aspect is being true to who I am, and being able to be a hundred percent of who I am to everybody I encounter, not just seventy-five percent or fifty percent of my personality. People didn't know all of me. They didn't know all of what I liked, and they had false perceptions of who I was.

—Michelle

In my family when I was growing up the phrase was, "Children are to be seen and not heard." And that's how it was; my mouth was always shut. That's why now I'm trying to talk about everything. If I think something is important I'm going to talk to the whole world and let people know, "Hey, you know, this means something to me."

—Renee

The best thing about being gay is being able to hold another man and not worry about what I'll be called because I know who I am and I know what this means and my masculinity and my manhood's intact. A lot of straight men can't truly hold another man without having that concern, will someone think I'm gay? Well, I'm already gay. If they think I'm gay, they're thinking correctly. That's the best part. The fact that I can love another man and I can love him openly.

—Dan

Certain obstacles in my life were like walls that I could jump over or get around. But being gay was a wall so big that I just couldn't go around it. I really had to break through. I was a junior in college when I realized I was the one that was ultimately responsible for doing that, and I think I'm a much stronger person now. I'm much more sure of what's important to me than people who haven't had to do that.

—Quang

celebration

Once you have found support and a comfortable self-acceptance, things generally start to get better and better. You realize that being gay is not only *OK*, it's often terrific. It is a thrilling experience to discover a world where you can be your real self.

When Dan competed in the Gay Games, he describes how he "felt whole for the first time":

> What really did it was walking to the closing ceremonies. It was dusk and the sky was that purple color. And as I walked into Yankee Stadium I looked up and I'm like, DAMN! Because Yankee Stadium is packed, I mean packed—over 60,000 people—and everyone's just clapping and cheering and yelling for you. I will always remember that experience. It was just amazing.
>
> It was the first time in my life I was able to be both gay and an athlete. And no one expected me to explain how I felt because they all knew. I didn't have to be the token gay boy in the athletic world. I didn't have to be the token jock in the gay world. I was like everyone else and we were being celebrated for being athletes and for being gay and for being strong enough to be both.

Doe describes going to her first community event where there were many lesbians:

> I practically wet my pants when I walked into the room and saw three hundred women. God! Number one, they're beautiful. And I was so excited there were Black women there. And they were my age. I knew there were a lot of lesbian writers, like Pat Parker and Audre Lorde,[1] but I didn't have any connection with other Black women my age. So going down to this Dinah Shore Golf Tournament, I mean it

Pat Parker (1944–1989) published five volumes of poems, including *Jonestown & Other Madness* and *Movement in Black.* She was an early and powerful voice for feminists, lesbians, and African-Americans. In the late 1980s, she was the Director of the Oakland Feminist Women's Health Center.

[1]A note about Audre Lorde appears in Chapter 3, "Reaching Out."

hurled me over the edge. I wanted to just run up and start kissing women. I love you! I love you! I love you!

As Margaret sums up:

I feel like I've come into an entirely different culture. Maybe this is heaven.

The process of coming to validate and celebrate yourself is rarely a straight line. And like so much else in life, your path may be clear only in hindsight. During the time that you are making your way through the difficult process toward self-knowledge and self-acceptance, you may not even know that this is what you're doing. Sometimes it's not until later that we can see the courageous and meaningful labor in which we've been involved.

So if your own journey seems less tidy than this general plan, as it probably will, or if you feel that you're not doing it right, give yourself a break. You don't have to have all the answers yet. Your ability simply to ask the questions, to think about your life, your feelings, your hopes and fears, is an accomplishment in itself.

Cathy Cade © 1995

3
reaching out

There are people who take the heart out of you,
And people who put it back.

—Elizabeth Davis

We all thrive when we are loved and accepted for who we truly are.
The more you can find people who appreciate you, the better off
you'll be. Reaching out is important if you are having problems, but
it's also essential for creating a healthy and fulfilling life.

The most critical step on the road from denial to a celebration of
being bisexual, lesbian, or gay is connecting with others. It's hard to
reach out when you feel vulnerable or need help, but it's almost
impossible to become comfortable with your sexual orientation all
alone. When you connect with others and hear positive and affirming

messages, your sense of yourself usually deepens. You are more able to recognize your strengths and special qualities. And you begin to build a life based on honesty and authentic relationships. As Doe says:

> The most important advice I can give to young people is to believe in yourself. And don't think that you're the only person out there, because you're not. The key is to find the community and surround yourself with people that love you, not people who hate you. If you feel trapped, hang on. There's a pot of gold waiting. It's like a beautiful cool lake on a hot, dry day. It's just around the corner. You have to walk a few more steps. It's out there.

Here are ideas about how to reach out, find support, and meet other young people (see the Resources, starting on p. 367, for ways to connect with groups or organizations).

gay youth support groups

At the top of the list—as one of the best ways to meet other lesbian, gay, and bisexual young people—is a gay youth support group. There are youth groups all over the country, in virtually all major urban areas and many smaller communities as well. Contact the lesbian, gay, bisexual community center nearest you to find out about youth groups or other ways for young people to meet. Your school may have a support group as well.

If you find a group you can get to, GO! Talking to others who are dealing with similar challenges is an excellent way to break through isolation, meet new friends, and feel good about yourself. Chris describes how he immediately felt better after his first meeting:

> For the first time I wasn't alone. I didn't have to bottle everything up. I could laugh about the hard times. Plus, it wasn't a big secret anymore. The more I went to BAGLY [Boston Alliance of Gay and Lesbian Youth], the more my confidence grew. In the past I had never been able to sleep well because that's when all the feelings would come up. But after my first meeting, I went home and for the first time I went to bed happy and I fell asleep.

Although support groups make a big difference right away for many people, others feel uncomfortable at first. It can be a good idea to stick with a group for a while before you decide whether it's right for you. Joselin attended the same group as Chris:

> My first time was awful, a terrible experience. It was uncomfortable because it was new. People there were not the most friendly people in the world. There was a clique. But I did meet one person who started talking to me, so that was pretty cool. We began to go together every week cause we both were new. It's been two months and things are better now. I'm starting to know people.

There are different kinds of youth groups. Some are support groups where you talk about what's going on in your life or about gay, lesbian, and bisexual issues in general. Others are social groups, designed for young people to meet each other. There are also political groups that focus on educating people about gay issues and working for positive changes. These are often on school or college campuses. They may organize projects such as a gay and lesbian information booth during orientation week or sensitivity trainings with students and faculty. And some groups are gay/straight alliances, where straight supporters join in to work for justice for gay, lesbian, and bisexual people.

If you live in an area where there are numerous groups, you can try different ones. For most people, participating in any kind of gay youth group will offer the all-important peer support. Jonathan went to the gay group at his college, even though he was "scared to death the first time":

> The group provided an outlet. I could talk about my life, about growing up and the experiences I had gone through. And I got to hear other people's stories as well, and I could relate them to my own. I would come home and just be in amazement. Because all this time I felt that I was so alone, like I was the only one. And here were all these people sharing the fact that they'd gone through the same thing.
>
> At the end of the school year, the current president of the group moved away, and so they needed a new leader for the group. Believe it or not, everybody in the group nomi-

nated me to take over and kind of reluctantly at first I went ahead and I accepted. It hasn't even been a year yet since I've graduated from high school, and I've come so far.

For a few people, support groups may not work at all. Craig felt out of place in the group on his college campus because his experience was so different from that of the other students. He was living part of his life in a secret—and painful—world that he couldn't talk about:

> The people there would talk about how they have all these new friends and they feel so liberated and their relationships have gotten so much better and more honest and whatever. And I didn't feel like that at all. I felt like an outsider. I didn't want to tell them I was going out on the streets for sex. That wasn't what they were doing. Everyone in that group was dating each other and having fun. That wasn't what was going on for me.

If groups don't work for you—for whatever reason—keep reading. There are other ways to get support.

◇ ROLE MODELS

Positive role models can make a big difference in helping you develop your sense of who you are and who you might become. They can be people that you actually know, like the leader of a gay youth group or your own uncle or aunt, who you recently discovered is gay.

Jason was impressed with two young lesbian and gay speakers who came to his school:

> It took a lot of courage for them to stand up there and say they were gay. They sounded so natural and self-confident. Although I wasn't ready to come out yet, it gave me a real sense that it was going to be possible for me too.

Jonathan found an important role model in his own family:

> During the summer between eleventh and twelfth grade I went to Michigan and I met my second cousin for the first

time. As the night progressed, he came out and told me, "Well, I'm gay." And this shock, this thrill just went through my body. I'm like, "Oh my gosh, here is someone else. I'm not the only person in the world." All of a sudden, not only is there another homosexual in the United States, but he's a family member. I kind of scampered around and finally I said, "I think I am as well."

We were up until three-thirty, four in the morning with him giving me information I needed to know, telling me what it was like to live life as a homosexual. He said, "I know it's really rough right now, but you're going to go away to college and you're going to make friends and there's a wonderful gay community."

It was the most amazing thing to me. Whereas before I didn't want to get up in the morning, now I couldn't wait to get up. Because every day that I spent was one day closer to getting to move away from there. And getting to where I could find my place in the gay community.

And people started to give me less of a hard time. They weren't accepting, but they were more tolerant. Though I never did come out. I was just so comfortable with myself that they backed off, because nothing they could do affected me anymore. They lost their power over me.

A role model can be a well-known athlete, like Martina Navratilova or Greg Louganis. Or it can be a performer, like Bessie Smith, or a political activist, like Bayard Rustin. Renee's role model is the poet Audre Lorde who died in 1992:

Martina Navratilova (b. 1956) was the top-ranked woman tennis player in the world in 1979 and 1982–86. In 1984 she won seventy-four straight matches, an all-time record.

Greg Louganis (b. 1960) was only sixteen when he won a silver medal for diving at the 1976 Olympics. Since then he's won four Olympic gold medals, six Pan American Games gold medals, and five world championships.

Bessie Smith (1894–1937), known as the Empress of the Blues, was the most successful blues singer of the 1920s. She was hearty, forthright, raucous, and totally uninhibited in her performances, as well as in her life. One of her own songs sums up her attitude well: "T'Aint Nobody's Biz-ness If I Do."

Bayard Rustin (1910–1987) was a civil rights and peace activist. An associate of Martin Luther King, Jr., he organized the 1963 March on Washington. When Rustin was denounced by a homophobic senator for being gay, King himself stood up for Rustin.

Audre Lorde (1934–1992) wrote eloquently from her experience as a black lesbian poet, mother, and fighter for freedom. Her best-known works include *Zami: A New Spelling of My Name, Our Dead Behind Us*, and a life-affirming essay, *Uses of the Erotic: The Erotic as Power*.

One of my major role models, because I like to write, is Audre Lorde. Whoa, she's cool. I keep track of all the books she wrote and all the articles she was in, and try to base my life after hers, because she was amazing.

The singer Melissa Etheridge was a role model for two lesbians living in abusive families. These young women were in love and struggling with severe problems when they read that Melissa Etheridge had come out. They said to themselves that if Melissa could do it, they could too—and they moved to a large east coast city where they were able to begin a healthier life.

Melissa Etheridge (b. 1961) is a popular and passionate rock and roll singer who came out publicly. Her albums include *Melissa Etheridge, Never Enough, Brave and Crazy*, and *Yes I Am*.

Role models can even be fictional—from books, comics, movies, or TV shows—like Neil in *All American Boys*, Northstar, the Marvel comic book superhero, or Jeffrey in the movie of the same name.

You can be a role model too. Luna, a nineteen-year-old gay man, is a peer educator at the Hetrick-Martin Institute, a program for lesbian and gay youth in New York City:

Harvey Milk (1930–1978) was San Francisco's first openly gay supervisor. Sincere and charismatic, he was a national spokesperson for justice for gays and lesbians. He was assassinated by Dan White, a homophobic ex–city supervisor, who also killed San Francisco mayor George Moscone.

When younger gay and lesbian youth come to me with questions or feelings, it's like I'm a father or mother to them. I enjoy that. It's like how my teacher at the Harvey Milk School was to me. He made me feel good about myself, and I believe I do that for a lot of the young people that come here.

Hyde is a college activist who has facilitated a youth group at the Billy DeFrank Lesbian and Gay Community Center in San Jose:

> One time there were a couple of fifteen-year-old baby dykes hanging out with me. They said, "There are no role models, but there's you. You're our role model." And I about cried on the spot. I was so touched. I tried not to be so sappy about it. I wanted to uphold my dyke image. Yeah, right.

We all need positive role models. They inspire us. And they help to counteract the prevalent negative stereotypes about gay people.

gay and gay-friendly people

In addition to being part of a group, you might want to talk to gay-friendly people. Choose someone who is lesbian, gay, or bisexual or who you know to be comfortable with gay people. Here are some suggestions about how to find those people.

PFLAG (Parents, Families, and Friends of Lesbians and Gays) is a wonderful resource with over 340 local affiliates all over the United States and in eleven other countries. Contact them to find the chapter nearest you. You can talk with someone on the phone or you could go to one of their support meetings. They welcome gay people, as well as family and friends.

Some school counselors, teachers, coaches, or ministers are also gay-friendly. You may have a family friend who is understanding. Or you might find someone to talk to through the gay community center in your town or nearby. If you want to keep what you say private, be sure to establish that at the beginning.

For Nancy, talking to a supportive adult was the start of finding affirming information about being a lesbian:

> The first time I said anything I was fourteen. I told this social worker. I told him I had feelings for women, I had feelings for girls. I didn't even know what to call it. He was really cool. He ran around giving me all this information and he gave me the number for the gay and lesbian center. He helped me a lot. He opened the door.

Volunteering with community programs is an excellent way to meet other supportive people. And you'll be doing important work you can feel good about. After a beloved family friend died of AIDS, Matt began to work at his local AIDS organization, with some unexpected benefits. It was there that he first came out and felt accepted as a gay person:

> I got such positive reinforcement. It's just like, "Hey, a lot of people are gay here. It's OK, don't worry about it." I feel lucky to have this place where I can talk to people about my life and feel good about myself.
>
> Also, I was able to go there with my parents' knowledge even before I came out to them. They thought I was volunteering because I care about AIDS. Since I do care, it wasn't a lie, but it was kind of a convenience that while I was helping, which I felt great about, I got to talk to people about being gay.

As with meeting all new people, use some caution. Even though most people are respectful, a few are not. Some people may try to take advantage of your natural desire for understanding by befriending you in ways that conceal a sexual agenda. Even within the most respected institutions there can be an occasional rotten apple. So whether you're talking to a priest, a teacher, a psychiatrist, a counselor, or a volunteer at your local gay, lesbian, and bisexual community center, get to know someone before you give them your total trust. And if they do anything to make you feel uncomfortable, protect yourself. You deserve to be supported and respected, not exploited.

HOW TO TELL IF SOMEONE IS A GOOD PERSON TO TALK TO

◇ Are they affirming of gay, lesbian, and bisexual people?

Your feelings are personal and deserve to be heard with respect and consideration. Especially if you're having a hard time, you don't need to deal with people who are insensitive or judgmental. If you're not sure someone is gay-friendly, it's a good idea to check it out before you reveal your sexual orientation. You can bring up the subject in a general way by mentioning an event in the news or making a comment about a public figure who is lesbian or gay. If you get a positive reaction, that gives you some indication that that person may be receptive to your concerns. If it's negative, you know to look elsewhere for a sympathetic listener. (For more about this, see "Testing the Waters" on p. 128.)

◇ Are they good listeners?

The people you talk to should do a lot of listening, especially at first, letting you say what is on your mind. They should ask you questions to learn more about your thoughts and feelings.

People often respond with a lot of advice. That advice may or may not be right for you. You get to decide. If their advice is useful, great. But if it's not, you can still take in their care and support. If you're lucky they may be able to share information about being gay, lesbian, or bisexual or hook you up with other resources, such as groups or books.

◇ Are they trustworthy about confidentiality?

If it's important that they not tell anyone about what you've shared, make that clear in advance and ask for their commitment to keep the conversation private. Professional counselors are required to maintain your confidentiality except in situations of extreme danger or abuse. With others, you'll need to make it clear that what you share is confidential.

◇ Are they free of hidden agendas?

It's important that the people in whom you confide aren't out to get something from you in return. They should *not* be trying—however subtly—to convert you, cure you, come on to you sexually, or take control of your life in any way. Understanding should be offered without strings attached. The only thing they should expect in return is mutual respect.

◇ Are they positive, encouraging, and affirming?

You should leave the conversation feeling positive and understood. The basic message needs to be that you are great the way you are and that there are many other young people like you. If someone starts to make you think your same-sex attractions are wrong or bad, get yourself out of there! If you want to, you can explain what wasn't helpful and what you need instead. But if that person still can't hear you, try someone else.

talk lines

A good place to find support is from a telephone talk line that offers information and advice to young people. Often connected with gay youth organizations, these lines are usually free 800 numbers and they commonly operate in the evening hours. Those who are answering the phones are often other young bisexual, gay, and lesbian people who have been trained as peer counselors. They are available to talk about your concerns as well as to provide information and referrals to local resources. As Quang says:

> When you call a talk line you're talking to someone you don't know. So it's totally anonymous. Just being able to say, over the phone, "I think I'm gay," makes such a big difference. It's a very empowering step.

pen pals

Writing to another gay, lesbian, or bisexual young person can enrich your life. The Los Angeles Gay and Lesbian Community Services Center has a pen-pal program for youth. And in Indianapolis there is the Lesbian and Gay Youth Pen Pal Network. Both programs are open to youth throughout the country.

In order to correspond with a pen pal you'll need an address where you can receive mail. Of course, your home address is the most convenient, but if that's not private enough you might want to try a rental mailbox or General Delivery, where you pick the mail up at the post office. Another possibility is to use the address of a trusted friend.

computer bulletin boards

Many young people who have access to on-line computer bulletin boards have found valuable information, support, and friends on the gay, lesbian, bisexual chat lines. As Tommy, living isolated in rural South Carolina, relates:

> The very first day I got AOL [America Online], I used the key word "gay" and a whole new world opened up for me.

Patrick describes how he came out on-line, at age fifteen:

> I went to America Online, first to the gay and lesbian community forum. I'd make a separate screen name that wasn't mine at all and delete it right after I got done. I would just look around. There's a gay and lesbian chat room, and you can talk to other people.
>
> After a while I posted that I thought I was gay. I got a lot of stuff in my mailbox. I met one person on-line who works for the National Gay and Lesbian Task Force. She said she was willing to talk to me about whatever I wanted to talk about. So I started sending her a lot of e-mail and we kept talking back and forth. She sent me snail mail and we started corresponding and for the first time I was really able to talk to someone about my problems. In the meantime I was talking on-line all the time and I was learning so much.
>
> America Online is something inside your house that's easily accessible. It's two-way communication, but at the same time you can be so anonymous and you can feel totally safe. You can get all the information that you need and you'll feel a lot less alone.

PATRICK'S STORY: COMING OUT ON-LINE

Subj: 15 and need support
Date: 93–07–01 04:09:59 EDT
From: Pat 1

I am a 15-year-old gay teen in San Jose. I just started confronting the fact that I'm gay this week. As a result, I literally feel sick because it seems like there is no one to talk to. I don't know how to deal with it or how to meet other gay teens my age. Please send me e-mail if you're willing to talk.

Subj: Come out
Date: 93–07–23 23:17:05 EDT
From: Pat 1

Thanks for all the support guys. I've decided to come out. I've talked to some people and I'm going to do it once I've finished reading all the books I've got on being gay.

Subj: Congrats to you too
Date: 93–07–25 5:30:17 EDT
From: Pat 1

It feels so good just to know I won't have to hide who I really am anymore. But I'm going to go to Billy DeFrank [the San Jose Lesbian and Gay Community Center] and make sure I've read enough books so I'll be as prepared as possible. I'm going to do it next week. . . .

Subj: I'm OUT!
Date: 93–08–07 04:17:35 EDT
From: Pat 1

I told my parents today that I'm gay!
They took it wonderfully!!
They still love me and everything! They're ready to join PFLAG and everything!!!!
I love you all!!

Subj: Yet more congratulations!
Date: 93–08–07 19:30:12 EDT
From: R Student

A festive mood on AOL tonight! The on-line party's burning bright! Congratulations, Pat 1! My Dr. Pepper is raised to you, and a big hug as well. And a second congratulations to your parents—they obviously love you very much, and deserve praise for raising a wonderful and honest kid like you, and sticking to their own values of love and acceptance . . . so both to you and them, my love! :)

Subj: Kudos Pat!!!
Date: 93–08–07 22:41:13 EDT
From: CAG 16

Congrats Pat on taking that big yet wonderful step in being yourself. I'm so happy for ya!! I would give you a big old hug right now. . . . but I think that's kinda difficult through a computer screen. :) So I'll give ya an Ehug instead {{{{{{Pat}}}}}}. I guess this means I'm next . . . to take the step. I'm going to prepare by empowering myself with as much info and support as I can muster. I'm glad your decision turned out to be a GREAT one. That gives me some hope.

◇ A WORD OF WARNING:

Sometimes people who meet on-line will want to meet in person. This can lead to valuable new friendships. But in some situations, it can lead to instances where you might be taken advantage of by others. Anni suggests some commonsense guidelines:

> Be very careful. There are some older people looking just for sex. There are a few people who get on there and they put out the image they want, but you don't know if they're telling the truth. You need to find out about the person. First talk on-line a lot. Then if you think you'd like to meet, from the computer go to talking on the phone. That's the best way. You'll find out more what their true personality is like. So talk on the phone a lot too. Don't give out your full name or address. Then if you still like them, have a group meeting where you bring your friends with you if you can, and make sure it's at a mall or public place so you're not alone with them. You might meet some wonderful people that way, but be very, very cautious.

books, magazines, music, and movies

Some bookstores, especially those near college campuses, have special sections on gay and lesbian issues. Books can also be ordered through the mail—and sent in plain brown wrappers. And don't forget the public library. When Matt was in junior high school, he was determined to get some information:

> The first time I got a gay book off the shelf at the library, I was looking over my shoulder. When no one was in the aisle I grabbed it, put it in my shirt, and ran to a hidden table. I didn't check the book out. I was afraid to do that because then it would be on the computer that I took it out. But I did get to read it.

In addition to books, there are an increasing number of magazines such as *OUT* and *10 PERCENT*. Also, new zines written and produced by youth are springing up all the time. Not only might you enjoy reading them, but you might consider contributing an article, story, or poem yourself.

Gay and lesbian music has also supported many a newly emerging person through the upheaval—both wonderful and awful—of coming out. When Stone came out she played her mother's old Cris Williamson tapes for months. They all heard "filling up and spilling over" day and night until she finally moved on to k.d. lang. And one young gay man has seen *Priscilla, Queen of the Desert* eight times. It's unlikely that he holds the record.

Cris Williamson (b. 1947) set the tone for a whole new genre of music with her first album, *The Changer and the Changed,* which has been the number-one best-seller in women's music. Her songs sparked the idea for the women's recording company Olivia. Chris continues to record with her partner, Tret Fure.

k.d. lang (b. 1961) is a Canadian country-rock singer with a resonant voice and high energy. Her albums include *Shadowland, Absolute Torch and Twang,* and *Ingénue.*

don't give up

If your first efforts at reaching out don't pay off immediately, don't give up. Be persistent and keep trying to find the connections that are right for you. If you don't like the gay youth group, try it again in a few months; there'll be new people by then. If the gay-friendly school counselor is someone you just don't get along with, call PFLAG for a supportive adult to talk to. If you don't have a computer, write to a pen pal. Be creative, be determined, utilize *all* the options and make up some of your own. You're worth the effort. If you keep trying, you'll find what you need.

HOW TO SHOW YOU'RE GAY-FRIENDLY: FOR ALL ALLIES OF GAY, LESBIAN, AND BISEXUAL YOUTH

◇ **Say the words.**

Use the words "lesbian," "gay," and "bisexual" without it being a big deal—work them into your casual conversation. Mention gay people in a positive way. Talk about gay-related history, current news, or media events.

◇ **Keep your language free of heterosexual bias.**

Using inclusive language is hard work at first. It involves a shift in how you think about things. It is more than just changing certain pronouns and phrases. For example, it reveals a straight bias to ask a young woman if she has a boyfriend. Instead ask if she is dating or involved with anyone. If a young man talks about someone he is close to, don't assume it's friendship if he is talking about a boy and romance if he is talking about a girl.

◇ **Wear a button.**

Pin on a button that is a symbol of gay pride like a pink triangle or a rainbow flag. Or wear any kind of supportive button like "Straight, But Not Narrow" or "Hate is not a family value."

◇ **Display gay-positive materials.**

Hang a rainbow flag outside your door, glue a bumper sticker on your car, put up posters in your office, post news clippings, leave books on your coffee table, set out informational pamphlets and flyers in easily accessible places.

◇ **Be prepared for inquiries.**

When people ask you about the button, the flag, or the poster, be ready to explain its meaning. You may also get asked if you are gay. Whatever your answer, offer it without embarrassment and make yourself available for future discussion.

◇ **Come out.**

If you are gay, lesbian, or bisexual yourself, come out as much as you can in as many different situations as possible. This may be the *most* important thing you can do to make the world a safer place for gay kids.

If you have a bisexual, lesbian, or gay family member, talk openly about that person.

Cathy Cade © 1995

4
if i live, i'll be great:
making it through hard times

> Have patience toward all that is unresolved in your heart and
> . . . try to love the questions themselves.
>
> —*Rainer Maria Rilke*

If you are questioning your sexuality or recognizing that you are bisexual, gay, or lesbian, you are acting in a profoundly courageous way. Acknowledging a part of yourself that goes against what most people feel comfortable with truly is a brave thing to do. But being brave and courageous does not mean you aren't scared. It's only human to be nervous in the face of new or challenging situations.

Being brave is about *continuing* to do what you need to—in spite of the fear. So give yourself credit.

Most young people go through some rough times as they recognize their same-sex feelings. And the younger you come out, the harder it's likely to be. For John:

> Ninth grade was the worst. I wasn't accepted. I knew I was gay, and I knew everyone else knew because they told me I was a faggot every day. But I was still trying to be straight with the friends that I did have. I stopped doing homework and didn't pay attention in school. I felt like something was exploding inside of me. I started smoking pot too. I was trying to hide from what I really felt.

With a great deal of determination, John got himself into the federal Job Corps program and was able to get his life on track. He is now twenty-two years old and studying for a degree in nursing at a college in Maine.

Even once you're comfortable with your same-sex feelings, life continues to present problems and challenges. But if you're having a terrible time—for any reason—remember, you can make it through. It won't be this hard forever.

above all, don't hurt yourself

Don't judge yourself for feeling miserable if you're in a miserable situation. Instead, think about the safe and unsafe ways to deal with that suffering. There are healthy ways to cope with very difficult times. Acknowledge your feelings. Don't try to pretend there is nothing wrong.

The unhealthy ways you have heard about a million times: drug and alcohol abuse, becoming isolated, engaging in behaviors that are highly dangerous like driving drunk, having unprotected sex, or being sexual when you don't feel good about it.

Devan describes how he was hurt while trying to survive:

> I got involved with prostitution for a while. You know, you do what you have to. And, I would sacrifice myself for the sake of other people. There were a handful of these young, innocent people that I kind of took under my wing. I felt

like I'd already been through the degrading, demeaning, and disgusting acts of it all. I didn't let these kids do those things. I did them instead and paid for a place for them to sleep.

I did all these things without feeling anything. Because if I felt it, it would have hurt too much. I'd already had so much hurt I decided I wasn't going to feel anymore. I didn't feel anything—good, bad, or indifferent. I turned off the emotions. It wasn't an easy thing to do, but I did it.

Now the feelings are getting turned back on. Since I went to Project Offstreets I've started to heal.

You are worth too much to hurt yourself. If you're used to hearing messages that you're no good, it may take some time for you to believe in yourself. But the truth is that you are a special, unique, and valuable person and you deserve to be treated—and to treat yourself—with respect and tenderness.

When you're suffering, the desire to escape from those painful feelings is powerful. That's what makes drugs and alcohol so attractive. But although drugs and alcohol may offer temporary relief, they don't bring you closer to self-acceptance. And, they may endanger both your judgment and your health. Often you wind up in even worse circumstances than before. As Beth recalls:

By high school I was a really, really heavy drinker. And I did drugs until I fried myself. I was hard core. I started drinking heavy when I started dating guys. I never made an association, at the time, with the fact that I was gay. I just knew that when I was with a guy I had to be high.

When my best friend who I was really in love with moved away to Pennsylvania, my whole world was crushed. I would drink before I left the house to go party and drink more. I was so unhappy and so messed up that I started having these fears that I was going to flip out and kill someone. I was feeling completely insane. I ended up being such a basket case I couldn't be left alone. I felt so out of control.

Beth finally reached out for help and found Alcoholics Anonymous (AA), which became an important part of her life. She has been clean and sober for eight years and has recently married her long-time girlfriend and reports that she is healthier and happier than ever before.

If you've gotten into abusing alcohol or drugs for *any* reason, reach out for the support you need to be safe and to stay in control of your life and your choices. There are AA and NA (Narcotics Anonymous) groups in almost every city and town in the country. And in quite a few places there are even gay and lesbian AA meetings, as well as meetings specifically for young people.

stay alive!

Many lesbian and gay people have hated themselves for being gay, tried desperately to change, and sometimes, when the conflict became unbearable, killed themselves. We have lost too many bright and promising young people already. It is imperative that we don't lose YOU.

When you're in enormous pain, you may feel that continuing to live is more than you can bear. When you're feeling so discouraged it can be hard to imagine that you have a future worth living for. These are real feelings and it's important to acknowledge them. But don't act on them.

No matter how bad you feel, no matter how grim or desperate your situation seems, no matter how much you think killing yourself is the answer to your problems, *don't give up*. Remember:

◇ There are happier days ahead, even though it may be tough getting to them.
◇ Your life has value, although that may be hard to realize right now.
◇ You are strong. You've come this far and fought hard to get here. You are capable of making it through to better times.
◇ You may be the person who discovers the cure for AIDS, writes a great novel, or makes some other contribution you can't even imagine from here. Give yourself the opportunity to find out.
◇ Rotten though it may be, you will grow from this experience, and maybe even use it to help others in ways that are lifesaving and life-changing.

Our community needs you. We need your particular energy and talents. Please don't leave—stay with us.

Other young people have made it through and you can too. Their despair—and the positive changes that have taken place in their lives—can reassure you that you too will get to a better place. Renee remembers her lowest point:

When I started to realize that I was a lesbian, all of a sudden these tapes started playing in my head—about being a bulldagger and this other negative stuff and all these jokes that people were saying in school. It came to be too much for me. I just couldn't handle it. I tried running away from home because I didn't have any support at home so, hell, why be there? I kept running away and they kept sending me back home to people not happy being my family, who hurt me. Every time I ran away something bad would happen to me. I just couldn't deal with it, so I tried to kill myself.

Renee survived and with some help she went on to find a foster home with a lesbian family. Now, at eighteen years old, she is determined to be the first person in her family to attend college.

Matt came from a loving family, but still he struggled with suicidal feelings:

I was feeling hopeless. I was feeling that I was always going to be alone. I was feeling like it's not worth it anymore. When I realized I was definitely gay, that was a real desperation time. I was thinking, what am I going to do from here, because I can't be gay. I can't, I can't be gay. After I started meeting some gay people I realized that suicide wasn't an option. If people can't deal with me for who I am, it's their problem, not mine. I used to think it was my problem, I have to change. Now I know they're the ones who need to change, to not be homophobic.

With support Matt was able to turn his life around. He now has many friends, is working part time as an administrative assistant at his local AIDS agency, and is preparing to go to college next year.

Jonathan is also thriving now. He's doing well in college, has good friends, and feels at peace with himself. But he went through real anguish as well:

In the spring of eleventh grade I decided that it was time. It was time to die literally. I was at the point where I was about to do it, and I knew I was. I was sitting in the house all alone; I was just bawling. And I was thinking how I could kill myself, how I could do it; what would be the easiest way. I was thinking about what my parents would think when they came back. Did I need to leave a note, did I need to just do it, did I need to go somewhere else to do it, or should I do it in my room? I was thinking those things and it just freaked me out.

I called my mother and I was just bawling hysterically on the phone. I said, "Mother you've got to come home now, you've got to. If you don't come home right now, you're probably going to regret it for the rest of your life."

Later she told me she drove ninety miles an hour. It was absolutely the longest time I've ever spent. Just seconds ticking, everything was slowed down. I've never been in that state again in my life, and I hope I never return there.

My mother came to the door and I was sitting there at the kitchen table crying frantically, shaking violently. She said, "You've got to tell me what's wrong." I said, "Mother, I'm about to do it, I'm about to kill myself. I almost did it, just a few minutes ago. Something told me to call you." Being a religious person, I think it was the Lord stepped in and said, "Look Jonathan, no. Uh-uh. Hang in there. Call your mother."

Jonathan's mother was supportive and took him to their family doctor who was sympathetic and helpful. Hanging in there was the best thing that Jonathan could have done. And it's exactly what we want you to do too. Even if your family is not supportive, there are people out there who are.

It's OK if you don't feel hopeful. It's OK if you don't feel better. For today, just stay alive.

IF YOU'RE THINKING ABOUT SUICIDE

Tell a trusted person how desperate you are feeling. If the first person you talk to isn't any help, talk to someone else. Keep trying. Let people know what's going on with you.

Although you may not want to, make a decision to stay alive today, one day at a time. You can always rethink this decision at a later time, but if you die today there will be no later time.

Decide to reach out for help. Make a plan for connecting with at least one person with whom you can share your feelings.

Call for Help Now

◇ Call a local suicide prevention hotline, listed in front of your phone book under "Community Services" or "Emergency Numbers."

◇ Call one of the gay youth talk lines listed on p. 367 of Resources.

if you're in desperate circumstances

If your home situation is abusive—physically, sexually, or emotionally—or if you've been kicked out or run away without a safe place to go, you need—and deserve—help. There are agencies that can help, people who care, and services available to you. Sometimes these are relatively easy to find. More frequently, it may take some persistence on your part to find the resources you need.

Please read "Getting Help from Your Community" beginning on p. 311 and see the listings beginning on p. 372 of the Resources.

be kind to yourself

Even if you're not feeling desperate, you may be hurting. If you're struggling with feelings about your sexual orientation and coming out, if you're having a hard time with your family, friends, or romantic relationships, you may be upset, lonely, or sad. Reach out for support. And try taking these suggestions to make it a little easier on yourself.

◇ LOVE YOURSELF

First of all, be gentle with yourself. Tell yourself encouraging, self-affirming things. If you say positive things to yourself, even when you're feeling rotten, you start to believe the good things a little bit more. Remind yourself of your strengths. You may be a loyal friend or care about the environment. Maybe you're a terrific dancer, a good listener, or you love animals. Whatever! Being gay doesn't take away your fine qualities. You're still the same wonderful person you've always been. Yevette speaks from her own experience:

It's OK, the growing pains you're going through. There's always light at the end of the tunnel. And you'll get to know you, which makes it OK. Just love yourself. If you love yourself first, everything else falls into place. It doesn't help to beat up on yourself. I've been there so I know.

When you're going through hard times emotionally, it's even more important to remember basic self-care: eat regularly, get plenty of rest and exercise. Sometimes it's difficult to do these things for yourself, but they help when you feel like you're falling apart.

You don't have to be totally on top of things. Just do the best you can. Each step you take makes it easier to take the next one—and even little ones count a lot.

◇ IT'S NOT ABOUT YOU

This concept can be hard to grasp, but it's very, very important. Oprah Winfrey said that when she became famous, she was disturbed by the negative things written about her in newspapers and magazines. Then she talked to her friend Maya Angelou, who told her, "It's not about you."

This advice is true. When people say insulting things to or about others, it often has nothing to do with what that person is really like, who they really are. Public figures get slandered in the press. Gays and lesbians get taunted and threatened. Women get obscene remarks yelled at them. And none of it has to do with who those people really are.

As best you are able, don't take it personally. Of course that's easier said than done, but it's essential that you understand that it truly is not about you. It hurts you. It hurts your feelings. It may even be making your life miserable. But the things that homophobic people do or say have nothing to do with who you really are. Those things are reflections on themselves—or on the misinformation that they've been taught. Sometimes, just knowing that can help a lot. As Jonathan says:

After meeting my gay cousin on my summer trip I was a brand new person. He introduced me to a new word, and it was called "homophobia." So now I had a word for them that also started with homo. And it was wonderful. You know, you're homo-phobic. Though I never did say it openly.

◇ EXPRESS YOURSELF

Creativity can sustain your spirit in the face of painful experiences. It's a way to take what is destructive and turn it into something constructive and meaningful. Insults and harassment are meant to put you down and make you feel terrible. But when you utilize your creativity, you turn it around. You create, rather than destroy.

One way to communicate your feelings, even when there is no one to talk to or correspond with, is to keep a journal or diary just for yourself. All you need is paper, a pen, and a private place to keep what you have written. You don't have to be a good writer. You don't have to spell well or use correct grammar. Just write down whatever you are really thinking and feeling.

You can write about what's going on in your life. You can write song or rap lyrics. You can write a short story, poetry, or a play. You could make up a futuristic fantasy about how you wish the world could be. The devastating dialogue that you endured in school yesterday, precisely recorded, could be the opening chapter of a Pulitzer Prize–winning novel.

Renee began writing when she was in a shelter waiting for placement into a foster home:

> I started out with a pen and a notebook and then they gave me a typewriter to put in my room. I would sit at my typewriter all day. That's how I healed myself. I wrote everything. I wrote poems. I wrote stories. When I came out of that shelter I was a totally different person. I was still sad, and I still felt lonely, but I was a thousand pounds lighter because I was able to put this on paper.

If you like drawing, painting, or sculpting, try to get the materials to pursue those avenues. Again, you don't have to be an artist to paint. You don't even have to make recognizable forms. Instead, you can use colors and shapes to express your feelings. Get a hunk of clay and roll snakes like you did in elementary school. Pretend they're hissing at your tormentors or coil them into a bowl to hold your rainbow-colored freedom rings. Or create a board game where the gays, lesbians, bisexuals, and their allies work together to fight homophobia in all its nasty guises.

If you sing, sing the blues. Or gospel. If you've got drums, drum out your feelings. If you dance, put your soul into it. If you're especially talented, that's great. But if not, you can do it anyway. Keep in mind the African proverb, "If you can walk, you can dance. If you can talk, you can sing."

◇ KEEP UP ACTIVITIES YOU CARE ABOUT

Often when you feel lousy, you lose interest in the things you usually like to do. It can take a real effort to make yourself do those activities even when you're not feeling like it. But it's worth the effort. You may like to play the piano, play computer games, raise pigs, or sew—it doesn't matter what.

Michelle had always been an avid swimmer:

> When I was feeling terrible I got out of my regular environment by going to a swimming camp. We were training six hours a day. When you're swimming you can think about anything, you don't have to talk to anybody. It was a time to take myself out of the problems I'd been in and just excel at something I enjoyed.

Even if you can't get away for an extended period of time, a couple of hours doing something that feels good can help a lot. Go for a run with your dog, soak in a hot bubble bath, read a mystery novel.

Whether you're interested in sports, theater, music, or getting good grades in school, keep pouring your energy into what you really care about. Although it won't make the difficulties go away, it will keep them from occupying the entire landscape. You may be a kid under siege, but you're also a young adult creating a meaningful life.

The flamboyant pianist Liberace was the object of much ridicule, but he was so successful that people used to joke that he "cried all the way to the bank."

> Liberace (1919–1987) played popular songs and what he called *Reader's Digest* versions of the classics in concerts and on TV, breaking attendance records at Radio City Music Hall. With his trademark candelabra, lavish costumes, and custom pianos, he was an obvious flamer. Yet he stayed closeted, even as he died of complications due to AIDS.

◇ FIND WAYS TO LAUGH

Singer and songwriter Kate Wolf once said, "You have to keep your sense of humor about life or it isn't funny." Oppressed people have always used humor to keep up their spirits and to point out the ignorance of bigoted people.

Scientists have found that when you laugh and smile, your brain releases the chemical seratonin into your body, which actually makes you feel better.

IT FEELS GOOD TO LAUGH

According to gay comic Tom Ammiano:

> The definition of "homophobia" is the irrational fear that three fags will break into your home and redecorate.

◇

Feminist humorist Kate Clinton[1] tells this story about her niece Grace:

> Grace, who's five, has a friend over and I hear her say to her friend, "Let's pretend we're gay." The friend goes, "What's gay?" And Grace says, "Gay is when two girls get together, dance, and have fun."

◇

Comedian Bob Smith tells this story about coming out to his family at Thanksgiving:

> Then my Aunt Lorraine said, "Bob, you're gay? Are you seeing a psychiatrist?"
> I said, "No, I'm seeing a lieutenant in the navy."

[1]Look for Kate Clinton's forthcoming book, *Point of No Routine*.

◇ ONE TICKET OUT

If you are in high school and having a hard time, one of the best ways out is to become a serious student and go to college. If you are isolated in a homophobic town, if your school is not a safe place to be out, if you're getting harassed or rejected by your peers, going to college is an excellent route to finding a more diverse community. As Richard says:

> Go to college and leave. That's the only thing I can say. That's the way I did it, and I don't know how to tell anybody else any different.

Attending a gay-friendly university opened up a whole new world for Doe:

> When I came to college it was like a warm, cozy, fuzzy blanket. I had a place to go where other women would be there to check me out, and there wasn't any pretending, there wasn't any hiding. There was the softball team, and the Stonewall meetings that I went to, and awareness week that I helped put on. I hit the scene and I gobbled it up. You know, like crackers.

You don't have to be supersmart to be a college-bound student. If you can read this book you have the skills and intelligence to go to college. There are scholarships, student loans, and low-tuition state schools that can help make it possible. And your grades don't have to be top-of-the-line fabulous in order to get into many schools.

If you've already dropped out of high school, you can get a high school equivalency diploma and go to a community college. Check with your local school district's adult education office about how to get started.

If you're at the beginning of high school, college will seem very far away, but sometimes it can help just to know that you're working toward something real—and much better—in the future. We can't overemphasize how liberating college has been for many gay youth.

◇ GET A JOB

Many gay, lesbian, and bisexual people who were miserable in their home towns have moved to larger, more cosmopolitan cities, gotten jobs, connected with the gay and lesbian communities there, and gone on to make satisfying lives for themselves.

This was true for Amy when she left her conservative town in Illinois:

> When I moved to Washington, D.C., and went to work in a homeless shelter, it was the first time I met anyone who identified as gay, lesbian, or bisexual. I began to learn posi-

tive things about queer people instead of the negative stereotypes I grew up with. And being out on my own made me more confident. Because I was physically and financially independent from my family, it became easier to come out to them.

After that I moved to Boston. I started working in a temporary job doing data entry and it led to a better, permanent position. Temp work was a good way to find a job without having a college degree. It was in Boston that I found a queer youth group and the gay community.

Beth has achieved independence and satisfaction through her work:

After I graduated high school, I went to work at a ski resort in Idaho where they provided room and board. Once I saw that I did OK there on my own, I learned that I could do anything and be whatever I wanted. For the next couple of years I moved around a lot and tried out many, many jobs.

It's when I got to LA that I really came out. I was detached from everyone I knew and what they thought I should be, so it was easier to be myself. Now I have two of my own companies. One is catering for the movie industry. The other is mail order merchandising to raise money for HIV-positive women with children. It's been a long journey, but I'm very successful. My life is so abundant.

Many of Beth's jobs were low-paying, and she often had to carry more than one at a time, but she was resourceful, determined, and, ultimately, successful.

◇ BE AN ACTIVIST

When you're alone and harassed, you're a victim. But when you join with others to combat oppression, you become an activist. If you're being tormented, one avenue is to take your anger and channel it into fighting for the rights of all gay, lesbian, and bisexual people. Not only does this help achieve important social change, but it also takes the emphasis off of what's wrong with you and puts it where it belongs—on what's wrong with the world.

It is very empowering to become part of an activist community. It's a good way to meet people, do important work, and, as Chris relates, contribute to your own healing:

I got asked to speak at a big rally for gay and lesbian student rights. I faltered a few times, but apparently it came off as being emotional, so it worked. When I was ending my speech I said, "I'm queer, I'm here, I'm a survivor, get used to it." Then I started crying. It was like I've made it. They can't hurt me anymore.

If you're not ready to be visible in an organization that works for equal rights for gay people, or if there isn't one in your town, other progressive causes are a good choice. You might want to work with a group like the Sierra Club, Amnesty International, or Planned Parenthood. Or you could volunteer with a service agency that feeds the homeless or assists older people. Socially responsible, progressive groups tend to draw more tolerant people who welcome diversity and are willing to stand up for what they believe is right.

WE ARE THE FUTURE

Even if you're having a hard time, know that there is a future for you. Hold onto your dreams.

It's my hope to have a partner and a family, and I'd like to raise kids—whether that's with a man or a woman. That's a traditional part of me. On the larger level I want to take the healing I've done inside myself and use it to heal a world that I think is very fragmented. I think I have a very authentic voice to speak from. It's my hope that I use that to provide healing.

—Sara

Ever since I was five I always wanted to be a famous singer. My high school is the high school of music, and I jump at every opportunity I get. I'm holding onto my dreams.

—Anthony

I know I want to stay in the creative arts, that's my field; probably be some famous photographer or something. Because I'm HIV-positive I've recently been exploring holistic health. I just want to live, that's all. Anything else I'll do later.

—Luna

I'm in the process of applying to graduate school, a Ph.D. in art history. But it wouldn't surprise me if I ended up with a masters degree in astrophysics. I don't know where I'll be in fifteen years.

—Alessandra

I have three political goals in my life. The first is to advance the gay youth movement, which I am doing now. The second is to reform high school education in California. And the third is to build a high-speed rail network across the United States. If I can accomplish those, I'll be happy.

—Rick

part 2

friends and lovers

Joan Bobkoff © 1995

◇ ◇ ◇ ◇ ◇ ◇ ◇ ◇ ◇ ◇

5
friends

A friend is a person with whom I may be sincere. Before him, I may think aloud.

—*Ralph Waldo Emerson*

Everyone needs friends. You don't need to be voted most popular, homecoming queen, or president of the senior class. But everyone needs one or two—or, if you're lucky, a few—good friends.

Real friends have a bond that's based on something sturdy between you. It may be shared attitudes and opinions; honest communication; involvement in an activity that's important to you both, like sports or computers; a way in which you inspire or encourage each other; or just really enjoying each other's company.

Within deep friendships, you experience the satisfaction of getting to know another person and of being known. Beyond these close friends, you may have a wider circle of friendly acquaintances. With these casual friends, you may do things together or hang out with the same crowd, but you don't necessarily reveal your deepest self.

Although it's not uncommon for gay and lesbian youth to experience some harassment or rejection from their wider sphere of acquaintances, many have friends who appreciate their courage and are truly supportive. As Jason relates:

> There are a couple guys who I used to play basketball with who've been obnoxious. But other than that, my friends have been great. I've known my best friend since kindergarten and I don't think anything could get between us. I think people who are secure in themselves tend to be more accepting anyway.

Brooke has also found support among her friends:

> My friends have been real good. The other night I met a lot of new people—we were all playing poker. There was a straight couple there, and I was with my girlfriend, and it seemed like an equal kind of thing. I'm lucky and I chose my friends well.

coming out to friends

Coming out to a friend can be frightening. It means exposing your deep feelings and, sometimes, risking rejection. How big that risk will feel depends a lot on your own situation. If you've fit our culture's expectations of how a boy or girl should look and act and you've always enjoyed a lot of friends, coming out may be daunting. You may feel like you're giving up the ease and reliability of the acceptance you've always known—at least superficially. Dan and his boyfriend Steven decided they weren't ready to expose themselves to possible harassment:

> We weren't public about becoming boyfriends. That was something we weren't ready for. We were public about being really good friends and I think some people guessed. But we were two jock boys and we went to a big school, and people didn't really pay attention to anyone outside their group.

On the other hand, if you've been isolated and lonely, coming out may be the first time that you find your way to real connection with others. Stacey describes her joy at finally making friends at the age of eighteen:

> After all those years of being so absolutely lonely and alone, I found friends. I was hanging out in Cambridge with all the punk rockers, and half of the kids happened to be gay. All of a sudden, I was with people who felt like me. I could be sitting next to them and the air felt comfortable. They understood the way I walked, the way I dressed, the things I felt, the dreams I had. From that day forward I don't think I lied about anything.

For Christopher, one of the rewards of coming out was more meaningful, honest relationships:

> The hardest part about coming out is telling something that's so deep in your heart with the realization that at any point they could say, "You're immoral, you're wrong," and turn around and walk away. And that's scarier than anything else that I've ever experienced.
>
> But what's wonderful is that finally you're not lying. You're being completely honest and they're sharing that joy with you. After the thumping of the heart in your throat, that's what makes it worthwhile.

The risks involved in telling a friend that you're gay, lesbian, or bisexual are rarely as severe as those involved in telling your family. Your friend can't kick you out of your home or cut off your financial support. Though you may care deeply about a friend, you can make new friends with more ease than you can get new parents. Although friends are very important, if one friend is not accepting, others will be. And, most basically, a friend who doesn't accept you isn't really a friend.

Even so, coming out is not the best choice in all circumstances. As Jonathan relates:

> I came back to Arkansas wanting to tell everybody. I wanted to say, "Look, I'm gay and it's alright and you people are just going to have to get over it." But I had to hold back because it's such a homophobic place.

Although it's great to be able to share all of who you are, only you can decide when—and to whom—you're ready to come out.

◇ DECIDING WHO TO COME OUT TO

You know your friends. You probably have a pretty good idea already of who is likely to be supportive and who isn't. People do surprise us, but thinking about what you already know gives you some useful information.

It's also a good idea to do some testing before you take the plunge. As Richard advises, "Be very cautious in whom you choose to confide, but still confide. You can test it out." (For more on this, see "How to Tell If Someone Is a Good Person to Talk To" on p. 36 and "Testing the Waters" on p.128.)

Matt has come out to some of his co-workers at the AIDS prevention agency where he volunteers, but he hasn't yet told any of his high school friends. He's concerned not only about his friends' reactions, but whether they would be able to keep his confidence.

Most people are not very good at keeping secrets. If you're not ready to make the news about your same-sex feelings public information, it's wise to assess your friend's ability to keep what you've shared confidential before coming out. Realistically, you can't be totally sure that there will be no leaks. Even well-intentioned friends may slip. If you absolutely can't deal with others finding out, you may want to wait a bit—or confide in a friend at a different school or in another town where your peers won't accidentally hear.

◇ DIFFERENT APPROACHES TO COMING OUT

People take different approaches to coming out. Some take their time and are very selective about whom they tell. Others, especially once they're in college or in the workplace, don't hide their sexuality, but they may not go looking for opportunities to come out. As Christopher explains, "I decided I'm not going to flaunt it, but if people ask me, I'm not going to say, 'Oh God, no!'"

Yevette, on the other hand, takes a very direct approach:

If I decide that I'm close enough to someone that I actually want to use their name and the word friend in the same sentence, then I tell them. And I say, "If you have a problem with this, please let me know right now." Because in the past, I've been really good friends with people and somehow or another it comes out and they lose their ever-lovin' mind. I don't need that around me. Let me know up front.

And Daphne comes out immediately:

> When I first meet people, the first thing I tell them is, "Hi, my name's Daphne," blah blah blah, where I come from, all this kind of stuff, "by the way, I'm a lesbian and I have a girlfriend." That way if they don't like me, that's fine with me. We don't become friends and it doesn't hurt my feelings.
> And you never know, you may end up saying that to someone and they're going to say, "Oh I'm gay too." I've had that happen.

Over time, the process of coming out may become a process of *being* out, simply being yourself, your whole self, in any situation. As Sara describes it:

> I'll be talking and they'll say, "Are you dating anyone?" and I'll say, "Yeah, I'm dating this really great woman." Then they do a double take and I'll say, "Yeah, I date both men and women." For me it's never this thing about, "Let me sit you down and tell you." It just depends on how I first know them. If I meet them when I'm kissing a woman then that's how they're going to meet me. But if they meet me in another place then it'll just be the first time it comes up.

Even once you are quite experienced with coming out, there is often a moment of choice when you, almost involuntarily, weigh the risks against the rewards. Though it may only take a heartbeat, most gay people notice that moment of self-awareness as they decide to reveal their sexual orientation.

How you come out will be individual. What's right for one person isn't going to be right for another. For most young people, a workable approach falls somewhere in between the extreme of wearing your purple button that says DYKE on the first day of school and, at the other end of the continuum, keeping yourself unnecessarily isolated.

I Get By with a Little Help from My Friends

I remember telling Janelle during that Christmas of our senior year. We were walking down the street, it was nighttime, and I said, "Janelle, I want to tell you something." And she said, "What?" And I said, "I'm afraid that you won't like me because . . . well . . . I'm gay." And she said, "But you mean so much to me. How could you think that? How could you actually think that I could leave your life?" I was crying in the middle of the street and she was holding me and crying too.

—Hyde

Someone on the swim team made some kind of remark about me and my boyfriend being "bum chums." And Mark, another guy on the team, said, "So what if they are? They can still kick your ass in the pool." Now my boyfriend was a really good water polo player. He got a scholarship to play in college. And I'm a national level swimmer. So the accuser had to back down. But it was the fact that it came from Mark, someone whose heterosexuality was beyond doubt, that made it so effective.

—Dan

My best friend had been mad at me for three months because I hadn't told her and she didn't know what was up, but she knew something was wrong. Everything I did was wrong. She screamed at me. She was just ready to kill me. I finally figured that it couldn't get any worse so I might as well tell her now while she hated me. I told her and she looked at me and said, "I knew there was something you weren't telling me." She was thrilled and very happy for me and immediately wanted to go about meeting my girlfriends.

—Stone

I had never been to a gay bar and I wanted to go, but I didn't have anybody to go with. And there was no way at nineteen that I was going to go to downtown Minneapolis at ten o'clock on my own, much less could I get a car for that amount of time, plus what would I tell my parents? So I got all my friends to go with me. I think they were just basically curious to see what it was like and I think they had a good time. The more that I look back on it, the more I appreciate that.

—Christopher

Earlier this year I was in the park with five of my closest friends
from my ninth grade class and I said, "OK, sit down. I know this
might make some of you uncomfortable, but, I'm bi." And my
friend Patrick was like, "Are you coming out? Are you coming out?
Oh my God, it's my first coming out!"

—Margaret

We were driving around and I said, "Josh, I really need to talk to
you about something. I think I might be bisexual." I wasn't really
sure what I was feeling, and I thought this would be a way to stay
in the middle. And he pulls over to the side of the road and turns
to me and goes, "I'm so glad you brought this up because I know
that I'm gay." I was just in shock that we had come out to each
other at the same time. It was just wonderful. We gave each other
the biggest hug for a long time, just because we knew we were
there for each other. And after that we stuck together even more.

—Gillian

WITH FRIENDS LIKE THESE, WHO NEEDS ENEMIES

I was in my first year in college and I decided to give my roommate
some time to get to know me before coming out. I thought, if he
gets to know me then maybe things will be OK. He had two weeks
before the rumor mill got to him. He came to me and said, "I heard
this rumor. I was talking to this guy and when I told him you were
my roommate, he said, 'Oh, he's a fag.' I told him, 'No, there's no
way. My roommate's not a fag.'"

I should have known to stop there. But I didn't. I got up my
courage and said, "Well, it's true. I am. I'm gay. But it's not like
I'm going to jump you at night." And he said, "Oh, I don't have a
problem with it." And then he proceeded to spend the night at his
girlfriend's apartment. He avoided me for two days and then he
told me he was moving out. That really hurt.

—Christopher

Marsha and I were going to the prom, and Marsha was going to
wear a tux and I was going to wear a dress, and Shannon, our best
friend, went off on, "Why can't you both just wear dresses and go
as friends?" And I asked, "Why should we? Would you want to wear
a tux with your boyfriend and go to the prom just as friends?" And

she goes, "Well, no. He's my boyfriend." I said, "Marsha's my girl-friend. Does it make any difference?" And she got really pissed off and stormed out of the house.

—Daphne

◇ THE COSTS OF HIDING

Although there are obvious difficulties in coming out, there are also deep costs involved in staying in the closet. Some of these costs have to do with our own sense of ourselves—if something has to be hidden, we can feel that it's shameful, bad, or wrong. Thinking that the truth about yourself is unspeakable reinforces internalized homophobia. And it's only a small step from feeling that your sexual orientation is not OK to feeling like you're not OK altogether.

The emotional cost of living in fear—and living a lie—is enormous. Al Ferreira, director of Project 10 East, a program for gay, lesbian, and bisexual students in Massachusetts, says, "Living with lies destroys the fabric of who we are as people. It imprisons us spiritually—and that's a terrible thing to do to other human beings."

There is also a price we pay in our relationships with others. As Richard explains:

When you have a lot of things to hide from people, you're very cautious about entering friendships. I'm still very hard on people, and people have to prove themselves to me.

Protecting yourself from exposure can be very stressful. It necessitates maneuvering conversation away from dangerous subjects—or even lying. For Richard, this evasion is a deeply embedded pattern:

I was very skillful at knowing everything about other people. They knew very little about me. I was on guard and watching everybody. I think a lot of people have a hard time letting their guard down and turning off the manipulation if they learned how to do it at such an early age.

Although we all have the right to keep information about ourselves private, it's a burden to have to hide our same-sex feelings. As Nancy says:

I would suggest to everyone to come out, but I know it's not always easy. If you think your situation will be bad, don't do it. But for me, coming out was the best medicine for my life. When you're in the closet, you're plugged up with one issue, when there are so many aspects to you as a person.

working it out with friends

Sometimes the reactions of friends are painful, but over time, more understanding is reached and the caring outweighs the difficulties. Christopher relates:

> My friend Shannon wrote a letter to friends of ours saying that she could not handle my "lifestyle" and that if I continued to act the way that I was acting, she could no longer be friends with me. That hurt really bad. The friends invited me over to dinner, handed me the letter, and stared at me while I read it. I couldn't say anything. I was devastated. I thought, this is the end of our friendship, a ten-year friendship just down the tubes. I didn't call her for the longest time and then eventually she called and apologized and said, "You know, I've been talking to my parents and they have a really negative attitude about this and they influenced my thinking. I don't understand it and I don't know if I agree with it, but I accept you and I love you and I'd like to be friends again." So being the nice person that I am, I took her right back. It was a happy outcome, but I still have that letter.

At first, Doe's best friend from high school didn't understand how she could be gay:

> She questioned me. She wanted answers, and some I could give her and some I couldn't. Like, why? Why would I want to date a woman versus a man? What do you mean, why? Because I do, you know? I realized that she had no clue.
>
> And that was always a conflict for me. I felt like Collette should go out and learn this herself, but where is she going to learn this? Why shouldn't I share this with her? She needs to know. She needs to get this from someone who she feels comfortable with, but it was always a conflict, because I felt drained from giving myself.
>
> As she started to do some signing for disabled student services on campus, she began to see things in a more politi-

cal way. It wasn't until she was able to parallel the struggles
of disabled people with similar struggles of gay liberation
that she was able to understand my life a little bit more.

With perseverance from both sides, Doe and Collette have been
able to keep communicating. Coming out is a process that takes
time, not only for you but for the people you care about.

WHAT CAN YOU DO? YOUR FRIEND JUST TOLD YOU "I'M GAY"

STOP TELLING QUEER JOKES	HELP YOUR FRIEND FIND AN UNDERSTANDING ADULT	DON'T GO AWAY
Because they're based on lies and may be hurting someone you care about	Because realizing you're gay can be confusing and lonely—we all need support Remember, not everyone will be helpful....choose carefully	Because your friend is in need of someone to lean on Trusting you is a sign of friendship

Adapted from a poster by Wingspan Ministry, Saint Paul, Minnesota

ADVICE FOR THE FRIENDS OF GAY, LESBIAN, AND BISEXUAL YOUTH

My advice to friends of gay kids is just to remember that we're no
different five minutes after we told you than we were five minutes
before—except ten minutes older, and that doesn't really matter
much. And remember that this does not mean we are in love with you.

—Stone

Be understanding, and don't think so much about yourself. I would
say that to both parties, not to think so much about what you are
going through, but about what the other person is going through.

—Rick

Let the person who's coming out just talk. They may not have had a chance to talk about this to very many people at all—maybe no one. Ask questions neutrally, not demanding questions but like, "How long have you been thinking about this?" And assure them that they can talk about anything with you.

—Brooke

Remember that coming out is a very hard thing. For someone to bring you into that circle of trust is a really big step.

—Quang

The friends I remained close with embraced it as part of my life. They asked if I was going out on dates. They asked me questions. They engaged me in conversations. Even if they were uncomfortable, they wanted to talk about it.

I had this boyfriend, and a couple housemates of mine would never ask me about it. So finally I told them, "Look, I'm always asking you about this person you're dating and that person, and you're not going to ask me any questions? You don't want to hear any dirt?" And finally they caught on.

—Craig

it's getting better all the time

In general, the younger you are the harder it is to be out. Young people who come out in junior high usually have a very tough time of it. Coming out in high school can still be extremely difficult, depending on where you go to school. But sometimes, by then, there are subgroups of people with like minds where it's possible to find an accepting niche.

In college, and out in the work world, people develop friendship circles based on their own values and affinities and don't have to relate as much to those with whom they don't get along. As you grow older, you have more control over your circumstances. And people are usually less demanding of rigid conformity. If they don't actually become more accepting of differences, many of them become more civil about how they act.

In high school it can look like the cool people will be cool forever. But it doesn't always turn out that way. Some of the most terrific, talented, successful, and well-loved people were desperately unhappy in high school. And some of the ones who were popular did not go on to lead very satisfying lives.

The good news in this is that you're getting older all the time. If you're in a situation now where you are experiencing harassment and rejection from your peers, it's important to know that *this will get better*. This is not to minimize the pain you may be going through now, but it can help to know that you won't have to put up with this forever.

I'M SO MUCH HAPPIER NOW

I'm so much happier now that I'm twenty-five. I have a lot more resources—both internal and external. The internal work has been about accepting myself. I've stopped being so self-critical. The external part is about moving away from where I grew up, getting to choose the community I live in and finding meaningful work that validates my political beliefs and emotional experiences. It took time for all this to happen. I needed to understand how the world I live in had affected me to be able to get past it.

—Sara

It's gotten better just in the fact that I don't feel so isolated anymore. Isolation was the hardest part. Now I'm more honest with everyone and I don't have to hide and it's great. As I get more mature, I learn, every day, to be more like who I believe I really am. Like I know that I don't have to be a *GQ* gay guy. Some are, but that's not me—though I do love to go shopping.

—Christopher

Even now at sixteen it's so much different. I feel like I've really settled into myself. A lot of aspects in my life have stabilized. I have a group of friends who know that I'm gay and they've known long enough that it isn't really an issue anymore. And I don't have to work so hard just to get through the day. I still get comments about being queer, but somehow it doesn't touch my perception of myself anymore. It still hurts, but I don't have to stop and tell myself that I really am a good person, regardless of what they say, because by now I know that.

—Stone

Looking back I feel like the hard times were a training to become the person I am today. So many of my positive traits—like learning not to judge others by outside appearances—were formed when I was the brunt of so much teasing.

Moving to Memphis meant that I no longer had to pretend to be someone I'm not in order to fit in. I've surrounded myself with people who love me and accept me for who I am. It's important to me to take a stance—to come out of the closet—I refuse to go back to that other place. I won't apologize for who I am. I'm very open and honest about who I am, and I feel so much better now.

—Jonathan

making new friends

For gay, lesbian, and bisexual youth who have felt isolated and lonely, meeting other young people who are gay or gay-friendly can feel really wonderful. When Chris went to BAGLY, the gay, lesbian, and bisexual support group in Boston, his life improved dramatically:

Since then, my life has taken a major turn. I've started doing the things I'd always wanted to do with my new friends. Like go to the movies. I went to the BAGLY prom. I even wore a tux.

If you've been suffering in isolation, if you've felt that you had to hide your true self, finding friends that you can be honest with is likely to feel terrific. As Matt describes it:

I don't know where the concept of "it's a lonely life if you're gay" came from, because that certainly has not been my experience. It hasn't been lonely at all. Before I was out, I pretended. I hung out with my friends and just didn't share this part of my life. But it was an incredibly hard thing to do. And it was very lonely. Since I've come out, I'm able to talk with some people, I'm able to completely share my life with them.

Cathy Cade © 1995

Joan Bobkoff © 1995

6
love

Fill our gold cups with love
stirred into clear nectar

—Sappho

> Sappho (b. 612 BC), the
> most famous woman poet
> of all time, was born on
> the Greek island of
> Lesbos, from which les-
> bians got their name. Her
> lyrics celebrate women's
> experience, and she writes
> of her love for women
> with passion, sensuality,
> and wit.

Special feelings for another person can start when you're just a small child. As Richard relates, "I remember having a crush on my close friend Jeffrey in kindergarten and wanting to pet his hair." As you grow up, you notice that there are people to whom you're drawn in a way that's different from "just friends." What it is that makes us feel that way is pretty much a mystery. But eventually we all have the experience of wanting to be with someone in a special way. We're happy in their presence. We long for them when we're apart. And we feel somehow enriched, enhanced when we're with them.

As Johnny Mathis sang way back in the days when records were played on turntables, "When I am with you . . . I am everything I ever wanted to be—and more."

> Johnny Mathis (b. 1935), an African-American singer, won enormous popularity in the 1950s with his first recordings, *Wonderful, Wonderful* and *Johnny Mathis's Greatest Hits*. He's best known for his velvet voice and melow ballad-style love songs.

i've got a crush on you

For some young people, same-sex attractions first become apparent with crushes. As Stone remembers, "I was thirteen when I fell in love with a friend at her birthday slumber party. I was watching her sleep on her pillow."

Kids can develop crushes on friends, teachers, movie stars—just about anyone. Chris relates that he once had a big crush on Arnold Schwarzenegger: "I think he's absolutely disgusting now, but back then I thought he was really cute."

Often crushes are on someone unattainable. Although unrequited love may be painful, it sometimes teaches you about yourself, as when Arwyn fell for a straight girl at her high school:

> It really hit me, my freshman year, when I totally just fell in love with this senior girl. She was the most popular girl in the school. She was like a poster girl for heterosexuals, so it was doomed from the beginning, but I completely tumbled for her. I mean to this day I still remember the first time I saw her and what she was wearing and everything. I didn't think it was sexual or anything like that, but after a while it got to the point where it was just obsession, there was no other way to put it, and I just said, "OK, fine, I'm bisexual."

Dan had his first big crush in seventh grade:

> I remember being in drafting classes seventh period and the door opens and I turn around and there is this really cute

boy, named Steven. He transferred from another school and I was like, literally, be still my heart. I really flipped for this boy. He was in all my classes, but I had already started to consruct this wall between me and straight boys, not that I had any gay male friends. I didn't let myself get close to anyone. I always thought that if I became really good friends with Steven, everyone would be able to tell what I was feeling just by looking at my eyes when I was around him.

Sometimes, happily, you may have a crush on someone who returns your feelings. As Nicky describes it:

I had a big crush on him. And finally I told him toward the end of seventh grade, "I really care about you." This guy was someone that every girl wanted. He was really shocked. I asked him, "Why don't we go some place, just so you can get to know me a little bit better?" He said, "Fine." We went to the mall. And we went to go see the movie *The Bodyguard*. And that's the first day that he told me that he cared about me also. It was just wonderful.

meeting boyfriends and girlfriends

Gay and lesbian teenagers usually don't have as many opportunities to explore their feelings and get to know boyfriends and girlfriends as their straight peers do. They may be limited by a lack of other openly lesbian and gay young people with whom they can socialize, by the homophobia in their families, schools, or communities, or by their own reluctance to acknowledge their sexual orientation.

Generally, the younger you are, the harder it is to meet boyfriends and girlfriends. There can be a monumental difference between the difficulties of meeting potential dates at fourteen and at twenty-four. Some young teens find that they just have to wait a little while before they're able to do much dating. Others pair up within the limited options available.

And some are lucky to already know the person they're attracted to—and to have it be mutual. As Michelle relates:

Victoria and I had been friends since elementary school. We had grown up together. She's in all of the major memories in my life. I was fifteen when I realized that I was attracted to her.

Best friends evolving into lovers seems more common among girls. As Daphne says:

> We moved here two years ago. And my first day of school I met my now girlfriend, Marsha. She called me and asked me to go rollerblading, and from that day on we were inseparable. Every day we spent together. She went home at ten o'clock at night, and then the next day we were together all day. It was in November, when we went camping, that I realized my feelings for her were more than just friendship. She has a phobia and she was having a bad night. So I was holding her. She was asleep on my lap and I was rubbing my fingers through her hair and I thought, oh she's so gorgeous.

Any situation in which you have the opportunity to connect with others is a place where it's possible to meet someone to date. Meeting people through a shared activity is often a less pressured, more comfortable way to connect. The emphasis is on your activity, rather than each other, giving you both a chance to get to know each other naturally. Quang met Alex volunteering for a youth organization:

> One night, after the training, we went to a cafe. We were just talking and talking. And there was a certain point at which I realized that there was something special going on. I felt like he was listening to everything that I was saying. He was really interested. And I was sitting on the edge of my seat and really listening to him, wanting to know about him also.

Of course one of the oldest ways to meet someone is to have friends introduce you. Christopher describes his feelings when his friend arranged for him to meet another young man:

> She told me who he was and said, "Well, you can call." Of course I was just too nervous. I could never, ever do that. So I made her call him. Then she brought me over there and I was so nervous I didn't know what to say. I mean, gosh, what do I talk about? I instantly fell in love, and it was wonderful.

And then there is chance. You might meet someone in the grocery store, at the laundromat, taking your dog to the vet, or at work. Sometimes love comes when you least expect it.

dating

Rigid rules about dating have all but collapsed. In same-sex relationships, it's even less clear as to who asks whom out, who pays, who
takes whom home, and all the rest. The good part of this is that you
get to do things the way you want to, you get to make it up. You
can flirt and hope the person you've got your eye on makes the first
move. Or you can ask them out directly.

If you're not sure if someone is gay, you can do a quick test for
homophobia. If they pass, you can come out. In that conversation,
they'll often reveal their sexual orientation too. Or you can ask if
they're gay or lesbian without letting them know that you're interested in dating them.

More Dykes to Watch Out For, Alison Bechdel, Firebrand Books, Ithaca, N.Y. © 1987

Dating has been somewhat out of vogue. Instead, people often
skip that getting-to-know-each-other stage. As Stacey says, "I kept
having these—'Hello, I've only known you for five minutes, but I'm
going to marry and be with you for the absolute rest of my life.'"

But dating can give you a chance to see how much you really
like someone before becoming too involved. It can also be a lot of
fun. As Jonathan describes it:

> I began to date for the first time, kissed a boy for the first
> time. And that was the most amazing thing because I was

afraid. I always had in the back of my mind that little inkling that the first time I dated somebody, it might not feel right and I might not be gay after all. So, I went out on a date, had a great time, everything. It was just the most comfortable thing I'd ever done. And I knew then, yes, this is definitely me.

After the first date, you may be crazy about the other person and he or she may be only lukewarm about you—or vice versa. If you're brand new to dating, it may even take some time before you're able to read the signals that help you to know what's what. One very young lesbian fell head over heels in love with her first date, an energetic activist for justice for gay people. When the date said she didn't have time to see her and didn't return her calls, this girl didn't have a clue. She told her mother, "It's hard to be in a relationship with an activist. You hardly get to see them."

"flaunting"

Being affectionate in public—or even just being clearly together on a date or as a couple—is not something that gay, lesbian, and bisexual people can take for granted. Outside of gay events or the gay sections of a few large cities, even simple activities like holding hands or walking with your arms around each other are met with stares at best and insults, harassment, or even violence in the worst cases.

Finding the level of visibility that's most comfortable for you can be difficult. On the one hand, you have the right to live your life as you choose regardless of what other people think. On the other, you may not always want to deal with the reactions of others—and sometimes you need to take your own safety into consideration. At first, Anni was surprised at how difficult she found this balance:

> I had thought I would be so cool and so wonderful and I'd walk down the street with my girlfriend and not have any problems about it. I found that wasn't true. I was uncomfortable. Not so much so that it held me back, but I was nervous about kissing her in public. I got over that, though. I became more sure of myself and proud of who I was. After a while it became kind of fun if people did double takes when they saw us kissing. We'd wave at them.
>
> I hear a lot of, "I don't want it shoved in my face," and I really find myself trying to project a good image. It's silly,

and I shouldn't have to. Every heterosexual on the street is
sucking face, and a little peck on the cheek is not serious,
but I find myself wondering what everybody's thinking and
how they're going to judge the entire queer community
because of what we're doing.

Even when you're quite relaxed yourself, there may still be circumstances when you determine that it's not advisable or safe to be
openly affectionate. One mother of a gay son expresses her outrage
about this:

Straight people get to run around and be visible, sexually, all
over the place and if gay people are visible in that way,
they're accused of flaunting. About a month after Brian came
out to me, I was in this coffee house and there was this
young heterosexual couple in front of me holding hands,
arms around each other, heads on shoulders, nuzzling. And I
was thinking, if this was my gay kid with his boyfriend, he
would get harassed, stoned, maybe arrested. This is offensive to me—not what they were doing, but the double standard. It's offensive to me that some damned straight people
say, "Why do those queers have to flaunt it?"

It strains our relationships when we are forced to hide our genuine and spontaneous feelings of affection. The division between
public and private time can feel like an international border instead
of a natural transition. This is one reason why it's good to have
places in our lives where we are free to express ourselves openly.
Gay events, social groups, and time with friends who are either gay
or gay-friendly give you a chance to be around other people with
your boyfriend or girlfriend in a natural way.

How Do You Introduce Your Sweetie?

lover? boyfriend?   girlfriend? significant other?   honey?
housemate?   **partner?**   long-time companion?   domestic
partner?   spouse? *roommate?*   wife?   *husband?*
friend?   mate?   *someone special?*   gal pal?   **sugarplum?**

*We still don't have the all-purpose word we need. Write in with your sugges-
tions and we'll include the best ones in the next edition.*

healthy relationships

The things that are important in developing healthy lesbian, gay, and bisexual relationships are no different from what's important in any romantic relationship: love, respect, good communication, physical attraction, mutual support, affection, a balance of intimacy and independence, and fun.

◇ RESPECT

Respect is an essential element in healthy relationships. Respect means thinking very highly of the other person, as well as yourself, and fully considering the other person's welfare. It means caring about their well-being beyond its impact on you.

In a respectful relationship, you can feel secure that your trust will not be betrayed. When you expose intimate feelings, they won't be ridiculed or ignored. You can rely on each other to be honest. You respect each other's wishes and boundaries. You don't push each other to move the relationship forward beyond what you're both ready for.

In a respectful relationship you don't try to make the other person over to fit your ideal. You honor your differences. And neither of you sees the other as property or a prize. You don't decide for each other who to be friends with, how to act, or what to wear. Although you share your love, you don't "belong" to anyone but yourself.

◇ COMMUNICATION

Good communication is a learned skill—and a real accomplishment. It's difficult to communicate clearly and well—especially when emotions run high—but honest communication is a key ingredient to a healthy relationship. As Daphne describes it:

> This is the best relationship I've ever had. Not only are we best friends and I can tell her anything, but the closeness that we have, the warmth in our relationship, the fact that we can talk so well, communicate so well with each other, it amazes me.

There are two essential parts to communication—talking and listening. In the talking department, you need to be aware of how you really feel—and brave enough to say it. You need to expose your honest thoughts and feelings in a considerate way.

As the listener, you need to be able to acknowledge the other person's point of view, even when you don't agree with it. This is what turns a fight into a dialogue. Then you can work together to find creative solutions and compromises for whatever challenges you face.

To do this, you have to be able to go back and forth between your own point of view and that of the other person. You need to convey your care for each other, even when you're angry. In order to accomplish this tall order, it sometimes helps to have a cooling-off period between an upsetting incident and the follow-up discussion.

Gay, lesbian, and bisexual young people may have an advantage in learning communication skills because they have had to look inside themselves honestly and wrestle with issues such as *Who am I?* and *What is right for me?* at an early age. That increased self-awareness can be a real asset in communication.

◇ MUTUAL SUPPORT

Supporting each other's endeavors and encouraging the best in each other are meaningful parts of a healthy relationship. This is easy to do when the other person's goals mesh with what you want anyway. It's much harder when your girlfriend or boyfriend wants to do something that won't be easy for you. For example, if your boyfriend wins a scholarship to a college several hundred miles away, you may be upset at the idea of being so far apart. You may even be jealous. If you think only of your own desires, you could try to influence him to forget about college, stay with you, and get a job. But that wouldn't really be supporting him or his goals. True support means helping the other person achieve his or her dreams even when that's difficult or requires compromise on your part.

◇ INTIMACY AND INDEPENDENCE

Healthy relationships have a balance of connectedness and independence. You are able to share yourselves, to know each other, to feel close, and to be intimate. And you are also able to maintain yourself as an individual, with your own interests, friends, thoughts, and feelings. Just where you set the balance will vary from person to person and from relationship to relationship.

The teenage years are notorious for close friendships where the friends are inseparable. So it's no wonder that many young people go overboard on the togetherness part of this equation and skimp on the separateness. And at the very beginning, lovers of all ages often go through a time when all they want is to be together. But in sustained relationships, the time comes when your individual self needs to emerge and you must balance times of intimacy with times of independence.

◇ FUN

Although lasting relationships require a willingness to work through difficult times, the good times should definitely outweigh the hard ones. Anything that makes you feel good and glad to be alive is fun. It can be things you like to do together—like riding bikes or cooking. It can be talking on the phone all night. Or reading poems to each other, taking a walk, or sitting at a cafe in the sun. Enjoying time together is the best reason to be together.

breaking up

You may like—and even love—someone very much, but that person may not be the one for you forever. Breaking up with someone you care about is painful. It's hard even if you're the one initiating the breakup or if it's mutually agreed, but of course it's even harder if it's not your choice. Nicky's boyfriend ended their relationship a year ago, and his heart's still broken:

> I still love him. I'm not going to say that I don't. It's just the memories I get when I hear songs, or I see something that we once did together. I've asked him, "Why can't we be just friends?" But he said, "I don't want to see you. I don't want to talk to you."

This kind of rejection feels devastating, but even kinder breakups can hurt a lot. Yet breaking up is something almost everyone does—and usually more than once. As Renee says:

> Part of growing up is learning that there are people in your life who might be good for you at one point but that are not

good for you anymore. Let them go. You learned something from them. Now it's time for you to move on.

GET OUT OF ABUSIVE RELATIONSHIPS

If your relationship is abusive or disrespectful, it's important that you get out. You deserve respect and care from anyone with whom you're intimately involved.

Abuse can be physical—including being hit, shoved, or threatened. It can be sexual—including forced sex or sexual humiliation. It can be emotional—including being insulted, ridiculed, lied to, manipulated, or overly controlled.

If any of these things—or things like them—are happening in your relationship, it's *NOT* OK. The abuse needs to stop *right away* and not be repeated, or you need to end the relationship.

Often people are angry as well as hurt in breakups, although this doesn't always have to be the case. You may be able to end your relationship in a way that's caring and respectful of both partners' needs. As Jonathan describes it:

> The relationship ended because of our age difference. I was eighteen years old and he was twenty-seven. Both of us wanted to keep progressing, but we were holding back because of the age. And so, we ended crying and holding each other. Very tender, and it wasn't a fight. It was a decision, a mutual decision that this was the way it needed to be. I still keep in contact with him even now because he was such a friend.

At its best, breaking up can be seen as a time of change in the definition of your relationship—making the transition from lovers to friends. Remaining friends is an affirmation of the fact that you really did like each other—beyond your romantic or sexual attraction. And it allows us to keep a continuity in our lives that is special and satisfying. But it usually takes some time for the heart to mend and feelings to cool down before former lovers can be friends. And sometimes, it's just never possible.

Dykes to Watch Out For: The Sequel, Alison Bechdel, Firebrand Books, Ithaca, N.Y., © 1991

Longevity is not the only measure of a relationship. The fact that it doesn't last forever doesn't mean a relationship has failed. The real measure of success in relationships is about caring, mutual respect, and growth.

Every relationship teaches us something. We learn more about ourselves—both what we like and what we don't like. We learn about what we want from the people we become involved with. And we learn what *we* bring to our relationships that enriches them, as well as what makes them difficult.

There's a saying that good judgment comes from experience and experience comes from bad judgment. So your mistakes are part of the process by which you become wise.

commitment

Although some people choose to be single or date casually, many people want to make a lasting commitment to someone special. Because our homophobic society often condemns or fails to recognize gay and lesbian relationships, there can be extra challenges to overcome in sustaining our relationships. Yet healthy, fulfilling relationships are absolutely possible, as Quang describes:

I've been so fortunate. My relationship with Alex is something that I never realistically dreamed of having. Growing up, from the time I started to realize that I was gay, I always idealized having a loving romantic relationship, but I don't think I ever truly thought that it could happen. It was always like a dream.

Lifelong love and commitment is something that many people hope for. Marriage is not yet legal in the United States for gay and lesbian couples, but concerted efforts are underway to make it so.

You may be aware that at one time marriage between different races was also illegal in the United States. It's only in the last forty to fifty years that state by state those laws have been stricken down, and now, of course, race is no longer a legal obstacle to marriage.

In 1996 the State Supreme Court of Hawaii is scheduled to consider a case which argues that preventing people of the same gender from marrying is a form of sexual discrimination and, as such, against the law. Although the outcome of this case is still unknown, it is only a matter of time before gays and lesbians will be able to be legally married.

In the meantime, gay and lesbian couples have created their own ceremonies and covenants to pledge their love and to honor their relationships. Some couples make private promises to each other. Others want a more public ritual. By sharing their vows with family and friends, gay and lesbian couples engage the ongoing support of their community. Increasingly, clergy are conducting such ceremonies and providing their blessings and the validation of their religious institutions.

And there are many couples that have been sharing their lives—without all the ceremony—for ten, twenty, thirty years and more!

BETH'S STORY: MY MARRIAGE TO BECKY

Becky and I married in a very traditional way. I was wearing a beautiful white dress. She wore a zoot suit. We got married in the woods in Oregon, and Becky said that when I came through the trees I looked like an angel. Everyone was crying. It was incredible to have our closest friends and family just surrounding us with love. My father is very eloquent, and he performed the ceremony. He planned a long ritual, which started with everyone holding hands, but he had to cut it short because he was so choked up he couldn't speak.

Thank God we hadn't prepared any long vows because I couldn't have gotten out two words.

The commitment that we made to each other was to love and honor and respect each other every day, one day at a time, for the rest of our lives. It feels just right, like all of my dreams coming true. I've always been an independent person, but it makes me feel even stronger because I know there's someone besides God in my corner, one hundred percent, no matter what.

We've taken this commitment slowly, one step at a time. We did premarital counseling where we shared our ideas of marriage that we had grown up with and we came to some common understandings of what our marriage meant to us. We have so many hopes and dreams—saving money, buying a house, having kids. And we're going to take all those steps slowly also.

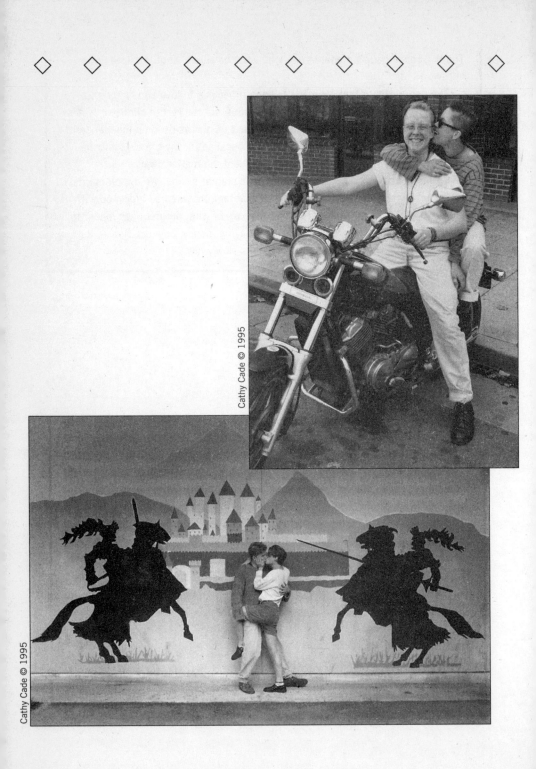

Cathy Cade © 1995

Cathy Cade © 1995

◇　　◇　　◇　　◇　　◇　　◇　　◇　　◇　　◇　　◇

7
sex

I mind how once we lay such a transparent summer morning,
How you settled your head athwart my hips and gently
    turn'd over upon me,
And parted the shirt from my bosom-bone and plunged your
    tongue to my bare-stript heart,
And reach'd till you felt my beard, and reach'd till you held
    my feet.
Swiftly rose and spread around me the peace and knowledge
    that pass all the argument of the earth . . .

                               —*Walt Whitman*

Walt Whitman (1819–1892), one of the greatest nineteenth-century American poets, was a pioneer in abandoning most of the conventions of earlier poetry to create a new form. In *Leaves of Grass* he celebrates the cultural diversity of America, democracy, freedom, the self, and the joys of living.

Whatever happens with us, your body
will haunt mine—tender, delicate
your lovemaking, like the half-curled
    frond
of the fiddlehead fern in forests
just washed by sun. . . .

. . . your strong tongue and slender
    fingers
reaching where I had been waiting years
    for you
in my rose-wet cave—whatever happens,
this is.

—*Adrienne Rich*

Adrienne Rich
(b. 1929) is one of the foremost poets and
feminist theorists of our
time. Her poetry reveals
the individual personal life
as inseparable from a
wider social condition.
Among her books are *The
Dream of a Common
Language, A Wild Patience
Has Taken Me This Far,* and
*An Atlas of the Difficult
World.*

Practicing safe sex is a matter of life and death. Because it's so important, please be sure to read the chapter that follows this one, "HIV, AIDS, and Safer Sex."

Sex is one of the sublime experiences of life. At its best, sexual ecstasy transports us out of our own limited being and we feel at one, not only with our beloved, but with all of creation. When the context is right, making love nourishes us physically, emotionally, and spiritually.

But when the circumstances aren't right, sex can hurt us. Sex is a powerful energy, and like many strong things, it can be used both for good and for harm. Learning what's necessary for us to experience the joy of sex and to protect ourselves from harm is one of the important lessons of adult life.

Young people who first explore their emerging sexuality in peer relationships that are loving, respectful, and not pressured are fortunate. This kind of positive, pleasurable, caring beginning makes it easier to develop a healthy, vital sexuality. But even for people whose first sexual experiences were not positive, it's possible to achieve a healthy, fulfilling sexual life.

the joy of going slowly

The ways in which you express physical intimacy will depend on your age and your experience. What's right for you in your early teens may be totally different from what's right for you in your twenties.

And you don't need to be embarrassed about being a beginner. You don't need to be as experienced as Madonna. Sometimes young people rush into sex just so they can lose their virginity and find out what all the fuss is about. Or they may be longing for validation or for intimacy. On the whole, this hurry-up approach isn't as satisfying as a gradual process of discovery and unfolding. As Stone relates:

> It was our third date and we still hadn't kissed. We were just holding hands all the way to San Francisco and back. Four hours. And I loved every minute of it.

Often young people are told to wait to have sex. The reasons are often repeated: you're too young, you're not old enough to be responsible about safety, and it's immoral. These reasons may or may not be meaningful to you, but there's another reason, rarely mentioned, which is very important. Taking your time getting started with sex—and going slowly, savoring each small step—can be the most delicious entrance into sex, as well as one that will lead to pleasure, satisfaction, and joy in your future sexuality.

FIRST KISS

We were sitting out on the stairs by my house and I said, "I really like you, but I've never even kissed a girl before." She leaned forward and it was the most incredible feeling. I was sitting there shaking and sweating. I was in some other world. I was like, oh my God. She leaned forward and she kissed me. A simple kiss. It was not a french kiss or anything. It was just a kiss. I was just like, holy cow. This is it.

—Mickie

In tenth grade, I'm still around Steven. It was lust at this point, pure unadulterated I wanted him. He was in my math class, and for homework we had to make a dodecahedron. So we're in his room, sitting at his desk next to each other. It was hot and we were both wearing shorts. And I was thinking how nice his legs were, because by this point Steven had gone through one whole year of swimming and water polo and the boy was a god. We're shaking our legs, and first our knees are hitting each other and pretty soon our legs are hitting and then they rest longer together and a little longer and pretty soon they're just together, thigh touching thigh and knee touching knee. I held my breath.

I remember looking at his profile and thinking how long his eyelashes are. He has really beautiful blue eyes, and I see him look out the corner of his eye back at me. And then he turns his head to look at me and I'm just looking at him and our legs are still together and it was like this pull, this magnetism, and neither one of us said a thing. I remember thinking, oh God, don't let me be wrong, don't let me be wrong about this one thing in my entire life.

I leaned forward. I half closed my eyes and then willed them to open again so I could see everything, but then I closed my eyes and landed on his lips. And that was my first kiss. It was accompanied by a rush of air through my body, like electricity, but not electricity. It was a rush kind of like if someone throws their hand into your face and stops right there. I remember thinking, don't think about what's happening, just do it.

—Dan

don't do anything you don't want to do

Kissing, hugging, touching, and all the rest of being intimate should feel good. If it doesn't feel good, don't do it. If you feel rushed, scared, unsure, or just don't like it—STOP.

Don't allow yourself to be pressured into sex that you aren't sure you want. Listen to your body, listen to your heart, and listen to your mind. You need them all to know what's really best for you.

If the person you're with can't respect your feelings or your limits, then he or she is not the person you should be sexual with. The pace should always be set by the person who wants or needs to go the slowest. Someone who would pressure you to have sex—or to do sexual things you don't want to do—isn't a good choice for an intimate partner.

Anyone who truly cares about you will want you to be fully present, comfortable, and happy. Jonathan describes the first man he was in a relationship with:

He was so respectful of me and respectful of the fact that I was young. I was very honest with him to let him know that he was the first person I'd ever dated and that he would have to go very slow, and we did.

Sex screams at us from billboards, advertisements, movies, sit-coms, talk shows, magazines, and CDs. There is enormous hype, giving the idea that everyone is having lots and lots of sex. Yet many people don't feel satisfied or joyful in their sexual lives. You are not likely to get a very clear picture about sex from the media. Nor are you likely to get much guidance for your own sexual life.

Instead, you will need to look inside and think about your own feelings, your values, and what you really want. People are not all the same sexually, just as they're not all the same in every other way.

In order for sex to feel right for you, it has to fall within your own value system. So if you believe that sex is something best reserved for a permanent committed relationship, you're not going to feel good about having sex without commitment. As Jonathan explains:

> Because of my religion, I have different attitudes toward sex, and that's part of the reason why I have not engaged in it. I want to be monogamous and be in a relationship before I do it. And it's caused me some problems. Some people want to be able to just go to bed. And I say, "No, I don't do that."

If you feel that love is an important part of sex, then you're not going to feel good having sex with someone you don't really care about—or who doesn't truly care about you. Patrick reports:

> I just had so much sexual tension inside me that I said, "OK, fine." I knew he did not want to be my boyfriend. He wanted to play around. At the time I didn't care. But now, looking back, it was hurtful, because I didn't really like him. I wasn't that attracted to him. I just did it because . . . I don't know, I just didn't even think about it.
>
> Afterward I realized that was exactly what I did *not* want to be doing. I really wanted to love. I wanted a boyfriend, not just sex.

The more you are able to be in touch with your emotions, listen to your body, protect yourself, remember your own basic values, and use your best judgment, the better. As Jessica relates:

> I got sexual real early, but I hated it. Now, with my present girlfriend, I've gone real slow and just enjoyed each thing we do. Even just kissing or holding hands is such a thrill. Before I just didn't feel anything. Now I get to feel everything we do, and we only do things when we're both ready.

Whether you are sexual because of lust or romance—or both—recognizing your own values and your own needs is an important part of becoming mature. Although what's right for you may be different from what's right for someone else, the bottom line is that sex has to be mutually respectful and safe.

If you have already had sex that was unsatisfying, frightening, unsafe, or otherwise not what you really wanted to be doing, you're not alone. And you don't have to keep doing it that way. Even if your beginnings were painful, you can start to make changes now that will enable you to have a healthy, fulfilling sexual life.

talk about it

Communicating about sexuality is a tall order for most people—regardless of their age. It can feel daunting to say what you like, what you don't like, what's enough, when to stop, when to go. But it's crucial that you manage to communicate. Not only do you need to talk about safer sex, but it's also important that you let your partner know what you want—and don't want.

If you can't always get it out in words, use body language. You can push away, pull closer, or get up. Or exchange lists of what makes you feel good. As Stone relates, there are all kinds of ways to communicate:

> After my girlfriend and I had been together a little while we started talking about sex on the phone because we were still too embarrassed to talk about it in person. And I remember I'd blush and blush. I was so glad she couldn't see me.

If your communication isn't so suave, don't worry. Most people have a hard time talking about their intimate feelings. You don't need to be graceful—blurting out what you feel is a fine start.

what's love got to do with it?

Sex without caring—or without a minimum of respect—can be harmful and can leave you feeling very hurt. As John relates:

> We had had sex and he told me that I gave very good head. I was so upset. I thought he'd say, you know, you're a very nice guy, I like talking to you. Instead he said that. It was a scary thing for me.

Jessica also got hurt by sex without love:

> I thought if I had sex with her she'd love me. I thought having sex *was* love. But it turned out that she was only into sport sex. And I was crushed. Just devastated.

Sex without a caring relationship can sometimes give you a brief feeling of being wanted, of being important, but that validation doesn't last very long. And the aftermath may feel even worse. As Patrick describes it:

> I felt like I wasn't really worth anything. I thought if I could get sex that it would validate me. And if I was cute enough to actually be able to have sex then I was really worth something. But after I went to the Castro and realized how easy it is to get sex, I realized, oh no, that's not it.

Yevette wishes she were in a loving relationship, but until then, she'd rather be alone than with people she doesn't really care about:

> I don't date much. I'm not into wham bam, thank you ma'am. Never have, never will be. And I haven't really run across a lot of women who aren't already in relationships who want the same thing. The loneliness is really bothering me. Waiting for the right one. I have friends who say, "Well, why don't you just date? Just go out with somebody even if you're not interested in them." But I wouldn't want anybody to do that to me. I would be insulted. So I don't even want to go that route. If I'm not even halfway thinking about being with you for a while, I don't want to go there.

Michael, a twenty-four-year-old gay man, describes how love enriches sex:

> Sex is always better with someone you really care about and respect. As gay men, it's not difficult to find somebody to have sex with, probably every night if you wanted to. But it's not easy to get through that with some sense of your body and your soul intact. It's better to allow the emotional and the physical to progress together so that the sexuality is complementing the emotional buildup. Whereas a lot of times we do the opposite. We jump into bed first and then expect emotions to follow. We often feel like we have to use our bodies to keep somebody, that if we don't do it now, it's not going to happen. There's a sense of urgency—which I understand, which I've been part of. But I now realize that it's OK to move slowly. It's better when it does, it's more rich.

Trying to fill deep human needs through more and more sex doesn't work, no matter how much sex you have, because the needs aren't sexual needs in the first place. We all need to feel important to others. We need to feel there's a place for us in this world. We need a sense of belonging. We need to feel that we're basically good and lovable and worthy. These are universal, profound needs. They can't be met through a frantic search for sex. But you *can* meet them by reaching out for meaningful connections with people who are able to appreciate you as the unique person that you are.

the impact of homophobia on sex

While using sex to meet other needs is something that straight people do as well, there are other painful sexual experiences that are unique to gay youth. Because of homophobia—both internal and external—gay and lesbian young people sometimes try to avoid or cover up their same-sex attractions by engaging in heterosexual sex. Hyde describes how she tried to deny her lesbian feelings:

> I would have done anything to get rid of how I felt. But they're feelings and I couldn't get rid of the feelings. That's why I had sex with guys at so young an age. I lost my vir-

ginity to men when I was thirteen, in a group setting.
Because at the time I believed that my actions were going to
change my emotions. I had sex with ten to fifteen different
men in high school to prove that I was not gay.

Craig was so confused and distraught about his sexual orientation
that he decided to let fate determine the outcome—in a dangerous
setting:

> I knew that if you stood out on certain corners, you get
> picked up. And I decided that was my route to go. I didn't
> know whether I was going to get picked up by women or
> men. And from the corner I was on, it was definitely possi-
> ble either way.
> I was sixteen. And very upset about my sexuality. I
> thought that my first sexual experience would determine
> whether I would be gay or straight, and I was leaving it up
> to God. It was just going to depend on who ended up pick-
> ing me up off the street.
> It never occured to me to have sex with a friend.

The lack of an acceptable social context for same-sex attractions
leaves gay youth especially vulnerable to encounters that have no
basis in affection or caring. This is what happened to Christopher:

> In eighth grade, I was getting to know this young man in my
> class. And one day, we were in the bathroom together, and
> he told me to give him head, basically. He said that if I didn't
> do it, he would hit me. So I did it. And he was shocked. I
> remember him saying to me, "Wouldn't you rather be hit?
> Wouldn't you rather get beat up than do that?" And I said,
> "Well, no. I'm not stupid." After that he would call me and
> we would go over to my grandma's apartment and have sex.
> And it was never my gratification. It was always his.

These encounters, disconnected from feelings and even a person's own sexual satisfaction, can have a negative impact on sexuality for many years, making it difficult to form emotional bonds or to
share mutual sexual gratification.

Sex that's separate from emotion is easier to label as experimenta-
tion, fooling around, or even, as in Christopher's experience,

power—forcing someone to do something for you. But if there's tenderness, affection, and caring, then it becomes harder to deny the homosexual feeling. And that can be too threatening. Julio describes how he and another boy avoided recognizing the extent of their feelings:

> For two or three years we'd get together every day after school. And we did everything. Everything. It was clear to both of us that we really enjoyed it, it was something we wanted. But we never kissed. Kissing would have made it like this big thing, that's what you did with girls, the first time. That's what you saw straight people do. And also it seemed like kissing would bring it all out into the open because that's what you did in the open. What we were doing you did behind closed doors.

Yevette became sexually involved with her first girlfriend when she was twenty-one. They wrote poetry to each other, talked every day on the phone, and spent a lot of time together, but her girl-friend could never acknowledge that they were dating.

> After six months she ended the relationship—because of her parents and also because she was engaged to a man. She said she had to do what was expected of her and that she would always love me but that she could never act on it again. It was a complete surprise.

Homophobia can distort our own perceptions as well. Sometimes people feel guilty about having sex—or may even feel that sex is dirty or bad. Dan describes:

> In all my sexual experiences, I felt like I was seducing these boys instead of it being a mutual thing. I always felt I was the initiator and I almost never was. I guess that's my own internalized homophobia that I felt somehow that I was cor-rupting them. It's so weird because I never thought it was wrong to be gay, but I guess that's how it manifested itself.

The lack of knowledge about gay relationships has also made it hard for young people to develop healthy, comfortable attitudes toward sex. As Quang explains:

I didn't know how to negotiate sex in a gay relationship. When I say negotiate, I mean how do I approach someone? How do I let them know that I'm interested? How do I let them know what I want to do sexually? How do I myself know what I want to do sexually? It's a process that I for the longest time couldn't even imagine figuring out, because there was so much fear and confusion and just lack of knowledge, from not having heard of it anywhere.

Although becoming self-aware and confident in the sexual realm takes some time for all young people—straight and gay alike—the scarcity of visible role models and frank, open discussion makes a gay youth's journey that much more difficult.

SEXUAL ABUSE AND RAPE

Approximately one in three girls and one in seven boys are sexually abused before the age of eighteen. Sexual abuse happens to children from all kinds of families—from every culture, race, class, religion, and geographical location. Abusers may be fathers, uncles, grandparents, siblings, cousins, mothers, aunts, teachers, clergymen, neighbors, baby-sitters, friends of the family, or strangers. Although some offenders are women, the great majority of sexual offenders are heterosexual men.[1]

If you have been sexually abused the most important things for you to know are:

◇ You're not alone.
◇ It wasn't your fault.
◇ Healing is possible.

Everyone reacts somewhat differently to sexual abuse, but for most people, such assaults have a profound impact. However, it's important to note that sexual abuse doesn't determine someone's sexual orientation. Homophobic attitudes sometimes lead people to look for negative "causes" of homosexuality, but in reality no connection has been established between abuse and sexual orientation.

Sexual abuse and rape can leave you with negative or distorted messages about yourself, intimacy, sexuality, and relationships. And because sexual violation can affect your ability to know or to express what you want or don't want in sex, childhood abuse can leave you vulnerable to exploitation. If it is difficult for you to say no—or yes, if you feel bad or ashamed after sex, or if you keep having sex that you don't really want or doing sexual things that you don't want to be doing, reach out for help and talk to someone safe. If you were sexually abused, or raped, you have a right to support and understanding in working through any aspects of that violation that may still affect you now.

In your present-day relationships, it's especially important to be aware of your feelings and respectful of your needs and boundaries. Often it takes real commitment and work to overcome the effects of rape and abuse. But it's possible to heal and to enjoy a healthy sexuality. You deserve that. (For more information about healing from sexual abuse, see p. 372 of the Resources.)

[1]For information about the scope of child sexual abuse, see David Finkelhor, *Child Sexual Abuse: New Theory and Research* (New York: Simon & Schuster, 1984); Judith Herman, *Trauma and Recovery* (New York: Basic Books, 1992); Diana Russell, *The Secret Trauma: Incest in the Lives of Girls and Women* (New York: Basic Books, 1986); and Anna C. Salter, *Transforming Trauma* (Thousand Oaks, CA: Sage Publications, 1995).

exploitation

There is a stereotype that gays and lesbians prey on young people. This is simply not true. Being gay does not lead people to exploit youth. Indeed, the vast majority of sexual offenders are heterosexual men. But that doesn't mean that most heterosexual men are sexual offenders—most are not. And most gay people are not either.

However, there will always be those who will try to take advantage of the vulnerabilities of young people. And sometimes young people don't recognize how vulnerable they are. Even if you are a strong person, you can still be hurt. No matter how tough your exterior, we *all* are tender inside.

In a homophobic society most gay youth have far less opportunity to date and form romantic relationships with their peers than straight youth do. If you are feeling isolated, unable to explore your feelings of same-sex attraction with others your age, and hungry for connection and affection, your judgment about who to get involved with may be impaired. If you need money or don't have a home, you're even more vulnerable.

When Craig was sixteen years old, he met a much older man who invited him to his house. Craig was confused and deeply distressed by his conflicting feelings:

We got a couple blocks from his house and he put his hand on my leg. All of a sudden the knowledge of what was going on, that he was picking me up, totally came through to me. I felt really stupid. I started to cry. I had an erection like nobody's business. And I knew I wanted to be sexual, but I hated it. I felt totally horrible.

I cried my way through the whole thing. Crying and kind of shut down. He was just doing whatever he was doing and I was like, well, just get it over with and let me out of here. I felt trapped. I cried my way home like I'd just been doomed.

After that, I kept repeating the same thing. I kept going on the streets. I'd go and trick, sometimes for money and sometimes not.

Some gay teenagers have been exploited by older people under the guise of consensual sex. But although the teens may have agreed to have sex, or even wanted to have sex, it often didn't turn out to be in their best interests. Rick was fifteen when he ran away from home and was picked up by an older man who gave him a place to stay and then seduced him:

I still don't know how I feel about it. It hasn't screwed me up. But I just wasn't attracted to him. I would have preferred to have done it with a guy my age. For a lot of young men, they don't know other young gay guys, so they go sleep with older men just to have sex. I don't regret it, but I didn't feel like I was consenting. Knowing what I know now, at twenty-four, I wouldn't do it again. I would search for someone my age.

It's easy to see how a young person could be seduced by an adult's attention. It can be flattering to think that someone more established and experienced in the world would be attracted to you. It can make you feel important and special. Being close to people we admire can make us feel like we have a little of what we think is so terrific in them.

Having a sexual relationship with an older person may be tempting because it can give you access to a lifestyle that you couldn't create on your own. You may have more money, opportunities to travel, and an invitation to adult activities. And if you haven't gotten the attention and affection that you needed from your own parents, a relationship with someone who is significantly older can seem like a way to create a fantasy parent—someone you believe will give you the nurturing you missed out on.

But there are serious hidden dangers in such relationships. In healthy relationships the power dynamics are fairly even. In fact, this is one of the great advantages in same-sex relationships—there's no power difference related to gender. But there are other elements of power related to age that are important to consider, such as who has power and influence in the world? Who has the financial power? Who has the greater independence? Who makes the really important decisions? It is extremely unusual for a young person to have the kind of power that an established adult has.

Age differences are more significant the younger you are. Although a ten-year difference may not mean much once you're well into your twenties, it does when you're a teenager. The difference between fifteen and twenty-five is enormous—much greater than between twenty-five and thirty-five.

If there is a significant age difference between you and a potential sexual or romantic partner, it's a good idea to ask yourself some questions. Look hard at what's in it for you, what may be in it for that person, and how it may leave you feeling. Being used and then abandoned, feeling second rate, like a sex object or like you can't quite measure up, is a deeply painful experience.

You deserve better than this. If you're in an exploitative relationship now, think about how you can safely get out. Get help if you need it. And, as always, remind yourself that mistakes are part of how we learn.

PROTECT YOURSELF FROM EXPLOITATION

◇ Don't spend time alone with someone until you know that person well. Stay in public places.

◇ Meet new people with other friends along.

◇ Be very careful about alcohol and drugs—keep your judgment sharp.

◇ Don't go anyplace that you can't get yourself away from. If you don't have a car, be sure you have money for a bus or cab—and know how to find or call them. Often you can tell a situation is beginning to look unsafe or uncomfortable before it escalates into a truly dangerous situation. Don't wait. Make your exit as soon as you notice such clues.

◇ Be willing to look uncool or foolish. Sometimes walking out or saying no feels embarrassing. But that short period of embarrassment may save you long-lasting pain.

the value of relationships that aren't sexual

In our sex-obsessed culture, there's not much support for nonsexual relationships—or even for getting to know someone well before you have sex. Instead, we often jump into bed before we know very much about each other, before there's an opportunity to build trust, to share experiences, or even to learn to care about each other beyond initial attraction.

Yet relationships that are close and loving without being sexual can be very fulfilling. And for anyone who's felt that his or her self-worth was previously tied up with being sexual, these nonsexual relationships can be healing. As Devan relates:

> Brad was a blessing because he was so uninterested in sex. It turned out he was afraid of it, but it worked out perfectly for us. He learned about sexual identity without having to actually do it. And for me, it was a healing thing, because I didn't have to have sex with this person to have him accept me and like me and know who I was and learn about me.

In her teenage years, Sara had "a lot of dreams, fantasies, interests, crushes" but didn't have sex:

> I didn't do a lot of sexual experimenting. I avoided situations that would put me in a place where sex would be coming at me. I had serial relationships with women and men who were like my best friends, and it was a totally intense relationship. It was that kind of dynamic. The way we talked, the work we did about our relationship was almost like we were dating, but we didn't have sex.
>
> During that time I had a very rich fantasy life. I felt like a very sexual person. Even today, at twenty-five, when I'm not expressing myself sexually physically, I still feel very much like a sexual person.

If you're not ready for sex, if you need to take a break from sex, if you don't have a lover for whom you care deeply and who feels the same about you, if for any reason it's not right for you to have sex now, respect that. You deserve a healthy, rich sexual life—and sometimes the best way to achieve that is to wait until the time—and the person—is right.

positive first sexual experiences

In spite of the odds, lesbian and gay young people do have positive sexual relationships and experiences that include genuine feelings of affection and pride in their sexual identity. Here is how Doe describes her first sexual experience with a woman:

> We went out for yogurt and she invited me back to her house. The attraction that I had for this woman and how she made me feel was unlike anything that I'd ever felt before. When she was touching my shoulder or giving me a back rub, I would melt. And I hadn't felt that with one of the guys that I dated in high school. I was very attracted to them, but it always came to a wall. But this experience was amazing. I practically bawled in bed. I was totally crying. I'm like, "Whoa." It was a combination of just: What am I doing here? What are my parents going to think? What's my granny going to think? Oh, wow, this feels so good. Oh my God, this is way intense. Jesus, wow, my body never felt like this. This is incredible. I mean, it's like everything was in that bed with us. Everything. The world, politics, how am I going to be looked at.
>
> When I walked from her house to my house the next morning, I felt completely exposed. I felt naked. I felt like everybody knew. Of course they didn't. But I knew. And I knew this had to be good. There was no way that there could be anything wrong with how I was feeling.

Some sexual experiences mark the beginning of a long relationship. Others may happen only once. As Jason relates:

> I met him at work. He'd come in to buy a backpack. He asked me out and we went to the movies. Just sitting next to him my heart was beating so fast I could hardly breathe. By the time we got back to my room we just fell on each other. He was leaving the next day and we knew it would be just that night so we made the most of it. He was a special person, very, very tender. And it was a special night.

Michelle and Victoria had been friends for a quite a while before they became lovers:

I really liked being close to her. I liked holding her hand, and sitting next to her, and leaning on her. Over time, it became more intense, more of a sexual attraction.

I had a coming out experience that was like the ideal. We were in my room and it was late and it was a candlelit evening with incense and a massage, which eventually graduated to a sexual encounter which lasted until the wee hours of the morning.

The first time we saw each other after that was really awkward. We didn't know what to say. And we didn't know if that was a one-time thing or if it would become a relationship. It did end up being a relationship for two years.

Although it wasn't a romantic relationship, Richard enjoyed having sex with his friend John:

I met John at the movie theater that I worked at. We would kind of clown each other affectionately and it had sexual overtones. We started hanging out together and we became friends. Then his dog died. I decided to make dinner for him to make him feel better. I ended up falling asleep on his bed and he just crawled in under the covers. In the middle of the night we had sex. I wasn't in love with him, but it was a nice experience.

For Dan, being with Steven was a dream come true:

I remember looking at him and caressing his body and it just didn't feel real. I had to squeeze him to realize he was actually there, like this wasn't a fantasy or dream. I couldn't believe I was with Steven. I'm one of the lucky ones who got to be with his most desired person.

Afterward I was thirsty and he went downstairs to get me some water. When he didn't come back right away, I followed him. It was nighttime and Steven was standing naked in front of the refrigerator, the light coming from the refrigerator, with his huge back, little white butt, because he has Speedo tan lines, and then white tube socks. His back was so big you could watch a movie on it. That's how I'll always remember Steven.

You deserve a full, healthy sexual life. The more you are able to value yourself, take your time, and use your best judgment, the more joyous and satisfying your sexual experiences are likely to be.

Cathy Cade © 1995

8
HIV, AIDS, and Safer Sex

I really believe that the worst thing that could happen to us is to despair and to stop living and loving and fighting.

—*Cleve Jones*

> Cleve Jones (b. 1954) is founder of the NAMES Project, which sponsors the AIDS Memorial Quilt. The Quilt was created to memorialize people who have died of AIDS and to educate about AIDS, grief, and the essential goodness in people.

Young people today are coming of age in a time when there are serious dangers to being sexually active. In heterosexual sex, there's always been the fear of pregnancy. And sexually transmitted diseases are not new. But since the AIDS epidemic, the dangers have not only increased, they have become lethal. This is a reality that must be integrated into your life and sexual practices. It's not fair. It's understandable to be resentful, sad, and angry about it. But it's real.

AIDS is deadly, but it is preventable. Being careful and safe *all the time* demands an awareness, control, and commitment that's challenging, even for mature adults. Yet it is essential that you know how to protect yourself against HIV infection and that you practice safer sex consistently.

what you need to know about HIV and AIDS[1]

HIV stands for *human immunodeficiency virus*. This is a virus that attacks the immune system, eventually making a person susceptible to many infections. HIV might not produce symptoms for many years, but once a person is infected, there is no cure. Virtually everyone who is infected with the virus eventually develops AIDS and dies. You can't tell just by looking if someone is carrying HIV. People can look and feel healthy and still have the virus.

AIDS stands for *acquired immune deficiency syndrome*. When a person experiences symptoms of a certain severity as a result of HIV, we say he or she has AIDS. People with AIDS don't actually die from AIDS, but from these infections and diseases from which their bodies can't heal.

The process of dying from AIDS-related complications is usually agonizing. It's long, slow, and filled with enormous suffering.

Worldwide there are between fifteen and twenty million people infected with HIV. In the United States, a very conservative estimate is over a million. Although in the United States, AIDS has hit the gay male community especially hard, worldwide AIDS has affected more straight people than gay.

The number of people with AIDS continues to increase. The cases that we are aware of now reflect people who were infected some years ago. People who are being infected today won't show up in these statistics for five, ten, or fifteen years. So although most people with AIDS are adults, many of them became infected with the virus when they were much younger. *Today, young people make up one of the fastest growing groups to test positive for HIV.*

[1]Numbers for AIDS information helplines and AIDS organizations are listed in the Resources. See p. 371

transmission

HIV can't be transmitted through casual contact the way some other viruses can be. A cold or flu, for example, can be passed to someone else through sneezing, sharing food, shaking hands, or using a water fountain. But HIV is different. It can't survive in air, food, or water. It can survive only in certain body fluids. So a person can get HIV only by a direct exchange of infected bodily fluids. There are four bodily fluids through which HIV can be transmitted: blood, semen, vaginal fluids, and breast milk. Scientists generally agree that other body fluids, such as saliva, tears, sweat, and urine, do not appear to contain enough HIV to be able to transmit the virus.

The most common ways HIV is passed are through sexual intercourse, by sharing needles or syringes, and from mother to child during pregnancy, birth, or breast-feeding.

You don't have to be gay to get AIDS. Anyone who exchanges one or more of the four body fluids with someone who has been infected with HIV can get AIDS.

It's not who you are but what you do that puts you at risk for HIV. Although in the United States there's a far greater incidence of HIV in the gay male population, bisexuals and lesbians are also at risk. *Anyone*—straight, gay, bisexual, or lesbian—can get AIDS. So just because you may be in a lower risk group doesn't mean that you don't have to protect yourself. You do. Lower statistical odds aren't good enough protection. It's important that *you* don't get AIDS.

prevention

The most common way HIV is transmitted is during sexual contact. So the surest way to be safe is not to have sex.

If you don't practice abstinence, the most reliable protection is to limit your sexual activities to ones that don't involve an exchange of the four bodily fluids that can carry HIV.

Because we live in a world where heterosexuality is the standard by which things are measured, sex tends to be defined as intercourse. But intercourse—be it vaginal, anal, or oral—is not the only way to have sex. By using your creativity, you can share sex that is loving, exciting, passionate, intimate, satisfying, and completely safe. You can still enjoy sexual pleasure. And you can be sure you're protecting your life and the life of your partner. Open your mind. Be creative. Explore. Enjoy.

SAFE SEXUAL ACTIVITIES

◇ Massage
◇ Touching, caressing, hugging
◇ Masturbation
◇ Kissing
◇ Sharing erotic fantasies
◇ Bathing together
◇ Dancing

Note: If you have cold sores or cuts in your mouth (including bleeding after brushing your teeth or bleeding from braces), it's possible that deep tongue kissing could be risky. Also, don't touch your partner's body fluids without a latex glove.

SAFER SEX

I've seen entirely too many gay teens with low self-esteem go out and have unsafe sex because they don't feel that they're worthy people. They don't feel that they want to live, so they have dangerous sex. And I would just like to say, "Don't have unsafe sex, period!" If it's because you have low self-esteem, go talk to someone, go read a book, go call a hot line, but don't have unsafe sex. I've seen someone die of AIDS and I've seen the progression of HIV in people and it's not pretty. It's terrible. Don't do anything that's going to get you in that situation.

—Matt

The best thing is to practice with a condom by yourself so you don't find yourself in a situation where you're not even sure how to unroll it and you're embarrassed about that too and you just don't use it. You need to practice those things on yourself.

—Quang

Last year I had two of my friends die within two months of each other from AIDS, so it really rocked my world. They were sick sometimes, but they weren't sick very much. I'd call and say, "How are you doing today?" "Oh, I'm OK today. I'm not throwing up." So it was like, "Hey, that's good." And then all of a sudden, bam. That really devastated me.

Even though my friends were older, they got HIV when they were younger. And that's the thing that people need to understand. Some of my friends say, "I won't have sex with an older man, because I'll be more at risk for HIV or AIDS." They think if they only have sex with young men, they're safe. But that's not true at all.

—Renee

When I first meet somebody, I always tell my HIV-positive status, and I know that helps a lot with people. With boyfriends, when I've mentioned my status, they get closer and they trust me more. I've been going out with Curtis for almost two years now. And we have so much in common. It's fun. And yes, I practice what I preach. Safer sex has become a way of living. You have to. It's the nineties. People think just because they're negative they don't have to, but they should. It's just important that everybody use protection. And you learn to make it fun. Use your imagination.

—Luna

For a while I was really scared that I might be infected. I don't know how many people the first man I had sex with was with. And I have a history of being unsafe.

I've been tested four times now. I was really scared. When I went back to get my results, she said, "You're fine. You're healthy." I was shaking. Even though I was fine, I'd broken through my immortality complex. When I'd gone in for the test and she was taking that blood, I almost felt the life draining out of my arm, and it just hit me, that I could die today, tomorrow, whenever. I was so relieved that I'm not going to die.

Now I only have safe sex. It's recent, but I feel better about it. It's like we have a condom or we don't do it. A lot of it has to do with self-esteem. Before, I wasn't in a position where I wanted to ask. I felt like I would be rejected if I asked. Now, it's my safety. It's my life.

—Christopher

We went out and just casually in the conversation she mentions that she's married and that her husband doesn't mind. I'm going, Aaggghhh, noooo! Don't you understand? If you're cheating, he's cheating too, and that's too much dirt. I think if I hadn't been an AIDS educator I may have actually ventured in that direction, but no. Why even go there?

I just don't believe that the information on lesbians not having HIV is accurate. The government doesn't bother to ask women if they're lesbians, so how can we know?

> It's made it real important to me to get to know somebody first as opposed to acting on the first sexual impulse. I've learned that if I wait a few weeks, sometimes the impulse just leaves. I realize that I don't really like this person.
>
> —Yevette

> We have to come up with ways to say, OK, granted, we've all messed up sometime, but we have to talk about it. There are a lot of men out there that have had unprotected sex—I know I certainly have—and you feel so guilty and you don't want to be chastised, so you don't tell anyone. And then a lot of men say, "Well I've had unsafe sex once, so I might as well have it again, and again and again." Because we're not allowed to talk about it. We need to work on why we didn't use protection instead of just saying bad, bad, bad.
>
> —Dan

safer-sex guidelines

Activities that involve any of the four bodily fluids—semen, vaginal fluids, blood, and breast milk—can expose you to HIV. For this reason, sexual intercourse, whether it is vaginal, anal, or oral, carries a risk of getting AIDS.

Vaginal intercourse places both partners at serious risk for getting HIV, as the virus can easily enter through small or invisible sores or cuts in the vagina or penis.

Anal intercourse is *especially* dangerous because HIV passes into the large intestine more easily than it does into the vagina or penis. *Anal sex is the highest risk sexual behavior.*

Oral sex—between men, women, or a man and a woman—can also spread HIV. Studies suggest that there are not a great number of HIV-infected people who engaged in only oral sex, but it's still not completely safe.

Mutual masturbation carries the least risk (if there are no open cuts or sores), but it's still safest to use condoms and/or latex gloves.

There is no way to be 100 percent safe when bodily fluids are involved. But properly using condoms, gloves, and barriers—depending on what kind of sex you're having—*greatly* reduces the chances of getting AIDS.

Men should use a latex condom during anal or vaginal intercourse and during oral sex. The condom should be latex, *not* lambskin, as the virus can pass through lambskin. A new condom made of polyurethane is being tested now and may be effective for people who are allergic to latex, but the results are not yet established.

It's also important to put condoms on correctly. Use each condom one time only. If you have sex again, use a new one. And never use two condoms at a time, as this can cause them to break.

Age and heat weaken condoms, so don't store them in your wallet or glove compartment and don't use them after the expiration date. Use a water-based lubricant, such as K-Y Jelly. Don't use oil-based lubricants such as baby oil or vaseline, as these can damage the condom. Nonoxynol–9, a spermicide, kills HIV so it may give extra protection. But nonoxynol–9 alone is *not* sufficient to protect against HIV, and some people have an allergic reaction to it.

Woman-to-woman transmission of HIV is less prevalent, but it *does* happen and so it is important that lesbians practice safer sex with each other. HIV and other sexually transmitted diseases can be transmitted through vaginal fluids and blood, including menstrual blood. Women should use a latex or plastic wrap barrier for oral sex. Regular plastic wrap that you buy in the grocery store is the easiest to find and it's cheap (be sure to get the kind without little holes), but you can also use dental dams or make a barrier by cutting a latex glove or condom into a flat square. For vaginal or anal stimulation or penetration by hand, use a latex glove. And if you share a vibrator or dildo, use a condom on it or wash it in bleach and rinse it thoroughly.

Comedian Sara Cytron tells this story about being on the road:

I see a lot of road signs. And very often I see a sign that says "Adopt a Highway." When I see this sign, I always wonder, "What if you're a lesbian? Is it legal to adopt a highway? Isn't there a danger that somehow you'd influence the highway and it would become a lesbian highway?"

Actually, I was on a lesbian highway recently. I was driving in North Carolina, when all of a sudden I saw a sign that said "Entering Charlotte." Thank God, I just had time to reach into the glove compartment and grab some latex.

"Adopt a Highway," © Harriet Malinowitz and Sara Cytron, from the show *Take My Domestic Partner —Please!*

How to Create Safe Barriers for Oral Sex with Women

LATEX BARRIERS	GLOVES	CONDOMS

LATEX BARRIERS are six-inch square pieces of latex also known as dental dams.

1. An alternative is to use *plastic wrap* cut to fit your needs

Note: you can get "harnesses" to hold the dams in place

Enemies of Latex

Do not use:

Vaseline	animal fats
Crisco	whipping cream
hand lotion	chocolate sauce
mineral oil	peanut butter
baby oil	liqueurs
vegetable oil	massage oil
olive oil	oil based
butter	perfumes
	suntan oil

GLOVES are made of latex and come in different sizes.

1. Cut the 4 fingers off the glove and do not cut off the thumb
2. Cut the glove on the seam along the pinky

3. Rinse the talcum off. Now you have a latex barrier. You can stick your tongue in the thumb area for oral/anal sex

CONDOMS are made of latex. Do not use lamb-skin condoms. Ribbed/textured condoms tend to tear easily.

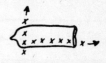

1. Unroll an unlubed condom and cut off the tip, then cut up along one side

2. Unfold and place lube on the side that goes on her vagina

Adapted from "Safer Sex Handbook for Lesbians" by The Lesbian AIDS Project—Gay Men's Health Crisis

◇ SEX, DRUGS, AND ALCOHOL

Drugs and alcohol can impair your judgment. Sometimes people do things when they've been drinking or using drugs that they wouldn't do sober. It's essential that you practice safer sex all the time. Don't compromise your safety by having risky sex when you're high on drugs or alcohol.

◇ COMMUNICATION

It's essential that you be able to talk with your partner about safer sex. Although it may feel awkward at first, you'll not only keep yourself—and your partner—safer, but you'll also be building real intimacy between you.

The best time to talk is *before* you have sex. Talk about your own limits and what you expect from each other. Your partner should respect your feelings and your boundaries around sexual activities. If he or she tries to convince you to do something you're not comfortable with, don't allow yourself to be pressured. Make it clear that although you want to be intimate, you're not willing to put either of you in danger of getting AIDS.

How to Use a Latex Condom

Make sure the condom is right-side-out with the roll on the outside. Put a drop or two of water-based lubricant in the tip of the inside of the condom.

Pinch a half inch of space at the tip before you roll the condom on the hard penis. Make sure there's no air inside. Roll the condom as far down the penis as it will go.

Apply plenty of water-based lubricant to the condom covered penis. Never use oil-based lubes like vaseline or baby oil. After ejaculation, and while you're still hard, hold on to the base of the condom as you pull out of your partner. Never reuse a condom. Use a new one every time.

Adapted from pamphlets by the San Francisco AIDS Foundation and Los Angeles Gay and Lesbian Community Services Center

◇ BETTER LATE THAN NEVER

If you've already had unsafe sex, begin to practice safer sex now. Don't let the fact that you've engaged in risky behaviors in the past stop you from taking care of yourself—and your partner—now. It's extremely dangerous to have unsafe sex even once, but it's much more dangerous to continue to have unsafe sex.

DAN'S STORY: THE IMPACT OF AIDS

My older brother Tim is HIV-positive. And that's when I realized it's everywhere. This sounds really scary to say, but I don't think in a few years there'll be anyone left who hasn't at least been touched by it. You'd have to live in some remote part of New Guinea or Antarctica to say that you don't know someone personally who has AIDS or has HIV. And it gets me angry. It's really hard for me to get sad. I'm just filled with anger.

I strongly believe that a lot of people didn't care about it because it was marginalized people who were getting the disease and dying. It's like, oh it's those Black IV drug users, it's the gay men, well, whatever. It's just amazing how it flourished and now it's everywhere. It's scary to think of and I'm mad that for me and for everyone younger than me, we can't think about sex without thinking about death.

WHAT IF MY PARTNER SAYS . . . ?

What if he says: "Condoms aren't romantic."

You could say: "Just give me those condoms and I'll show you how romantic they can be!"

or

"Worrying about AIDS isn't romantic. With condoms we won't need to worry."

◇

What if she says: "You don't trust me."

You could say: "It's not a matter of trust. It's a matter of health."

or

"It's important to me that we're both protected."

◇

What if he says: "I don't use condoms."

You could say: "I use condoms every time."

or

"I don't have sex without condoms."

◇

What if she says: "But I love you."

You could say: "I love you, too. We still need to practice safer sex."

or

"Being in love can't protect us against AIDS."

◇

What if he says: "But I know I'm HIV-negative."

You could say: "The best way to stay that way is to practice safer sex."

Adapted from information from the San Francisco AIDS Foundation and the California AIDS Clearinghouse.

if you know all about it and you still don't do it

Some young people have all the information about protecting themselves from HIV but still don't practice safe sex. There are many reasons why the information alone may not be enough to insure that you protect yourself. You may think you're immortal. You're young and you think death isn't real. You may be willing to play the odds. You may feel so desperate for love and attention that you can't risk being rejected if you insist on using protection. You may feel so driven by your hormones that you ignore what you know and can't see beyond the moment. Or you're so disconnected when you have sex that you aren't present enough to take care of yourself.

Life may be so tough that you feel like you don't really care if you live or die anyway. You don't want to live past thirty because you think you'll be old and not beautiful and you've decided you'd rather live in the fast lane and die young. You've internalized the homophobia around you and think you don't deserve to live. You're embarrassed to talk about safe sex, it's awkward to learn to do things differently, and you think it'll be less pleasurable. Because the consequences don't show up right away, they don't seem real to you. Your judgment is influenced by drugs or alcohol. You've already slipped once, so you figure it doesn't matter if you slip again.

If you don't practice safer sex for one or more of these reasons—or for another of your own—you can start *now*. You can begin by looking at why you do things that can kill you. Then work on figuring out how to avoid situations that put you at risk. You may want to consider not having sex for a while until you are able to keep yourself safe.

You are too valuable to throw your life away. No matter how much emotional pain you're in, how much you feel like you don't care what happens to you, how overwhelming your need for sex feels, *you* are too precious, too special, too unique to risk losing.

SARA'S STORY: I AM WORTHY OF LOVE AND OF LOVING

As an AIDS educator, I know how you get HIV and how to use a condom. My father died from HIV so I am very aware of the consequences and of mortality in general and mine in specific. Yet I was having very unsafe sex. I was ashamed to tell anyone because I, of all people, should know better.

Finally, I told my best friend, also an AIDS educator. His concern made it real for me. I finally got how serious my behavior was and spent the evening crying. The next morning he guided me through figuring out what was going on while I was having unprotected sex.

After hours of replay, I figured out that I just disappear when I'm having sex, especially with men, with whom I'm the most likely to engage in the highest risk behaviors. After a certain point in being sexual with someone, depending on how safe I feel with them, I disappear and it seems like everything from that point on just happens to or around me.

So my friend came up with an idea. First, I agreed to stop having casual sex, particularly when I felt unsafe. Then he suggested that when I'm in a situation and I start to disappear that I take all the bracelets I wear on one arm and put them on the other arm. The bracelets were all given to me by people whom I love and who love me. This act brings me back into myself—just *doing* something—and reminds me that I am worthy of love and of loving.

AIDS and drugs

Sharing needles can transmit HIV. When a person injects drugs, a little blood or fluid always flows backward into the needle and syringe. If another person then uses that needle, the blood or fluid can be injected into his or her body.

Shooting drugs is seriously bad for you and for your health. The best way to eliminate the risk of infection from dirty needles is not to shoot drugs. But if you're going to inject drugs, don't share needles or syringes with anyone. Use sterile, disposable needles once and then throw them away. If you can't get a new syringe, clean the one you have three times with bleach and three times with water, alternating between them and finishing with the water. Many communities now have needle exchange programs—contact your local AIDS agency for more information.

piercing and tattooing

If you are going to get a tattoo or pierce your ears or other body parts, always go to a professional who uses one-time-use sterilized needles for each client. Tattoo artists should pour ink into clean, disposable containers and throw them away after each client. If you have any questions about the safety of the procedures, go elsewhere!

testing

If you have ever engaged in any behaviors that would put you at risk for HIV, it's important to be tested. The testing process itself is simple. A small amount of blood is taken from your arm, and the blood is tested to see if you have become infected with HIV.

Emotionally, being tested for HIV is not so simple. It's frightening to think about the possibility that you could be HIV-positive. But there are important benefits to being tested. Knowing the results of your test allows you to be more complete in communication with a sexual partner, and if you are HIV-positive, there are treatments that are helping to maintain health and extend life. Many people are now living ten and more years since being diagnosed as HIV-positive.

Choose a testing place where you're not required to give your name or any personal information, where the results of your test are guaranteed to be anonymous, and where there is counseling available.

◇ IF YOUR TEST RESULTS ARE NEGATIVE

If your test results are negative that means there's no evidence of HIV in your blood at this time. However, it can take up to six months for HIV antibodies to show up, so your test only tells you your status as of six months ago. If you haven't engaged in *any* behaviors that could possibly put you at risk over the past six months, you can assume that you're still negative. Otherwise, it's necessary to be tested again in six months. If you continue to practice safer sex (and don't share needles), then you're likely to remain free of the HIV virus. But it's still important to be tested regularly.

Even if you are in a monogamous relationship and you've both tested negative, it's a good idea to continue to practice safer sex. If either of you has sex with someone else *even once,* you could contract HIV and give it to the other. It can be hard to tell the truth if you've had sex with someone other than your partner. Practicing safer sex all the time is the best way to protect both yourself and your partner.

◇ IF YOUR TEST RESULTS ARE POSITIVE

If you are HIV-positive, that means that your body is carrying HIV. It does not necessarily mean that you have AIDS. It does not mean that you are about to die. Many HIV-positive people—and people with AIDS—live vigorous, productive lives for many years. But it does mean that if you have unprotected sex (or share needles), you can give HIV to other people. It's essential that you let potential sexual partners know about your status and that you practice very safe sex.

If you test positive, there are steps you can take to keep yourself healthy longer. A good diet, exercise, enough sleep, and avoiding drugs and alcohol can all help prolong healthy, high-quality life. Also, there are medical treatments that are helping HIV-positive people to stay healthy and live longer. If you are carrying the HIV virus you should have good ongoing medical care.

Occasionally the results of testing are not accurate. If you test positive, especially if you haven't practised high-risk behaviors, there's a small possibility that the results are mistaken. Have the test repeated to be sure.

Finding out that you have HIV is frightening and can feel overwhelming. You need and deserve emotional support. A counselor or a support group can listen to your feelings and offer help with the important decisions that you face. You don't have to handle all this alone.

LUNA'S STORY: LIVING POSITIVE

I was fifteen and I met this man. He was thirty. I saw him all the time because I would walk my dog and he would walk his and we would say hello. And then we got to the point where we started talking as our dogs played together. And then it came to a point where I took my dog home and I went out to meet him. We had things in common. We both liked Bette Davis, but I'd say Marilyn Monroe was my favorite and we'd debate.

Then one day he started kissing me on the neck. I kept pushing him away, saying "No, we're friends." To make a long story shorter, we did engage in sex. And then I never saw him again. He never walked the dog again.

When I got sick, I had no idea what was going on. My mother took me to the hospital. My doctor asked if I was homosexual, bisexual, heterosexual, and I, back then, didn't even know what those words were, so I said, "I don't know." Then she went back to my parents and told my mother I was homosexual, so that's how I came out to my parents. The doctor did it for me. She said, "We'll do the AIDS test," and they did it and I turned out to be HIV-positive, from just that one experience.

My parents were ignorant about HIV. Whenever I would use a glass, my father would boil it. Whenever I used the toilet my mother would wash it down with Clorox. So I started reading and I began to educate them. I taught my parents about being positive and about being gay, and they learned because they love me. It was harder to get through to my father. At first he wouldn't even look in my direction. He said once that he was disappointed in me because I was the one that was supposed to do good in the family. I'm his favorite. So I said, "What makes you think that I can't still do all those things?" And he just turned away. But he's really good now. He's learned a lot.

After I took the test the doctor said I had about two years to live, so I almost gave up. I didn't want to go to school, because I thought, what's the purpose? But I'm not like that now. I try to do everything I can. And it turns out the doctor was wrong. I'm almost on my eighth year being positive and I'm living. I don't have AIDS yet. I'm really healthy and I'm so happy. I'm doing good.

I started going to Hetrick-Martin Institute in New York City and I graduated from Harvey Milk, an alternative high school. Right now I'm working with Stand Up Harlem. It's an educational center and people come there to get information about HIV prevention.

I'm involved in the creative arts, photography, writing, art. I do theater with a gay youth troupe, Revelations. We do improvisational pieces about our lives, different issues as gay and lesbian youth, and dealing with HIV. This is my therapy. Talking and teaching actually help me. I've learned to breathe to deal with my anxiety. Breathe. And I work it all out through art.

I know that if I put my mind on something, I can do it. That's actually helped a lot dealing with having the virus. I have a positive attitude about myself and my life.

family

◇   ◇   ◇   ◇   ◇   ◇   ◇   ◇   ◇   ◇

Cathy Cade © 1995

◇   ◇   ◇   ◇   ◇   ◇   ◇   ◇   ◇   ◇

9
coming out to your family

It takes two to tell the truth: one to say it and another to hear it.

—Henry David Thoreau

Families are an extremely important part of our lives. If your family is working well, it is a supportive environment in which to be yourself. A healthy family is a safe place to explore your thoughts and feelings and to learn the skills you need in relationship to others.

In healthy families, you experience yourself as lovable, precious, and valued. Although much of this critically important

Henry David Thoreau (1817–1862), writer and naturalist, is best known for *Walden*, an account of his experiment in simple living, and for the essay "Civil Disobedience" whose doctrine of nonviolent resistance influenced both Gandhi and Martin Luther King, Jr.

nurturing takes place in early childhood, in your teen years you still need love and affirmation as you begin to separate from your family and become your own person. Ideally, your parents will provide support, reasonable rules, and some protection as you move toward independence. Even after you have separated from your parents and are living independently, their advice, approval, and acceptance continue to have profound importance.

In reality, families vary greatly in their ability to offer loving support. Some families are critical, rejecting, or abusive. Everyone deserves consistent love and caring, but not everyone gets it. Although this is painful and unfair, part of the lifelong work of maturing is coming to terms with the families we have. As we recognize what is and isn't possible within our families, we can look to other healthy sources for the support we need.

Whether your family is accepting and nurturing, critical, or abusive, there's no denying their influence on your life. For most people, family acceptance—or rejection—of their sexual orientation is very significant.

HATE IS NOT A FAMILY VALUE

The phrase "family values" is used a lot these days. In many cases it's distorted to imply that it's OK to insult, reject, and discriminate against people who are not like you. But the real meaning of family values has nothing to do with such behavior. Real family values are about unconditional love, mutual support, and caring for each other through thick and through thin. Real family values are about bonds of affection, loyalty, and understanding.

Gay, lesbian, and bisexual people have been portrayed as a threat to the family. But in reality, virtually all gay people care very much about their families—and when there is alienation, it is the straight relatives who are rejecting them, not vice versa. Fear, hatred, and misinformation are the true threats to family unity.

---

thinking about coming out

We all want to be loved and accepted for who we are. We want to be authentic in our relationships. We don't want to have to hide important parts of ourselves. Coming out is a way to share ourselves, a gift of honesty. Coming out can bring families closer, improve communication, and help you feel better about yourself.

Chris Kryzan, Executive Director of !OutProud!, The National Coalition for Gay, Lesbian, and Bisexual Youth, describes the pain that many gay youth endure in their families before they come out:

> Sometimes, what makes it so especially hard for gay teens is the very thing that protects them, their invisibility. What Jewish family would sit around casually commenting on how God condemns the Jews? But lesbian, gay, or bisexual teens, sitting there in their cloaks of presumed heterosexuality, laugh outwardly, or join in expressing shared disgust, while yet another chunk of their self-esteem has been chiseled away.

Ideally, almost all gay, lesbian, and bisexual people want to tell their families. Although it may be difficult, they're willing to go through some hard times for the benefit of having a more authentic relationship. Julio decided to come out to his mother in his junior year in high school:

> She had already guessed a hundred and ten times about this guy, David, in my life. But not being out made my interaction with her very hard because I couldn't be honest. She was the person I'd always gone to. She's my best friend. So I thought, if I want to communicate with her, I have to come out.

Like Julio, many gay, lesbian, and bisexual youth are no longer willing to hide their real selves from their families. They want to be seen for who they are.

For some young people, the decision to come out is difficult because they know this news will be hard for their parents to understand and they don't want to cause them pain. As Manny says:

> I knew she would have to accept me because she wants me to be happy. But that was definitely the hardest part, knowing that she was suffering.

It's true that many parents go through a difficult time when they learn that their child is lesbian or gay. But most parents would rather have an authentic relationship than avoid the pain and not know much about your life. Rick has thought a lot about this issue:

> If your family loves you, then they wouldn't want to see you hurting. Despite whatever their own views may be about

homosexuality in general, if that love is there, then they
would want to help you through it.

Although it's upsetting to see your parents in distress, your own
life and well-being are important. Ultimately, we all have the right—
and the responsibility—to be true to ourselves.

deciding whether to come out

In general, families react in character when you come out. If your
family is basically understanding, supportive, and respectful, they're
likely to be that way now, too. Even though there may be some difficult feelings to work through, deeply nurturing families aren't
likely to reject their children.

But in families where there is little tolerance for differences and
few skills for working through conflict, coming out can be a time of
crisis. When there is a history of poor communication, neglect, or
abuse, a parent may even reject a gay or lesbian child outright.

Because every family is different, coming out in your family won't
be exactly like coming out for anyone else. It is important that you
think through your own family situation to assess whether it's in
your best interests to tell your family that you're gay.

If you decide to share this part of your life, put some time and
effort into preparing and planning. If, on the other hand, you decide
it's not right for you to come out to your family, it's important that
you know why you've made that choice. And if you decide not to
come out now, you may, of course, change your mind at a later
time as circumstances change.

Remember, this is *your* decision to make. Friends, support
groups, or even counselors may have strong opinions about
whether you should or should not come out to your parents. But
don't allow yourself to be pressured one way or the other.

You know your family—usually much better than the person
who's giving you advice. There are no absolute rules about coming
out. Trust your own reasoning.

◇ THINK ABOUT YOUR FAMILY

In deciding whether to come out to your family, it's useful to
think about the kind of family you have. Basically, how do people

in your family treat each other? When there are problems or differences, do they work to communicate and resolve them cooperatively and with respect? If someone strays from the expected behavior, how is that person treated? What kind of skills does your family have for communicating about difficult issues?

Brooke had reason to feel confident that her mother would accept her sexual orientation:

> My mom and I lived alone for a long time after she was divorced and we became sort of like roommates. We pretty much knew what was going on in each other's lives.
>
> I was a little bit scared. My heart beat a lot. But essentially I knew it was going to be fine. My mom has always been the kind of person who said, "You're so wonderful," "You're so intelligent," "You're so outstanding," in whatever I was doing.
>
> When I said, "I'm bisexual," she cried. My mom cries. She cried when I got my period for the first time. It's about my growing up. She said that she was glad that I knew that about myself. She said she was really proud of me.

John, on the other hand, knew there'd be trouble if his stepfather found out he was gay. He had never been kind or caring. In fact, he'd been abusive—to various members of the family:

> I was thrown out five days before Christmas. My stepbrother told my stepfather that I was gay and he kicked me out immediately. I was in bed. It was eight o'clock in the morning and he said, "You're a lazy good-for-nothing faggot." Then he picked me up by my nightshirt and punched me. When he looked at me, his eyes, I swear to God, were red. He said, "If you're not out of my house when I get home tonight you're going to be dead."

In families where communication is strained and difficult topics are not discussed, parents may be unwilling to talk about your sexual orientation at all. Hyde knew her father had always been "a man of very few words." When she told him she was lesbian, he said, "I don't need to know about that. That's your life." And he wouldn't discuss it any more.

◇ WHAT IS YOUR FAMILY'S GENERAL ATTITUDE TOWARD HOMOSEXUALITY?

Over the years it's likely that you've heard members of your family make a remark, tell a joke, react to something on TV, or in some way indicate whether they are generally open-minded or homophobic. Renee remembers how her mother made it clear that it wasn't OK to be gay:

> I had a cousin and my mom would always tell me, "I don't want you around her." And I would be like, "Why?" And she said, "Because she's a bulldagger." And I'm like, "What's a bulldagger?" I didn't even know what the word meant.

In contrast, Jason talks about his father's positive attitude:

> My father's best buddy in Vietnam turned out to be gay. He told me that he'd never thought about gays as really being *people* before that. But he knew this guy well before he came out—they'd been through so much together—and it opened his mind. He always told us, "Never judge a book by its cover."

Thinking over what your family has already revealed will give you some information about what you might encounter should you decide to come out.

◇ TESTING THE WATERS

Opinions sometimes change over time, so gathering current information on your family's attitudes toward lesbians, gays, and bisexuals is a good idea. If you bring up the topic in a general way, you will usually get a sense of your parents' thinking. Michelle suggests a way to do this with anyone:

> I would test the waters first with a gay concept. I would expose them to, say, a gay character in a book, or I would bring up gay or lesbian issues in some way that wasn't related to me; for example, that I had gay friends, or tying it into the conversation like, "Oh I went out with Jenny and her girlfriend last night," so it didn't reflect specifically on me, but I could see what their attitudes were.

Testing the waters will give you general information, but it won't be absolutely reliable in predicting how your parents will react to the discovery that *their* child is gay, lesbian, or bisexual.

TESTING THE WATERS: A SAMPLE SCRIPT

You: There was an interesting Oprah show this afternoon.

Mom: Oh?

You: She had some kids on from a gay high school. What do you think of that?

Bring up the subject in a neutral way—just state the facts—asking your parent's opinion without offering yours.

Mom: What do you mean, gay high school? What's that?

You: It's a special school for gay kids cause they couldn't make it in regular high school.

You answer the question, giving just the information asked for, but no opinion one way or the other.

Mom: What do you mean they couldn't make it in regular school?

Mom is asking for more information. This is often a good sign. So you provide information in a neutral way.

You: Well, they got harassed by the other kids.

Now, or soon, it's likely that Mom will reveal something of her feelings.

Mom (negative response): Well, it's good they put them all together. They don't belong with normal kids anyway.

If Mom's response is negative, you can grunt, say "Whatever" or something else noncommittal, and change the subject. You haven't revealed anything about yourself, and you've gained some useful, though very painful, information.

Mom (positive response): That's good. Those kids can use some support. Isn't it a shame that people still treat gays so badly.

Even if your parent has a positive response like this, you don't have to rush into coming out that very instant. It's still worthwhile to take the time to prepare. You can say, "Yeah, I think so too." And feel good that you've taken a first step.

Mom (unclear response): What will Oprah think of next?

In this case you haven't learned anything, but you haven't lost anything either. You can try again another time.

◇ DON'T COME OUT IF YOU'LL BE IN DANGER

In some families, it would be dangerous to come out. Before you tell your family—or unconsciously allow them to find out—think realistically about the likely consequences. If you still live at home or are supported by your parents and there is a real possibility that you will be physically harmed, kicked out of your house, cut off from financial support, or that your parents would attempt to hospitalize you in a psychiatric institution, it's much wiser to wait until you are independent before coming out.

Chris had been highly visible in campaigning for gay student rights when his father saw him on a television news broadcast:

> My father was channel surfing and I was on NBC News and he figured it out. He went out and got blitzed. Really, really drunk. He started banging on my door, saying, "I don't want a faggot in my house." He came at me with the butter knife. It wouldn't have done any harm, but it was the symbolism. He said, "I don't want to see you. I don't want you around me." And I was scared because I had seen what he had done to my brothers. I'd seen him beat my sisters. And I remember leaving the house and going into town. I was standing at the pay phone right across from Tower Records and thinking, this is a scene from a movie—me standing at a pay phone after I'm thrown out of the house. What's next?

Although it's great to be honest, sometimes it's necessary for your own well-being to keep information about yourself private. This is not hiding. It's not cowardly. It's not less politically correct. This is wisdom. This is survival. This is taking good care of yourself.

◇ IF YOU DECIDE NOT TO COME OUT NOW

There are many valid reasons to postpone coming out to your family. Even if your parents wouldn't reject or punish you, you simply might not be ready to take on this difficult emotional struggle.

If you decide not to come out to your family now—for any reason—that doesn't mean you're committed to staying in the closet forever. Quang waited until he graduated from college to come out to his parents:

Being gay is something that my parents do not understand. We immigrated to the United States from Vietnam when I was three. They're a little bit older than most parents and they're also from a different culture. Before I could tell them, I needed to be in a situation where I wasn't dependent on their reaction. I guess a lot of it was just growing up.

◇ WHOOPS!

If you're not ready to tell your parents, don't tell them unconsciously. Sometimes if you really want your parents to know and accept you—or if you're angry that they don't—you may do something that causes them to find out without realizing that's what you're doing. One teenager who insisted that she didn't want to tell her mother *anything* habitually used her mother's desk to write personal letters and "forgot" them there.

Sometimes parents really do find out accidentally that their child is gay, but you can minimize the odds of that happening by using some caution. You know your family. If your mother is going to rifle through your underwear drawer, don't put a gay-lesbian-bisexual-transgender manifesto in there.

◇ TAKE YOUR TIME AND COME FROM A POSITION OF STRENGTH

It's usually best if you work through some of your own feelings, fears, and concerns before you talk with your parents. If you feel comfortable with who you are, it will help them to become comfortable. You'll also be better able to hear your parents' feelings and fears as their own and to remain secure in your own perspective.

Doe notes that her security with herself helped her withstand her fear of coming out:

It was scary as shit. I mean my heart was pounding, my mouth cottoned up, my mom looked at me like her heart broke. But I was secure and positive in who I was. I had really come into my own, as an individual, along with being in love with this woman. I was like a new person. And so they couldn't rattle me.

One father, whose son came out at eighteen, echoes this:

> The reason why I took this seriously was because my son did
> this from a position of tremendous strength and courage. He
> stood there like, this is who I am and you deal with it. By the
> way he presented himself, I thought, this is something for me
> to contend with. He was very serious about this.

Although coming from a position of strength is generally a good idea, there are exceptions. If your parents are truly understanding, open-minded, and welcoming of diversity, it may be possible to enlist their support as you work toward your own self-acceptance. Ideally, it would be good to have your family's support all along, even as you share your questions, conflicts, and doubts. If you are lucky enough to have parents like this, take advantage of your good fortune.

coming out with consideration

Choosing to tell your parents about yourself is an act of faith in them. People will often live up to your expectations. How you share this information can have a big influence on what you get back. If you are caring and respectful and expect them to be also, it will improve the chances of a positive outcome. But even your best efforts can't always guarantee your family's understanding and acceptance. You can only do your part and know that the rest is not in your control.

If you decide to come out to your family, take your time and think about the best way to do it. Remember, you have the opportunity to think about this for as long as you want. The people you're telling don't.

◇ BE SENSITIVE TO YOUR PARENTS' FEELINGS

It is a sign of your emerging adulthood that you are able to consider your parents' needs and feelings as well as your own. Amy describes the intensive thought she put into preparing for her visit to tell her parents:

> I would just sit there and no matter what I was doing, it
> would come to me that in two months, six weeks, ten days,
> I would be talking to my parents. And I was trying to figure

out how to do it. And asking everybody I knew and reading whatever I could get my hands on.

My housemate had told me, "Pick a public place." And then I read something that said, "Don't pick a public place," and really explained how that might humiliate my parents. It might intensify their negative feelings rather than give us a chance to talk.

That changed my perspective. All of a sudden I realized *it wasn't just me doing this*. This was going to be pretty big for them to deal with. Here I am taking three years to come out to myself and expecting them to accept it all of a sudden. I had to think about how to make it work for them.

◇ EXPLAIN THAT COMING OUT IS AN ACT OF LOVE

Let your parents know that you're telling them about your sexual orientation because you care about your relationship with them and want to be closer. Most parents want connection with their children very much. The idea that you want that too may help them be willing to work through any difficult feelings they might have.

Drawing by Alyx Flatley. Words from *PROJECT 10 Handbook: Addressing Lesbian and Gay Issues in Our Schools* (Los Angeles: Friends of PROJECT 10, 1989).

◇ PICK A PLACE THAT IS PRIVATE AND A TIME
THAT IS UNHURRIED

Jack, whose daughter came out on the way to the airport, quipped, "They always tell you in the car."

Although this may be the easiest way for you to come out—on your way out the door—it probably won't be best for your parents.

◇ DON'T COME OUT IN ANGER

Coming out in anger will maximize the potential for your parents to do everything that you *don't* want them to do—or to say something that they don't necessarily mean. If your parents are provoking you and you get angry, don't blurt out that you're gay. Being gay is not a weapon to be used to hurt someone.

◇ CONSIDER ENLISTING AN ALLY

You might want the help of a relative or friend as you come out to your parents. An ally can support you or can be someone your parents could go to for support.

If you have an aunt or uncle, older sibling, or family friend who you *know* is understanding and accepting, you might want to tell them that you're planning on coming out to your parents and ask for their help. Amy calculated that she was going to need support coming out to her ultraconservative parents:

> About a month before my visit home, my parents all of a sudden found religion again. They hooked up with this very right-wing section of the Catholic Church. I had a conversation with my parents on the phone where my father told me how the pope was being plotted against by this left-wing group that wants birth control, that wants abortion, that wants to justify homosexuality.
>
> I said, "Oh God, how am I going to do this?" So I talked to my sister. We planned that I would go home and I would spend three days showing them how happy, healthy, perky I was in general. Which I did. The first three days all they could comment on was, "Oh you seem so happy," "Oh this new short haircut, it's great." And then, Tuesday night, my sister was going to come over and just be in the house while I told them. So if I needed to leave, I could go to her apartment.

Amy's parents were not thrilled that she was a lesbian, but her mother said she still loved her and that of course she could stay, and her father, somewhat begrudgingly, agreed.

◇ PROVIDE BOOKS FOR YOUR FAMILY

Accurate information can go a long way toward dispelling fears. Over and over again parents have expressed their appreciation that their children brought them books when they came out. As one mother from Oregon relates:

> My husband and I took a batch of books and we took off up into the mountains and put up the tent and piled in and started reading. We stayed up there for about a week and we read and we read and we read. And we traded books and we read to each other. And we talked and we read and we read. And we came back with a lot more education.

◇ HAVE INFORMATION ABOUT PFLAG AND OTHER SUPPORTIVE GROUPS OR PEOPLE

Being able to talk to other parents of lesbian, gay, and bisexual youth has been one of the most helpful things for many parents. Most parents will appreciate information about PFLAG (Parents, Families, and Friends of Lesbians and Gays). And even parents who are hesitant to go into a group situation might welcome an opportunity to talk to another parent individually. If you call your local PFLAG chapter, there's sure to be a parent who would be willing to invite your parent to have coffee and talk one-to-one.

◇ BE WILLING TO ANSWER THEIR QUESTIONS

Some parents don't want to hear very much about being gay, but others will have a lot of questions. Jason talks about his coming out conversation with his mother:

> My mother said she wanted to know how long I had had these feelings, and I told her that I'd had them from way back, but I hadn't realized what they meant until I was in high school. She wanted to know if I had a boyfriend. She wanted to know if I knew any other gay people.

Sometimes your parents may ask you questions that you don't know how to answer or don't want to answer. Hyde relates this dialogue:

> My mother got on this kick, you know, "Life is short, you got to be who you are." And I thought, oh my gosh, this is it, if I'm going to tell her, I've got to tell her now. And I'm like, "Um, Mom," and I started bawling. And she said, "What honey?" and she had me in her arms and she was crying, she didn't know why, and I was crying. "I have something to tell you." And she said, "What?" I said, "I'm gay." And she said, "Well how much gay?" "I don't know, Mom. I'm just gay." She was like, "Are you half gay? Are you mostly gay?" "I don't know, just, I'm gay, that's it." Then she said, "Well, what do two women do in bed anyway?" And I said, "I'm not going to tell you. I don't ask you what you do in bed."

Hyde didn't answer everything her mother asked, but she didn't get angry at the questions either. She set her boundaries where she was comfortable and was relieved to have gotten coming out over with.

Even questions that seem inappropriate or bizarre may be genuine. Hyde continues:

> A couple of months ago my mother asked me, "Do you consider yourself a man?" I wanted to get angry, just go off. Of course I don't think I'm a man! I'm a woman! I never got a sex change. But I'm trying not to read her the whole Riot Act, because it was a genuine question. So I just said, "Well Mom, no. I don't see myself as a man. I see myself as a woman who loves women. You can still refer to me as 'she' and 'her.'"

You are the teacher in this situation, and any question—however weird—is an opportunity to educate.

◇ IT'S NOT NECESSARY TO BRING UP THE MOST DISTURBING TOPICS POSSIBLE IN THE FIRST CONVERSATION

Your parents are hearing information about you that is new to them. You can make it a little easier on them by not initiating discussion of the hardest topics right away. Amy explains how she got into terrain that she later felt she could just as well have left alone:

> I explained that I was telling them because I wanted to be closer to them, so that I could tell them about the things I was involved in, so that when I meet the woman who I want to settle down with and have children with, I can share that with them. And this was the only time my Dad spoke. He asked, "How are you going to have children?" So I launched into a whole explanation of adoption and insemination, which was just not appropriate at that moment.

◇ CONSIDER YOUR PARENTS IN YOUR DECISIONS TO COME OUT TO OTHER RELATIVES

If your parents are still reeling from your initial disclosure, they may ask you to wait before telling other relatives. You, ultimately, are the one who gets to decide who and when you tell about your sexual orientation, but if your parents are doing their best to absorb this new information and ask you to hold off on spreading the news, you may want to take their feelings into consideration.

◇ TRUST YOUR OWN JUDGMENT

All these suggestions can help make the process of coming out a positive one, but you know best how your family works. You don't always have to do things strictly by the book to have a successful outcome. Here's Jonathan's story of a basically positive experience:

> Now about coming out to Mom. I had to mark it down in my calendar because I never wanted to forget the day. See, right here, *out with mom, 2:30 a.m.*, on the sixteenth of July.
>
> I was driving home from college to Arkansas for a visit, and I just felt that this was the time. So I got home and as normal, we had dinner and then we sat around the kitchen. My father had already gone to bed, and my mother and I were talking about my new apartment and about my being on my own. I told her that I was involved in a lot of things that people here wouldn't accept very well. I said, "I want you to know that if there are certain aspects of my life that

you want to ask me about, that I'm at a point in my life that I can answer. Nothing that you ask is going to offend me in any way." And she said, "Well, what do you mean by that?" I said, "I don't want you to feel that parts of my life should be closed off to you. We've always been close, you're not only my mother but you're my best friend."

She got all teary-eyed, and she said, "I feel like you're wanting me to ask you something, so I'm just going to ask you." She couldn't ask me if I was gay, so she said, "All those things they said about you in high school, is it true?" And I said, "Yes, I'm gay."

coming out to brothers and sisters

The friendship, love, and understanding of brothers and sisters is very important. When Matt came out to his twenty-year-old brother, he was pretty sure that he'd be accepting because his brother's attitudes are very liberal. Still, it was difficult to begin:

> I was mumbling, "This is very hard. This is very hard." And he said, "Relax, it'll be all right," because he thought I was talking about something else. And I said, "No, that's not what it's about." He said, "What then?" And I said, "I'm gay." Boom. Just like that.
>
> His first words were, *"Really?"* And then he said, "I love you. You're my brother. It doesn't matter to me." He's very straight, just redundantly heterosexual, but he was smiling and it was very clear he was happy for me. One of the things he said was, "I'm glad you felt you could come out to me."

Next Matt came out to his oldest brother, whose views are not so open-minded:

> The very first thing he said to me was, "I love you. You're my brother and that's really all that matters." We talked for a long time. There were a few things he said that I didn't like. One was, "Don't commit yourself to this. You're kind of young. This might be a phase, so maybe you're not old enough to know." I said, "Well, when did you know you were straight?" That shut him up. And when he thought

about it, he came to the conclusion that, "Yeah, I knew when I was twelve years old too." He said, "I'm your brother, I'm going to be supportive of you, but I don't support the gay community." I really didn't like that, but he came from such a conservative group of friends that I was just impressed with how accepting he was.

Quang very much values his sisters' understanding and patience:

Both of my sisters have been wonderful. Coming out to them has been a great, great experience. They had known or suspected for a long time, but they didn't try to get it out of me or press me on it. They gave me the room to do the work that I needed to do while they tried to keep our relationships comfortable—like not asking me about girlfriends all the time—so that I could eventually come out to them. I really respect them for that. Not forcing me into saying anything, but giving me the room to say it, shows a lot of love and respect on their part. I really appreciate that from them.

When Rick told his younger sister that he was gay, they both cried—and then celebrated:

My sister was taking a shower and I wrote her a note. I couldn't say it to her, but I could write it. She started crying and she said, "Oh, you know I love you. I kind of thought you might be gay, but I'm glad you told me." I started crying too, and she gave me a really big hug and we went out to McDonald's. She loves McDonald's.

Not all brothers and sisters are this accepting, of course, but if you are fortunate enough to have a sibling who can share in your life, that relationship can be a source of strength and joy.

Joan Bobkoff © 1995

10
your family's response

... Could I ever praise
My father half enough for being a father
Who let me be myself?

—Robert Francis

In an ideal world, a parent's response to a child coming out would be, "I'm so glad you know this about yourself and that you wanted to share it with me. You know it's not important to me who you're in love with. What's important to me is that you're happy."

Unfortunately, this kind of solid acceptance and understanding is rarely a parent's initial response. But what your family says at this first talk is not necessarily where things are going to wind up. Over time it usually gets better—and sometimes a great deal better. In some families change takes years, but in others there can be a real improvement even within a few months.

what is a good reaction?

Some parents are immediately comfortable with their child's sexual orientation—even nonchalant. As Arwyn describes her experience:

> I was in the kitchen on the phone with my friend Jen. And my mother was there making dinner. Jen said, "You know, I think you should tell your mom right now." I was like, "Really? You think I should tell her right now? OK, hold on." And I said, "Mom, what would you do if I told you that I was going to start dating girls?" And she looked at me and said, "What am I going to do? As long as it doesn't cost me any more money than your dating guys, I don't care."

© Karl Anderson, 1995.

Jason's parents also found it easy to accept their son's sexual orientation. My father said, "Why didn't you tell us sooner? What made you think you had to hide?"

But you don't have to get this kind of total approval for your family's reaction to be a good beginning. If your parents don't reject you, withdraw love, or alter their behavior toward you, that's a fine place to start from. As Nancy relates:

> My mother actually asked me one night, "What, are you gay?" It was five in the morning and I was coming home from a club, and I walked in and I couldn't say no. I said, "Yes." And she started crying. Then the next day she came over to me and she said, "I love you. You're my baby. And it doesn't matter what you are. I just wanted grandchildren and for you to be married and to be happy."
>
> It hurt me when she cried, because she didn't lose me. It's not like I died. But I can see from her point of view. These expectations she wanted for me maybe didn't come through and that was such a grief. But when she said, "I love you, it doesn't matter to me," wow, that was something I can't express. It was beautiful—like a sunset. And after that I thought to myself, I'm really lucky. Wow. Now I don't give a damn who knows.

Julio's mother had suspected that he was gay for some time—and had questioned him repeatedly. "She reads me like a book," he says, "She always knew and she always rejected it." When Julio finally came out, his mother did a whirlwind race through the stages of acceptance:

> I came home and I said to her, "You always taught me my entire life to believe in myself and regardless of what other people say that I should stand up for myself. Well, this is what I'm doing. I think there's a big possibility that I might be gay."
>
> And that's it. That's what I told her. In a period of fifteen minutes my mother went through denial, completely denied it. For five minutes she screamed at me and said, "No, you're not. No, you're not. What about all these girlfriends that you had?"
>
> I said, "Yeah, they're just a face." For five minutes she screamed at me. And then for five minutes she went into complete shock and just cried and cried, "Why me? Why?" She went through the whole stage of, "It's my fault, your father left us, I left Brazil, I should have been a good wife, I should have been"—the whole bit.
>
> I told her, "Don't go there. None of it is your fault. You're

the best mother I could ever have because if you hadn't given me the strength to come out to you the way I have, then maybe I could suffer for the next twenty years of my life. Would you prefer that I did that?" I kind of made it hard for her to say yes.

So she went through denial, then she went through her rage and crying, and then in fifteen minutes, "Fine, let's go on with our lives."

Some parents may be very upset initially, but their distress is not enduring. Alice, the mother of a gay son, describes it this way: "I thought I didn't like gay people, but when I found out it was *my* kid who was one, I decided it must not be so bad."

Sometimes parents want to be understanding and supportive, but their feelings aren't really there yet. This was true for Michelle's father:

When I finally told him, I said, "Are you OK with that?" And he muttered something to the effect of, "Sort of." But his tone of voice didn't say he was OK with it. For the next few months we couldn't get along about anything. We would say hello in the morning and that would turn into a screaming match. I remember getting into a completely blown out argument about something like I wasn't feeding the cats because I was gay and my sexuality was more important than my chores.

If your parents' response is not all that you wished for, give them time. It almost always gets better. A year and a half later, Michelle and her dad marched together in the annual Gay Pride celebration and he couldn't stop grinning the whole length of the parade.

For Better or For Worse © Lynn Johnston Prod., Inc. Reprinted with permission of UNIVERSAL PRESS SYNDICATE. All rights reserved.

weathering a bad response

Even loving parents sometimes have a very difficult time when they first face the fact that their child is gay. Anthony, who is bisexual, describes his mother's terse reaction:

> When I was fourteen I sort of came out to my mother. I said I might be bi. She said, "I don't want to hear about it ever again. Do what you want to do, but don't discuss it with me."

And Mickie's mother cried, "Oh my God, what have I done to deserve this?"

If your parents' response is angry, blaming, or if it otherwise deeply hurts your feelings, you're likely to feel pretty upset. If you thought they would handle this well, their negative response can be especially jarring. So do your best to take care of yourself. Try to be assertive in surrounding yourself with gay-positive people outside your home. Get some extra support from people who think you're great exactly as you are.

If your parents continue to be demeaning and insulting about your sexual orientation, if they constantly tell you you're no good, sinful, or a failure, your pain can be as deep as if you were physically assaulted. And it's just as important that you be protected. Reach out for help.

RESPONDING TO COMMON REACTIONS WHEN YOU COME OUT

Parent: Are you sure?

This question is sometimes a genuine inquiry. On the other hand, it can imply that they are hoping that you're really not gay. If you're still questioning your sexual orientation, talk about your feelings. But if you've waited until you really know you are gay, say something simple like:

You: I've thought about it a lot and I'm sure.

◇

Parent: What did we do wrong? I always knew I shouldn't have let your father take you fishing *or* I knew I shouldn't have bought you that doll.

This is an opportunity to reassure your parents. Say:

You: You didn't do anything wrong. It's just who I am. And there's nothing wrong about it. In fact, you did a lot right, which is what makes me able to talk to you about this.

◇

Parent: It's not true. It's just a phase. You're too young to know. So and so influenced you. It's a fad.

If your parents present one or more of this denial quintet, it's best to say, with as much patience as you can muster:

You: I know it may be hard for you to accept, but I've thought about this a lot and I'm sure. Just like you knew you were straight, I know I'm gay.

This may be a good time to share a little of what has made you realize that this is who you are.

◇

Parent: It's wrong. It's sinful. Let's pray.

If you expect your parents to present some variation of the sin and prayer response, read the Spirituality chapters to get an idea of what gay-positive religious leaders are saying about homosexuality. You may even want to line up someone who'd be willing to talk with them. Initially, though, it's often better to stick with simple statements like:

You: I'm sorry you feel that way. I hope you'll be willing to learn about some different points of view because this is who I am. Please don't make this a contest between my faith and my feelings.

◇

Parent: How could you do this to me?

If your parents think that everything you do is about them, this is a good time to remind them that's not true. Say simply:

You: This isn't about you. It's about me being true to myself.

what to do if you're in danger

Even with thoughtful assessment, people can surprise us. Hopefully, you won't be faced with a threatening response, but if you are, it's important to keep yourself safe. If there is any violence—if your parent hits you, shoves you, or threatens to be violent in any way—you need to protect yourself. Usually it's best to remove yourself quickly from a dangerous situation. Sometimes a short cooling-off period will help.

If you are threatened with abuse, get help from a trusted adult to secure protection and safe housing. If your parent talks about psychiatric hospitalization—locking you up to cure you of being gay—it's important that you get help right away. There may be a teacher or counselor at your school who can help. Call your local chapter of PFLAG. If you're under eighteen, call Child Protective Services. Although there aren't always easy solutions to such serious problems, enlisting the aid of capable adults increases your odds of working out a safe next step. (See "Getting Help from Your Community" beginning on p. 311 and "Psychiatric Abuse" on p. 316.)

◇ HONESTY IS NOT ALWAYS THE BEST POLICY

If you are living at home and your parents react in a violent, threatening, or extremely hostile way to the information that you are gay, lesbian, or bisexual, one option is to deny your sexual orientation. Although this isn't going to work in all situations—sometimes the circumstances are such that your denial wouldn't be believable—often it is possible to say that you really aren't gay even after you've said you are. If your safety is at stake, you can say that you thought you were gay, but now you realize you're not. Or you can provide another explanation that fits your situation.

Telling the truth is an important value, and being an honest person is an important part of one's character, but there are times when honesty is not the best policy. In child protection programs, small children are taught that it's OK to lie to someone who is trying to hurt them in order to get away safely. This is true for teenagers and adults as well. It's OK to hide your same-sex feelings if there are circumstances that aren't safe enough to reveal your true self.

◇ STAY CLEAR IN YOUR OWN HEART

Throughout history there have been times when people have had to conceal their true identities to save themselves from harm. For example, some Jews during the Nazi regime were able to pass as Christian and thus save their lives. Many of these Jews carried the truth inside them even as they hid it from the outside world.

If you need to hide your true identity for a time, it will be important that you have ways to preserve the truth inside you until you are in a more favorable environment.

Being in the closet has its costs. It hurts to have to hide parts of who you are, but with the support and affirmation of caring people, those hurts can heal.

And while you're maintaining yourself, do the things that will help you get to more advantageous circumstances. Study hard at school, work and save your money, write for college catalogs, make realistic plans to get out to a better environment as soon as you are able.

◇ DON'T LEAVE HOME WITHOUT IT

Although leaving home before you can support yourself is rarely the best option, there are some extreme circumstances—such as physical, sexual, or emotional abuse—where an alternative living situation may be preferable to staying at home. But don't leave without thinking realistically about your options. Do you have a relative—aunt, uncle, grandparent, older sibling—who might be willing to offer you a home until you're able to be on your own? Might you qualify for help from a social service program, a foster home, or a group home? Can you enter a vocational training program, like the Job Corps, where housing and food are provided?

Unless you can arrange to live with a responsible and trustworthy adult, then moving out of your family home is unlikely to be a safe choice. Minimal requirements for independent living are safe and affordable housing and a steady, reliable job. (For more on finding help in these situations, see "Getting Help from Your Community" beginning on p. 311.)

◇ BUT WHAT IF I'M KICKED OUT?

Sometimes when young people disclose their sexual orientation to their parents—or when their parents have found out—they've been kicked out of the house. If you don't have a friend, family member, or other trusted adult to go to, begin looking for help immediately. Call a crisis hot line or youth talk line. Call your local PFLAG chapter. If you're under eighteen, call Child Protective Services.

Remember, you are precious and valuable whether people are treating you that way or not.

responses of brothers and sisters

Many gay, lesbian, and bisexual young people have received mean-ingful support from their sisters and brothers. It feels really good to know that the people with whom you grew up, played, fought, laughed, and cried, accept you and love you just as you are.

But of course, not all siblings have this kind of loving relationship even without the issue of sexual orientation. Nancy says that her brother is OK with her being a lesbian most of the time, but when he's angry with her, he taunts her:

> We'll be having a fight and he'll throw it in my face or call me something in Spanish and it hurts me. Or I'll say things like, "Oh you're jealous because I get more women than you do," and he gets mad.

This kind of fighting—using sexual orientation as a way to insult—hurts. And it hurts, especially, from someone in your family.

Sometimes, once brothers and sisters get to know more gay peo-ple, their attitudes change. Daphne describes her brother's response when he saw her kissing her girlfriend in the kitchen:

> I said, "Well, I guess you know now." He goes, "I guess I do." I said, "Well, how do you feel about it?" And he said, "It's OK. I kind of suspected for a while." He asked a lot of personal questions about what we do behind closed doors, how our relationship was. He wasn't so much homophobic as he was uneducated on the subject. He had been in the military, and he had a couple of close friends that he found out were gay and lesbian. That made a big difference because before that he had always been all, "If I ever see them gay people I'm liable to go off on their heads."
>
> But he was more concerned about our welfare than he was the fact that we were gay. And what he said that almost made me cry was, "I'll stand up in front of a room with a hundred thousand people and say, 'This is my sister and not only has she accomplished all this stuff in her life, but she's also gay and I'm proud of her.'"

Nicky hasn't yet come out to his parents, but his brother's absolute acceptance has been deeply reassuring:

Before I told my brother I had no one. I still felt that what I was doing was really bad and I was scared to tell him. But now that I know he accepts me completely, I'm able to be more open and more myself. He told me that whenever I wanted to, I could always move in with him and my sister-in-law. It makes me feel that I can be myself around them and not be scared. I no longer have to worry, if I get caught, do I have someplace to go? Is someone going to be there to help me out? Someone is going to be there.

Often in families where the love is strong, sisters and brothers can offer acceptance and support even if they're not entirely at ease with the idea of homosexuality. Yevette says her sister is able to accept her, "just because I'm family."

it'll kill your grandmother

Don't be so sure. Although not every grandparent will be accepting of your same-sex feelings, our stereotypes that older people will not be able to understand simply aren't true. Sometimes age means that people are more understanding and less judgmental.

And sometimes you may be surprised that your grandparents have a thing or two to tell *you*. As John relates:

I worked in a nursing home and my great-grandfather was a patient there. I was starting to feel pretty good about my gayness. So I'm brazen enough to tell my great-grandfather. And he said, "You know, I had a boyfriend until I was thirty, and then I came to the United States and I married this girl." He showed me pictures of him and his lover from high school until they were in their thirties.

He said, "Back when I was a kid you had a boyfriend because you didn't want to spoil the girls. The girls were meant for babies. The men were fun." He said, "But I don't think you like that idea, do you? You always liked men, didn't you?"

I said, "Yeah I did." It was great.

Doe's grandmother surprised her in a different way:

After I came out, my grandmother and I were in the living room and she was telling me about this talk show where they had these lesbians on. And she said, "You know, they talked about everything but what you do in bed." This is my grandmother asking me what we do and how we do it. She wanted to know if we had pleasure. So of course I was embarrassed, right? I mean totally embarrassed, not wanting to tell her, but kind of wanting to tell, too.

I said, "Well, Granny, we use our hands and mouths and, you know, other stuff."

"So why not just do it with a man?"

I'm like, "Well, because we don't want to be with men. We want to be with each other."

And she got the drift. She got the scoop.

Even when grandparents are judgmental, their love often overrides their judgments. As Mickie relates:

My grandmother was like, "Ah, Jesus. Oh my God," all this stuff. She said, "I think that if you go to church and pray to God, you won't be like that anymore."

I just sat there saying, "Grandma, I can't change it. This is who I am."

She sat there. "I don't approve of it, but I deal with it because you're my granddaughter. You're my favorite one."

And so I'm like, "Thank you very much."

"As long as you don't do anything in front of me, OK?"

I was like, "You got that right."

coming out issues over time

Coming out does not begin and end in the particular moment that you tell your family that you're gay. As Amy says:

You don't just come out to your parents. You come out to them over and over again, forever.

Each time you tell someone else in your extended family, each time you bring up a gay subject, when you bring a boyfriend or girlfriend home, when you meet new people and make introductions—all these are occasions when your parents will, once again, encounter the fact that you're gay.

If you find yourself feeling frustrated that your parents aren't already relaxed with your sexual orientation, try to remember that really becoming comfortable can take some time.

◇ COMMUNICATION

Sometimes parents will act like the coming out conversation never even happened. You've made this earth-shattering revelation and they ignore it. You know they know, but they avoid mentioning anything to do with gay or lesbian concerns, ask no questions, and are generally silent on the subject. Or they may even make comments that imply that you're straight. This may leave you feeling invisible and abandoned.

If it takes some time before your family is able to do much talking or reaching out, try to be patient. Christopher relates that although his mother was accepting when he first came out to her, she wasn't at all ready to have gay and lesbian issues be a natural part of their lives:

> I had all these books in the closet, literally in the closet, so after I came out to my parents I pulled all this stuff out and I totally let loose. And then I happened to be watching some talk show about lesbians and I thought, well, this is OK now, I don't have to change the channel every time they come into the room. But my mom was getting ready for work and she came in and said, "Would you just knock it off! Stop. I need some time." I was not prepared for that. I had let down my whole guard. I was happy, gay, and me. She said, "You're doing this on purpose and I don't appreciate it. "
>
> So I said, "I'm sorry. I know you need time." That's the one thing that I want to give them. So I gave her a ride to work and I kind of cried on my way home. And I put my books back on the shelf and I decided that maybe for now their knowing is enough.

Wanting to talk freely and openly with your family is an understandable desire. But if you can't talk naturally and in depth with them now, it doesn't mean that it will never happen. In the meantime, you need to decide how—and how much—to bring up the subject of being gay. You'll need to strike a balance between wanting to let them know who you are and giving them space to work through their feelings.

One strategy is to bring up the subject now and then so they can begin to get used to the idea. Let them know about your plans to attend a gay pride march or a dance at the gay and lesbian center. Tell them a little about the report you're writing on gay history. Introduce a friend by saying she's from your gay, lesbian, and bisexual support group. Weave it into the conversation naturally as you would any other events from your life.

If your parents don't say much in response, that's OK. You're still normalizing the discussion of your sexual orientation, and that's a positive step.

◇ GIRLFRIENDS AND BOYFRIENDS

Bringing home your special someone to meet your family is usually a big event. And sometimes it's not so easy. Your parents may be adjusting to the fact that you are gay theoretically, but actually meeting your romantic partner and spending time with the two of you can be challenging. Meeting the person that you're involved with makes your being lesbian or gay a lot more real.

Although you may be nervous—and your parents and your girlfriend or boyfriend may be nervous too—first meetings can turn out to be warm and welcoming. As Hyde relates:

> I picked up Shelly from the airport and I brought her to my Mom's office because I needed some cash. So I said, "Mom, this is Shelly," and my mom went after her with this big open-armed hug and just said, "Hi, Shelly. I've heard so much about you." Very friendly and open. Very welcoming. Which surprised the heck out of me. I was in the background thinking, Oh my God, what's she going to do? when she had her arms open. Is she going to go over there and choke her?

Some parents want to meet their children's dates and encourage them to spend time with the family. Stone notes:

> My parents have wanted to meet everyone, so they'd invite them over to dinner. I'd sit there really nervously, going like, my girlfriend is sitting here, my parents are sitting here, my six-year-old brother is throwing food across the table—could somebody please just shoot me? They were very good. They didn't make anybody feel too embarrassed.

Many young people have related how their families have grown to be very attached to their boy and girlfriends. As Luna says:

> My whole family loves him. Sunday was my niece's birthday, and my boyfriend wasn't there yet because he had to get his work clothes ready for the next day. My brother and sister kept asking. "Where is he? Is he going to show up?" He's really part of the family now, and I like that.

When Michelle's girlfriend moved in with her family, it actually brought Michelle and her father back together:

> My girlfriend got along with him better than I did. She could say the exact same things that I did, except that they could actually talk about things without fighting. And that brought him full circle.
>
> I remember sitting in my room one day and he knocked on my door and he said, "You know, Michelle, I learned a lot from you." And he walked back down the hall. I closed the door and I just sat there going, "Wow."

Girlfriends and boyfriends can build meaningful relationships with siblings, as well. Daphne's fourteen-year-old sister, Daisy, explains that Daphne's relationship has been an important role model for her.

> Daphne and Marsha have a really strong relationship because they were friends first. They know each other really well. They talk about everything. When I get older I hope I can find a relationship like Daphne and Marsha have. Not with another girl, with a boy. That would be a dream come true, to have that strong a relationship, to have someone that I feel so comfortable with.

Your parents—like most people—have probably not had many opportunities to see and get used to lesbian and gay relationships. They're not used to seeing two women or two men holding hands, sharing a special smile, or being affectionate—even in ways that are appropriate and accepted in your family for straight couples. But with a little time, most families get used to it. As one parent says:

In the past I didn't think I could handle him kissing a man, but I handled it fine. I've seen it done. It's OK.

Again, your patience, compassion, and perseverance will usually help your parents become more accepting. Patience doesn't mean that you have to stop doing what you're doing. It doesn't mean that you should stop bringing dates home in order to keep your parents comfortable. Patience means that you respect their feelings just as you want them to respect yours. You are compassionate, even as you continue to assert the legitimacy of your relationships.

POSITIVE CHANGES OVER TIME

My mom has become my best friend. I will sit here in the kitchen and I'll tell her what we did for our anniversary, that we took a bath together and that we want to move in together, that we want to have kids and that we argued—everything. It's so incredible. She'll tell me things to do, she'll give me advice.

And my dad is just the same. He stood right there in the doorway and we were talking about Lily and me moving in together. I said, "Well, she doesn't like soft beds, she likes hard beds." And my dad was like, "Well, you can go to Levitz and buy a hard board for the bed." I couldn't believe my dad.

—Mickie

My dad and I always had a bad relationship. I put him down. I'd call him a jerk. And he wouldn't do anything back. I always thought I didn't have any feelings for him at all, but now I realize that I did, but I hid them because I figured there was nothing I could do to make myself the kind of son he wanted. I created a shell where I didn't have to worry about these feelings. But now we're starting to connect. I can admit to myself that my dad is important, and we're both trying to bring more understanding to each other.

—Patrick

My mother went through a period where she felt as though there was something she did wrong to make me gay. She was calling me every other day. Some days she would wake up, she was fine with it. Other days she would wake up absolutely bawling. But now she's gotten things in perspective, and she's comfortable with it. She says she progresses daily. And she really does. She says she's real proud of me for everything I've done. She's my mother of course, and we love each other, which I am so fortunate for.

—Jonathan

I came out to my mother when I was seventeen, and she reacted very negatively. She sent me to a psychiatrist. She forbade me from even thinking about talking to my father about it because she thought it would destroy him. The situation got so bad that I left Brazil and came to Florida to live with my girlfriend and her parents.

Now, six years later, both my parents are coming around. We're working to bridge the canyon between us. They send hugs to my girlfriend any time I talk to them on the phone. And last summer, when I went to visit, my father said, "You know, people forget the Bible was written by people. God didn't write it." I was in shock because I didn't expect that level of understanding from my father.

—Alessandra

Now I know more about my sister. It isn't like she's hiding something. I know all of her and it feels a lot better. And she and Marsha don't have to hold back if they want to kiss each other. They can hold hands, stuff like that. So that makes me a lot more comfortable too.

—Daisy, Daphne's sister

I knew my mom really truly was fine with us being gay when she told her friend. One of her friends came to my mom upset because she has lesbian twins and she knew my mom had gay children. This woman is Vietnamese and my mom's Chinese. And my mom's like, "What? How are they disgracing the family? Are they good daughters?" She's like, "Yea, they're good daughters." And my mom's like, "Look at them, they got accepted to private college, they're getting scholarships, they're making you proud. And just because they like girls, does that mean they're not your daughters?" And the woman said, "No, of course not." My mom said, "Think of what you have. Just think. They're honoring you. You should never think anything bad about them."

My mother had never verbalized any of these feelings toward us, but apparently she had found her own way of dealing with it—like, they're my children and I'm not going to stop loving them because they like men.

—Dan

◇ FAMILY EVENTS

Emotions often run high around family gatherings and celebrations. Whether it's your graduation, your parents' twenty-fifth anniversary, your cousin's wedding, or your grandfather's birthday party, it's likely that members of your family will have a big investment in how the event turns out. They want everyone to love each other, to be comfortable, and for things to go well.

Sometimes a big family event is the first time that your relatives will see you after you've come out as gay, lesbian, or bisexual. Or it may be the first time that you've brought a romantic partner to a family occasion. It's natural that you may feel some apprehension or concern about how your family will respond.

At the same time, others, including your parents, may have big expectations or concerns about the occasion that don't have anything to do with you. All in all, feelings can be intense, and it's easy for you—or others—to feel hurt or disregarded.

To the extent that you're able, be clear about your needs while being considerate of the feelings of others. You have a right to be yourself, including your sexual orientation. You deserve to be treated with respect and you have a responsibility to treat others with respect. It may take a little—or a lot—of extra effort to work through arrangements if your whole family hasn't yet incorporated your sexual identity.

For starters, don't spring any surprises on the day of the event. Don't announce that you're bringing your sweetie when everyone is vying for time in the shower that morning. Let people know what you want and what you plan beforehand. Talk it out. Listen to their feelings and make your own needs clear.

Dear Miss Manners:
What am I supposed to say when I am introduced to a homosexual "couple"?
Gentle Reader:
"How do you do?" "How do you do?"

Copyright © 1986 by Judith Martin

If you resent that you have to put out this extra effort while straight people can just assume acceptance, those feelings are understandable. It isn't fair. But this is an important opportunity to educate your family and to affirm yourself.

In general, the more comfortable and confident you are—and the less defensive or angry you are—the more comfortable everyone else will be.

How to Communicate That You Want Your Special Someone to Be Invited to Your Cousin's Wedding

Sometimes people don't know how to handle inviting same-sex partners to family events. They may never even have thought about it. Although this may hurt or infuriate you, you can often get very good results once you open up communication and make your needs clear.

If you've been invited to a family celebration and your partner wasn't included in the invitation, find out if other family members are bringing their partners. If no partners have been invited, then it's understandable that yours wasn't either. But if your sister's live-in boyfriend is coming, it's reasonable to expect that your long-time companion would be welcome as well.

If you're ready to talk about this in your family, call your cousin, and after a little chit-chat about how happy you are for her, say something like this:

You: I don't think you know, but I live with Joe—we moved in together a year ago—and of course I'd like us to come to your wedding together.

Be casual and positive, leaving no room for a negative response. And don't be afraid of silence. Take a few deep breaths as you wait. A positive response that leaves you home free would be something like:

Cousin: Why of course. Joe would be welcome.

If she hesitates, stammers, hems and haws, you may want to suggest that she think about it:

You: This is probably a surprise to you, so maybe you'd like to think it over. Why don't you call me in a couple of days?

Although you don't want to rescue her, you also don't want to back her into a corner. Sometimes people respond more favorably if they have just a little time to digest what you've said.

If the answer is no, you may need to think over your choices. In difficult situations like this, you're likely to feel better about your decision if you take your time. Say something like:

You: I'm really sorry you feel that way. It seems unfair to me and hurts my feelings. I need to take some time to think about this. Maybe you could think about it more, too.

In the meantime, you may have allies in the family that can work on your cousin. Do you have an aunt, uncle, or other relative who could ask her, "What are you doing? Have you thought about how this is going to hurt our family?"

When you talk again, if she's changed her mind, thank her:

You: I really appreciate your changing your mind. This means a lot to me.

If she is still not willing to include your partner, you have a choice to make. If it's more important to you to be there, even without your partner, you can go alone and express your disappointment:

You: I'm really disappointed, but I also want to celebrate your wedding. I hope the next time this comes up you'll feel differently.

If you choose not to go, you can say:

You: I'm really disappointed. I would have loved to be there and share in your happiness, but I can't come. It would be dishonoring my relationship and I couldn't do that. I hope it's a lovely event, and I'm sorry I can't be there.

If you decide not to attend, you may want to have your allies tell the truth about why you're not there. And know that although you didn't achieve what you wanted this time, if you were able to stay kind, loving, and firm throughout, you are likely to have made quite an impression on people's thinking.

Of course this kind of direct challenge is an approach that demands a lot from you. If you're not ready for a face-off yet, you needn't raise the issue of your partner. You can simply go alone or make an excuse as to why you can't be there. This won't be the last family event at which you can take a stand.

◇ LIVING YOUR LIFE IN A HEALTHY WAY

Assuming that your family's most fundamental concern is for your well-being, one of the most effective ways to demonstrate that being gay or lesbian can be fulfilling and satisfying is to live your life now in a healthy way.

Luna is doing just this:

> I was the first one from my family to graduate from high school. So I proved to my parents that I was succeeding. Now, my mother comes to see shows that I do. She came to to an exhibit of my photography. So they know that I'm doing stuff and they're happy with that.

If you do well in school, or at work, are respectful at home, spend time with friends who are also making healthy choices, your parents will probably be reassured that you really will be OK. But no matter how well you do all these things, you can't control your family's response. Ultimately, all you can do is to live your life in the best way you can, and enjoy the rewards. As Jessica relates:

> I know I'll never have my mother's approval, but I've created a new life for myself with my dad. I've been clean and sober for over a year, I'm in school part-time at community college and I work part-time at a video store. I've got a wonderful girlfriend and I'm beginning to make some real friends. From where I started out, I never imagined that life could be this good.

We all want our parents' approval and support. But whether that is offered to you or not, you have the power to create a life rich with inner satisfaction, accomplishments, and respectful, loving relationships.

◇　◇　◇　◇

Joan Bobkoff © 1995

11
our pride and joy

For Parents of Gay, Lesbian, and Bisexual Youth

Your children are not your children.
They are the sons and the daughters of Life's longing for itself.
They come through you but not from you,
And though they are with you yet they belong not to you.

You may give them your love but not your thoughts,
For they have their own thoughts.
You may house their bodies but not their souls,
For their souls dwell in the house of tomorrow,
    which you cannot visit, not even in your dreams.[1]

—Kahlil Gibran

[1]Sweet Honey in the Rock, a truly inspiring a capella group of five
    African-American women, has made this poem into a powerful song.

This chapter speaks directly to your parents. You can learn a great deal about their experience by reading it. You can also give it to them to read.

For many parents, the feelings of love and care that we have for our children are deeper than in any other relationship. Our children's happiness gives us great joy. And we ache for them in their sorrows. We want to be good parents. We want to feel that we've helped them grow into healthy, whole, independent adults.

Sometimes it's easy for us to support and affirm our children. Other times, it's much more difficult. And there are times we just don't know what to do. But when we approach our children with an attitude of unconditional acceptance and a willingness to work together through the difficult places, it's likely that the outcome will be one of increased understanding, respect, and mutual appreciation.

You may be reading this book for a variety of reasons. Your fourteen-year-old daughter may have just told you that she's a lesbian and you went to the bookstore and asked for help. Or you may think that your son in college is gay and you want to prepare yourself in case he wants to talk to you about it. Perhaps your daughter came out recently and gave you this book, knowing that you're having a hard time. Or it may be that you've known your son is bisexual for a long time and you're just now ready to learn more. Whatever your situation, if you're reading this book, you care about your child very much. And that will take you a long way toward understanding—and affirming—your child.

When parents first hear that their child is gay, lesbian, or bisexual, their responses vary widely. You may be concerned for your child's well-being. You may be upset, confused, angry, guilty, or shocked. You may be frightened about AIDS. You may be disbelieving, relieved, accepting, or have a combination of conflicting feelings. It's helpful to remember that your responses reflect more about you than they do about your child. As one mother said to her child, "Whatever feelings I'm having about this, they're mine."

We are all products of our environment and our experiences. Your values, your thinking, your feelings are all shaped by your conditioning, your assumptions, and your access to information. At the same time that you are facing new and important information about your child, you are also learning a great deal about yourself—perhaps more than you ever wanted to know!

Although this time may be tumultuous and challenging, it need not be destructive—for you, your child, or your family. Over and over again parents report that the sharing and communication that resulted from their child's coming out—though it may have been very difficult—led to relationships that are close, honest, and richer than they had been before. As this mother said:

> My relationship with my daughter has been enhanced a thousand percent. I've been invited into the dialogue. I've been invited into the community. I've been invited into her life. It's not like I have to beg to see her.

If your child has chosen to tell you that he or she is gay, that child cares enough about your relationship to want to be honest and authentic. This is a gift. Accept it as an affirmation of the love and trust between you.

creating an affirming home before your child comes out

None of us knows whether we're going to have gay, lesbian, bisexual, or straight kids, so it's a good idea to establish a home environment that is affirming to all young people. If it happens that we do have gay children, they will grow up with a feeling of belonging. And if our children turn out to be straight, they will be tolerant and accepting people. Also, a strong attitude of open-mindedness and understanding will make it easier for our kids to bring up *any* difficult issues, not just those about being gay.

Richard, now a freshman at college, has always remembered a comment that his mom made when he was in grade school, that she wouldn't mind if her kids were gay:

> It was definitely comforting to me in years to come. I think it gave me a sense of strength or certainty that other people didn't have.

This single positive remark was powerful enough for Richard to carry it through the years as reassurance and support. If your child brings up an issue related to sexual orientation, don't ignore it. Make room for discussion. One mother from the Midwest, Ruth, describes her regret at not realizing that her daughter's seemingly off-the-cuff question was actually an important overture:

> When Margie was in junior high school, she asked me how I felt about the gay couple who owned the house next door. I said that it was a really important issue that I hadn't had time to think about. Looking back, I realize that I told her, "I don't have time to think about the thing that's most important to you."

Many parents of gay children echo this regret that they had no idea what their children were going through, that their children had to struggle alone. As one mother, Clare, expressed it, "Nobody ever told me I might have a gay son."

But don't assume that your child is gay just because he or she brings up a gay issue. If you respond positively to what you think are hints or clues that your child is gay, and this turns out not to be true, you've simply demonstrated your belief that everyone deserves equal rights and acceptance. If, on the other hand, it turns out that your child *is* gay or lesbian, you'll have helped to create an environment that affirms his or her self-esteem.

Remember, making your home a safer place for gay and lesbian children does not increase the likelihood that your child will be gay or lesbian. It simply lets your child know that your love and acceptance are unconditional and that respect is due to all people.

◇ NOT HAVING A CLUE

Sometimes parents have reason to suspect that their child might be gay, lesbian, or bisexual. But very often, they don't have a clue. Carroll, a mother from Canada, relates:

> My daughter asked, "Well didn't you know, Mom?" and I said, "The buzz haircut, the Doc Martens, the jeans with the knees gone and the ass hanging out? I thought this was a new fashion statement." You know, we went through the pink stage, we went through the white wicker stage, we went through the black and white stage, we went through saving the whales, so I thought this was another statement. It's like I was standing so close to the wall I couldn't see the building. I didn't know what I was looking at.

And sometimes parents don't get the hint even if their kids make it quite obvious. Here is Clare:

> Brian was very involved in ACT UP, and the International AIDS Convention was in San Francisco. ACT UP was not invited to be present so they decided to do a direct action. As the keynote speaker came up to the podium, they disrupted the speech.
>
> The next day Brian called me and said, "Mom, I'm on the front page of the *New York Times*." And there was the photograph with a shadow of a protester with upraised arm and clenched fist, a silhouette. And, if you knew Brian, you knew that was him. I, however, still didn't get it that Brian was gay. I thought he was just a political activist.

◇ IT'S USUALLY BETTER NOT TO ASK DIRECTLY

Although you may be prepared to totally accept your child's sexual orientation, it's usually better not to question him or her directly. Even if your child is gay, he may not be ready to acknowledge those feelings—even to himself. When Clare finally realized that Brian might be gay, she thought a lot about how to open communication:

> I came up with a way to give him an opportunity—without backing him into a corner. I said, "So, Brian, it seems to me that your involvement with ACT UP and the gay community has been very important in your life." And he said, "Yeah." And I just waited. I stayed quiet for what seemed like a long time. And then he said, "Well, you know I'm gay, don't you?"

Every family is different and no one rule works for everyone. Many parents have asked their children directly if they were gay with positive results. If your intentions are good and you are accepting of your child, however you bring up the topic is likely to be successful.

when your child comes out

Your response—both initially and, especially, in an ongoing way—is likely to be a very influential factor in the ease or difficulty your child experiences being gay, lesbian, or bisexual. Although many parents worry about how hard a gay life will be for their child, they themselves may inadvertently do the most to make their children's lives difficult. You don't have to repeat this painful pattern. Gay youth need acceptance from their families. Life is tough enough—don't make it any harder on your child.

Instead, by providing a positive foundation of support, you can help your child face any difficult situations he or she may encounter. At the same time, you will strengthen and enrich the relationship between you.

Here are some suggestions and reminders that may help you to assimilate this new information and to communicate with your child:

◇ REMEMBER: THIS IS STILL YOUR SAME CHILD

As Susan, a mother from the Southwest, relates:

> I keep by the side of my bed a photograph of both of my kids when they were about one and two. They are just these precious little creatures. One of the things that really helped me was to go back and keep remembering how I felt about my daughter when she was born. All that incredible love and wonder and excitement, those overwhelming feelings. I kept going back to that and saying to myself, this is the same, she's the same. She's unfolding in a different way than I thought she would, but if I loved her as an infant and child, then surely I can love her even more now. She's the same person. She's just growing up.

◇ REAFFIRM YOUR LOVE AND ACCEPTANCE

It's OK to be confused or upset. You don't have to pretend to take this all in stride—you probably couldn't fool your child even if you tried. But you can affirm your love and the assurance that you'll hang in there together. Julio describes his mother's response:

> She said, "I'm going to respect you for who you are because I love you and because you're Julio." Her attitude was that everything else we'd deal with. She was a parent who was struggling, who was in shock over what she thought she had done wrong, a parent who probably wished I was different,

but she did the best thing she could, both for her and me. She made it really clear that, regardless of what you are or who you are, I'm going to love you. That gave her some space to think about it all.

Over and over young lesbian, gay, and bisexual children describe how much they needed their parents' love and acceptance, how painful it was when they didn't get that, and how reassuring it was when they did. When Chris was sixteen, he let his mother know he was gay. Her expression of love was crucial in helping him begin to face himself and her:

My mother kept following me around the house saying, "I want to ask you a question." And I knew what she wanted to ask. I kept saying "No" and walking out of the room. Finally she grabbed me in the living room and said, "I want to ask you a question." And I remember, I hugged her really tight and I said, "What?" She asked me, "Are you gay?" And I said, "Yes." And we both started crying. We were sitting in the recliner and I was hugging her as tightly as I could, didn't want to let go, cause I didn't want to see her face. I didn't want to see her cry. But I could tell she was. I said, "Yes." The weight was lifted, but a knife was put in my heart. It's like, OK, now she knows, but I've killed her. I finally said, "I can't do this," and I ran upstairs and locked myself in the bathroom.

My mother called my therapist and my therapist thought I was going to kill myself so she sent my mother up to talk me out of it. And my mother started pounding on the door. I remember, the first words out of her mouth were, "I love you anyway." I wonder whether the therapist told her to say that, but still she said it, which helped. So I made her turn off all the lights. And still it took her half an hour to talk me out of the bathroom.

Although your child may not show how much your reactions mean to him or her, every child has a strong need for acceptance. And as Meyer, a father of a gay son, advises:

If your child is gay, believe me, acceptance is a lot easier than rejection. The pain that you will suffer if you cut yourself off from your child is infinitely worse than what would come from the acceptance.

◇ DON'T BLAME YOURSELF

Charles describes his agony when his daughter first came out:

> My first thought was that I turned Barbara off men because when she was in high school she and I did not get along at all. And furthermore, my parents were bigots, terrific bigots, and they taught me that all Blacks, Jews, Catholics, and so forth were no good—and the worst of all were homosexuals. And so I put these two thoughts together immediately and thought, OK, I am responsible for forcing Barbara to live the rest of her life in utter depravity. And I felt terrible. I just felt a horrible feeling of guilt.

Whatever your situation, it's easy to find something about yourself to blame. As Meyer sums it up:

> Then we started to blame ourselves. We must have done something wrong. Alice said I wasn't assertive enough, and Alice thought she was too assertive.

In reality, you are not the cause of your child's sexual orientation. The idea that parents' behavior can cause homosexuality is false. Our best understanding at this point in time is that our sexual orientation is very basic to our nature, and environment alone cannot cause a child to become gay, lesbian, or bisexual. One father from the Midwest explains:

> The fundamental thing to know about being gay is that it's a given, like eye color or left-handedness. And it's an academic curiosity about why it's a given. When we know why I'm straight, then we'll know why my child is gay. That's a very interesting question for research, but it's not an important question for life, for how we live our lives and how we react to each other.

In a supportive environment children may be able to recognize and acknowledge their sexual orientation earlier and with less

anguish. So if your child is telling you that he is gay, you've probably provided an environment that allowed him freedom to take an
honest look at himself and to feel that his relationship with you is
strong enough and safe enough to risk telling you. You did something right, not wrong.

When I told my Mum I was gay she blamed herself.

Now she wants to take all the credit.

Adapted from a poster by the Australian Federation of AIDS Organizations and the
Victoria AIDS Council.

◇ ALLOW YOURSELF YOUR FEELINGS

When your child first comes out, you may be so overwhelmed
that you don't even know what you feel. Carroll describes her state
of shock:

> I remember when she said, "I'm gay," I went, "As long as
> you're happy, dear." Afterward you realize the silliness of it.
> But I was so confused. And I felt that I had to say some-
> thing. If you put a million dollars in my hand and asked me
> what I did the rest of that weekend, I couldn't tell you.

Many parents go through an initial period of grief. Even parents
who grow to celebrate their child's sexual orientation may at first
feel deep pain. As Bunny, a mother from Arizona, describes it:

When I heard the words over the telephone, I was so surprised at my reaction. I didn't fall apart to her, but I was hys-
terical. I cried and I carried on for many months. I did a lot
of crying. To my daughter I said, "I love you, it doesn't make
any difference." And I meant that. But the hurt and the
grieving I felt was for *my* dreams that were dying. I was
grieving for the dream that I knew I wasn't going to have for
her life. The husband. The wedding under the chuppa. The
children. This was my grief and my sadness.

Even parents who now feel comfortable with their child's sexual
orientation may have a difficult time in the beginning. One parent,
who is now an outspoken advocate for equal rights for lesbians and
gays, relates:

Today I'm so comfortable with these issues that there's a
danger that I make it sound too easy. So it's important to say
it was two years before I was able to make the shift. I
dragged my feet.

If you are initially upset, your feelings are understandable, but
they are not necessarily an indication of how you'll feel in the
future. In the meantime, be gentle with yourself, make room for
your feelings, learn more about gay and lesbian people, and talk to
others.

◇ GET SUPPORT FOR YOURSELF

If you find it painful or confusing to realize that your child is gay,
lesbian, or bisexual, you need—and deserve—a supportive environment in which to explore your feelings. You don't have to be isolated in your struggles. Choose someone who can affirm your child's
good qualities and the bond between you. Avoid people who are
going to act like this is a disaster. You don't need someone else's
prejudices or even their excessive sympathy. This is not a death or a
tragedy. It's a challenging passage through which you deserve support and understanding.

One of the most helpful things you can do is to go to PFLAG
(Parents, Families, and Friends of Lesbians and Gays). Talking to
other parents has helped thousands of parents of gay and lesbian
children to work through their pain, disappointment, and fear—or

simply to become more informed about gay, lesbian, and bisexual people. PFLAG is a national organization, representing more than thirty thousand families, with affiliates in more than 340 locations. PFLAG's purpose is to support the health and well-being of lesbian, gay, and bisexual people, their families, and their friends.

PARENTS WHO GOT SUPPORT FROM PFLAG

The first thing that struck me as we got to talking to a few people was, I didn't see any evidence of insanity. And then I was surprised to hear them talking about their gay and lesbian kids as if they were human beings, that they weren't depraved, they weren't animals. They didn't do terrible things. They talked about kids going through college and having nice homes and good relationships, and that was utterly amazing to me. I said to myself, hey, the things they're saying about gays and lesbians are totally different from what my parents always told me.

—Charles

Seeing the pain of gay and lesbian people made me realize what a struggle it is for them to acknowledge who they are. It took the onus off of, "Why did my children do this to me?" It gave it a whole different perspective. So meetings were wonderfully healing for me, supportive and healing.

—Bunny

When we left that first PFLAG meeting, we talked all the way home, seventy miles. We talked all about gay and lesbian things, our own families, everything. I'd been working at this lumber mill for two years where the main conversation was, "What's your favorite kind of beer?" Lo and behold I met people who could talk on subjects other than Budweiser. It was like a breath of life, people who could talk directly about real things and be open and honest. I don't think I've ever talked as much since.

—Chuck

I didn't need a healing because I accepted it from the beginning. So for me, PFLAG was an education. Now that I knew that my daughter was one, I had to understand what they were. I did have, as all of us do, preconceived ideas, so it was time for me either to

> acknowledge those as being true or to find out what the situation
> was. Being around gays and learning what was going on, I found
> that pretty much they did the same thing I did. There was really
> very little difference, other than who they loved.
>
> —George

If there's no PFLAG chapter where you live, you might want to start one. Or you may be able to drive to another city. Even if the nearest chapter is too far to go weekly, a monthly meeting may provide the kind of support and connection that makes the drive worthwhile.

You can also look for like-minded people in other ways. Corky, a mother from a town of eight hundred in rural Montana, was creative in her search for people to talk to. First she met a person who worked for a domestic abuse hot line, and that led her to a training for self-esteem. She figured that these kinds of groups might draw open-minded people—and she was right. She met a friend who was understanding and accepting.

Another mother who was isolated called a parental stress hot line. The person she talked to happened to know of another parent with a gay son and introduced the two mothers.

If you can't find a way to get support in your area, look for connections outside your community. You can read the PFLAG newsletter, attend the annual PFLAG convention, or share with other parents by phone, on-line, or in letters. Don't let the limitations of your locale keep you unnecessarily isolated.

◇ YOU MAY EVEN FEEL RELIEF

Sometimes parents have been suffering because they've known that something was going on but they couldn't figure out what it was. When their child finally comes out, they feel great relief. As Corky describes it:

> We had been really, really close, and something was falling apart, and I had no way of knowing what it was. And I couldn't do anything for him at all. Nothing.

Corky had been very worried that her son was on drugs. Finally he wrote her a letter telling her that he was gay:

When I first read it, I felt such relief. That was the very, very first thing—aside from I'm reading this in black and white and I don't like it, I mean, oh my God, he really is—but at the same time I felt this huge relief. It's not drugs. Oh, he's just gay.

It was wonderful. I was distraught and going oh God, no, he can't be gay, But he's just gay, that's it. That's what the whole damn thing was. And it was thrilling.

David experienced a different, but also wonderful, release in finding out the cause of his daughter's distress:

My wife and I went through years of self-doubt and questioning because here's this terrific person who's really unhappy with us. Therefore we are at fault. We went through all this, "Ooh aah, what is wrong with Mary? How have we failed?" So when she came out, we felt a sense of relief. Oh, well, that's it. That's what had been bothering her. Maybe we aren't such terrible parents after all.

◇ EDUCATE YOURSELF ABOUT GAY AND LESBIAN ISSUES

One of the most helpful things for parents who first hear that their child is gay or lesbian is information. As Alice, mother of a gay son, says, "How do intellectual Jews deal with this? You get books!"

All of us living in this culture have absorbed a number of negative stereotypes about gay people that make it harder for us to see and recognize the truth about real gay people. Carroll describes how unprepared she was to hear her daughter say, "I'm gay":

I had no idea what that meant. I thought gay only meant men. I remember her saying, "If you have any questions please feel free to ask me." I didn't even know what to ask. I had no point of reference, so I thought, now she's going to be walking around the house in men's boots and driving a Harley Davidson.

I told her, "I feel like I'm learning a new language so if I say something wrong, please correct me. I would never intentionally hurt you. But all these new words, what is a dyke, lesbian, what the hell is all this? I feel like I'm a Martian and I'm in a whole new environment."

As you begin to replace misinformation with accurate knowledge about the lives of gay and lesbian people, you are likely to feel some genuine reassurance. Charles, father of two lesbian daughters from Oregon, relates how important it was for him to meet other young people who were his daughters' friends:

> After both of our daughters came out to us, they invited us to join them for Christmas. They had a potluck at their home in which they invited about a dozen friends, some being hetero and some being homo—men and women. And the thing that struck me so much was that nobody really cared in that group what sexual orientation anybody was.
>
> And the other thing was that when I got to know these other gays and lesbians, I came to realize that they are decent young people too. And once again, this thing kept going through the back of my head. Hey, all this stuff that my parents used to teach me about all homosexuals being depraved monsters simply is not true.

We often fear what we don't know about. Help yourself by beginning to learn more.

◇ EDUCATE YOURSELF ABOUT AIDS

It is natural that parents of young people be concerned about AIDS. And it's particularly frightening to learn that your child may be in a high-risk group for this fatal disease. And so it is important to become informed about HIV and AIDS. Fears mushroom in ignorance, and information helps us to cope with our fears and to support our children in staying safe.

Gay men are in a high-risk group for getting HIV, and lesbians are in a low-risk group. But *anyone* can get HIV, whether they are straight, gay, lesbian, or bisexual. People get HIV by engaging in certain behaviors, not because they have a certain sexual orientation.

Although AIDS is a deadly disease, *it is preventable.* Educate yourself and educate your child about transmission and prevention—or ask your child to educate you. And do all you can to affirm and support your child. The more self-esteem your children have, the more likely they will care enough about themselves to protect themselves.

As with all the serious dangers our children may face, it helps if we can find a way to put our fears in perspective. Alice, the mother of a gay man, relates:

> As soon as I learned about AIDS I sent information to my son. Then I started talking to him about it and he assured me that he was protecting himself. Now if that's not perfect, that's the way it is. He's been mugged in New York City and he could have other things happen to him. He could have cancer. He could have an auto accident. He's probably more cautious about AIDS than he is about anything else.

As parents we are well aware that anything could happen to our children at any time. Yet we do our best to protect them and then remind ourselves that the future is beyond our control.

◇ DON'T MOURN LOSSES YOU MAY NOT ACTUALLY HAVE

Don't jump to the conclusion that everything you hoped for is now impossible. You may be grieving that your daughter won't have a big wedding, only to find yourself addressing engraved invitations to her commitment ceremony. You may feel deeply disappointed because you think that you'll never have grandchildren, only to find that your gay son adopts twins. You may acquire in-laws (some families call them *out*-laws) that you grow to love and rely on. Here's evidence of this process from Bunny:

> It took me many months and lots of reading before it dawned on me that these dreams were mine and they wouldn't make my daughter happy. That was a big turning point for me. And then it dawned on me that she *can* have those things, but they'll be different. She can have a commitment ceremony. She can have a committed relationship with another woman. She can mother and raise children.

There may even come a time when you realize that everything you really wanted, you already have—only the faces in the family album weren't the ones you anticipated.

◇ BE HONEST IF YOU'RE HAVING A HARD TIME

It's better to admit that you're upset than to shut off communication with your child—or to get angry about the wrong things. Matt's parents were loving the night he came out to them, but the next days were rough:

> I thought it was all going to be fine. But on day two and day three my parents were not talking to me. And they started to get angry about things. They just screamed and yelled about the lawn not getting mowed when it was clear that that wasn't the issue at hand. I felt real abandoned.
>
> For them to be upset about me being gay is normal. I never expected them to be like, "Yeah, that's great," but I did expect them to talk about it. I imagine that if we could talk about it, things could get better. It's like, don't yell because the lawn didn't get mowed. If you need to, yell because I'm gay. Yell for the real reason.

◇ TRUST THAT YOUR FEELINGS WILL EVOLVE

It's common for parents to experience grief, loss, and fear, but over time your feelings will change. One gay man described how his parents had insisted that his lover was not welcome to visit. Finally, fed up with spending holidays apart, he brought his lover anyway. The parents got along so well with the boyfriend that they couldn't even remember their earlier rejection. When it was time to say good-bye, they told him how much they liked him and questioned their son, "Why didn't you ever bring him before?"

From where you are now, it may seem impossible to get to the place where you feel good about your child being lesbian, gay, or bisexual. But what now seems incomprehensible may feel natural with time. As one father, Joseph, from Massachusetts describes his experience:

> At one point shortly after the time that Elizabeth had come out, she was getting picked up and taken somewhere by some person. I asked, "Is that person gay?" After a period of time elapsed, a similar situation occurred and my question was, "Do they have seat belts?" So the thing had progressed to the point where this was part of the furniture, part of the scene.

◇ BE COMPASSIONATE IF YOUR CHILD IS HAVING A HARD TIME

Our primary job as parents is to foster our children's self-esteem and self-confidence so they can feel good about themselves and hopeful about their ability to handle life's challenges. Your children's needs to be nurtured don't vanish when they acknowledge their sexual orientations. Susan's daughter, who was only fourteen when she came out, needed her mother's reassurance that she was fine just as she was:

> As we were taking the skis back to the rental place and pulling out of the parking lot, she turned to me, "Mom, I don't like boys. Do you know what that means?"
>
> And I said, "Yes, I know what that means."
>
> She said, "No, but do you really know what that means?"
>
> I said, "Yes, that means you don't like boys."
>
> She said, "I don't like boys in that way."
>
> I said, "I know. It means you're attracted to girls." And of course, my heart just sank.
>
> And she said, "Do you hate me?"
>
> And I said, "No, of course not. I could never hate you. You're my daughter."
>
> And she said, "Well, do you think I'm a freak?"
>
> And I said, "Absolutely not. You're not a freak. You're a lesbian."
>
> She'd never heard the word lesbian. She didn't even have a name for it.

◇ ACTIONS CAN SPEAK AS LOUDLY AS WORDS

If you are an action-oriented person and find it hard to express yourself in words, there are still many ways you can communicate acceptance to your gay, lesbian, or bisexual child. You can offer to give your teenager a ride to a gay function or invite your son's boyfriend to dinner. If he's living away from home, you can ask him to bring his companion home for a visit.

You can demonstrate acceptance, even if the words don't come easily. A hug for your daughter *and* her girlfriend will go a long way toward making it clear that you accept them. A holiday card addressed to them both will communicate your recognition of their relationship.

◇ THE UNEXPECTED BENEFITS

Although your child's coming out may present challenges, there are often unexpected benefits as well. If your family has been laboring under the strain of an unnatural silence, you may find that family relations become a lot more comfortable. As Ruth describes it:

> There had been a glass wall that was increasingly apparent. We'd be having a conversation and then suddenly this wall would go up and I would never know why. That wall came down the morning she came out. It was very dramatic. And clearly, looking back, the glass wall was her need to protect herself, this secret about herself.

For Meyer, his son's coming out made it possible for him to really communicate the depth of his love:

> Larry was very concerned about how I felt about him. I can remember specifically telling him, "Larry, you're the most important person in my life. You're the person for whom I feel the most anguish when you're hurt." I wanted him to know how much I loved him. And he cried and he hugged me. Although I had tried to make it known to him before, this was the first time he really believed that I felt that way about him.

And Martin, a father from Connecticut, relates:

> Because we had such deeply felt things to work through together, it's brought a depth to our relationship that we never would have had otherwise. It's not what I expected, but I thank God that my son turned out to be gay. It forced me to know him—and to let him know me—at a whole different level.

◇ ENJOY THE REWARDS OF PARTICIPATING IN YOUR CHILD'S WORLD

Many parents have found that by embracing their child's sexual orientation, meeting their friends, and participating in their activities, their lives have been enriched. As Jack, a father from Washington, relates:

As we got involved in the gay and lesbian world it was like an old movie that's going along in black and white and all of a sudden it switches into technicolor—and that's the world that was exposed to us, that we didn't know existed. It's changed our perspective enormously at a pretty late stage in our life, too.

Jack's wife, Frankie, adds:

And it's a lot of fun. We're on the gay circuit. We could go out every night. We get invited to all these young people's birthdays, all these wonderful birthday parties and commitment ceremonies, and they're very touching.

Parents who have entered into the gay and lesbian community have been received with enormous praise and gratitude. As one mother describes her experience:

I never thought I would be loved just because I accept my child. I've had lesbians and gay men come up to me and say, "I wish my parent was like you. You're so courageous." Sometimes I feel like it's not deserved, because I have been just doing what each of us parents should be able to do, which is just love our kids, but it's been real wonderful for me.

◇ RECEIVE THE GIFT OF YOUR UNIQUE CHILD

Over time you may come to appreciate just who your child really is. Clare expresses this sentiment:

I lost the son I thought I had, but the fact is that the one the universe sent me is so much better. I thought Brian was going to get married and have a family and a job and two-point-three cars or two-point-three kids, I forget which, a dog and a cat. That kind of storybook life. That's who I thought I had.

Now, who I really have is just fabulous. He is so thoughtful. He thinks about life. He thinks about what it means to be human, to be a person in our society. He's so caring and so committed. Two-point-three kids and two-point-three cars is not even in the ballpark.

◇ IT'S NEVER TOO LATE

It's never too late to offer your child understanding and affirmation. It's never too late to open communication. If you wish that you had done or said things differently, it's never too late to acknowledge your mistakes, your lack of information, or your shortcomings.

It's impossible to overestimate the profound healing that takes place when parents acknowledge their limitations and resolve to make changes. Whether your child is fifteen or twenty-five, thirty-five or fifty, your absolute acceptance is a priceless gift.

We have all grown up in a homophobic world, steeped in ignorant and judgmental attitudes. And as parents of gay or straight kids, we all have expectations that cloud our ability to appreciate, accept, and unconditionally love our children. If you didn't do things the way you wish you had, begin to do them that way now.

your kid is still a teenager, even if he's gay

Setting limits for gay, lesbian, and bisexual young people is pretty much the same as setting limits for any children who still live at home. Whatever the expectations, rules, and privileges are in your family, you should treat your gay child similarly to the way you would if he or she were straight. As one mother, Susan, explains:

> The standard that I kept using, what I kept trying to say to myself, was, OK, she's fifteen. Is this appropriate for a fifteen-year-old, regardless of whether they're homosexual or heterosexual? And, if she were going out with a boy instead of with a girl, would I react differently?

Your child may not always be thrilled with the limits you set, but that's to be expected. As in other areas of parenting, your job is to set the limits; their job is to push against them. Stone describes her parents' response when she came out first as a lesbian, then a year later as a bisexual:

> Their response to the lesbian and the response to bisexual are so close to identical that when they said it, I started laughing. I thought that somebody was playing a broken record. "I'm glad you know. Girls can't spent the night." "I'm happy you know. Boys can't spend the night."

I said, "Mom, you're making this very difficult on me." We eventually worked out platonic friends that I couldn't possibly be even the least little bit interested in could spend the night.

Christopher says:

My dad explained that he didn't care if I was staying with a man or a woman, that I should not be spending the night somewhere else while I lived under his roof, not at twenty. Which I thought was nice. He wasn't saying, "You can't stay because you're gay." He was saying, "Because I don't think it's right."

Over time this will all feel perfectly natural—because it is.

◇ TESTING, TESTING, TESTING

Kids may do some outrageous things as they explore their identity. Testing is a normal part of the developmental process. Sexual orientation may provide the content for this testing, but the process is typical of the teenage years.

Your son may come to a family wedding in drag. Your daughter may shave her head and pierce her nose just in time for Christmas dinner. Fifteen-year-old Margaret has this vivid fantasy of how she'd like to come out to her relatives:

I'd really like to shock them. You know, some Thanksgiving bring home my new girlfriend, six feet tall, extraordinarily butch, and just like kiss each other all the time and really shock them, make them angry. My family is just very neutral about pretty much everything.

I want to get a reaction out of them. If I told them, some of them might be like, oh that's horrible, you're a bad person. And some of them might be like, oh that's great. Now you're a really wonderful person. If I can get them all into one room and tell them all at once, then I'm sure that it would create a huge hullabaloo. They'd all just start screaming. That would be pretty neat.

Sometimes kids choose behavior so extreme that you feel like they're doing it just to hurt you. In some cases this may be true. If your child feels rejected by you, it's possible he or she may try to hurt you back in a hostile cry for acceptance. But usually your child's style of dress, taste in music, or behavior has nothing to do with you.

The best response to most behavior meant to shock is to notice it but take it in stride. You need to react—otherwise your kid will have to take it further to *get* a reaction—but keep it low key.

If you're getting ready for your nephew's bar mitzvah and your son comes down the stairs in a T-shirt that proclaims WE'RE HERE, WE'RE QUEER, GET USED TO IT, you might want to sit him down, put your hand on his hand, look him in the eye, and say, "Look, this makes me uncomfortable. Everyone's going to be dressed up and it isn't the place for a T-shirt with a political message. I'd really appreciate it if you'd change." Let your child know this is important to you and then give him a few minutes to think about it on his own. It's usually easier for a child—or anyone—to back down if you back off. If, after considering it, he refuses to change, you might as well say, "This is going to be really hard for me, but you're my kid and I want you with us, so let's go."

Be selective in your fights, and limit the major battles to behavior that is truly dangerous. Wearing conventional clothing but snorting coke in the bathroom is certainly not preferable to showing up in something outrageous, but being responsible about drugs and alcohol. Throughout the generations hair and dress have been badges of identity and ways that teenagers have distinguished themselves from their parents. Hair grows; clothes get changed. In fact, if hair and clothing are your greatest problems, count your blessings. As one mother, Judith from Minnesota, said:

> He's dressing in the black cape and he's wearing eyeliner. It just drove me up a wall. I knew if I said anything to him that he would do it more. So I never said—or I hardly ever said—anything about how he dressed, as long as he went to school.

You don't have to like or agree with everything your children choose, say, or do. And you don't have to defend their outrageous behavior to others. You can say nothing about it at all. Or you can say, "I'm not crazy about it, but this is my kid."

coming out to others

It's healthy to share what is real and important in your life and in the lives of your children with people you care about. You tell them that your child is accepted into college or moves to another city, gets a promotion at work or is engaged to be married. Hopefully, you're proud of your kids and you're glad to have opportunities to talk about them. Although the fact that your child is gay, bisexual, or lesbian is only one piece of information about him or her, it's something worthy to be shared, just as you'd share other significant things.

Talk about your gay kids in the same way that you'd talk about your other kids. If you'd normally remark to a friend that your teenager went on a backpacking trip with his junior class, then mention that he's going backpacking with his gay youth support group. If you'd say your kid sings in the church choir, then say your kid is in the lesbian and gay chorus. If you'd mention that your daughter's heartbroken because she just broke up with her boyfriend, say the same thing about her breakup with her girlfriend.

If you're just beginning to come out as the parent of a lesbian, bisexual, or gay child, start by telling the people you're most comfortable with and who seem to be the most open-minded. In most cases, if you talk about your child with casual pride, it's likely that the response will be casual acceptance. Many parents find that the most comfortable way to come out is to include information about their children in conversation.

You may be surprised how often other parents will tell you about their own gay child. Ruth has had this happen more than once:

> I was having lunch with a woman that I know somewhat casually through our church. She was asking me about the kids, and as I was telling about Marge and her commitment ceremony, this woman was very quiet. She is a former politician and is never quiet. It turned out that her child had just come out.

Parents have had positive experiences talking to people where they work, as well. George, a sales representative, has been outspoken in support of his lesbian daughter, including going on talk shows. Although he has occasionally lost a client, George's attitude is that speaking up is well worth it:

It doesn't bother me that it's cost me business. It's part of the price that you pay. Everybody pays a cost on this thing. If you're silent you pay a higher price.

Jack has also been open in his workplace, where he is a lawyer:

It was just fine. People said, "Wow, that's real interesting," and "I appreciate the fact that you told me." They were real supportive. Of course, I was the head of the office, so there's not a hell of a lot they could do about it.

The more people have the experience of knowing and loving gay people—and their families—the more the world is changed. And your kids benefit. Sometimes there are unexpected perks as well. Bunny relates this story:

We have PFLAG cards that say "Your business has just been supported by the loving family of a gay or lesbian person." When we go to a restaurant or we do business and we buy goods, we give those cards out. Or when I pay bills, I stick it in with my checks. It's advocacy, and it's educational.

A couple weeks ago I flew to LA. And I rushed to the gate because we were late. I get in line at the check-in, and there I'm facing this nice-looking young man. I handed him my ticket and I gave him a card. He looked at it and he put it down next to my ticket and he says, "Would you like an aisle or a window seat?" And I said, "Well, I believe my travel agent has already secured my seat." And he doesn't hesitate and he doesn't miss a beat. He says, "I've upgraded you to first class." And I said to him, "Thank you." And he said, "No, thank *you!*"

It's important for parents to be able to talk freely about their bisexual, gay, and lesbian children, but if your children aren't ready for you to tell the world yet, respect their wishes. This is, after all, their life, and they get to set the pace at which they come out.

we're here, we care, get used to it: parent activists

Learning that your child is gay, lesbian, or bisexual can change the way you look at the world. Things that you didn't think about before become important—because now they affect your child. People who are already social activists almost inevitably take up this issue. For others, public or political involvement may happen farther down the road or not at all.

Speaking out as the parent of a gay, lesbian, or bisexual child is a powerful agent of social change. As one father describes it:

> At my thirtieth college reunion we were at dinner with eight or ten people at the table, and one of them started to tell homophobic jokes. This person is a nationally known comedian and he's very, very clever. And my wife immediately took him on. She said, "I don't like that. I have a gay kid and I really don't like that." And it stopped him.

Chuck, stepfather to a gay son, admits that he loves controversy, so he's taken some pleasure in educating his coworkers in rural Montana:

> We went to a human rights conference where they were selling stickers. I bought a pink triangle and one that said, "Not tonight, honey. It's a felony." That really got to me because it's still a felony in Montana, inactive, but it's in place. So I just slapped the "Not tonight, honey. It's a felony" on the front of my hard hat and the pink triangle on the back. And got lots of comments. I would ask the guys I work with, "Do you know what that pertains to?" Then I'd get out the soapbox and we'd have a little discussion about it. It had absolutely no adverse effects at all. If anything, it was probably positive in that I gained more respect from them.

Not everyone will find it as easy to speak up as Chuck did. Parents, like kids, need to go at their own pace, but ultimately, our job as parents is to do what we can to support our children. As one parent says:

> I never heard of a parent being beat up or shot or fired over the fact that they have a gay kid. Of course there's lots of gay people who have lost their jobs or been shot or beat up. And I think for parents to hide under whatever they're hiding under, that they'll lose a friend or whatever, is so wrong. When parents who are not in jeopardy at all won't speak out

in defense of their kids—who potentially *are* in jeopardy—I just can't believe it.

For a growing number of parents, the knowledge that their children are at risk for harassment and violent attack and are still deprived of basic civil rights leads them to become political activists. Bunny speaks for many parents as she explains her motivation:

> It is so awful that I have to advocate for the rights of one of my children, where I have three children who were born and raised the same way in the same household with the same religious upbringing and two of them are guaranteed equal protection under the law and one of them is not, simply because of who she is. To me, it's that basic.

There are many ways to advocate for equal protection under the law. And as a parent you're in a uniquely effective position to speak out. One Canadian father relates:

> There were a couple of holdouts on the Alberta human rights commission who did not want sexual orientation included in their nondiscrimination statement. So I'm there in my starched blue power suit, white shirt, red tie, the whole thing. And there was an interesting thing about this, because I was not asking for anything for myself. I said, "I'm here on behalf of my child." I talked about the illogic, how people say, "Well, gays are against family values," and here we are asking for permission for gays to form recognized households and adopt kids. I said, "These cannot be true at the same time. There's a real logic problem here."
>
> And afterward, one of the staffers said, "We never thought about the parent's point of view. Gays have parents and they come from families and everything." And I thought, this is amazing. I'm the first person to communicate this?

Speaking out in your local community is a powerful way to change hearts and minds. Many parents have joined speaker's bureaus in their local communities, making presentations to schools and community groups in order to educate about gay and lesbian people. Audiences—both young people and adults—are usually very interested in the perspective of parents. The model of a parent who offers unconditional love and acceptance is a powerful one.

The results of speaking out are often very positive. And you never know where your allies will come from. Although lesbian, gay, and bisexual people are a minority of the population, if you consider that each of these people has some combination of parents, grandparents, brothers and sisters, children, aunts, uncles, cousins, friends, and others who care about them, it becomes clear that almost everyone loves someone who is gay—whether they know it or not.

The voices of parents are profoundly important in the journey to greater understanding and full civil rights. As one parent said, "I have a big mouth, which has always been a liability, and when our kid came out we finally found a good use for this big mouth."

Each activist parent has a slightly different perspective on how and why they got involved in working for respect and justice for gay people, but they would probably all agree with this father when he says simply, "It's a question of what we think is right. And since somebody has to take up the fight, then we're here."

THE REWARDS OF BEING OUT AS A PROUD PARENT

When you march along in Gay Pride and the people on the side are applauding the parents as we go by, you can see what it means to have parents who care. We were applauded along the whole length of Market Street. I got more applause for being a proud parent of a gay son than than I've gotten in my entire life for everything else I've ever done.

—Meyer

I think what touches me is that I feel like I'm the mom to every gay person who doesn't get the love and support from their family. And I'm so glad that I'm able to do that, but I'm so sad that they don't have their family there for them.

—Bunny

When we realized the commitment ceremony was going to take place with or without us, we decided to get involved. It turned out to be one of the really all-time great moments in our life. If parents ever want to be heroes, you need go and pay for something like this, because Margie's friends were just in awe that her parents did actually participate. It turned out to be certainly a major roadmark in our journey of understanding. And there was such warmth, such a wonderful feeling at the ceremony and the reception.

—Dave

If you're visible and proud as the parent of a gay kid, not only will your kid love you, but all their friends will adopt you. You don't just get welcomed, you get made into this king or queen, an honored person. You don't deserve it, but you get it.

—Clare

◇

part 4

school

◇ ◇ ◇ ◇ ◇ ◇ ◇ ◇ ◇ ◇

Cathy Cade © 1995

12
school daze

I didn't belong as a kid, and that always bothered me. If only I'd known that one day my differentness would be an asset, then my early life would have been much easier.

—*Bette Midler*

Though not a lesbian, Bette Midler is held in special affection in the gay community. She got her start singing in gay clubs where her bawdy, outrageous style and sharp humor made her a hit. Now that she's a mainstream success, she's remained loyal to the gay community, performing at benefits and speaking out for justice.

Ideally, school should be a safe, supportive environment in which to explore ideas, learn skills, and prepare for satisfying work. It should be a comfortable place to make friends and enjoy activities—with open-minded students and understanding teachers.

For most gay, lesbian, and bisexual young people, this picture of an enlightened school is a far cry from their experience. But many schools are making significant positive changes toward becoming more accepting and supportive of gay youth. Programs that teach tolerance are being introduced to help students learn to appreciate and respect diversity. Some teachers are becoming aware that anti-gay remarks are not acceptable and are responding appropriately. Administrators are adopting policies that prohibit discrimination on the basis of sexual orientation. Gay youth support groups and gay/straight alliances are being formed. Students are standing up for their lesbian, gay, and bisexual classmates. And some brave students are bringing their same-sex dates to the school prom.

For Better or For Worse © Lynn Johnston Prod., Inc. Reprinted with permission of UNIVERSAL PRESS SYNDICATE. All rights reserved.

Stone's experience in eighth grade gives us a glimpse of the possible future:

> What's really nice is when your friends stick up for you. I was in a small private middle school where I had just come out. Almost everyone was real supportive except this one guy. We were playing baseball, a sport I'm terrible at and hate playing. I can never hit the ball. I was up there and there were two outs and I had two strikes. I wasn't doing well. I just wasn't real happy. Then this guy yells at me from behind the fence, "Hit the ball, dyke." And everyone on the field, everyone on my team and everyone on the other team, all turned around and stared at him. They were all totally furious with him. He shrank into the ground. After that nobody dared say anything. It was wonderful. I was thrilled. I still didn't hit the last ball.

When Jessica transferred to her present high school, she felt safe and accepted for the first time in school:

> The guidance counselor is an out gay man, and that just sets a tone where you know it's OK to be whoever you are. No one makes fun of him. He's just so respected. I couldn't believe it at first, but it's really great.

Jason helped to start a gay, lesbian, and bisexual awareness forum at his high school. When the school planned a Cultural Diversity Fair, their group set up a booth with information about local resources, pictures of famous gay people, and postcards for a letter-writing campaign:

> Because there was something for people to *do*, both students and teachers came up to the booth, asked questions, and actually wrote out cards. We had several issues that people could write about: one to support "My So Called Life" that was getting criticism for having a gay character, one was to protest Cracker Barrel's policy against hiring gays in their restaurants, and one to support the Marriage Resolution. We got over three hundred postcards!

Jason is excited about going to college because it's clear that he'll find a supportive environment there:

> I got the Evergreen orientation schedule, and that first week there's a workshop on diversity, talking about culture, race, sexual orientation, gender. As soon as I read that, I knew I'd made the right choice.

the worst of times

Unfortunately, only a small number of young people are lucky enough to attend schools that actively support and protect gay students. For most, the scenario is grim. In spite of the myth that your high school and college years are supposed to be "the best years of your life," if you're lesbian, gay, or bisexual, being young can be the worst of times. As Chris describes his experience:

I got called faggot and fairy every day. I kept my head down. I became a wall. I learned how to not let it soak in until I got home. And even then, I could sometimes not deal with it for months at a time. Then I'd have one big break-down where I'd put my fist through the glass coffee table or throw a clock against the wall. And I'd scream at my mother and wouldn't let her touch me, wouldn't let her hug me.

I didn't talk in class because I was afraid they would tease me. I slouched around in black jeans and black turtleneck, sunglasses, a black hat. Didn't want to be seen. And got C's and D's.

When I was in my freshman year I wrote down a poem that I carry with me to this day, four years later. It's called "We Wear the Mask" by Paul Laurence Dunbar. "We wear the mask that grins and lies, it hides our cheeks and shades our eyes." It's about slaves during the Civil War, about how they'd hide their real feelings from the master, keep their feelings inside.

Gay and lesbian students have to go to school every day, where they are expected to work and socialize with other kids while being taunted, threatened, and occasionally physically harmed. In spite of this harassment, they are expected to stay focused on their assign-ments, while teachers and administrators usually condone or ignore the fact that they are being insulted or even beaten up. If the way they dress or act indicates that they may be gay or lesbian, they may even be blamed for "provoking" harassment. They may be coun-seled to change their appearance or behavior, while those doing the tormenting are not held responsible.

If they have private same-sex feelings but appear straight, they are not the object of harassment but they have to keep their true feelings a total secret from everyone—sometimes even themselves. They live with fear that if the truth were known, they would be sub-jected to the same torture they see inflicted on those who appear gay. And they hear the insults that they know are meant for them as well. As a result, they are conditioned to keep silent—or risk being attacked. They too experience school as an unsafe place.

◇ IT'S LONELY

Being isolated, fearful, and the object of harassment is a terrible situation to live with every day. Is it any wonder that so many gay students find it impossible to walk through those school doors every morning? Nancy describes her experience:

> As I was realizing I had a crush on my best friend, I went through a very hard time. It was hard to keep that in. I would cry a lot. I couldn't get to my schoolwork. I was always thinking about it. And my grades failed because I didn't want to be around school, where I thought I was the only gay person in history. The only one. I would prefer to cut, and my best friend would be along to talk about things. We'd just sit and hold hands and be together. We couldn't do that at school like the straight kids could. I didn't know anyone else at school like me. No one was openly gay in my high school.

Devan was so unhappy at school that he left. But the consequences of that decision weren't clear to him until several years later:

> Because people gave me such a hard time, school was really miserable for me. And I had no concept of how important education was. I didn't realize that it was going to be important later. Earning money wasn't a concept to me at the time. I just had no desire to go back to school and suffer anymore.

Loneliness can be acute even for students who are not overtly tormented. Being betrayed or spurned by people you thought were your friends is very painful. Alessandra tells this story:

> I was very, very happy about the relationship developing with Susie, and I told my best friend who told another friend about it. This other friend told the whole class when I was out of the room. Between fifth and eighth period I went from very popular to not having any friends. It was absolute hell. Most people wouldn't talk *to* me but there was a lot of talk behind my back.

Michelle was hurt by the indirect way that her former friends pulled away from her after she came out:

> People would subtly disassociate with me, and that really hurt. That was really spineless and sleazy. "Oh, I'm your

friend, I just um ..., uh ...," and they'd sort of drift off with no explanation. I felt ostracized, not in a verbal way, because I went to an upper middle-class, white monochromatic school and we needed to be politically correct. So people weren't going to outwardly gay-bash me and physically beat me up. It wasn't cool to do that, so instead they drifted away, noncommittally.

The number of bisexual, gay, and lesbian students who are willing to be out in high school is growing. However, the numbers are still very small. For every student who is out, there are many more who are closeted or still privately questioning. As Hyde said: "The main feeling for gay youth in high school is isolation. Feeling that we don't fit in, that we're different in some way."

◇ WALKING THE LINE

Young people who aren't perceived as gay or lesbian sometimes steer a course in between pretending to be straight and coming out. Yet even for popular kids with strong self-esteem, it's not always easy to manage the balance. As Dan relates:

I never said I was heterosexual. I couldn't do that to myself, and I certainly couldn't do that to some unsuspecting girl. I was taught to be proud by my older brothers and sisters because I saw that they were proud to be gay. I could never bring myself to play the role of the closet case, but I knew I had to be quiet about it. Being half Chinese, we know when "silence equals gold," as my mom used to say.

So it was a badly kept secret. But still it was a secret. Everyone knew, but I had never actually said, "I am gay," so people still had this lingering feeling, well, maybe he's not, maybe it's just a rumor. Actually, they just didn't want to see it. I swam. I went out for water polo. No one questions your manhood if you play water polo. I was popular, and I did have girls who liked me, so somehow I became straight in other people's minds.

Sometimes I was called fag, but then so were a lot of people. It was just a hurtful word slung at you. I was like, "Yeah, whatever." I never said, "What are you going to do about it?" I never got into a fight. I just let it slide off my shoulders.

But I remember every once in a while someone would say it, really meaning that I was gay. And that did hurt because I would wonder, how do they know? And I'd think, oh my God, what's going to happen to me? I had all these horrible pictures of just hell, because my sister, who's six years older than me, came out when she was in high school and she was driven out of the school Frankenstein-style. So I knew the horror story of what could happen.

TO BE OR NOT TO BE . . . OUT AT SCHOOL

When I first came here to UCLA I wasn't out to everybody right away. I needed to meet people as a straight person first and then come out. The pro side is that it let me feel my way through things. The con is that I was closeted.

—Julio

I stood up in my first class where I was supposed to say my name and something interesting about myself. "Hello. My name's Stone and I'm a lesbian." It was a very amusing class. The teacher's mouth dropped open, closed, dropped open, closed. It was the first class, first period, first day, first year in high school, but I didn't really think about it.

I got a reputation as "the dyke." I figured that I'd have it for two months max and after that everybody would be bored with my sexual orientation. I was really wrong. I got harassed a lot. I don't recommend this approach to anyone, but I didn't have a choice. I'm not capable of being in the closet. I can't do it.

—Stone

If your high school is anything like the high school I went to in Louisiana, you just don't come out at all. To do so would probably mean certain death, very literally. In those situations it's best if you tell trusted friends outside of school, but not in school. And that's sad, really sad, but it's true.

—Daphne

The reason I came out at school was because I felt I really didn't have anything to sacrifice. I wasn't friends with anyone I cared about anyway so I figured I'll just come out as fast as I can, it doesn't really matter what my feelings are. I wore a "Click and Drag Queen" T-shirt and a button that said, "I can't even THINK straight." That obviously brought the issue to attention, but it wasn't good because it made me a one-dimensional person, just a gay icon. Emotionally I wasn't ready to come out, so it was easier for me to be an icon than to be real. One time a girl asked me what the pink triangle meant, and I literally started shaking because I just wasn't ready. I couldn't even tell her.

—Patrick

I decided to be out. If somebody asked me who I went out with, and I went with my girlfriend, then I'd say so. If I went to the gay community center, then that's what I'd say. I stopped telling all those lies. I took the fake cover off the lesbian novel I was reading. I just stopped hiding myself. At school there were rumors that I was a lesbian, but nobody took the rumors seriously even though they were coming from me. They thought, "She doesn't look like one." I'm very, very feminine. I wore high-heeled shoes and dresses. It took quite a while for them to believe it. And then I had to deal with passive-aggressive behavior and being ostracized by my peers.

—Michelle

One high school that I went to, in the last part of the year they started to have a gay support group. Even then it still wasn't OK to be out. We had to *not* publicize what day it was on, and *not* publicize what room it was in, for fear that people might be gay-bashed. I never even went to the group because I was too afraid—what if someone finds out? So I was never out at school.

—Renee

I came out in eighth grade, and basically I had all the guys hate me and the girls admire me. I even had a few girls come up to me and say, "We really respect you cause you're not afraid." And in my yearbook two girls I barely knew wrote that they really appreciated all that I'd done and were glad I stood up for what I believed in. So that made me feel good, especially being only fourteen.

—Anthony

◇ HARASSMENT

Insults are a common form of harassment. And you don't have to be out to be harassed. Young people who are perceived to be gay or lesbian—whether they are or not—are vulnerable to attack. And contrary to the old saying about only sticks and stones being hurtful, name-calling can be devastating. This kind of ridicule can start very early for those who are perceived as gay. Here is Luna's experience:

> I always thought how I felt, how I acted, was normal, but the kids would pick on me. Even back in second grade, it was always there. They would call me names, they would say faggot and all different things. Stupid things. It was always when I would speak. I remember in sixth grade the teacher asked a question and when I answered all the kids started laughing. And I never understood why.

Whether the name-calling is yelled or whispered, to your face or behind your back, it all hurts. Brooke recalls her first year of high school:

> I was having a really hard time that year. My grandma, who I was very close to, was dying. One good thing was that I was in my first relationship with a girl, but people would make fun of us as we walked down the hall. That was complete hell. I felt trapped and scared. I was upset about things and on top of that to get yelled at in the hall, or hear comments muttered just loud enough for us to hear after we had walked by, was totally, totally painful.

Sometimes kids pick on those who appear to be gay as a way to defend themselves against their own insecurities. It's "the best defense is a good offense" strategy. This tactic often works to keep the focus of harassment off the person hurling the insults. Sadly, there may be students who themselves are lesbian, gay, or bisexual who are the worst tormentors. Jonathan understood this instinctively:

> I remember sitting in English class in seventh grade, and right across from me was this guy Jaime, and he's making fun of me. I said to him, "Why are you calling me a fag? You have a girl's name. You're evidently struggling with some-thing, that's why you're doing this." I was kind of picking up

on some psychology, right there. Well, he came back with this wonderful word, "Well, you're just a stupid butt pirate." The name stuck, and I heard it all throughout high school until I graduated.

Having to face this day after day, week after week, is a torment no one should have to endure.

Vicious harassment isn't limited to name-calling. It can include obscene gestures, gay-bashing jokes, or finding nasty notes on your seat or locker. It can also escalate to physical threats or actual violence. All too often young people have had things thrown at them, been spit on, shoved, kicked, beaten up, and sexually assaulted.

coping and getting help

Bisexual, gay, and lesbian students have found different ways to cope with the harassment they face at school. Cutting classes or dropping out of school are common and understandable reactions. But finding ways to make school at least tolerable—or even, possibly, OK— is a much better option.

Most young people prefer to handle things themselves if their peers are treating them badly. Daphne learned the hard way how to respond effectively to verbal assaults:

> I found the best way to handle it is not to run away but to confront people. If you confront them, they'll usually quit. If you run, that just gives them more ammunition because then they know you're scared.
>
> But don't be defensive, because then they know you're upset and it just gets worse. You need to take it in stride, walk up *nice and politely,* and inform them you don't feel their attitude is appropriate. The thing I mostly said was, "I don't holler things at you, and I don't try to hurt your feelings. I have no reason to, I don't know you and I have no personal feelings for you at all, whether you're a nice person or not I don't care one way or the other. However, I do care that you've seen fit to holler things at me, when you don't know me either. I don't judge you, so you don't judge me, and I think that's only fair." Then turn around and walk

away. And it really works when you say this all very calmly and don't show the least bit of it fazing you.

Remember, when they're in groups they're more macho, so wait until you find that person alone and confront him then.

As Daphne advises, it usually works best to talk to people individually. In groups, people tend to show off for each other, but one-to-one they're more likely to hear what you're saying. Even so, it can be hard to speak up for yourself. Unless you're a person who thrives on confrontation, it's stressful and takes enormous effort to challenge those who attack you.

Sometimes humor can work to defuse situations, but sarcasm or smart-mouth retorts can also backfire. Chris reports:

> I had started to learn things from the drag queens at BAGLY [the Boston area youth group]. If someone is nasty to you, you go nasty right back. I remember the first time it snapped. Some ugly little straight boy comes up to me and he goes, "You want to sleep with me, don'tcha?" And I was like, "Honey, pleeeze!" He was shocked, I mean he didn't know how to react, so he just walked away. But I paid for it later. He started leaving me nasty notes, and then the physical harassment started. Blocked in the hallways, pushed into lockers, you know.

If you feel good about yourself, you are less vulnerable when verbally assaulted or rejected by others. Daphne talks about how her own attitude of self-acceptance helped her weather the taunts at school:

> As a way of supporting other gay kids, my girlfriend and I decided in our senior high school year to be out. At first people screamed things at us. It really hurt our feelings, and Marsha and I would handle it by going somewhere and just crying and holding each other. After a while it became kind of funny because we didn't let it get to us anymore. It all depends on your attitude. If you have this attitude of "I am not normal and they have a right to do those things to me," then it's going to hurt you. Because it's reinforcing those ideas that society puts in your head. But if you have the atti-

tude of "There is absolutely nothing wrong with me. These people are the ones with the problem from their ignorance," then you'll be OK.

No matter how good you feel about yourself, cruelty still hurts. But it won't shake you up nearly as much once you believe in your own worth.

◇ WHEN ADULTS WON'T HELP

Although adults can—and should—be of help in dealing with harassment, too often they are like the three monkeys with their hands over their ears, eyes, and mouths—hearing nothing, seeing nothing, and saying nothing. Almost every kid who has been called names has seen school staff act like it's not happening. Renee describes a common scenario:

> The teachers would hear people screaming "dyke" as we're walking down the hall, and they'd just go in their classroom and shut the door.

While racist and sexist harassment is beginning to bring consequences, homophobic acts are still largely ignored or condoned. Even when the harassment is brought to the adults' attention, often nothing happens. Stone tells this story:

> Every morning I was greeted with this one guy leaning his head out the third story window screaming "dyke" at me. That was my "good-morning." I told the teacher about it and she refused to look and tell me who it was. Totally refused. I was so furious.

Jonathan was angry at being abandoned by school staff:

> The sixth grade was literally the beginning of hell for me. In a nutshell, everybody knew I was gay except for me. For the first time I heard the word "fag," the word "queer," the word "homo," and they stuck. They would call me names because I was more effeminate, and I would openly start bawling in class.

The teacher I had, I blame her a lot for it because she just ignored it. The school counselor was more sympathetic than the teacher, but she didn't do anything. I was going in there and telling her that people were calling me gay and things like that, and I was obviously more effeminate than other people, so I mean it wouldn't take much of a college degree to figure out, hey, we may have somebody here who is struggling with their sexuality. I mean if this group of sixth graders could figure it out, then why can't a professional counselor figure it out?

This incident from Chris's saga shows how even trained counselors often just don't get it:

Finally I went to my guidance counselor and I said, "I can't do it." I told her how bad it was, how I'd try to disappear, hide in the stairwells or in the basement instead of going to classes. She said, "You need to go to class." I said, "I can't." She said, "You need to go to class or you're going to flunk. You aren't going to make it to college." I remember thinking to myself, "Honey, I'm not going to make it to the next day."

When the harassment of lesbian, gay, and bisexual students elicits corrective action from top administrators, it is likely to improve the situation. However, the *pretense* of a corrective response from administrative personnel can send the wrong message. Here's what happened to Chris when the assaults became violent:

Finally I went to the principal. I'd saved all the death threats and I brought them to him. After he heard the story of all that had been going on he said, "We don't want this to continue." I told them who had thrown me down the steps, and they brought them into the office and asked them: "Chris said you threw him down the steps. Did you?" And they said, "No." So then the principal said, "OK, you can leave." And that just made it worse cause the kids knew that the administration was going to let them get away with it. So I got picked on worse and got spit on a lot more. That was the worst thing the principal could have done.

This situation leaves students feeling betrayed by the very adults charged with keeping them safe.

◇ ADULTS CAN HELP

Although adults will not always respond helpfully to your problems, it is their job to create a school environment that is safe for *all* students. Dan tells this story:

> I was in the jock English class. There were about fifteen of us—two girl jocks and all the rest were boy jocks. It was just horrible. I had this boy sit behind me who's a football player, and he'd spout all these racist, sexist, homophobic things. One day I got sick of it and I went to my teacher after class and I said, "I don't feel safe in this class when you allow people to say really racist, sexist, and homophobic things without letting them know that's not going to be allowed here. It's not about censoring ideas. It's about making it a comfortable forum for everyone." And I told him, "I'm saying this as a gay man."
>
> He looked at me and kind of smiled and I'm like, "Don't think I'm telling you this because you're my confidant. I just want you to know so you can take the proper steps so I can feel comfortable, because frankly I'm afraid of him."
>
> And he let it be known, he did a good job of responding. He set limits.

If the first person you approach isn't helpful, you may have to talk to more than one person, but don't give up. When you're singled out for severe or chronic harassment, you need—and deserve—the help of responsible adults. It's their duty to provide protection so that you can focus on getting an education. Daphne shares some more of her hard-earned wisdom on dealing with this issue:

> There are times you have to take it to the administration. When they threw a rock and hit me on the head and left a gash, it was time. If you don't, it's just going to get worse. It's kind of scary going to administration because then those people are going to be angry with you for getting them in trouble. But if they care about being in school, they're not going to mess with you anymore, because they don't want

to get suspended or expelled. I think we had a total of seven people disciplined.

If you are being harassed, talk to the principal and the vice principals. If they're not helpful, go to the counselors or teachers. Don't give up.

Harassment is not as universal in college, but it still happens too often. Christopher attended a college where students were required to live on campus. But he had problems with other students in his dorm for several years. After trying to work it out himself—with no success—he requested special permission to live off campus:

> I wrote a letter to the Dean of Student Services. I listed my reasons for wanting to live off campus, including my sexual orientation. I said that I had to put up with all this stuff three years in a row because people couldn't handle my homosexuality.
>
> I dropped the letter off, and the next day the Dean called me into his office and said, "OK. You can move off campus." No questions asked, none whatsoever. He said he was sorry for all the stuff that happened to me. It made me mad that he didn't try to make it so I could stay.

Christopher had good reason to be angry. Although his request was granted, the offenders were not held accountable in any way. Stacey had a better response from the administration of her college.

> I walked on campus the first day and somebody had seen me on a talk show, so immediately everybody knew I was gay. I had never been a person who had hidden it. There was a lot of harassment. "Hey, are you a dyke?" And of course I was like, "Yup, deal with it." I got pushed and shoved. I had two hockey players trap me in the basement of the dorm and push me around. I went to the Dean. The coach ended up sitting down the hockey team and football team and saying, "If you harass her again, we're not going to let you play." It stopped them because football is much more important than harassing a lesbian.

If your parents are supportive, this is a great asset. Enlist their help. Sometimes school administrators will pay more attention to the concerns of parents than they do to students. Stone had this experience:

> I told the principal what had been going on, but he was kind of pathetic. After my mother went in and told him, in no uncertain terms, that he had to do something, then he did. Mostly it was the janitor who helped actually. I gave him a list of names, and he gave them hell, which was wonderful.

Brooke rejected her mother's offers to intervene, but in retrospect feels it was a mistake:

> I got a lot of shit at school. My mom was very positive in that she offered to talk to the principal or my teachers. I felt like that wouldn't help anything. I thought, I have to handle it when it happens, in the situation, with the kid it's coming from. And I didn't want my mom going in and fighting my battles. But she offered a lot of support, and if I had taken her up on those offers, it would have been good for me.

Supportive parents will usually be glad to try to help make school a place where you are comfortable. And they can be effective in reminding the school administrators of their responsibility to provide a safe learning environment for all students.

◇ YOU'VE GOT TO HAVE FRIENDS

It only takes a few hostile people in any group to create an unfriendly or threatening situation. Those few can create a lot of problems and make you truly miserable, even though most of the group may not be participating. Having a real friend who will stick with you in such hard times is a great gift and can help you make it through—not just in facing harassment at school, but any time. Jonathan had one such friend:

> Kristen was my best friend in school. She always protected me. We became friends in seventh grade. She was a twirler, a majorette, which was almost as glamorous as being a cheerleader. So the football players loved her. She was my protection from that world. Here's one of the most popular

girls in school who is friends with "the school fag." That helped. By my senior year they weren't accepting but they were more tolerant of me because she forced them to be. She said, "Look, he is my friend. You can't say those things around me."

When a group of boys told Anthony that they were going to beat him up after school, he asked his friend Abdul for help:

Abdul and his friend Hugh were good fighters, but they only loved fighting for a good cause. And they're both six feet tall, muscle-bound, OK? So these three guys are outside ready to jump me, and I walked out with these two big guys standing side by side. Then Abdul starts talking this, "We're all brothers, we're all sisters, we got to love each other." The other guys were like, "That's right, but Anthony better stop being with guys." Then they left. Abdul and Hugh walked me to my house, and after that Abdul started walking with me to school.

If you have a good friend, or friends, be sure to let them know how much it helps to have them in your life. Don't hesitate to ask for their support when you need it. And don't neglect being available to them too. Sometimes our most meaningful relationships are created when we are able to assist each other in times of need.

If you are feeling friendless, think about who you know, in school or from some other place in your life, with whom you'd like to become better friends. Invite that person to do something with you. It's hard to reach out, but you can do it. If you are very shy, think about calling someone who seems shy also. Find out if you have any activities in common that you could do together regularly. It doesn't matter if it's shooting hoops in the park, playing guitar, computer games, or going shopping at the mall. Having even one friend you can count on can make a tremendous difference.

◇ FIND THE OPEN-MINDED KIDS

Sometimes there'll be a group of students in a particular club or extracurricular activity who are more welcoming. Spending even part of your day in a place that is safe, with people who are accepting, can make the difference between school being bearable or unbearable. Julio used the creative arts as a way to find a supportive environment in his high school:

> I hung out with the artsy crowd. Artsy people have this path where it's OK to explore; where you can be whatever you want to be.

Think about where the most generally open-minded kids hang out at your school. In some high schools the easiest place to find this group is in the theater. As Richard says, "Join drama. If you're gay in high school—especially in a rural area—join drama."

It could also be the dance club, school newspaper, peer counseling classes, or maybe something unexpected. Although he didn't come out to them, Jonathan found acceptance with kids in the school band:

> That's where I found my first true friends as far as being able to feel more comfortable about being who I was. We all just had a good time together. We didn't have people trying to be Mr. Macho. Everybody could be themselves and just have a good time. Now if other people were watching us, we all fell back into our roles. But in the band room, that was a safe haven for all of us. I don't know of one other homosexual that was in my band, but we were all allowed to detour from our normal roles, and it was a safe haven to be crazy.

◇ THE SUPERSTUDENT ROUTE

Some students who are dealing with harassment or loneliness are able to direct their energy into their schoolwork. It helps to keep your eye on the prize that will help get you out of a lousy situation and increase the options for your future.

It's been said that living well is the best revenge. Jonathan became a superstudent, and it brought him some pleasure:

> Because of the constant torment, I wasn't able to have much social interaction with people, so I focused on my work. And I made excellent grades. Of course, everybody hated the fact that I'm at the top of the class. Here I am the school fag, and I'm at the top of the class. They're competing with me for grades, and I'm blowing them out of the water.

Succeeding in school is extremely worthwhile—both in the present and for the future—but for some young people, the superstudent route has had a hidden downside, as well. Some gay students feel they need to do perfectly in school as a defense to conceal what they believe is their deeper "flaw" of being gay. The pressure of this can be overwhelming. You don't have to be a perfect student—or a perfect person—to make up for being gay. You're OK just the way you are.

◇ CHANGE SCHOOLS

If your school situation continues to be intolerable in spite of your efforts, you might want to consider the possibility of changing schools. Sometimes there are schools in your same area that are more accepting and supportive. In big cities there are sometimes special-focus schools—such as fine arts or science—that have more tolerant attitudes. Even in smaller communities, there may be alternative schools that attract students who feel—for a variety of reasons—isolated from their peers.

When Brooke was being hassled unmercifully at her high school, she looked for a way out:

> I wanted to just forget about the teasing. I thought, it'll just go away, but it didn't. It definitely affected my actions. I started ditching school. It was so unpleasant to be there. That was when I decided to switch schools. My mom offered for me to go to private school, but the ones nearby were really pretentious. That's when I decided to go to the public high school in the city next to mine, which has a liberal reputation. I was excited to have a whole new scene. I went from being afraid and somewhat in the closet to being much less afraid and much less in the closet. Most of the people I met knew I was bisexual within a few weeks of having conversations with them.

After suffering through many months of increasingly serious harassment and physical assault at school, Chris finally decided to tell his mother what was happening:

> My mother was angry. As she put it, "How dare they? They're hurting my son." So she called the principal. My

mother was nice, but she said, "My son's told me about what is happening at school, and I want to know what you are going to do about it, cause I don't want my son to drop out of school." He said, "OK, we'll take care of it." I went to school the next day but the same things happened, and they continued for the whole week. Finally I walked back into the principal's office and said, "Do something or I'm leaving." He said, "Well, perhaps you should look for another school." I walked out of his office, slammed the door, called my mother, and said, "Come pick me up, it's over." I remember sitting, waiting for her. It was a very, very cold day and I didn't have a jacket on.

At first Chris did home study. He decided he couldn't attend any high school because "all high schools are the same, all teenagers are the same." But he didn't do the work and he felt guilty. After a few months he heard about an alternative school program:

It's called EDCO Youth Alternative, and the way the pamphlet put it, it was a school for kids who couldn't make it through normal high school. I thought, "Well that fits me." I called the director, and he called me in for a meeting. As I walked in the door I heard one kid call another a faggot. I was like, "I'm leaving." But a teacher was right there, and the teacher said, "You know the EDCO rule. You take a time out." He explained to the kid why that word was offensive. And I was like, "OK! This is a new thing."

One of the first days a girl sitting next to me asked if I had a girlfriend. I said, "No, I'm gay." She said, "Oh, that's cool." She didn't freak out about it, and the rest of the class did not freak out about it. I remember thinking, "What a contrast from my old English class where I was attacked all the time." There are some teachers who came out to me. It's a very supportive environment. I wake up in the morning and look forward to going to school.

If there are no local schools that provide options for a better situation, you might want to consider the possibility of going to school in another area. One mother in the Midwest who watched her gay son endure years of torment at school tells this story:

I couldn't find a local private school to send him to, and he was going to quit. And to me, going to school was the most important thing in the whole world. A friend said, "I know a school, it's a Quaker school in the mountains of California." I was interested in that because the Quakers celebrate people for their differences. So I called and they accepted him, and for two years they gave him a scholarship.

Although she missed him a lot, this mother was pleased that her son began to rebuild his self-esteem and was able to graduate from high school.

◇ ATTEND A COMMUNITY COLLEGE

Another strategy that some students have been able to employ is to graduate early and begin attending a community college. This is what Stone did:

I went to my freshman year of high school, and then tested out. I was sick of being harassed, and it was getting to be quite absurd. I just finished my first year at a community college.

California has a high school proficiency degree that you can get—even before you are eighteen—by taking a comprehensive test. If this is an option that you want to consider, talk with your parents and with college admissions counselors. Explore all your options. The more information you have about what might be available, the better your chances of making a decision that will work for you.

◇ CONSIDER A LEGAL CHALLENGE

All students are entitled to a safe learning environment, If you are suffering fom harrassment, especially physical harassment, your school may be legally liable for the failure to provide that safe environment. In addition, the offending student themselves may be liable.

How the courts will rule on these lawsuits is not yet clear, as it is only recently that students have begun to challenge anti-gay violence in public schools. It's likely that if enough students pursue legal relief, schools will eventually be held accountable.

If you are being attacked by violent classmates and your school has not acted resposibly to protect you—and if you have the emotional support necessary to fight a legal battle—you may want to consider a lawsuit.[1]

◇ IF NOTHING IS WORKING

If all your attempts to improve a terrible school situation don't work out, it's especially important to establish some kind of positive life outside of school. And as you are enduring, know that this is likely to be the worst time of your whole life. If you can just make it through this, things will usually get better. So be gentle with yourself, look for healthy and enriching activities outside of school, and hang on. This too shall pass.

ooooh child, things are gonna get easier

The positive changes that are starting to happen around the country are exciting and encouraging. Gay and lesbian students are recognizing that they have the *right* to a safe learning environment and are demanding that their teachers and administrators provide it. Renee represents this energy:

> I've been harassed in my school. It's been physical sometimes. It's been bad. I've reported it and nothing's been done. This year when I go back to school, if I get harassed and nothing happens I'm on my school's case from now on. I've learned I have rights and I don't have to put up with that. I'm just now saying, "Hey, forget this!"

In a small number of high schools there are now weekly support groups for gay, lesbian, and bisexual students and their straight allies. Daphne recently graduated from a suburban high school, where she was one of the founding members of the gay and lesbian club. She tells of one of the benefits of the club:

> I had people come up to me who didn't have the courage to go to the meetings, but they said, "I just want you to know

---

[1] If you're interested in knowing more about this option, contact Lambda Legal Defense and Education Fund, 666 Broadway, 12th floor, New York, NY 10012, (212) 995-8585.

that I appreciate what you're doing. I'm not out, I'm very much in the closet, and I just needed to tell *someone*, and I thought I'd come out to you." They would tell me how it helped to have the club. It made them feel less alone even though they never came to meetings.

Some schools have an identified gay-friendly staff person who is available for confidential meetings. Nicky was cutting school a lot before he talked to the designated gay-sensitive counselor at his school:

It was really, really hard, but I talked to her and she understood. And then I felt that I wasn't alone. She told me about the group and other things to help me. Things felt much better. And I decided to come to school more. You know, I want to be the first person in my family to graduate.

A small number of teachers include positive information about homosexuality and gay people in their curriculum. Matt was "really impressed" with his social science teacher when he gave an unexpected essay assignment on a test:

We were doing civil rights stuff. For part of our test we were supposed to write about how you would encourage gay people who are fighting for equal rights to use the lessons of the civil rights movement. I was very happy about that. It took a lot of guts to do that.

Many college campuses have gay support, awareness, and education activities, and some colleges have classes on gay and lesbian subjects. Taking a gay studies course helped Craig understand his own experience and build self-esteem as a young gay man:

In my second year of college I took a class called "Homosexuality in Film" taught by a great teacher, Vito Russo. He was just the most incredible influence on my life. He helped me understand the pervasive negative stereotypes about gay people in this society. And he was a role model. He embodied such integrity and love. He was funny and witty and loving and interested in everybody. He was angry and honest and really loved life. I thought he was the best. I wanted to grow to express those qualities the way he did.

Although school has been a dreadful place for many gay youth, it doesn't have to continue to be that way. Gay student activists, dedicated educators, parents, and other concerned adults in the community are beginning to address the needs of bisexual, gay, and lesbian students. Hopefully, some of these changes will come in time to make your school years better ones. You may even be part of making that happen.

THE LESBIAN, GAY, AND BISEXUAL BILL OF EDUCATION RIGHTS

1. The right to attend schools free of verbal and physical harassment, where education, not survival, is the priority.

2. The right to fair and accurate information about sexual orientation in textbooks and other classroom materials.

3. The right to unbiased information about the past and present contributions of lesbian, gay, and bisexual people in all subject areas, including art, literature, science, sports, and history.

4. The right to positive role models, both in person and in the curriculum; the right to accurate information about themselves, free of negative judgment and delivered by trained adults who not only inform lesbian, gay, and bisexual students, but affirm them.

5. The right to attend schools where respect and dignity for all students, including lesbian, gay, and bisexual students, is a standard set by the Superintendent of Public Instruction, supported by boards of education, and enforced by every principal and classroom teacher.

6. The right to be included in all support programs that exist to help teenagers deal with the difficulties of adolescence.

7. The right to legislators who guarantee and fight for their constitutional freedoms, rather than legislators who reinforce hatred and prejudice.

8. The right to a heritage free of debilitating self-hate and unchallenged discrimination.

Adapted from Project 10 (Los Angeles Public Schools) and Project 21, GLAAD/SFBA resources.

Cathy Cade © 1995

13
making schools safe for lesbian, gay, and bisexual students

For Educators

Never doubt that a small group of thoughtful, committed citizens can change the world; indeed, it's the only thing that ever does.

—*Margaret Mead*

Making schools safe is not something that lesbian, gay, and bisexual youth can do on their own. It's essential that there be a partnership between students and educators. This chapter speaks directly to educators who want to create a supportive and respectful environment for gay students.

As a gay youth, knowing what your teachers and administration can do to improve schools will help you work in conjunction with them to seek your rightful place. You may also want to give this chapter, as well as the others about school, to your teachers, guidance counselors, and principals.

When schools are at their best, all students are treated with respect and are provided with a high-quality education that will help them fulfill their potential and contribute to society. This is what virtually every educator wants to provide. But because schools mirror the problems in the larger society, this is not always the case. Educators everywhere are grappling with problems that make it difficult to meet their goals, including increasing violence, racial tensions, and shrinking funds.

In addition to these well-known challenges, there is—*in every school in the country*—a group of lesbian, gay, and bisexual students whose particular needs and suffering are usually unknown or unattended to and whose education is at risk as a result.

A few schools have recognized that support for gay students is a critical part of their mission to provide a positive learning environment for *all* their students. These schools are important role models for what needs to happen everywhere. However, until supportive programs are commonplace, the school atmosphere will continue to be a harsh one for most lesbian, gay, and bisexual students.

Many changes are necessary to transform schools to safe and comfortable environments for learning. But, as the saying goes, "A journey of a thousand miles begins with a single step." There are many things you can do right now, to begin—or continue—this transformation.

what you can do as an individual

The best approach in dealing with any challenging situation is to be proactive rather than reactive. There are many things you can do as an individual educator to foster respect for all people and to integrate awareness of gays and lesbians into your classes. Daphne's English teacher put up posters about famous gay and lesbian people:

There was a little bit of an uproar, but she handled everything very well. When the class made comments she told them, "It's not for you to put down. It's for you to know that if you need support to come here. Don't go around making comments like that in my class, because I'll kick you out, and you need this class to graduate. So you have a decision to make. Do you want to graduate or do you want to sit here and make fun of these kids who have more courage and guts than you ever will?" She said it more politely, but that was the bottom line.

SCHOOL IS NOT A SAFE PLACE FOR GAY STUDENTS

A survey of four hundred high school students conducted by the Massachusetts Governor's Commission on Gay and Lesbian Youth found that 97 percent of the students heard homophobic remarks either very often or sometimes.[1] A study conducted by the Philadelphia Lesbian and Gay Task Force found that almost 60 percent of gay men and 30 percent of lesbians had been harassed or attacked in high school, junior high school, or college.[2] Another study found that 28 percent of young men who identify as gay or bisexual drop out of school altogether because they are so uncomfortable in the school setting.[3]

[1]Massachusetts Governor's Commission on Gay and Lesbian Youth, *Making Schools Safe for Gay and Lesbian Youth: Breaking the Silence in Schools and Families,* Publication No. 17296-60-500-2/93-C.R., (Boston: The Commission, 1993), p. 52.

[2]Larry Gross and Steven K. Aurand, *Discrimination and Violence Against Lesbian Women and Gay Men in Philadelphia and the Commonwealth of Pennsylvania* (Philadelphia: Philadelphia Lesbian and Gay Task Force, 1992). Cited by Anthony R. D'Augelli and Lawrence J. Dark, "Lesbian, Gay, and Bisexual Youths," in Leonard D. Eron, Jacquelyn Gentry, and Peggy Schlegel, editors: *Reason to Hope: A Psychosocial Perspective on Violence and Youth* (Washington, D.C.: American Psychological Association, 1994), p. 179.

[3]Gary Remafedi, "Adolescent Homosexuality: Psychosocial and Medical Implications," *Pediatrics* 79(March 1987). Cited by Ritch C. Savin-Williams and Kenneth M. Cohen, "Psychosocial Outcomes of Verbal and Physical Abuse Among Lesbian, Gay, and Bisexual Youths" in Ritch C. Savin-Wiliams and Kenneth M. Cohen, editors: *The Lives of Lesbians, Gays, and Bisexuals: Children to Adults* (Fort Worth: Harcourt Brace, 1996), p. 187.

There are a multitude of ways that you can introduce information about bisexual, gay, and lesbian people into your lessons. In art classes, you can point out great artists—such as Leonardo da Vinci or Frida Kahlo—who were gay, lesbian, or bisexual. In music classes, you can listen to the work of gay composers such as Tchaikovsky or Cole Porter. In literature classes, you can note that many of the authors you study are gay, lesbian, or bisexual—such as Herman Melville, Virginia Woolf, Marcel Proust, and Willa Cather. You can also include books with gay or lesbian characters. Choosing books where sexual orientation isn't the issue is an especially good way to make gay and lesbian people more visible.

Leonardo da Vinci (1452–1519) was an Italian Renaissance artist and scientist whose immense scope of achievement establishes him as the foremost creative mind of his time. His portrait *Mona Lisa* may be the most famous painting in the world.

Frida Kahlo (1907–1954) was a major Mexican artist whose powerful paintings—mostly self-portraits—speak directly to contemporary and feminist issues.

Peter Ilich Tchaikovsky (1840–1893), the eminent Russian composer, is best known for his ballets *Swan Lake, Sleeping Beauty,* and the *Nutcracker,* as well as the *1812 Overture.*

Cole Porter (1892–1964) was an American lyricist and composer whose songs have wit, sophistication, and technical virtuosity. Many have become classics, such as *Begin the Beguine, Night and Day*, and *I Love Paris.*

Herman Melville (1819–1891) is widely regarded as one of America's greatest and most influential novelists, best known for *Moby Dick.*

Virginia Woolf (1882–1941) was a distinguished writer whose works include the feminist essay "A Room of One's Own" and innovative novels such as *To the Lighthouse* and *Orlando: A Biography,* a fantasy that follows its protagonist through three centuries and one change of sex.

Marcel Proust (1871–1922) was a French novelist whose multivolume work, *Remembrance of Things Past,* has no equal. It is among the few novels that have revolutionized the genre.

Willa Cather (1873–1947) was a Pulitzer Prize–winning novelist whose work, often set in the pioneer American West, includes *O Pioneers*, *My Antonia*, and *The Song of the Lark*.

In math classes, you might give word problems in which students calculate the budget for a gay/straight alliance group or the rate at which people march in a Gay Pride Parade. You might also discuss important mathematicians, such as Alan Turing. In philosophy classes, it's natural to read Socrates and Plato. October is Gay History Month and a ready opportunity to point out important historical figures who were gay, lesbian, and bisexual or to study significant events in the history of the struggle for justice for gay people.

You can include positive information about lesbian, gay, and bisexual people in ways that don't need the cooperation or approval of anyone else. Although integrating gay issues into the curriculum in a formal way is a more lengthy and challenging process, individual educators are free to take teaching material from a wide variety of sources.

Alan Turing (1912–1954) was a British mathematician whose cracking of the Nazi's secret code was crucial to winning World War II. He was also one of the fathers of the modern computer.

Socrates (469–399 BC) and his disciple Plato (c.428–347 BC) are regarded by scholars as the founding thinkers of Western civilization. Both believed that the highest form of love was a spiritual one, which came from seeing into another's soul without regard for trivial concerns such as wealth, appearance, or gender.

Not only will these positive acknowledgements be supportive to your gay students, but they will also be meaningful for other students who have gay or lesbian parents, siblings, relatives, or close friends.

◇ TAKING A STAND AGAINST HARASSMENT

One of the most basic actions a teacher can take on behalf of all students is to take a strong stand against harassment. By establishing guidelines for respectful behavior at the outset, you can get ahead of the game. Clearly, it's much better to prevent problems than to wait until they occur.

The reasons why insults, slurs, and hate speech are not allowed should be explained clearly. As Sherri Paris, a university lecturer, explains, time should be spent in discussion with students:

> Students need to understand why this sort of speech is destructive. Otherwise, they see the rules against it as arbitrary—like adult hang-ups on gum-chewing or passing notes. I have learned over the years that in the course of such discussions, students inevitably come to the point where it is safe to allow them some ritual, like voting or a show of hands, where they voluntarily agree they will abide—as a group—by these rules to make the class better.
>
> I have also learned, painfully, that at least for older students, without the discussion the rules against hate speech don't work and are deeply resented by some students—both those with racist attitudes and those who just don't like rules.

It's remarkable how much even one supportive teacher can mean to a student who is struggling. Anthony makes this clear, saying that he wants to thank one teacher by name:

> Mr. Soriente was the only one in the whole school who supported me, and he isn't gay. In class one time people were calling me names and talking about humping the faggot. And he told the whole class, "Everybody except Anthony has an extra homework assignment tonight." He said they needed to show me respect. And they all had to apologize to me.
>
> Another time I was absent and when I came back to school I found out that he'd spent the entire period teaching them why they needed to respect gay people.

There are now federal laws against sexual harassment in schools, and these laws may cover the harassment of students on the basis of sexual orientation as well. In addition, a few states have their own laws against such harassment and Massachusetts has a law specifically protecting lesbian, gay, and bisexual students.

Gay students are beginning to seek legal relief for the harassment they suffer and national civil rights organizations are supporting these efforts. In order to ensure fair treatment for all your students and to protect your school from liability, you have a clear obligation to intercede when any bisexual, gay, or lesbian student is insulted, threatened, or otherwise harassed.

Teaching the fundamental principle of tolerance for all people, regardless of race, religion, culture, gender, sexual orientation, economic status, or disability, is well worth your efforts. Because the principles of teaching tolerance toward gay people are exactly the same as they are for any other group, you can simply include lesbian, gay, and bisexual people in any discussion of tolerance in general. The skills required are the same as those needed to handle incidents of racism or any other prejudice. The only additional work you need to do is to become educated about the specific issues involved for gay, lesbian, and bisexual youth.

WERE YOU EVER THE TARGET?

When students make remarks that are insulting to people of a particular race, culture, sex, or sexual orientation, it presents a wonderful opportunity to discuss the importance of extending basic respect to all people. You can ask students, including those who are the offenders, to talk about times in their lives when they were discriminated against or harassed. Ask questions, such as:

◇ Were you ever the target of discrimination, prejudice, or harassment because of your race, culture, class, religion, sex, sexual orientation, physical size, or ability?
◇ How did it make you feel?
◇ What assumptions do you think the person who discriminated against you made about you?
◇ What did you say back?
◇ What did you do?
◇ What do you wish you could have said or done?
◇ Has this ever happened before?
◇ Has this happened to any of your family or friends?
◇ Why do you think it happens?
◇ What do you think can be done?

◇ EVERYDAY HEROES

Ordinary people are making schools safer for gay youth. It's not a requirement that you have a grand vision or commit the next ten years of your life to this struggle. Though if you *are* ready for that—more power to you! All you need is to decide to take the step that is right in front of you now. Down the road you can choose if you want to take another step or not. Even little steps take courage and make you a hero for the students whose lives are improved as a result of your actions.

WHAT YOU CAN DO TO MAKE YOUR SCHOOL SAFER FOR BISEXUAL, GAY, AND LESBIAN STUDENTS

◇ **Remember that there are gay, lesbian, and bisexual youth in your classes.**

◇ **Examine your own beliefs.** Think about your assumptions and commit yourself to unlearning any prejudice you have internalized.

◇ **Show that you're gay-friendly.** Use the words "gay," "lesbian," and "bisexual." Keep your language free of heterosexual bias. Wear a button or put up a poster.

◇ **Talk to gay, lesbian, and bisexual youth.** Ask them what they want and need. Listen to their answers, and work to help them achieve their goals. If someone comes out to you, don't tell anyone else without that person's permission.

◇ **Challenge homophobic remarks everywhere and all the time.** Remind students—or others—that antigay labels, remarks, or jokes reflect prejudice and are hurtful. Use such incidents as opportunities to educate. Make it clear that you are offended by the name-calling and will not tolerate it. Let students know what the consequences will be if you hear any further insults. Follow through immediately with those consequences.

◇ **Order lesbian, gay, and bisexual books for the library.** Many people go first to the library when they want information but are not ready to talk about their concerns. More than one librarian has reported that gay books were "the most dog-eared, least checked out" books on the shelves. If there are budget constraints about library purchases, think about soliciting contributions or making donations yourself.

◇ **Write letters to school—or local—papers.** When there are current events that affect gay, lesbian, and bisexual people, write letters to the editor expressing your supportive point of view.

◇ **Sensitize other staff.** Arrange a viewing and discussion of an educational video, such as *Gay Youth,* for a group of your coworkers. Follow up with speakers from a local lesbian, gay, bisexual, or PFLAG speakers bureau.

◇ **Provide support and resource information.** Because you are someone who is showing yourself to be gay-friendly, students may come out to you verbally or in their written work. In addition to responding with emotional support and affirmation, be sure to inform the students of resources such as books and local groups.

a comprehensive program for school-based suppport

In the last decade there has been a growing number of teachers, administrators, school nurses, and counselors around the country—spurred on by students—who have become aware of the needs of gay youth and have responded with the development of programs to meet those needs. They recognize that such programs benefit not only the target group but the entire school community. Learning respect and appreciation for lesbian, bisexual, and gay people is part of learning respect for all marginalized groups. Teaching tolerance prepares students to interact more successfully in the world and helps to create a more enlightened society where diversity is embraced.

In order to make these changes, the involvement of *both* students and school staff is essential. Sometimes students inspire staff to show their commitment to providing an equal educational opportunity for everyone. And the staff models how to make positive institutional changes, motivates the students to participate, and provides continuity as students graduate and move on.

PROJECT 10: THE MODEL FOR ALL SCHOOL
SUPPORT PROGRAMS

In 1984, after an ugly incident at Fairfax High School in Los Angeles, long-time teacher Virginia Uribe invited gay and lesbian students to meet weekly at lunchtime for informal discussion about problems they faced in the school setting. As the lunch group shared their experiences, the students' needs became so evident that Virginia was inspired to found PROJECT 10, the first school-based program in the nation to address the needs of lesbian, gay, and bisexual students.

The focus of the program is education, the reduction of verbal and physical abuse, suicide prevention, and accurate information about AIDS. PROJECT 10 is committed to keeping students in school, off drugs, and sexually responsible. Because there is a high correlation between low self-esteem and high-risk behavior, PROJECT 10 works to improve self-esteem among lesbian and gay youth by providing accurate information and nonjudgmental counseling on issues of sexual orientation. Its services include workshops and training sessions for educators, counseling for students, outreach to parents, liaison with peer counseling, substance abuse, suicide prevention programs, and coordination with health education programs.

PROJECT 10 has since been implemented throughout the Los Angeles Unified School District and is the model for programs in other school districts across the country.

In order for there to be meaningful and sustained institutional change, there needs to be a comprehensive program that includes the following.

◇ TRAINING

Teachers, counselors, and other staff need to be educated about the needs of lesbian, gay, and bisexual students and the issue of homophobia. This mandatory training is essential. When educators are sensitized to the issues facing their gay students, they are able to respond in much more helpful ways.

Not all faculty need to become experts, or even totally comfortable with the concerns of gay students. Every teacher is not required to be all things to all students. However, the staff should be sensitive and affirming and know where to send the student who needs help or guidance.

Training workshops are also important because they help build the base of support necessary to make other institutional changes. It is common for there to be controversy about any discussion of gay and lesbian students. Therefore, the more you are able to educate people about the issues, the more likely it is that you will be able to overcome any political roadblocks.

◇ SCHOOL POLICIES

It's critical to develop school policies that prohibit harassment, violence, and discrimination against all students and staff, including those who are gay, lesbian, and bisexual. This protection also establishes a safe environment for educators to come out as positive role models for the students. Antislur resolutions and codes of behavior and discipline are important in the enforcement of any nondiscrimination clause.

◇ GAY-FRIENDLY STAFF

An essential step in any support program is to identify trained, gay-friendly adults at your school. These "safe staff" should be announced as the contact people for students, families, and other educators who may have concerns or questions about any gay issue. The sexual orientation of the contact people is not of critical importance. What's most important is that they be well-informed, sensitive, respected by the students, and easily approachable.

If you designate a cluster of at least three contact people in each school building, students will have a good chance of finding someone they feel comfortable talking with and the staff can support and encourage each other.

◇ WEEKLY SUPPORT GROUPS

Support groups provide a safe and confidential place for students to meet and discuss their feelings and experiences. They also offer an opportunity for students to educate themselves and the school community about sexual orientation and homophobia. High school groups need a faculty adviser, but the group content should be driven by the young people. College groups are generally run by the students themselves.

Support groups can be just for lesbian, gay, and bisexual students or can be open to straight allies. Both formats have their advantages.

If the group is solely for gay, lesbian, and bisexual youth, there's a special bond of shared experience and an affirmation of their shared identity.

"The beauty of the gay/straight alliance model is that it takes the pressure off kids to self-identify," says David LaFontaine, chairperson of the Massachusetts Governor's Commission on Gay and Lesbian Youth. "The kids like the idea that it's up to them when and how they talk about it, and they like the idea that their straight friends can be part of the group."

Al Ferreira explains another advantage to this model:

> The focus of our gay/straight alliance group is on education and information and being a safe haven. We never ask anybody their sexual orientation. If they want to reveal it, they can. If they don't, that's fine too. And it's important to have heterosexual allies to help make changes.

Kay Williams, a school nurse in Minnesota, describes how she was prompted by a lesbian student to begin a support group:

> It was in the fall when Erin was a freshman. She was thirteen years old and she came in and said, "I'm a lesbian and I want a support group like the other support groups here." I said, "OK." She walked out and I thought, "Oh dear, what am I going to do now?"
>
> First, I talked to my friend Sharon, a nurse at South High in Minneapolis, who had gotten a group off the ground the year before. Then I sat down with Erin and we made plans.

You can post fliers with information about the group and announce it over the PA system or in the school paper. (Don't be discouraged if the posters get taken down or defaced and need replacing many times.) This lets everyone know that gay students have administrative support for their concerns.

Jerry Bang, a high school counselor in Texas, used this strategy:

> I had an announcement read on the PA system, the whole school heard it. "Attention students, as you know Miss Bang has started several support groups, and there's going to be one added for the new semester." I wanted it to blend in, so

I sandwiched it between the other two. "There's an Alateen group, the new lesbian, gay, bisexual support group, and the Challenge group for people who want to kick a habit of some sort. If you are interested in knowing more about these groups, please come see me and I'll give you a schedule."

The programs—and individual efforts—that are beginning to make schools safer and more welcoming for lesbian, bisexual, and gay students enhance the quality of school for *all* students. Al Ferreira, a high school teacher, relates this story about a student who attends their support group meetings:

There's a kid who's considered a nerd and is isolated because he's academically talented. There's a tremendous amount of cruelty for anyone who's different. This student comes to meetings and is an active member. He's now recently identified himself openly as a heterosexual. I initially thought maybe he was coming to the group because he was gay, but he was coming because he's been marginalized. The one place he's found that he can be safe is our meetings.

SUPPORT GROUP ACTIVITY IDEAS

◇ Sponsor a Diversity Day in coalition with others.
◇ Create a gay history display for a school bulletin board.
◇ Invite outside speakers—such as openly gay community members or gay-friendly clergy—to attend group meetings.
◇ Participate in a school beautification project by planting flowers in pink triangle or rainbow flag designs.
◇ Organize a dance or other social event.
◇ Attend a Pride Day Parade.
◇ Go to movies, concerts, or plays together.
◇ Advocate for school policies, teacher training, and curriculum that improve life for lesbian, gay, and bisexual students.
◇ Raise funds to buy gay-friendly books for the school library. Or organize a book drive.
◇ Connect with other support groups for joint activities.

◇ Write an article about your group for the school—or local—paper.

◇ Present Certificates of Appreciation to school staff who have made a difference.

◇ Organize an Alumni Home-Coming Out Day.

◇ CURRICULUM

To foster lasting changes, we need to integrate gay, lesbian, and bisexual issues into all subject areas of the curriculum. Arthur Lipkin, Director of the Harvard Gay and Lesbian School Issues Project at the Harvard University Graduate School of Education, explains:

> If we don't touch the core of what students are being asked to inquire about, if we don't alter what's being presented to represent a more inclusive truth, then we will ultimately have failed. If students perceive that gay and lesbian issues are confined to Diversity Day and rules about insults and are never part of their serious academic study, then I think they get the message that this is some kind of fad that will pass.

Efforts to integrate lesbian and gay issues into curriculum may face some of the most entrenched opposition. (We are not the only ones who recognize that curriculum helps to create lasting changes in attitudes.) In 1993 the Massachusetts Governor's Commission on Gay and Lesbian Youth issued a report, "Making Schools Safe for Gay and Lesbian Youth: Breaking the Silence in Schools and in Families," which made five recommendations for schools. One of those recommendations was for the development of a curriculum that included gay and lesbian issues. Later that year the State Board of Education voted to take steps to improve the school situation for these students, based on the recommendations in the Commission's report. Three of the original five recommendations were adopted. Those that did *not* make it through were the suggestions to provide information in school libraries for gay and lesbian adolescents and to integrate curriculum into all subject areas.

Working for institutionalized changes toward more fully inclusive curriculum will take much effort and patience. Yet as an individual teacher, you can take steps immediately to introduce these issues in your classroom in appropriate ways.

GAY, LESBIAN, AND BISEXUAL ISSUES: A FEW GENERAL CURRICULUM IDEAS

ELEMENTARY SCHOOL

◇ Include lesbian and gay parents and relatives in any discussion of families.

◇ Challenge sex role stereotypes in children's play.

◇ Challenge gender assumptions in discussions of careers and family roles.

◇ Include lesbian and gay people in any discussion of discrimination and the struggle for full human rights.

◇ At Mother's or Father's Day, allow students with gay or lesbian parents to make two projects.

JUNIOR HIGH SCHOOL

◇ Discuss lesbian, gay, and bisexual issues in current events.

◇ Include lesbian and gay examples in mathematical word problems.

◇ Integrate lesbian and gay content into family life education.

HIGH SCHOOL

◇ Include readings with lesbian and gay themes in English classes. Note when authors are lesbian, gay, or bisexual.

◇ Teach about the struggle for equal rights for gay people in U.S. history.

◇ Include lesbian and gay examples in foreign language reading practice.

◇ Include the full range of sexual orientation in sex education classes.

COLLEGE (and some high school classes too)

◇ Include discussion of the influence of sexual orientation on the writings of lesbian, gay, and bisexual authors in literature.

◇ Discuss the different ideas about what "causes" sexual orientation in biology or psychology.
◇ Apply a social constructionist analysis to lesbian and gay issues in sociology.
◇ Study cross-cultural attitudes about lesbian, gay, and bisexual people in anthropology.
◇ Include sexual orientation when discussing the influence of lesbian, gay, and bisexual figures in history.

◇ COUNSELING SERVICES

Counseling services for gay, lesbian, and bisexual students and their families should be provided. Students who have lesbian or gay parents may also be subjected to harassment, and their need for help is often invisible.

◇ SOCIAL EVENTS AND CONFERENCES

Social and educational events for gay students and their friends can provide healthy opportunities to meet peers and build self-esteem.

◇ RESOURCE CENTER AND COORDINATOR

Establishing a districtwide resource center and designating a coordinator of services for lesbian, gay, and bisexual students promotes easy access to information, training, and counseling for students and staff.

◇ ADVOCACY AND NETWORKING

Communication among community agencies, task forces, commissions, parent groups, educational organizations, and teachers unions helps to secure the rights of gay, bisexual, and lesbian students.

separate schools

There are two schools in the country that have been established specifically for gay, lesbian, and bisexual students who feel so unsafe in their regular high schools that they cannot continue to attend. The first of these is the Harvey Milk School, which is a joint program of the Hetrick-Martin Institute, a social service agency for lesbian, gay, and bisexual youth, and the New York City Board of Education. This small, fully accredited alternative public high school was established in 1985 and was named for Harvey Milk, the openly gay San Francisco supervisor who was assassinated in 1978. The school has an enrollment of about thirty students, ages fourteen through twenty-one, and has two full-time teachers. To graduate, students must meet the same standards as in other public schools.

The other school is the EAGLES (Emphasizing Adolescent Gay Lesbian Education Services) Center, a High School Options Program of the Los Angeles Unified School District, founded by educator Jerry Battey in 1992. EAGLES Center is very similar to the Harvey Milk School. One seventeen-year-old student, Jerry, had dropped out of school four different times because of constant name-calling, intimidation, and threats of physical violence before he came to EAGLES. Jerry says, "I am finally comfortable coming to school. I don't have to pretend to be someone else."[4]

Both these schools provide an invaluable service to bisexual, gay, and lesbian students who would otherwise be unable to continue their education. There is a real need for such schools. However, this need exists because of the *failure* of regular high schools to provide a safe environment for all students. As Eddie, a student at Harvey Milk, says:

> Although having this school is fabulous, I hope there will be a day when there is no gay school. Because, you know, honey, there shouldn't have to be one.[5]

the challenge of coming out

> *This section is addressed to educators but is equally important for other gay, lesbian, and bisexual professionals who work with youth, such as clergy, social workers, and counselors.*

The most profoundly meaningful individual act a lesbian, gay, or bisexual professional can do is to come out. It's not an exaggeration

[4] "Teens Find a Haven in L.A. School," *Los Angeles Times*, January 10, 1994.

[5] "This School Is Out," *New York Times*, October 13, 1991.

to say that by being a positive—and visible—example you can save lives and help change the world.

Gay youth have an urgent need for role models. As Patrick expresses it:

> I didn't really know anyone who I knew was gay. It made it a lot harder, at the beginning especially. I only had a very negative, sensationalized view of gay life. I didn't have any gay role models, and I think that's sad.

Amy notes an unhappy irony in this regard:

> One thing that was the biggest tragedy for me, and I think is for a lot of people, is that I didn't meet role models until *after* I was past the critical point of needing them. It wasn't until I was in the gay community that I started meeting role models.

Respected role models can make a big difference. Luna tells about the influence of one of his high school instructors:

> There was this very flamboyant, out teacher. It was an obvious thing, everybody knew he was gay. He had this power and style of teaching where everybody would listen because he was so interesting and so much fun. I used to look at him and think he was God and put him up on that pedestal because he had a lot of respect from the younger people. And that's what I wanted. They didn't tease him, but they teased me. They didn't call him faggot or anything, so I wanted to be just like him. People were comfortable around him because he was so comfortable with himself. And he made me feel more comfortable about myself. I've learned to be more like him, and now I don't have problems when I meet people.

When teachers come out, it can be meaningful to all students. Joe Salvemini, a high school teacher in southern California, shares an incident that happened the day he came out in his classroom:

> A student in the class was a Native American, and he stayed after class and said, "You shocked me when you said you were gay. But I know what it's like to be discriminated against." I turned around to him and I said, "By knowing that I'm gay does it change your opinion of me? Or does it

change your opinion of other gay and lesbian people?" He said, "It doesn't change my opinion of you, but it does change my opinion of other gay and lesbian people because I know what it's like for people to have one perception of what you're supposed to be and that not being true." Well that made me glad I came out.

In schools where teachers are out the progress toward creating a safe environment for gay youth gains real momentum.

◇ WHAT'S GOING TO HAPPEN?

Fear is, of course, what makes coming out difficult for most people. A gay high school counselor, who recently came out to a few colleagues—and has been supported by them—explains why he is not yet out to the whole school: "That's the result of my own fears, my own homophobia. And, thank God, that is changing. My growth continues."

Even Virginia Uribe, founder of Project 10, started out afraid:

I put up a little thing that said "Lesbian and Gay" on the bulletin board. And I can remember shaking as I did it, thinking, what's going to happen if I put this up and then nothing happened.

It's natural to feel fear. But as with many other challenging things in life, the more we do them, the more comfortable we become. The more you work to create a positive environment for gay, lesbian, and bisexual students, the more natural it will feel for you—and them—to come out.

Al Ferreira describes the response when he came out at a staff development training:

In a panel discussion I talked about what my experiences had been and how some of my colleagues hurt me by making assumptions about my sexual orientation and using words that were really hurtful. I wanted that to stop. And I talked about how those attitudes were hurtful to young people.

I was really surprised at the response that occurred. For the most part it was very loving and supportive. One male teacher came down the stairs with tears in his eyes and apol-

ogized to me. That took a lot of strength of character to recognize that he had inadvertently said some really hurtful
things to me. I was really touched.

The only negative thing that occurred was the following
day a woman who had been professionally cordial in the
past refused to get in the elevator with me.

Gail Jaffer was hired as the principal of an elementary school in a
midsized district. She tells this story about her final interview by the
superintendent of schools, after she had met with the school board:

Apparently the board was concerned about why I had left
my last high-level job. So the superintendent of schools
called me in and said, "I need to ask you a few questions.
Are there any skeletons in the closet?" Those were his exact
words. I looked him straight in the face and I said, "No, I've
been out of the closet for a long time!" And he laughed.
Then he said, "So why did you move here?" And I told him,
"Because my partner took a university job." And he said,
"Well, that's reasonable."

That was so empowering. That was to me probably the
highlight of my life as a lesbian. To be able to tell the truth
before I was hired and not fear the consequences. Then
there could be no surprises. If I keep that a secret then it
becomes something that people can use against me. No one
could out me, because I've done it for myself. That provided
safe territory for me.

Joe Salvemini relates what happened after he decided to come
out to his students:

What really amazed me was that I didn't get all the rejection
that I had planned on. One of my most homophobic students asked if I was gay during a class and I said that I was.
And then I said, "Does it make a difference?" And this one
kid turned around and said, "You're still a good teacher." A
lot of other kids said, "Yeah" or "Right on" or "You bet" or
something accepting. It meant a lot to me.

Sometimes there is an initially negative response from administrators, but if a teacher is generally well respected for his or her work,
and determined about this issue, the administration will usually

come around over time. Ron Schmidt teaches English to eighth grade students. He came out to his principal about eight years ago:

> When the principal was able to work his jaw again, he said it would bring down the walls of the district if it were to become known that I'm gay, and he forbade me to talk about gay issues in the classroom. I have continued to talk about that, in the context of human rights, because I believe I have not only the right but the responsibility, and I ignored both for too many years.
>
> This same principal now sits in on sessions with concerned parents and assures them, "Mr. Schmidt has the same right to talk about gay issues as he does to talk about any other area of discrimination."

There are certainly some risks if you come out as an educator. Only you can evaluate your particular situation, and only you can make the right decision for yourself. But for each individual person, the chances of your worst fears being realized are actually very slim. Virginia Uribe expresses a common experience for educators who have come out:

> All of us spend so much time in the closet and then, most of the time, when we come out it's really no big deal. It makes you wonder why you were so in to begin with.

As with all other growth and change, validate yourself for the steps you've taken, assess the challenges ahead, and keep asking the question "How can I take the next step?"

IF YOU FACE HARASSMENT

If you do face harassment after revealing that you are gay, be sure to document the incidents *as they occur.* It's a good idea to send written copies of your documentation to at least two other people who are interested or involved, so that there is an indisputable record of your perception of the incidents. If you have union representation, use it. Create a network of allies. Since 1973 the National Education Association has offered free legal counsel to teachers harassed or discriminated against because of sexual orientation. The NEA phone number is (202)822–7700.

◇ THERE ARE MANY WAYS TO COME OUT

Sometimes when educators think about coming out, they imagine a public announcement of what feels like their private lives, but coming out does not have to be a proclamation to the entire assembly. It's possible to be honest about your life in natural, appropriate, and dignified ways.

Teachers have found that generally it works best to come out first to a few supportive peers, then to the administration and the rest of staff, and lastly to students. For some teachers this process happens fairly quickly. For others, it's a slower progression. As one high school teacher relates:

> I'm out to the teachers. It was frightening to tell them, but there haven't been any bad experiences. If anything, it's made people respect me more. I'm not yet out to the kids, though. Right now, today, I would feel afraid to take that step. But tomorrow, I might not. For me, it's a progressive thing. I'm out this far, and I'm going to keep opening up to this.

Sometimes teachers use a topic of classroom discussion to reveal their sexuality. Rodney Wilson, who teaches high school in Missouri, was conducting a lesson about the Holocaust when he said, "If I had been living in Europe in World War II, they would have put a pink triangle on me and put me in a concentration camp because I am gay." First there was silence, then one of the students said, "That was a very brave thing to say." Another student expressed a similar sentiment, and soon the whole class started clapping. Although a protest by some parents followed, it did subside, and Rodney Wilson became the first openly gay teacher to gain tenure in Missouri.

Occasionally there will be students who inquire about your life outside of school. They may ask whether you are married or where you got your tan on vacation. Those kind of questions are an opportunity to give honest answers about your life.

Keep your remarks brief and appropriate, of course. It makes sense to answer in ways that are similar to how your heterosexual peers respond to personal questions. Just talk in the same direct way about this part of your life as you do about other aspects of who you are.

STRAIGHT ALLIES CAN COME OUT TOO

There is an important message conveyed when supporters of bisexual, gay, or lesbian people are visible and positive role models as well. Talk about your gay family members or friends. Let it be known that you believe they deserve the same full civil rights as everyone else. Since heterosexual educators are less likely to face reprisals, you have a special opportunity to be out there raising consciousness.

As a teacher, it's not possible to be consistently aware of the enormous power you hold. Yet the influence you have on your students is awesome. We all remember certain teachers throughout our lives. We remember things they said, what they believed in, how they lived their values. Although the job can feel daunting, you have an opportunity to have an inestimable positive impact on the lives of your students and—it is not an exaggeration to say—on the world.

Cathy Cade © 1995

14
strategies for building
a support program

For Activists and Educators

There are moments when things go well and one feels encouraged. There are difficult moments and one feels overwhelmed. But it's senseless to speak of optimism and pessimism. The only important thing is to know that if one works well in a potato field, the potatoes will grow. If one works well among men [and women, we would add], they will grow—that's reality. The rest is smoke. It's important to know that words don't move mountains. Work, exacting work, moves mountains.

—*Danilo Dolci*

This chapter is for activists—students, educators, parents, and community members who want to create a school support program for gay, lesbian, and bisexual students. Making schools safe for gay youth is not something that can be undertaken alone. It requires the cooperation and efforts of everyone involved. This chapter will give you more ideas about how you can work together to make positive changes in your school.

Teamwork is the essential ingredient in making successful changes in schools. Students are the inspiration, but the participation of teachers and administrators is essential. And parents and other allies in the community can also lend valuable support.

getting started

It is often a brave and persistent student who inspires teachers to begin a support program for gay, lesbian, and bisexual students. Jerry Bang, a high school counselor, tells this story:

> Two years ago an out lesbian, who was a senior, came to me and she wanted to start a group. Although I was out to her, I said a flat "No," because I didn't want to come out publicly. Well she mentioned my name in passing as a counselor who is thinking about doing this group, and it got printed in a local gay community paper. I got flooded with phone calls, all positive. People sent me information about Project 10, which I never had heard of. I started getting all the statistics about gay youth on the streets and committing suicide and dropping out.
>
> So I reconsidered and said, "OK, I'll do it." By then my main concern was not me any more. I decided if this means that people label me, that's their problem. I'm doing this because the kids need it.
>
> So I give the student credit for starting it. She made me aware, whether I wanted to be or not: "You are a role model, so get over yourself." She was wonderful.

Daphne was one of a few students who searched for a teacher to help establish a support group:

> First we approached the adviser to the school paper, and he
> said he'd like to but he didn't have time. I talked to a couple
> of other teachers who said the same thing. Then I went to
> Mrs. Moore, who was my English teacher. She said, "I'd love
> to. And we'll put up a fight if we have to because you have
> as much right to a club as anyone else."

When students aren't able to find a teacher to work with them, they sometimes move ahead anyway. David LaFontaine, chairperson of the Massachusetts Governor's Commission on Gay and Lesbian Youth, reports,

> We've had many schools where the students formed a gay
> student group and they didn't even have a faculty adviser.
> The school was then shamed into appointing a faculty per-
> son to do it.

On the other hand, teachers don't have to wait for students to insist that their needs be recognized. There are young people in *every* school who are in need of positive acknowledgment, information, and support. Any educator can take the lead in initiating a program for gay, lesbian, and bisexual youth.

Educators around the country who have established support programs report that three basic strategies contributed to their success:

◇ Build allies (gay and straight) through education and organizing.
◇ Look for whatever angle will get you in the door and grow from there.
◇ Be prepared to deal with opposition.

building allies

As with any effort of significant change, it works best to start with a few people likely to be supportive. As they become more knowledgeable, enlist their help in educating others, and so on in an ever-widening circle. Expend the least effort on those who are the most resistant to your point of view, and concentrate on the people who are open to learning more.

◇ STUDENTS

Gay and straight students are an essential part of any effort to make changes. Students—including recent graduates—are highly effective advocates when they share their personal experience. Not only are they powerful spokespeople for their own cause, but as David LaFontaine notes, "The process of standing up for themselves and telling their stories becomes a way of making a transition out of the victim role, because the victims are the ones who are silenced."

Supportive students who are not gay—or not out—can help in many important ways, from individual acts of friendship and raising awareness to schoolwide actions. One high school newspaper in a suburban town in Texas ran a five-page section on gays, lesbians, and homophobia. It was part of a series encouraging students to understand and accept diversity in their school. Although the piece was well balanced and won a first-place award from the National Scholastic Press Association, it created a big controversy, including loud and persistent criticism on a local radio talk show. Still the student editor was pleased when he reported that, "Despite the outcry from the adult element of the community, the students (who were, after all, our target readers) read the section with interest and little commotion. Possibly its effect was even positive: the gay student we interviewed was elected Homecoming King." [1]

[1]"Whose News? Student Journalists Examine Gay Rights; Community Response Is Shock, Anger," *Teaching Tolerance* 3:2 (1994), pp. 24–27.

MASSACHUSETTS VICTORY

After an extraordinary campaign, involving nearly one thousand students, the Gay and Lesbian Students' Rights Bill—an act to prohibit discrimination against students in public schools on the basis of sexual orientation—was passed by the Massachusetts legislature and signed into law by the governor in 1993. The students gave powerful personal testimony at the statehouse. They held candlelight vigils and held demonstrations, carrying signs with statistics about the suicide and high school dropout rates of gay youth and demanding that legislators "Make Schools Safe." They conducted a letter-writing and a phone-calling effort. And on a special lobbying day, they gathered into groups and visited all forty state senators.

As reported in the *New York Times* ("Gay Rights Law for Schools Advances in Massachusetts," December 8, 1993):

In two previous years, the Senate had kept the gay rights bill in committee. What made the difference this year, said Marty Linsky, the chief secretary to Governor Weld, were the students.

"There were 1,000 young people up here endlessly," Mr. Linsky said. "And I think they were able to persuade members of the Legislature that the problem was real and that the solution was reasonable. Their stories about their own difficulties were very compelling, very persuasive."

◇ TEACHERS

When talking with educators, appeal to the fact that they care about and are committed to young people. You might start by talking to individual faculty and administrators about your concerns and ask them to take home a video like *Gay Youth* or *Who's Afraid of PROJECT 10?* Follow up by discussing their reactions, and supply them with written materials. Ask their support to educate a wider audience of staff, administrators, and friendly board members.

Often teachers have operated as lone rangers as they've attempted to improve life for gay students, but although individual efforts are extremely important, working in conjunction with others is crucial if we are to achieve widespread and sustained change.

Al Ferreira, a teacher at a Cambridge, Massachusetts, high school, organizes a school assembly annually in October for National Coming Out Day. Students who identify as bisexual, gay, or lesbian speak to the audience about their experiences. Kristin Sharp, a high school health teacher and straight ally, also invites gay and lesbian speakers to her school each year. She does preparatory lessons on the preceding days and follow-up discussions afterward.

Kristin is also part of her school district's task force for gay, lesbian, and bisexual student concerns that has provided diversity training for administrators in all the schools. In addition, this task force is using the standard annual curriculum reviews to introduce accurate and affirming information about gay people into all subject areas.

Rodney Wilson, a St. Louis high school teacher who was appalled at the failure of his 800-page textbook to mention *any* gay history, organized a grassroots network of teachers and community members across the country who began working to see October recognized as Gay, Lesbian, and Bisexual History Month. The National Education Association has given its endorsement, and activities are being planned in local communities across the nation.

◇ ADMINISTRATORS

The endorsement of people in key positions in the school district is very helpful. If they are willing to commit time and energy to the cause, their help will be invaluable. But even if they do not participate in the day-to-day work, their authority will add legitimacy to your effort.

In one California town there were several school district staff who were interested in starting a task force to establish gay student and family support services. They believed the Assistant Superintendent for Instruction would be sympathetic, so they approached her to be chair of the task force. The Assistant Superintendent was supportive but unable to make the time commitment. She suggested that she would "sign all the memos if the staff would do all the work." This arrangement has been successful and districtwide staff trainings are now being conducted.

At the very beginning, it can be wise to keep a low profile as you do the initial assessment, obtain basic support, and possibly build a little track record. However, once you start to undertake highly visible activities, everyone needs to be kept informed. Administrators, especially, don't like surprises. Keep them well informed of your activities and forewarned about any potential opposition.

Take the time to go through the proper channels, get the permissions required, and thank everyone who offers assistance. If you do need to go over someone's head to make progress, be sure you have tried hard to get their support first, and let them know of your intentions to move up the ladder.

TIPS FOR ADMINISTRATORS

◇ Administrators should have a firm policy of nondiscrimination at their school site.

◇ Harassment against gay, lesbian, bisexual, or questioning teachers or students should not be tolerated, whether it is between students, students and teachers, or among teachers themselves.

◇ Disclosing one's sexual orientation is a right that teachers and students have if they choose to exercise it. Administrators should respect this right and protect both staff and students from a hostile environment.

◇ Court cases have generally upheld the right of same-sex couples to attend school dances as long as their behavior is not

disruptive. The conventional wisdom is "don't make a big issue
of it."

◇ Discussing gay and lesbian issues in the classroom is not the same
as having a lesson on sex or reproduction. Clarify to teachers that
classroom discussion should not lapse into sexually explicit
information, unless that is the regular subject of the class.

◇ If a parent complaint should arise, ask them to put their
complaint in writing, specifically stating their objections and
the reasons for them. The administrator can then, calmly but
firmly, review the complaint in view of the suggestions mentioned above.

Adapted from *PROJECT 10 Handbook: Addressing Lesbian and Gay Issues in Our Schools* (Los
Angeles: Friends of PROJECT 10, 1989), p. 54.

◇ PARENTS

Parents are also very important within the school community and
should be invited to join any effort to make changes. Lesbian and
gay parents, as well as understanding heterosexual parents, can be
critically important in this struggle.

Parents of gay or lesbian youth who are being insulted or threatened should be encouraged to talk to the principal of their child's
school and to insist that their child's safety and right to a comfortable learning environment be protected. As one mother relates:

> I am so glad I finally went to school, but I wish I'd gone
> sooner. I had been thinking about how kids have to work
> things out themselves with their peers. But now I see that it's
> nothing like that. My daughter was being harassed—and
> that's against the law. The kids who were tormenting her
> weren't friends. There was no way she could work it out
> with them. And they toned it way down after the principal
> laid down the law.

If every parent whose child was harassed came to school and
protested, administrators would be much more aware of the scope
of the problem.

Supportive parents can become involved in the PTA or attend
school board meetings. Working individually with school board
members to provide information about the needs of gay youth can
be very worthwhile.

◇ ALLIES FROM OUTSIDE THE SCHOOLS

Allies from the general community are invaluable when you are building support for new programs and dealing with controversy. Since it takes time to build such connections, begin to work on this from the outset. Take your education campaign to local organizations such as liberal churches, human rights and antiviolence groups, and children's commissions. Talk to other minority groups, teachers unions, Planned Parenthood, NOW, PFLAG, ACLU, Amnesty International, groups of mental health counselors, public health professionals, and social workers. And enlist the help of your local gay and lesbian community center or group fighting for lesbian, gay, and bisexual civil rights.

Call on your allies to support the school program whenever it seems appropriate or needed. They can offer advice, write letters, make phone calls, attend meetings, or give testimony. Don't forget that if you want others to offer support for your issues, you must offer support for theirs as well. Working together to make the schools—and our communities—safe and welcoming for all people helps to create the kind of world we want for our children.

there are many possible points of entry

Project 10, the support program for gay, lesbian, and bisexual students in the public schools of Los Angeles, was conceived of primarily as a *school dropout prevention* program. In Massachusetts the State Department of Education is funding teacher trainings as part of the implementation of the *antidiscrimination* law protecting gay, lesbian, and bisexual students. Minnesota has developed school support systems as part of an *HIV/AIDS/STD prevention* effort, understanding that building self-esteem is as important as teaching the facts about the disease.

Substance abuse and suicide prevention can provide justification for locating a support project in the health and wellness or counseling departments. Project 10 East, in Cambridge, has found funding from federal *antiviolence* sources to help support the program coordinator. In schools committed to *teaching tolerance* and respect for differences, it is simply a logical extension to include gay issues. Wherever broad-based *diversity and human rights* issues are addressed, gay-related topics can be included.

Since all these aspects are truly part of the picture for bisexual, lesbian, and gay students, it doesn't matter where you begin. The important thing is to find an area where you already have some supportive connections and start working. Think about how other changes have been brought about in recent years and learn from those experiences. Some districts like pilot programs. Other school boards respond well to reports from advisory committees, where fair-minded professionals from the community have participated. Remember, no single strategy is guaranteed to work all the time. You need to analyze the situation, consider all the options, revise plans when necessary, and keep on keeping on.

dealing with opposition

Misinformed individuals and organized opposition can be counted on to protest programs that affirm gay, lesbian, and bisexual students. The controversy that they create can sometimes be very difficult and painful. The good news is that if they are making a fuss about your efforts, it means that you are having an impact. And you can prevail in the struggle.

Most people do not want youth to suffer. Keep the issue focused on helping *all* students to become good citizens, to stay healthy, and to have the tools they need to do well in the world. The issue is not whether being gay is right or wrong, and engaging in that debate is seldom useful. The fact is that there are gay, lesbian, and bisexual students in every school. In order to insure that they receive the same education as their peers, we need to end the abuse that they endure. As David LaFontaine says:

> It's a child welfare issue. We're talking about teenagers who could be anybody's kids, who could be anybody's students. You either support young people in the right to an education, the right to human dignity, or you're condoning, if not promoting, child abuse.

If you are dealing with organized opposition this is one time to call upon your allies. Meet with key people and your core group and anticipate the objections you'll be hearing. Develop answers that you can all agree on. Keep them very brief—we live in a sound-bite world.

It usually works best to appoint one spokesperson who is cool-headed, articulate, and can think well on her or his feet. But everyone who talks to those who oppose your efforts should resist getting hooked by personal attacks or sucked into heated arguments. Listen respectfully, respond with, "I understand what you're saying, but . . . ," and keep repeating your few main points.

Again, there is nothing more powerful than youth offering their own testimony about why there should be programs that address their needs.

Sometimes the media will become involved—they love controversy. If you are well prepared, interviews with the media will usually give you a chance to tell your side of the story. Virginia Uribe of PROJECT 10 notes:

> I happen to think if we're given our say we're going to come out on top because we're making sense and those other folks aren't making any sense. So I found the media to be a great asset. Lou Sheldon of the Traditional Values Coalition put PROJECT 10 on the map. It was just a teeny weenie program until the whole thing got attacked by the right wing.

How to Deal with the Opposition

◇ Be pleasant. Be firm. Stay focused. Don't get sidetracked.
◇ Offer information.
◇ Remind opponents that we are educators and that our responsibility is to serve *all* children.
◇ There are lesbian, bisexual, and gay students in every school.
◇ *All* children are deserving of dignity and respect.
◇ One mission of education is to teach children how to live peacefully in an increasingly diverse society.
◇ Personal beliefs *must* be separated from public policy.

Adapted from *PROJECT 10 Handbook: Addressing Lesbian and Gay Issues in Our Schools* (Los Angeles: Friends of PROJECT 10, 1989), p. 69.

◇ NOT ALL OPPOSITION IS OVERT

Dealing with a loud and vocal opposition that sometimes engages in disrespectful, or even hateful, behavior is certainly difficult. But it is a direct and open conflict, where you know what you're up against.

The passive resistance to change and the reluctance to provoke controversy that is present in almost every school system can be a more insidious challenge. There are some districts where most people are aware enough to avoid overt homophobic remarks and behavior. They may even give lip service to the concept that gay students deserve a safe and affirming educational environment, as do all students. However, when it comes to actually doing something, nothing happens.

Foot-dragging takes many forms. It can be as obvious as never making a plan for any concrete activities. Or it can be that a plan gets made—for example, a panel of gay speakers is invited to a Family Life class—but it is canceled for some convenient reason and never rescheduled. Maybe the committee planning Diversity Day has gay issues on the bottom of its agenda and always runs out of meeting time before that item is addressed. Or the library doesn't have enough money to buy the gay-friendly books on its list.

The way to deal with this invisible opposition is to be a vocal advocate all the time and to keep an educational campaign going to motivate your allies to be vocal advocates as well. Celebrate small successes, give yourselves lots of credit for your efforts, and keep each other informed about related developments all over the district—and the country.

the long haul

Ruth Ellen Luehr, who runs the Prevention and Risk Reduction program for the State of Minnesota Department of Education, describes the attributes that have made school advocates successful:

> They push and pull their faculty and administration along in gentle, nurturing, systematic, but deliberate ways. They don't let the issue die!

The effort to make schools a place where lesbian, bisexual, and gay students can learn instead of just struggle to survive is a long-term endeavor. This is not a sprint—it's a marathon. Homophobic attitudes have been around even longer than the concept of public education. It's going to take some time to turn things around. And even when gains are won, you'll have to keep working to maintain them. So hang in there, have faith, and keep working.

appendix

This appendix includes examples of staff trainings, nondiscrimination policies, and curriculum that can be used to raise awareness about gay, lesbian, and bisexual people. Feel free to use them as presented or adapt them to fit the needs of your particular school or subject area.

OUTLINE OF AN INTRODUCTORY ONE-DAY SCHOOL IN-SERVICE: "MEETING THE NEEDS OF LESBIAN, GAY, BISEXUAL, AND QUESTIONING STUDENTS"[1]

I. Group Exercise
Name and dispel common myths and stereotypes about lesbian, gay, and bisexual people.

II. Facilitator Presentation—Identifying the need[1]
A. There are lesbian, gay, and bisexual students in every classroom.
B. They are a population at risk for:
  1. suicide and isolation
  2. drug and alcohol abuse

[1]*FACTFILE: Lesbian, Gay and Bisexual Youth*, a one-page handout, cites statistics and sources, from the Hetrick-Martin Institute, 2 Astor Place, New York, NY 10003, (212) 674–2400.

3. family rejection and homelessness
4. HIV infection
5. harassment and physical abuse
6. dropping out of school

III. Panel Presentation[2]
A. Lesbian, gay, bisexual, and parent speakers make very brief (under five minutes) autobiographical statements about their own lives.
B. The audience asks questions and panelists answer based on their own experiences.

Lunch Break

IV. Group Discussion—Responses to the Panel Presentation

V. Video and Reactions
A. Show video *Who's Afraid of PROJECT 10.*[3]
B. Individual exercise—each participant spends two minutes writing reactions to the video.
C. Small group exchange—groups of three participants each take two minutes to express their responses to the video. (In order to create a safe environment for sharing, other group members are expected to listen respectfully *only,* not to react or discuss.)

VI. Small Group Brainstorm
Break into groups of four to six people and generate ideas about what can be done in our schools and classrooms, both immediate and long-range actions. Record the ideas.

VII. Group Reports
Each small group reports its ideas to the whole. Ideas are recorded by the facilitator or helper.

[2]Contact the nearest lesbian and gay community center or PFLAG for trained speakers. It is most effective if at least one of the speakers is a youth.

[3]Video available from Friends of PROJECT 10, Inc., 7850 Melrose Avenue, Los Angeles, CA 90046, (818)577–4553.

VIII. Closing

The facilitator passes around a workshop evaluation form and a sign-up list for those interested in meeting to discuss ways to implement the ideas generated by the group.

NOTE: The facilitator should have related materials available for participants to view or keep, including a list of local resources.

◇ ◇ ◇

A SAMPLE SCHOOL NONDISCRIMINATION POLICY

The St. Paul Public School District supports the diversity of students, staff, and parents that make up the stakeholders of our schools. The current [nondiscrimination] policies and practices of the district support this diversity, and any prejudicial behavior toward any minority or ethnic populations, including gays and lesbians, will not be tolerated.

◇ ◇ ◇

A SAMPLE HIGH SCHOOL CODE OF BEHAVIOR

Any kind of obscene, demeaning, abusive, or profane language, gestures, or acts (whether related to race, gender, sexual orientation, nationality, religion, ethnicity, language, physical appearance, or physical or mental capacity) are unacceptable. The penalties associated with this unacceptable behavior may include a warning for the first offense and suspension or expulsion for subsequent incidents. If appropriate there may be police/court involvement.

◇ ◇ ◇

CURRICULUM SAMPLE—GENERAL SENSITIZATION: A CONSCIOUSNESS-RAISING EXERCISE[4]

This lesson can be used to introduce gay and lesbian issues in the high school or college classroom. It's appropriate for social science

[4]Adapted from Dave Donahue and Meg Satterthwaite, *Breaking the Classroom Silence: A Curriculum about Lesbian and Gay Human Rights* (Lesson 1), Amnesty International, 53 W. Jackson, Room 1162, Chicago, IL 60604, (202)544–0200.

and health education classes. The exercise is designed to make students aware of what it's like to have their sexuality questioned as though there were something wrong with them. In the process, students are led to examine their assumptions about sexual orientation.

Ask students to read the following questionnaire and to take a few minutes to think about the questions and how they would respond. Most students will quickly realize that the survey casts commonly asked questions and concerns about homosexuality in a heterosexual context.

Also, as you begin the discussion phase, it's important to point out that the survey assumes that everyone answering the questions is heterosexual. Let students know that that is not likely to be the case in *any* classroom. But the questionnaire is still useful to help us all understand the environment in which we come to awareness of our orientation.

The following questions can be used afterward as a springboard for discussion:

◇ How did you feel while thinking about these questions? Why?
◇ What assumptions does the survey make about heterosexuality?
◇ In what ways are those similar to the assumptions that many people make about about gay, lesbian, or bisexual people?

sexual orientation questionnaire

1. What do you think caused your heterosexuality?
2. When and how did you first decide you were heterosexual?
3. Is it possible that your heterosexuality is just a phase that you might grow out of?
4. Is it possible that your heterosexuality stems from a neurotic fear of others of the same sex?
5. To whom have you disclosed your heterosexual tendencies? How did they react?
6. Why do heterosexuals feel compelled to seduce others into their lifestyle?
7. Why do heterosexuals insist on flaunting their heterosexuality? Why can't they just be what they are and keep it quiet?
8. Would you want your children to be heterosexual, knowing the problems they'd face?

9. Since almost all child molesters are heterosexual, do you consider it safe to expose your children to heterosexual teachers?
10. Even with all the societal support marriage receives, there is still a 50 percent divorce rate. Why are there so few stable relationships among heterosexuals?
11. Why do heterosexuals place so much emphasis on sex?

◇ ◇ ◇

CURRICULUM SAMPLE—LITERATURE[5]

Shake Hands
A poem by A. E. Housman

Shake hands, we shall never be friends, all's over;
I only vex you the more I try.
All's wrong that ever I've done or said,
And nought to help it in this dull head:
Shake hands, here's luck, good bye.

But if you come to a road where danger
Or guilt or anguish or shame's to share,
Be good to the lad that loves you true
And the soul that was born to die for you,
And whistle and I'll be there.

study questions

These study questions are appropriate for a high school or college class. They can serve as a study guide for students as they read the material, a preparatory guide for teachers planning lessons, a baseline of questions for classroom discussion, or a source for writing topics and exam questions.

[5]This lesson is one of many prepared by Arthur Lipkin, Harvard Gay and Lesbian School Issues Project, Harvard Graduate School of Education, 210 Longfellow Hall, Cambridge, MA 02138, (617)491-5301.

1. From the tone of such expressions as "shake hands," "friends," and "here's luck," what kind of relationship do you think Housman has had with the person to whom he addresses his poem?
2. What kind of response does Housman think he has been getting when he has tried to rescue the relationship?
3. In the first stanza find two examples of the poet's putting himself down.
4. Do the words "loves" and "die" in the second stanza influence you to change your first-stanza opinion of the relationship?
5. Why do you think Housman anticipates that his beloved will suffer guilt, anguish, or shame? Could it have anything to do with the breakup? Or with the nature of the relationship itself?
6. Why would Housman think his beloved was being good to him by sharing suffering in the future? Would that be a consolation to Housman?
7. How is line 9 both a prediction of possible future sacrifice and a description of current reality?
8. How does the last line affect the tone of the poem? Does it make Housman appear any less desperate?
9. Would the meaning of the poem change if you discovered it was written to another man?

suggestions for writing

1. Compare this poem to James Taylor's "You've Got a Friend" and "Every Breath You Take" by the Police.
2. Assume you are the beloved one who, after a year, is having a hard time. You have just received a letter from Housman asking how things are going. Write a letter in reply.

◇ ◇ ◇

CURRICULUM SAMPLE—MATHEMATICS: WORD PROBLEMS

This is an example of how gay and lesbian awareness can be integrated naturally into all subject areas:

The gay/straight alliance is planning to charter a bus to the Gay Pride Parade. The cost will be $900, and each member will share the cost equally. If the club had 15 more members, the cost per person would be $10 less. How many are in the club now? (Hint: Substitution will result in a single quadratic equation.)

Recently Tom and his boyfriend Steve spent their vacation in San Francisco, which is 540 miles from their home. Being a little reluctant to return home, they took 2 hours longer on their return trip and their average speed was 9 miles an hour slower than when they were going. What was their average rate of speed as they traveled from home to San Francisco?

spirituality

◇ ◇ ◇ ◇ ◇ ◇ ◇ ◇ ◇ ◇

◇   ◇   ◇   ◇   ◇   ◇   ◇   ◇   ◇   ◇   ◇

Joan Bobkoff © 1995

15
religious life

i found god in myself
and i loved her / i loved her fiercely

—Ntozake Shange

Religion is the place to which people often turn for comfort or strength in difficult times. But for many lesbian, gay, and bisexual youth, religious institutions have not been a source of support or nurturance. Instead they have been places of condemnation, rejection, and hatred. Ironically, religion, which should inspire feelings of love, acceptance, compassion, and community, has often been used to justify hostility toward gays and lesbians.

Gay, lesbian, and bisexual people have been told that they were immoral and that God despised them. They have been pressured to hide their genuine feelings. And they've been advised to pray to God to change them into heterosexuals. It has been a soul-wounding experience to be put in the wrenching position of feeling that they had to choose between their God, their spiritual connection, and their own integrity.

The terrible paradox is that this struggle is hardest for those for whom religion is the most important. The more people believe the teachings of their religion, the more they are attached to their religious community, the more painful their inner conflict can be.

Fortunately, although slowly, this is changing. In hopeful and exciting ways, gays, lesbians, bisexuals, and their straight allies are achieving positive changes within traditional institutions, as well as creating new faith communities in which the spiritual value of all people is affirmed and celebrated.

In their own hearts and minds, spirits and souls, many gay, lesbian, and bisexual youth are searching for—and finding—their own authentic spiritual connection. They are coming to their own understanding of God and affirming a spirituality that celebrates the value, dignity, and preciousness of all people.

the destructive impact of religious condemnation

Religious indoctrination has caused many young people to be plagued by fear, guilt, and self-hatred. Hyde describes this fear poignantly:

> I grew up Catholic, and I was so afraid I was going to hell. I didn't like the thought of being Catholic. I didn't like being gay. I remember being so afraid.

Daphne was also deeply troubled by the homophobia she had been taught:

> A lot of the reason I couldn't accept my feelings for Marsha was because of my Southern Baptist teachings. I knew that if I admitted these feelings I was sinning and I was going to burn in hell and I was a rotten person who had the devil in me. All my problems about being gay were in my religion.

And Rick still suffers from guilt:

> The other thing about Catholicism is the guilt factor. Everyone jokes about it, but it's true. I got really scared about going to hell when I was younger. My dad would give me those comic books that depicted gay people as in the Roman era with big huge earrings and lipstick and beards and long hair. They just looked really like vile creatures. They were dressed as women and chasing little boys. I was too young to identify as being gay, but that freaked me out—like God, I wouldn't even want to know somebody like that. That has to have an impact. Even now, a lot of times when I have sex I feel guilty afterward.

This kind of fear and guilt has caused many young people to suffer in terrible conflict and deep depression. As one young lesbian, who grew up Muslim, describes her experience:

> My mother caught my best friend and me kissing. She screamed. She kind of went crazy, yelling at me. But then she calmed down a little and told me Allah would forgive me if I never did anything again. So I've tried to fight the feelings, but I've been depressed a lot. I just feel like I'm dead inside.

Tragically, for some youth this agony has led to suicidal feelings—and, in alarming numbers, to suicide. One young man describes the pain he went through when he recognized his same-sex feelings of attraction:

> I literally tormented myself in adolescence and teenage years, tormented myself with prayer, agony, hoping that that would change, believing that it might. And then just pouring myself into activity as a good little boy in high school and church, an endless round of activity, seven days a week and seven evenings a week. Until finally I reached the point where I thought, this is not going to change . . . and I thought the easy thing to do for all concerned, the easiest thing, would be just to walk into the ocean and—and end it.[1]

[1] From a tape played at a PFLAG convention workshop, "Faith Communities at Work."

While some gay youth are tormented, others become angry about having to struggle to reconcile their deep feelings and their religious teachings. This anger can be a healthy defense against the condemnation of religion, as Ruth Eller, an Episcopal priest, affirms:

> It's OK to be angry. You can be angry at the church or your parents or God. It's OK to be angry as long as you express it and notice it for what it is and don't get yourself out of communication with the people who love you or with God.

praying to God to be straight

It is extremely frightening to think that because you are bisexual, gay, or lesbian you might be deprived of God's love and a place in heaven. Religious condemnation has been such a deep source of pain, many lesbian and gay youth have prayed to God to become heterosexual. Jonathan used to cry himself to sleep at night, begging God to change him:

> And I know I'm not the only one. I've talked to so many kids who have said that. The poor guy, He probably hears so many of those prayers, these kids crying for help.

All too often clergy and teachers have prayed right alongside gay youth. When Nancy came out to her Bible Study teacher, the teacher said, "We're going to pray and we'll study more and you have to just forget about it":

> It became a choice of my happiness or their happiness, and I want my happiness. And I guess I'll have to deal with my God and my beliefs. I can't be anywhere where they don't accept me.

Manny also prayed to be heterosexual:

> When I was little, I used to be very religious. I was all the time in the church and in the choir. I had little statues of saints. At the beginning of my struggle, I used to pray and say, "I want to be heterosexual." But that never happened. So that means that God doesn't want me to be straight.

Mickie believed there was something wrong with her:

> I used to kneel down in my room and pray to God to make those feelings go away. I used to cry and cry—make this go away or show me that it's not wrong.
>
> When Anna kissed me, that went away. Absolutely went away. I knew there's nothing wrong with me.

Mickie's prayers didn't stop then, but she began praying for something else:

> I had a crush on my best friend. I told her about it and she took me to church. One of the women put her hand over my head and was praying, trying to cure me. But I began praying for God to give me the strength to carry on with these feelings. I stopped asking Him to take them away. That night, I actually realized that I wanted them. I just wanted to have the strength to be able to make it through with everything that was going to come to me.

positive experiences with religion

In spite of the ways in which religion has been used against gay, lesbian, and bisexual people, some young people have been able to find strength and sustenance in their religious traditions. Jonathan has been able to draw on his basic faith in the presence of a loving God to sustain him:

> My mother is very active in the church, as well as my father. My grandfather is an elder of the church. I grew up in the type of family where you got up on Sunday morning and you knew you were going to church. You didn't ask. We went. Believe it or not, I'm so thankful for that. I drew on that to help me get through a lot of hard times.

For Sara, her heritage of pride in her religious and cultural identity has been supportive:

> I'm Jewish. So there is a cultural aspect there, a cultural stamina that historically goes against the grain. The greatest gift

I get from Judaism is that there's a pride, there's a history, there's a tradition, and there's this sense that this is who we are. We are Jewish. We are different. And there's a certain strength around that.

Quang has found that the teachings of Buddhism have been consistent with honest self-reflection:

Buddhism has been good for me because the spirituality is not as prescriptive and not condemning of any particular way of life. It's a process that you go through to try to understand yourself and to be yourself—just a process of thinking and developing and changing. It's not about "you can't do this" or "you can do this." I've gotten the benefit of spirituality without having to deal with some of the bigger conflicts or tensions that people have who want to find a spirituality or a faith within a religion that is more condemning of homosexuality.

If your religion helps you live in a meaningful and self-loving way, it is a blessing. Hold on to whatever nourishes you in the effort to become more of who you want to be.

How Youth Reconcile Sexual Orientation with Religion

I look at myself when I was younger and it amazes me because I used to be a fervent Catholic. I would go to the Catholic store every day. I would be so excited if they had a new Virgin Mary key chain. Whenever I prayed, I prayed to Mary. And whenever I got scared in bed, I'd sleep with my picture of Virgin Mary as opposed to a teddy bear.

But now I've lost my belief. I still believe in a higher power. I still believe people are always good at heart. I believe in an afterlife and all that, but the church I have no faith in. To me it's the biggest business in the world.

I believe God is a woman. And I don't think She cares about people being gay. It's basically, you live a good life. You try the best you can to help other people.

—Chris

I'm really religious, and when there's something that I really want—that seems almost impossible to get—I pray hard for it, and He will answer. That's why I believe in God. If God was so against my sexuality he wouldn't do half the things for me that He does.

—Anthony

At first I had to really think about it. And then I realized it's like being Black. Some people used the Bible to justify the idea that if you're Black you're automatically supposed to be a slave. If I don't believe that, why should I believe what people say about being gay?

I decided that God would love me for who I am because I was created that way. I don't need a church to tell me that, or anybody else. I'm not harming anybody. It's just another expression of love, so get over it. I couldn't find a reason to really hate myself for it, so I don't.

—Yevette

If God is love and God created me, then it must be fine to love whoever I am. I can't see God making anyone this way unless it was acceptable to Him. I don't go to church any more. I seldom read my Bible anymore. I know there's a God. I choose not to believe in a hell because it can't get any worse than this. Living in a homophobic society has got to be my hell.

—Daphne

I've just separated the institution from my relationship with God. And what's most important to me is my relationship with God. I just don't care what the church has to say about it.

—Joselin

In one of the first verses of the Torah in the book of Genesis, it says that humanity was created in the image of God. I think that each human being carries within a spark of divine life, in some sense resembles God, and that you should treat each human being with this in mind. I don't believe that God created in vain. I believe that I was created this way for a purpose. And I wouldn't change it for anything, because I believe that I'm part of the divine, part of creation, and God's partner in making this world a holy place.

—Michael

finding your place in a faith community

As a gay, lesbian, or bisexual person, you have the right to be treated with absolute equality within your church or temple. You should enjoy the same privileges and responsibilties as straight people.

Anni has been very active in Christ Lutheran Church. She's been in charge of the nursery and is a Sunday School teacher. She feels like the church is a second family:

> I was fearful that when they found out I was gay they would take away the children. I couldn't live without kids. I knew that my pastor would take it well. But I didn't know how the congregation would take it. Last week I came out to my pastor, and I'm happy to say I'm not going to hell. He said, "That's fine. And I think the church will take it positively. You'd be very surprised when push comes to shove how these people will act."

Anni has been able to stay involved in her church and continues to feel affirmed there. Yet not every congregation will be welcoming. How open or accepting your congregation will be is likely to vary greatly depending on your religion. Within the Quaker or Buddhist traditions, for example, where there is no doctrine condemning homosexuality, it will be somewhat easier to find an affirming faith community. On the other hand, in religions like Catholicism and Islam, where there are strong prohibitions against same-sex relationships, it is more difficult. In most religions, you'll find a wide spectrum of attitudes, depending on the congregation.

If your church is not supportive—if you are exposed to negative statements about gays and lesbians or if you feel forced to hide your real feelings—you may want to look for a faith community that is affirming. If you are still living with your parents and they object to you going to a different church, this can be difficult. But once you're independent, it's possible to find a spiritual home that's comfortable for you. As Hyde relates:

> I recently went to the local Unitarian Church. I walked in with my Catholic heebie-jeebies heaped on my shoulders.

But by the time we sat down, I was really comfortable. They didn't force the concept of God on you. And they were very gay-positive. It renewed my faith in Christianity.

It took Beth quite a lot of churches, but she kept trying until she found one that was right for her:

I was kicked out of a lot of churches because at Sunday School I would say, "If Jesus is the son of God, then we are all the sons and daughters of God and we are all good. My aunt is a lesbian and there is nothing wrong with her. God loves her." And I would get booted from one to the other. Finally I found Religious Science Church, and that's what I became comfortable in.

For people with a strong need to be part of a faith community, finding a welcoming church can be a powerful experience. Ruth Eller encourages gay youth to have confidence:

Be absolutely assured that you are made in the image of God and that God loves you. And somewhere in the world you will find a community of faith of other persons made in the image of God who will love you, who will be the love of God for you. You may not find it right away, because people are very confused about a whole lot of things and unfortunately one of the things they are confused about is sexuality. But you will find it. There is a home for you somewhere and a group of people who will love you and support you and help you in your spiritual growth.

Although religious institutions don't have a history of moving quickly or making change easily, change is clearly happening. It is a very personal choice whether to engage in the struggle to change churches and temples. There is always an inner cost in participating in an institution that, at best, is debating your right to be who you are. For some people, it is fundamentally unacceptable to be part of a religion or congregation that questions their full legitimacy. But for others, though they may at times feel frustrated and impatient, the changes that they are able to effect are satisfying.

VERY BRIEF RESPONSES WHEN YOU DON'T WANT
TO ENGAGE IN DEBATE

There are some situations where it's clear that no amount of discussion will influence someone to be more open-minded. In these cases, it's usually not a good use of your time and energy to become involved in debating religious issues. Instead, it's better to save your efforts for people who are open to real dialogue. Here are some ideas for closing down unproductive arguments:

If they say: Being gay is an insult to God.

You could say: Love is never an insult to God.

◇

If they say: Aren't you afraid you're going to fry in hell?

You could say: No. I believe in a God, or higher power, that gives blessings to my loving relationships.

◇

If they say: It says in the Bible that being gay is an abomination.

You could say: Thoughtful and intelligent people have been debating Bible interpretations for thousands of years. I respect your right to your interpretations, and I ask that you respect my right to interpret the Bible as I understand it.

groups that affirm gay, lesbian, and bisexual people

In most of the Christian denominations, there are liberal branches that are more accepting of gay, lesbian, and bisexual people. There are also congregations that have been established specifically to welcome and affirm people of all sexual orientations. The Universal Fellowship of Metropolitan Community Churches is an international denomination with over three hundred affiliated churches. Dignity is the largest national organization of gay, lesbian, and bisexual Catholics and their friends and families. Integrity is the organization of lesbian, gay, and bisexual Episcopalians. Both the Mormans and the Methodists have a group named Affirmation. There are also Lutherans Concerned, Evangelicals Concerned, and others.

In Judaism, the Reform movement has made the inclusion of all sexual orientations a policy, and in a number of major cities there are congregations with special outreach to lesbian, gay, and bisexual people. The Reconstructionist branch of Judaism is also accepting of gays and lesbians, and some rabbis within the Conservative movement have made positive progress. The Jewish Renewal movement holds the affirmation of all people as a basic tenet.

Because Buddhism emphasizes a way of being rather than prescribing a set of laws, Buddhist groups are generally accepting of gay, lesbian, and bisexual people. Buddhist teachings don't condemn sex between people of the same gender. They speak only of not misusing sexuality in any way that harms another. Gays and lesbians can be married, ordained as priests, and hold positions of influence within most Buddhist organizations. In many large cities, there are groups of gay, lesbian, and bisexual Buddhists who study, practice, and socialize together.

Unitarians and The Society of Friends, known as Quakers, have a tradition of welcoming people from diverse backgrounds. A number of Native American religions recognize a special and honored role for gay, lesbian, and bisexual people. And there are various other spiritual traditions from all over the world that hold less restrictive views of gender as well as more acceptance of gay, lesbian, and bisexual people.

For Better or For Worse © Lynn Johnston Prod., Inc. Reprinted with permission of UNIVERSAL PRESS SYNDICATE. All rights reserved.

METROPOLITAN COMMUNITY CHURCHES

The Universal Fellowship of Metropolitan Community Churches was created in 1968 to provide a church where gay men, lesbians—and "all other outcasts"—could be welcomed and affirmed.

From the beginning MCC has taken an active role in social action, working to change unjust laws that discriminate against lesbians and gay men, participating in the marches on Washington for equal rights, and providing ministry and counseling in prisons. It has also made a commitment to diversity and has worked for gender and racial equality. Lesbian and gay couples can receive communion together and can be married within the church.

Diverse Christian traditions are combined in MCC, and though it is essentially a Christian church, elements from other religions are sometimes incorporated.

THE ROLE OF RELIGION IN WORKING FOR SOCIAL JUSTICE

Some churches and temples are not only affirming of their gay, lesbian, and bisexual members but are taking an active role in fighting for equal rights for gay people. In many religions, there is a strong tradition of working for social justice.

In countries where there have been struggles for liberation against dictatorships, a radical wing of the Catholic Church has been at the forefront, supporting those seeking justice, even, at times, in defiance of the Vatican. Parish priests and nuns have taken great risks to work for freedom, sometimes literally giving their lives. And some religious leaders from the United States have joined them, taking part in sanctuary movements and other aspects of working for desperately needed social change.

Within Judaism, there is a strong commitment to *tikkun olam*, which means a healing or reparation of the world. This covenant has led Jews to fight in struggles for social justice over the centuries. The message of the Passover seder, about the Jews' escape from slavery, reminds Jewish people that because they know what oppression feels like, they are obligated to help others who are oppressed.

Increasingly, when the Holocaust is memorialized, the experiences of gays and lesbians are included in recognition of the fact that they too shared in that suffering. The cry "Never again," which insists that an atrocity like the Holocaust never be repeated, is understood by many to mean that such persecution must never again happen not only to Jews but to anyone.

The civil rights movement in this country cannot be separated from its religious foundations. The Reverend Dr. Martin Luther King, Jr., was a Baptist minister whose beliefs and power to inspire were deeply rooted in his spiritual heritage. After turning to Islam, Malcolm X became a crusader for social justice for his people. And freedom fighters like Rosa Parks and Fannie Lou Hamer were sustained and compelled by their faith.

More recently, the Reverend Jesse Jackson carried the banner and spoke at the 1987 and 1993 gay and lesbian marches on Washington. He and other religious activists for social justice in the African-American community, like Coretta Scott King and the Reverend Cecil Williams, have embraced the struggle for human rights for lesbian, gay, and bisexual people.

sex and religion

Dr. George Regas, an Episcopal rector, joked that people are given double messages about sex. They are told "Sex is good and beautiful, but let's not talk about it in church." Or "Sex is dirty. Save it for somebody you love."[2] With teaching like this, it's no wonder that many people, not just gays and lesbians, have mixed—and mixed-up—ideas about sex.

Until quite recently, mainstream religions have declared that sex outside of a heterosexual marriage is wrong. Because gays and lesbians have not been allowed to marry—and are not heterosexual—they have often felt intense pressure to hide their authentic sexual feelings. Yet this denial is destructive to our deepest capacities. Daniel Helminiak, a Roman Catholic priest and theologian, explains:

> To have to be afraid to feel sexual is to restrain that noblest of human possibilities, love. It is to short-circuit human spontaneity in a whole array of expressions—creativity, motivation, passion, commitment, heroic achievement. It is to be afraid of part of one's own deepest self.[3]

Each religious tradition has its own guidelines as to what is and isn't an acceptable expression of sexuality. But in sex, as in other areas of life, whether you are gay, lesbian, bisexual, or straight, the same standards apply. As Jonathan says:

> If I go out there, if I commit sins that are sins for those who are heterosexuals, they're sins for me. I don't feel that there's any difference. I don't think there's gay sins and I don't think there's heterosexual sins.

Most religious teachings emphasize love, respect, and commitment as a necessary basis for sexuality. Michael A. Latz, Program Director of the Hillel Foundation at Stanford Unviersity, explains:

> Because of my base in Judaism and the importance that Judaism places on family and relationships, I am very pro

[2]From his sermon "God, Sex, and Justice," delivered at All Saints Church, Pasadena, California, November 11, 1990.

[3]Daniel A. Helminiak, *What the Bible* Really *Says about Homosexuality* (San Francisco: Alamo Square Press, 1994), p. 18.

monogamous lifelong relationships. I think of the line from *Les Misérables*, "To love another person is to see the face of God." Not all of my sexual experiences are holy and God-like, but I do try and bring a sense of intimacy and trust and holiness to them, and respect for the other person's soul.

There's that excitement and that wonderful sexual energy when you meet someone for the first time and you go home with them that night and it's over and done with, and that in some sense is fulfilling on a primal level, but I don't believe that sustains one for a long time. It doesn't sustain me. And I think what most young men and women are really grappling for is something that's more enduring.

Discovering one's own authentic sexuality and spirituality can be part of the same journey. As Sara says:

As I become more comfortable with my sexuality I'm gaining the spiritual part. I think they're very connected for me. I first dealt with being bisexual politically, separate from my feelings. I'm very intellectual, and my mind is totally protective for me. That was safe. Now that I have that safety, I'm able to allow myself to be in a more essential place. It's a spiritual experience to be in touch with the essence of who I am—sexually, emotionally, intimately.

ADVICE FROM FATHER ED HOLTERHOFF

If you allow other people to dictate the direction of your life, you are in fact losing your soul. People give far too much attention to a possible destination in the future—about losing their soul then—and give very little thought, if any, to losing their soul in life. At some point many gay and lesbian people realize that they've listened to everyone else and thus have lost their own integrity. The hell they experience is here on earth, because hell is merely losing your soul.

◇

Feelings are feelings, and feelings are not bad. Feelings are signs, indices, that tell you about yourself, and you must take them as neutral information. You must listen to the information which is coming in. If you try to squelch that you do a tremendous disservice to yourself. If you have same-sex feelings, that is very important information, and you must listen to it.

◇

One's legitimacy cannot come from the outside, from an external source. Legitimacy must come from the inside. And you don't ask for legitimacy. You tell people you are legitimate, and they either recognize it or they don't.

Father Ed Holterhoff has been a Catholic priest for twenty-five years.

finding your own spiritual connection

Many young people look inward to find their own authentic spiritual connection. As Doe describes her experience:

> My journey with my own spirituality came after I totally abandoned Catholicism when I came out. I couldn't see how I could negotiate being Catholic and being queer. I didn't have a priest saying that it's OK, you can still be Catholic. It's like, OK, you're Catholic, you're gonna have to get rid of this homosexuality. And I'd rather get rid of the Catholic than get rid of the lesbian.
>
> That's where my personal journey to my spirituality began. That's when I started to pull different things from what I learned growing up, being Catholic. But it was more personalized. I was praying, but not necessarily to God anymore but just to the earth, or just to the sky, or just to whoever wanted to listen. It was a redefinition. I was creating my own.

Matt has found a philosophy that's meaningful to him:

> I need to be in a place where I'm going to be accepted for being gay and not told I'm an abomination or even told, "Yeah, that's what our book says, but don't worry about it." I can't do that. There are some people who can, who can say, "I just ignore that part," but I can't. So I left.

I've found Eastern philosophies welcoming. I've read a lot about Taoism. One of the things about Taoism is the idea to just be who you are. Just no pretenses, no pretending, just be who you are. I really liked that. My belief is that everyone, everything, is part of a universal spirit that runs through everything. Call it God, call it Tao, call it what you will.

Quang is, for the first time, examining his own religious tradition:

My grandmother, who I lived with most of my life, died just over two years ago. She lived her life in a way that was spiritually beautiful. She cared about people and shared with people in a way that I really admired. And when she passed away I felt a strong urge to look into the teachings of Buddhism and see how they applied to my life.

I've been in a process of learning and understanding and trying to look at my own desires and greed and things like that—examining more. I don't necessarily believe that I am Buddhist, but a lot of the teachings are things that I've come to respect and try to incorporate into my life.

Al Ferreira, a high school teacher, offers this advice:

I do a lot of reading centered on spirituality, but from all cultures. And I recognize there isn't any single truth. That's helped me a tremendous amount in my work today in talking with kids who face religious turmoil. The one thing you really should beware of in education or any situation in life is when any human being tells you that they have the truth. Run as fast as you can. No one has the truth. We only have perspectives on it.

Many people who don't belong to a church or follow the precepts of an established religion are enriched and guided by their ethical beliefs. As Jason relates:

I wasn't raised religious. In fact, my parents believed that organized religion was often a destructive force. But they taught us a very strong sense of what is right and wrong. What's right is what's fair and just and respectful toward all people, and what's wrong is what hurts people or takes advantage of them.

There are many ways that I'm different from my parents,
but I think they got it right about the basics.

In the midst of the AIDS epidemic, gay men and lesbians have
been at the forefront of extending care. Some have religious affilia-
tions, but many do not. Yet their actions are deeply connected to
the spirit. As Michael affirms:

> I've seen more profound acts of compassion and loving-
> kindness, of people acting God-like and caring for their
> loved ones, their sick and their dying. For all the faults that
> the gay community may have, the compassion we have
> shown, in not only taking care of our own but others with
> sick babies and drug addicts and hemophiliacs, and advocat-
> ing on their behalf, is a model for the world. I have a
> tremendous amount of pride for how we've responded to
> this epidemic. AIDS has certainly challenged my Jewish
> identity insofar as the responsibility of saving human lives,
> of compassion, of welcoming the stranger.

We all have guiding principles by which we try to live our lives.
Some people call this religion or spirituality. Others talk about it as
morality, ethical behavior, or social justice. Some call it philosophy.
And some don't talk about it at all. But these deeply held beliefs
concern what is most important or meaningful to us.

Although these principles may be elaborate, they may also be
very simple. The Dalai Lama summed it up in just one word when
he said, "My religion is kindness." In the Talmud it is written that
"The beginning and end of Torah is performing acts of loving-kind-
ness." And in the New Testament, Jesus explains that the two essential commandments, upon which everything else rests, are to love
God and to love your neighbor.

When we have the opportunity to hear from people who have
almost died, they all relate that at the point at which they were
dying, what they remembered, what they cared about, was the love
they had given and received. They rarely mention any other meaningful thing—not the satisfaction of a significant achievement, the
passion of some creative expression, nor even a moment of solitude
that was filled with peace. When all is said and done, it is love—
more than anything else—that counts.

At its essence, spirituality is life-affirming. It allows us to affirm
the richness of life and its preciousness. Some people experience

this most powerfully in church, but for others, sitting by a river, planting a garden, or singing fills them with spirit. As Renee describes it:

> I make my own religion as I go along, believing in the things that are important to me. Things that make me happy, like being out in nature. That's like a higher power for me because it takes me higher.

Each person's way is different. But whenever we are in awe of the magnificence and richness of creation, we are surely taking part in the spiritual.

Joan Bobkoff © 1995

16
the bible

There are more scriptural reasons to oppose homophobia than to oppose homosexuality.

—*Rev. Dr. Professor John B. Cobb, Jr.*

If you have felt conflict between your same-sex feelings and the teachings of the Bible—or if you want to know more about how religious teachers understand the Bible to be compatible with loving gay and lesbian relationships, this chapter will be useful to you. It will also arm you with specific information about what the Bible really does say, so that you can protect yourself from misinformed people who may try to use the Bible as a weapon against you.

However, if a discussion of what the Bible says about being gay is not meaningful to you, feel free to skip ahead. Not everyone is interested in debate about what individual passages mean. For many, the basic messages of love and kindness are what matter.

All too often the Bible has been used to justify the condemnation of people who are gay and lesbian. But those who believe it's wrong to be gay did not get their attitudes from the Bible. Instead, they have turned to the Bible to defend their homophobic attitudes.

"God's on our side"

It is dangerous territory to presume to know who or what God is for or against. Throughout history the name of God has been used to condone, and even incite, torture, murder, and war, and all too often the Bible has been used to uphold the most immoral and shameful institutions.

The Reverend Doug Ensminger, who has spent over twenty years as a Presbyterian minister and has founded the Community of Reconciling Churches, explains:

> During the period of slavery, people would find evidence in the Scriptures to support slavery and why it was God's will that white people should enslave Black people. People have used the Scripture to explain why women ought not to be the equals of men or be able to vote. By and large we've grown out of both of those abuses of Scripture. We still have people who are using Scripture—or abusing Scripture—to justify pre-existing attitudes in opposition to gay and lesbian people.[1]

The Right Reverend John Spong, Episcopal Bishop of Newark, explains that an absolutely literal reading of the Bible leads to a denial of reality and the persecution of people who attempt to enlighten us:

> Had I lived in an earlier part of history, I would have seen the Bible quoted to condemn Copernicus, who asserted that the sun did not occupy the center of the universe, and Galileo, who said that the sun did not rotate around the earth.[2]

[1] Steve Baker and Russell Byrd, *Always My Kid* (Houston: Triangle Video Productions, 1994).

[2] Daniel A. Helminiak, *What the Bible Really Says about Homosexuality* (San Francisco: Alamo Square Press, 1994), pp. 9-10.

No one continues to insist that the sun circles around the earth. And we no longer hear biblical justifications of slavery. Yet some people still claim that their judgment of gay, lesbian, and bisexual people is based on a literal reading of the Bible.

In truth, there is no such thing as a totally literal reading. Whenever we use language, we are always interpreting what we read and hear. When you look at the Bible, there are many words, statements, and teachings that make sense only when you understand something about the historical context in which these events took place. Daniel Helminiak gives an example from the Bible in which Jesus says, "It is easier for a camel to pass through the eye of a needle than for a rich person to enter the kingdom of God":

> It sounds as if nobody who had lots of money could ever get into heaven. . . . But in Jerusalem there was a very low and narrow gate through the city wall. When a caravan entered through that gate, the camels had to be unloaded, led through the gate crouching down, and then reloaded inside the city wall. That gate was called "the eye of the needle."
>
> So what was Jesus saying? Understand something about his everyday world, and his meaning is obvious. Jesus was simply saying that it would be hard for the rich to get to heaven. They might first have to unload their material concerns.[3]

what the bible says about homosexuality

In fact, the Bible says very little about homosexuality. Amidst the hundreds of thousands of other teachings, responsibilities, laws, and prohibitions, there are only a handful of statements that might possibly apply to sex between men—and none that address lesbian sexuality. The scarcity of references to homosexuality is so striking that comedian Lynn Lavner quipped:

> The Bible contains 6 admonishments to homosexuals and 362 admonishments to heterosexuals. That doesn't mean that God doesn't love heterosexuals. It's just that they need more supervision.

[3]Helminiak, p. 23.

Even when we look at these few passages carefully, we find no basis for condemning gay and lesbian relationships.

◇ THE OLD TESTAMENT

Sodom and Gomorrah

> The two angels came to Sodom in the evening; and Lot was sitting in the gateway of Sodom. When Lot saw them, he rose to meet them, and bowed down with his face to the ground. He said, "Please, my lords, turn aside to your servant's house and spend the night, and wash your feet; then you can rise early and go on your way." They said, "No; we will spend the night in the square." But he urged them strongly; so they turned aside to him and entered his house; and he made them a feast, and baked unleavened bread, and they ate. But before they lay down, the men of the city, the men of Sodom, both young and old, all the people to the last man, surrounded the house; and they called to Lot, "Where are the men who came to you tonight? Bring them out to us, so that we may know them." Lot went out of the door to the men, shut the door after him, and said, "I beg you, my brothers, do not act so wickedly. Look, I have two daughters who have not known a man; let me bring them out to you, and do to them as you please; only do nothing to these men, for they have come under the shelter of my roof." But they replied, "Stand back!" And they said, "This fellow came here as an alien [Lot was not originally from Sodom], and he would play the judge! Now we will deal worse with you than with them." Then they pressed hard against the man Lot, and came near the door to break it down. But the men inside reached out their hands and brought Lot into the house with them, and shut the door. And they struck with blindness the men who were at the door of the house, both small and great, so that they were unable to find the door.
>
> —Genesis 19:1–11

The story of Sodom and Gomorrah has been used to condemn gay men. In fact, it's the basis for the word "sodomy." Yet it has nothing to do with being gay. It is not about feelings of affection and attraction between men, nor does it have anything to do with consensual sex. The men of Sodom weren't interested in pursuing a sexual relationship with the strangers. They were threatening rape.

As feminism has taught us, rape is about power and violence, not about sex. As one survivor of sexual assault observed, "Sex and rape have as much in common as cooking and being hit over the head with a frying pan."

Don Sinclair, a minister in the United Methodist Church, explains:

> The tradition of Israel is that you must never allow a stranger to be in your midst and not be cared for. It's called inhospitality. When the prophets refer to the sins of Sodom and Gomorrah, they talk about things like greed. They talk about having wealth and not sharing it with those in need. They talk about the oppression of the poor within the cities. They never once mention anything sexual.[4]

Peter Gomes, an American Baptist minister and Professor of Christian Morals at Harvard, sums it up well when he says:

> To suggest that Sodom and Gomorrah is about homosexual sex is an analysis of about as much worth as suggesting that the story of Jonah and the whale is a treatise on fishing.[5]

And then there is Lot's willingness to offer his virgin daughters to be raped. At the time, women were considered merely property and guests were objects of moral obligation. Surely this alone should give us a clue that a literal reading of this story is not going to provide sufficient guidance for moral behavior today.

Leviticus

> You shall not lie with a male as with a woman; it is an abomination.
>
> —Leviticus 18:22

[4] Baker and Byrd.

[5] Peter J. Gomes, op-ed, *New York Times*, Aug. 17, 1992.

If a man lies with a male as with a woman, both of them have committed an abomination; they shall be put to death, their blood is upon them.

—Leviticus 20:13

The many prohibitions of Leviticus were a means of preserving the integrity of Jewish identity. They were a way to keep the Jewish people separate, to differentiate them from the gentiles and to keep their religious and cultural identity intact.

Also, in Biblical times it was imperative that the Jewish people produce babies in order to keep the population strong. Today just the opposite situation exists. In a world faced with serious problems of overpopulation, the historical imperative to keep increasing our numbers no longer exists.

The word "abomination" is very strong, but it is interpreted to mean unclean, a violation of the purity laws that kept the Jews separate from the cultures surrounding them. Things that were prohibited in these laws were not necessarily bad in themselves, but following these rules was a way to fulfill one's pledge to God.

As the Reverend Doug Ensminger explains, the Levitical code says:

> . . . that a woman is unclean during her menstrual period, that you're prohibited from eating shellfish, that you're prohibited from eating meat that still has the blood in it—in other words a medium rare steak would be out—that you're prohibited from wearing clothing that combines two different kinds of stuff, such as a cotton-wool blend. Most of the things that are dealt with in the holiness code are issues that we have come to recognize don't apply.[6]

And Dave, the father of a lesbian daughter, points out:

> I came to understand that an awful lot of things in the Bible were peculiar to the time it was written. Like Leviticus 11:7–8 that says, "The swine is unclean to you . . . and their carcasses you shall not touch," meaning you can't touch the skin of a dead pig. Well, that pretty well does away with the Superbowl.

[6] Baker and Byrd.

◇ THE NEW TESTAMENT

Jesus's teachings were extremely simple and very revolutionary. He taught that you could be a good person without following all the rules. Extensive laws, purity codes, rituals, and other religious requirements were not essential to purity of heart. Even time-honored practices such as circumcision and dietary laws were not what counted. Instead, Jesus taught that what really matters is being loving, kind, compassionate, generous, honest, and nonjudgmental.

Brooks Anderson, a minister in the Evangelican Lutheran Church and father to a gay son, points out:

> Jesus didn't say one word—not one word—about homosexuality. He did, however, have a great deal to say about love, compassion, and not judging others.

Romans, 1 Corinthians, and 1 Timothy

The Bible was first passed down through an oral tradition. Then, over a period of two thousand years, it was written down by many, many people, ending about two hundred years after the death of Christ. These documents were written in several languages, including Hebrew, Greek, and Aramaic. How the original language is then translated into English very much affects our understanding of some passages.

There are passages in Romans, 1 Corinthians, and 1 Timothy that have been used to condemn homosexuality, but many scholars refute such interpretations based on the difficulty of knowing exactly what the words in question were intended to mean. In fact, these passages have been interpreted in extremely different ways in various times and social climates.

For example, in the original Greek, there are words that are sometimes translated as "natural" or "unnatural." But these words do not imply moral rightness or wrongness. Instead, "unnatural" is likely to have meant something that was not common or customary. Likewise, the Greek word that is sometimes translated as "degrading" referred to things that were considered disreputable or socially unacceptable. For example, Paul uses the Greek word for "degrading" in describing himself and the disapproval he has experienced because of his commitment to Christ![7]

[7]Helminiak, p. 71.

Since there is such significant debate about how to translate the key words in these passages, it does not make sense to use them as a basis for judging gay people or same-sex love.

the tree of life

Although the Bible has been used to back up many unworthy causes, it has also been used to sustain and inspire great social progress. As Peter Gomes writes:

> The same Bible that the advocates of slavery used to protect their wicked self-interests is the Bible that inspired slaves to revolt and their liberators to action. . . . The same Bible that antifeminists use to keep women silent in the churches is the Bible that preaches liberation to captives and says that in Christ there is neither male nor female, slave nor free.
>
> And the same Bible that on the basis of an archaic social code of ancient Israel and a tortured reading of Paul is used to condemn all homosexuals and homosexual behavior includes metaphors of redemption, renewal, inclusion and love—principles that invite homosexuals to accept their freedom and responsibility in Christ and demands that their fellow Christians accept them as well.[8]

The Jewish concept of the Bible is that it's a living book with great opportunities for new interpretation, new teachings, and new understandings. Paula Marcus, cantor in the Reform movement, explains:

> It's a living book, *eytz chayim*, the tree of life. Now why would it be called the tree of life if it was supposed to be looked at one way and that way was already decided thousands of years ago? It wouldn't be living. It would be dead.
>
> Why do we read it over and over again? Wouldn't it be boring if we just read it the same way each time? Within our tradition we have a basis of communication. The rabbis argue over the generations, not only over space, but also time. There is no one interpretation.

[8]Op-ed, *New York Times*, Aug. 17, 1992.

same-sex love in the bible

Although we hear a great deal from homophobic people about how the Bible condemns gay relationships, we hear very little about the positive representations of same-sex love. The story of Jonathan and David is rich in the language of love. We are told that "The soul of Jonathan was knit with the soul of David, and Jonathan loved him as his own soul"(1 Samuel 18:1) and "Then said Jonathan unto David, Whatsoever thy soul desireth, I will even do it for thee" (1 Samuel 20:4). Later, "They kissed one another, and wept one with another" (1 Samuel 20:41). And after Jonathan's death, David said, "My brother Jonathan: very pleasant hast thou been unto me: thy love to me was wonderful, passing the love of women" (2 Samuel 1:26).

It is not possible to know for certain whether this relationship included a sexual expression of love, but it certainly demonstrates the kind of tenderness that we associate with intimate relationships.

Though the context is not a romantic one, Ruth's declaration to her mother-in-law, Naomi, is one of the most stirring expressions of devotion:

> Intreat me not to leave thee, or to return from following after thee: for whither thou goest, I will go, and whither thou lodgest, I will lodge; thy people shall be my people, and thy God my God. Where thou diest, will I die—and there will I be buried; the Lord do so to me, and more also, if aught but death part thee and me.
>
> —Ruth 1:16–17

Ironically, these words spoken by one woman to another express our ideal of love and commitment so beautifully that they are commonly included in heterosexual marriage ceremonies.

Joan Bobkoff © 1995

17
making changes in churches and temples

For Clergy and Congregations

The question is not one of acceptance, but one of forgiveness. It is not whether you will accept us, but whether we will find it in our hearts to forgive you.

—*James Baldwin*

James Baldwin (1924–1987) was one of the most influential African-American writers during the era of civil rights activism in the 1950s and 1960s. Among his best-known works are an autobiographical novel, *Go Tell It on the Mountain*, an essay collection, *The Fire Next Time,* and a 1956 novel about gay love, *Giovanni's Room.*

> This chapter is addressed to clergy and congregations who want to make their churches and temples welcoming and affirming places for all young people, including gay youth. As a gay, lesbian, or bisexual young person, you may want to read it to learn more about how churches and temples are changing—and the support that should be available to you. You may also want to give it to your religious leader or to open-minded adults in your congregation.
>
> Since the process of making changes is similar, regardless of the institution, the information in Chapter 14, "Strategies for Building a Support Program," and Chapter 19, "Creating Supportive Community Groups," will also be relevant.

For all of you who want to make your place of worship a safe, accepting, and welcoming home for lesbian, bisexual, and gay youth, the good news is that it can happen—it's being done. Your participation in that effort is enormously meaningful. Every step is important and helps to build a foundation for fundamental changes in attitudes and beliefs.

Becoming an affirming church takes the united efforts of both congregation and clergy. As a member of the congregation, you can make the initial push for change. You may be the parent of a gay man or lesbian, you might be a sibling, aunt, or uncle, or you may be gay, lesbian, or bisexual yourself. Change can begin with just one or two people. A handful of people for whom this issue is important can catalyze a significant transformation in a large congregation.

If you are a religious leader you play a key role in initiating change. Your influence as spiritual guide is extremely important in affirming gay and lesbian people and in setting the tone for a process of change that is respectful to all. Your attitude will be a model for the entire congregation. If you are clear about the need for positive change, the congregation will be more likely to agree. And if you are confident and reassuring that these changes, though they may be unsettling at first, will eventually be for the good of all, the congregation is more likely to see it that way as well.

where is your congregation now?

Most gay and lesbian youth are not open about their sexual orientation in their communities of faith. Generally, the way they know whether they will be rejected or affirmed is by observing the way their church treats adult gays and lesbians.

Avi Rose, who co-edited *Twice Blessed: On Being Lesbian and Gay and Jewish,* speaks about four stages—acknowledgment, tolerance, inclusion, and affirmation—that congregations go through in accepting and ultimately welcoming gays and lesbians. Although he is referring to Jewish congregations, these stages are replicated in all reconciling congregations.

> It wasn't that long ago that most of the community was dealing with the basic issues of acknowledging our existence, admitting that yes, there are Jews who are lesbian, gay, or bisexual (although, of course, always in someone else's family or congregation). Most of the Jewish community has moved past that initial stage of acknowledgment, though some have done so with reluctance or disapproval. It has been firmly established that we're here.
>
> Beyond that basic acknowledgment of existence, most of the community has moved along to tolerance. Tolerance is characterized by the notion that we shouldn't be overtly discriminated against, that we should be left alone. That's a lot better than overt persecution, but being left alone is exactly that—you are essentially on your own to be as isolated, excluded, and invisible as possible. Tolerance stops some of the overt oppression, but it does not build community.
>
> Beyond tolerance is inclusion, encouraging us to be visible, acknowledging our relationships and families, valuing us as participants and leaders and role models, which is all wonderful. But I've found that many of our institutions still operate, often subtly and seldom intentionally, in a way that falls short of full inclusion and doesn't go as far as full affirmation. There's often a message that "you" are welcome here as long as you fit in with "us." Don't challenge us too much, don't try to change too many things, don't expect the overall culture of our institution to shift.
>
> To look beyond inclusion to full affirmation is to envision something that is just beginning to come into being in our community. It is a place where "us" truly becomes all of us. It is a congregation where there are no reservations about joyfully celebrating ceremonies of same-sex love and commit-

ment. It is a community where the diversity of our families is truly valued and seen as a sign of the vitality of Jewish family life rather than a sign of its demise or as problematic in any way. It is a congregation where liturgical language and imagery reflects lesbian and gay sensibilities. It is a community where publicly affectionate same-sex couples are so much the norm that it's barely noticeable. And it is a congregation where young people grow up knowing that heterosexuality is not assumed for them and where they fully trust that they will be supported by parents, teachers, rabbis, and others as they grow to know their individual sexual orientation.

Clearly, most of our congregations have a long way to go, but just as clearly, we are headed in the right direction.

change is needed

Our religious institutions must change—because our children's well-being, and even their lives, are at stake. As one Muslim mother, whose son is gay, explains:

> Our religions *must* transform themselves. They've become instruments of torture. My son is suffering. And I'm suffering. I'm torn apart. And it doesn't have to be this way.
>
> As a feminist, I see it so clearly. Patriarchy has created a system where people dominate each other. And that's exactly opposite to the essence of Islam. Yet patriarchy has corrupted Islam, just as it has all the other religions. And it's hurting us. It hurts me as a woman. It hurts my son as a gay man. It's tragically ironic, because at the heart of Islam is an insistence on equality, a search for justice.

Brooks Anderson, a minister in the Evangelican Lutheran Church, speaks out passionately about why churches must address the needs of gay and lesbian youth:

> Youth is the issue. This is not an abstraction. We're talking about my son. We're talking about the sons and daughters of our congregations that we don't even know. And we are wounding them by our silence.

My son's story is a story I've heard a hundred times over. Of learning this ugly thing called "fag" and learning it's something evil, when he's twelve. And then, when he's thirteen, somebody calls him fag, and when he's fifteen—my God, I'm one of them. I'm a worthless piece of shit. And I can't get rid of this, and I could just as well end my life.

We've got to do something differently. Let's reach across some of these barriers and find the things we agree on.

ADVICE FROM MICHAEL A. LATZ

The more support that young people have from their religious communities, the more we will see the rate of teen suicide drop, the more we will see the rate of HIV infection drop. Because I believe that young adults who have support from their communities are less likely to engage in behavior both physically and emotionally that endangers their lives.

And I mean substantive support. I mean the minister or rabbi saying, "I condemn any interpretation of Leviticus that is used to judge homosexuals and I welcome you into my congregation." I mean having a PFLAG chapter at your synagogue or your church.

I say to those leaders who are afraid of taking risks, to stop for a second and really assess the reality of your risk. Is the risk worth saving a human life? Is the risk worth knowing that a child will not attempt suicide? Is the risk worth knowing you can prevent somebody from becoming HIV-positive? Assess it in realistic terms.

I think there are a lot of rabbis, ministers, priests, and educators who feel like they don't know enough. Most of the time if people come to you, they're not necessarily wanting answers, they're wanting to know that they'll be listened to. They're wanting a hug. They're wanting to know that you're there for them and that you'll help them find the resources. But they won't know it unless you tell them. Unless you state explicitly that you're here for them in a nonjudgmental way, they won't know it.

Michael A. Latz, a twenty-four-year-old gay man, is the Program Director of the Hillel Foundation at Stanford University. He will be attending rabbinic school at the Hebrew Union College–Jewish Institute of Religion in Jerusalem.

how to affirm gay and lesbian people in your congregation

◇ INCLUDE POSITIVE EDUCATION FOR YOUTH

It's important to include positive education about gays and lesbians in religious instruction. For heterosexual youth, this is a good opportunity to learn respect for all people. For young people who know themselves to have same-sex attractions or who are questioning their sexual orientation, such forums will provide reassurance that whatever their sexual orientation, they will be accepted.

Whether they are visible or not, there are gay youth—or young people with gay family members—in your classes. They need to hear affirming messages, not just about sexuality but validating everyone's basic dignity. Rabbi Rick Litvak invited gay and lesbian speakers to the confirmation class he teaches for ninth and tenth graders:

> The class is about love, sex, and marriage, a Jewish view. I think this is really important because we want to reverse prejudice that's in the culture, not to ignore the prejudice but to reverse it as part of religious education.

With young children, positive education can be presented by affirming different kinds of families rather than talking about sexuality.

◇ MAKE YOUTH GROUPS SAFE

Youth groups should be safe places. Make it clear that slurs against people with same-sex orientation will not be tolerated.

The Lutheran Youth Ministries passed a resolution declaring that all Lutheran youth groups were to be safe places for lesbian, gay, and bisexual young people. Find out if your denomination has such a policy. If so, publicize that in your congregation. If not, work toward the endorsement of this kind of statement.

◇ PLAN AN EDUCATIONAL FORUM

Invite speakers to share their personal experience and to educate the congregation. One father of a gay son relates:

> We put on a forum that drew a fabulous turnout of gays and
> lesbians and other members of the congregation. We had a
> full house and nobody left before eleven o'clock at night.
> That says something.

Such presentations serve two functions—they provide education
for the congregation at large and concrete support for gay, lesbian,
and bisexual members.

◇ UTILIZE STUDY GROUPS

Most denominations have enlisted members of their clergy and congregation to study the issues involved in including gays and lesbians
in the church. After much reading and discussion, these groups
have—almost universally—come to the conclusion that gays and lesbians deserve full equality and that the moral and just course of
action is to make changes in their religious institution to reflect and
encourage that. However, the findings of such groups have often
been rejected or ignored—because of homophobia. If your denomination has had such a study group, encourage your congregation to
read its findings and incorporate that wisdom into its policies and
procedures. If not, organize such a group.

◇ FORM GROUPS FOR SUPPORT AND ADVOCACY

Begin a group for gay and lesbian members of the congregation and
their allies to work toward increased understanding and positive
changes. Start a group for parents of gay, lesbian, and bisexual
youth. Paula Marcus, cantor at Temple Beth El and sister to a gay
man, was instrumental in getting a group started:

> We put up a flyer in the lobby that announced the group. It
> was a small thing to put that on the bulletin board. We didn't
> need any permission to do it. So now when someone comes
> in, there is something that shows outwardly, OK, there's
> somebody like us here.

In addition to support, such groups can provide opportunities to
be visible, contributing members of the community. Ken Plate, who
began the Gay Guild at Calvary Episcopal Church, relates:

We started an annual rummage sale. Last year we raised two thousand dollars. This year the money will go to the child care center that the church runs.

KEN PLATE'S STORY: THE GAY GUILD, CHANGING MINDS AT CALVARY EPISCOPAL CHURCH

The main reason we founded the Gay Guild was not for us. We founded it for the rest of the parish. It's our gift to them.

We did it because of young people. When teenagers are wondering about sexual orientation, they don't hear anything about it in their faith community. Also, we have some young people in our parish who have talked about gays and lesbians in disrespectful and terrible ways. So we wanted to provide positive role models. We wanted those young people—and their parents—to know that we were gay.

When the Gay Pride Parade was held, the Gay Guild made a banner to hang on the church saying, "Calvary Episcopal Church Salutes Gay Pride." Now 98 percent of our people had no problem with that, but it so happened that the parade was held on the day of a funeral, and they called in a retired clergy person to conduct the service. He saw the banner and told us to take it down. He gave the usual reasons of, "Why do you have to flaunt it?" and "Did it come before the governing board?"

Well, we had quite an argument, and finally we did take it down. We had not specifically cleared it with the rector, who has been very supportive of us, and we didn't want to get him into a whole lot of trouble.

When the rector heard about it, he said, "I wish you hadn't taken it down, but I understand why you did." And he called together this clergy person and a couple of others who were offended and the very next day we had a session together in his office.

He asked my partner and me to talk about what the church had done to us, what it meant to us, and how all of this happened, why we were active in the church today. My partner began speaking, and he was so eloquent. I started to tear up when he was telling about his Roman Catholic upbringing, how he hid his sexuality behind going into a monastery. And then he got married to hide it. He went into the military to hide it. At forty years old, he finally

said, OK, I am who I am. He told about how he felt so good at
Calvary Church and how it was so welcoming and affirming to him.
And then to have an incident like this happen, how that brought up
so much pain.

Well, by the time we were done those who were opposed to us
were weeping, some audibly. The rector led us in a prayer for
tolerance and understanding and love, and we all ended up
embracing at the end.

◇ AVOID THE ASSUMPTION OF HETEROSEXUALITY

Update paperwork, such as application forms and position papers,
to eliminate the assumption of heterosexuality. Substitute a word
such as "partner" for "husband" or "wife." Substitute "parents" for
"mother and father." If there are family membership rates, make it
clear that "family" includes gay and lesbian families.

◇ USE INCLUSIVE LANGUAGE

Use language in which everyone can find themselves reflected. This
is an issue that has become important to many women, as well as to
gays and lesbians. Increasingly, religious leaders are adapting the
language of prayers, sermons, and instruction to include the female
gender.

Although basic changes in the liturgy can be hard to get used to,
congregations can use their creativity to experiment with different
plans. Last year one progressive Jewish group debated about including the feminine form of God in the prayers for Rosh Hashanah and
Yom Kippur. Some people felt that it was essential to include the
feminine, Shekhina, while others were reluctant to lose the reso-
nance of the traditional, familiar language. In coming to a resolution
they employed a principle that can be applied to advantage in many
situations: when faced with a choice between A or B, choose A *and*
B. They included each prayer twice, first with the feminine, then
with the masculine language.

◇ PROVIDE AFFIRMING BOOKS AND PAMPHLETS

Buy books for your church library that affirm gay and lesbian people, as well as books that reconcile religious teachings with gay and

lesbian sexual orientation. In addition, you can create your own literature.

◇ SEEK OUT AFFIRMING IMAGES

Display artwork or other imagery that makes a positive statement about gay and lesbian people. Or sponsor an art show that includes work by lesbian, gay, and bisexual artists. The artists may be members of your own community, or you could include reproductions of work by great gay artists such as Michelangelo.

> **Michelangelo Buonarotti** (1475–1564) is one of the most famous artists and perhaps the greatest artist of Western civilization. In his sculpture of *David* and fresco of the *Creation of Adam* in the Sistine Chapel, as well as in many other works, he reveals his vision of the beauty of the human male.

◇ CREATE GAY-FRIENDLY EVENTS

Have a potluck dinner for gays, lesbians, and their friends. Publicize it in the church newsletter and announce it at services. You can also publicize it in the community at large—you may attract new members to your congregation.

Holidays provide good opportunities to socialize, as Laura Giges, a lesbian member of a congregation, relates:

> The next event was a Chanukah party. It was to continue the idea of letting community members know we were doing this outreach, and also it felt like a time of the year that a lot of gay and lesbian Jews feel particularly alienated—for being Jewish and for being gay and lesbian. So it was an important time to bring people together. We had almost a hundred people. It was a surprise. It was the only Jewish event I've ever been to where there wasn't enough food.

◇ SPONSOR A SINGLES EVENT

A brunch, a dance, or an afternoon hike gives gay and lesbian singles an opportunity to meet others of their faith in a wholesome, positive environment. Here again, you may publicize this event in the community.

◇ PREACH A SERMON

Preaching a sermon that affirms gay and lesbian people may feel daunting at first—particularly if you are someone who doesn't like to make waves. As in all challenging endeavors, it can help to break the effort down into manageable steps. To begin with, you could include gay and lesbian people in more general discussions of tolerance, respect, and an appreciation of diversity. You could also mention gay people in sermons on other topics where there is a natural connection, such as honesty, authenticity, relationships, being a parent, or family life.

If you feel ready to devote an entire sermon to an affirmation of gay people, it can be a general statement of acceptance and inclusion or it can be linked to an event in the news—such as the legal efforts to establish same-sex marriages or the rising numbers of hate crimes.

◇ ACKNOWLEDGE SAME-SEX COUPLES

Acknowledge the relationships between gay and lesbian couples in the same ways straight couples are acknowledged. Anniversaries could be noted in the church newsletter. Couples could light candles at services or stand together at events that celebrate their children, such as christenings, confirmations, or bar and bat mitzvahs.

◇ BLESS SAME-SEX UNIONS

There is no way to truly affirm lesbian and gay people without acknowledging and blessing unions between loving couples. It is another painful irony that gays and lesbians are criticized for their sexual behavior and yet are denied legitimacy for their committed relationships. Gay and lesbian youth need to see models of healthy, loving relationships and to know that this is possible for them.

Loving, faithful relationships are what all religions encourage us to strive for. Priests, ministers, and rabbis bestow upon heterosexual couples the blessings of God, instructing them to treat each other with respect and tenderness. They encourage these couples to care for each other during hard times, and they wish them the joy of good times. There is no legitimate rationale for denying spiritual and community recognition to same-sex couples. Yet there has been reluctance on the part of many religious leaders to extend their blessings to the unions of gay and lesbian people. Avi Rose powerfully expresses the pain and injustice of this:

As a gay man in the midst of this long and relentless epidemic, I, and my friends, have felt that it's very ironic and painful and angering to be in a situation where people are willing to bury us but not to marry us. Especially because so many of us know, in the most profound way, what a commitment to "in sickness or in health" really means.

Although many religious leaders do not sanction same-sex unions, an increasing number of ethical ministers, rabbis, and priests have recognized the responsibility of religious institutions to provide the same kind of blessings on gay and lesbian couples that are available to heteroseuxal couples.

Bishop John Spong has been outspoken in urging the Episcopal Church to support same-sex unions:

I regard the blessing of gay or lesbian couples by the church to be inevitable, right, and a positive good. We must be willing to relinquish prejudice and turn our attention to loving our gay and lesbian brothers and sisters, supporting them, and relating to them as a part of God's good creation. That will inevitably include accepting, affirming, and blessing those gay and lesbian relationships that, like all holy relationships, produce the fruits of the spirit—love, joy, peace, patience, and self-sacrifice. This is a step the church must take *for the church's sake,* to be cleansed from our sin of complicity in their oppression.[4]

Bishop Olson of the Lutheran Church observes:

Religious leaders are asked to invoke God's blessings on farms, homes, cemetaries, and people's pets. Prayers are offered at football games, conventions, and public gatherings of all types. What is so strange then about blessing the covenant of fidelity of two committed and loving persons who are gay or lesbian?[5]

[4] Parents, Families, and Friends of Lesbians and Gays, *Is Homosexuality a Sin?* (Washington, D.C.: PFLAG, 1992), p. 16.

[5] PFLAG, pp.16-17.

"GOD, SEX, AND JUSTICE"

From a sermon by Dr.George F. Regas, Rector, All Saints Church, Pasadena, California, 1990

This morning I want to engage you on a difficult issue. Among many ethicists whom I respect there is the growing conviction that human sexuality is the test case for communities of faith in our time. These complex issues of sexuality are placed forcefully on the Church's agenda: full equality and justice for women, abortion rights, sexual love outside of marriage, and the most controversial of them all, homosexuality. William S. Coffin, formerly the senior minister of Riverside Church in New York City and a leading prophetic voice in American churches, says the issue of homosexuality is probably the most divisive issue since slavery split the church.

The mandate of Amos and the prophets, and the imperative of Jesus and the Church to seek social justice will not allow us to forget the fact that discrimination and oppression continue against millions of gay and lesbian people in the structures of society, as well as within the Church. We must address that injustice. . . .

The really serious problem for the people of the Book is not how to square homosexuality with certain Biblical passages . . . but rather how to reconcile rejection, prejudice, hostility, and punishment of homosexuality with the unconditional love of Christ. . . .

At the core of the Christian faith is the simple and profound assertion: God loves you just as you are. This radical acceptance is of the total person—body, mind and spirit. Our body's feelings, our body's erogenous dimensions, our fantasies, our masculinity and femininity, our heterosexuality, our homosexuality, our sexual irresponsibilities as well as our yearnings for sexual integrity—all of this is graciously accepted by divine love.

That is the wonder and glory of the Christian faith. When we know God loves us just as we are and we put our arms around ourselves in acceptance and self-love, there is released in us enormous spiritual power—power to grow into wholeness, into that beautiful person God has created us to be.

After much study, reflection and struggle, I have come to believe that the ethical standards for sexual practice are the same for homosexuals as for heterosexuals. The core issue for sexual ethics is not the assessment of certain types of physical acts as right or wrong, normal or abnormal. The core issue is not whether genital love is within or outside of heterosexual marriage. The pivotal issue is the integrity of the relationship. This is true for us all. . . .

The ethic is authentic love for all of us. What is a good sexual act? It is honest and real—clearly conveying what the relationship really means, what its deepest meaning is. It is other-enriching, respecting the other person, never exploiting. It is faithful— "tonight's pleasures are not tomorrow's pain." It reveals a commitment, a trust, a tenderness for the other person. It is willing to take responsibility for sexual love's consequences—personal and social. Good sex connects us to the building of a good society. It is liberating, life-giving, joyous, fun, easy, ecstatic, fantastic. And it resists all cruelty, all exploitation, all impersonalization.

This kind of ethic for sexual behavior is appropriate, I believe, for both gay and straight Christians. . . .

I know many same-sex couples in this congregation. Some of them I know up close and down deep. I'm convinced, without any question, of the integrity and goodness of their relationship. I believe I should bless those unions if the request is made.

I certainly recognize we are not all at the same place. We need to share how we feel, our fears and our hopes, as we plan this important act of justice for gay and lesbian persons.

But it is for us all. Sexuality is vitally important to the dignity of each one of us. The issue isn't about "them" but about all of us. I'm confident that the more I live in the radical grace of God and trust myself, body and soul, to this loving God the more steadily I will travel on this adventure . . .

I look forward to that day when gay men and lesbians will be embraced fully and unconditionally in love with justice. And once more in this church those famous words of the prophet Amos will mark our corporate life:

Let justice flow on like a river
and righteousness like a never failing stream. (5:24)
Amen

how to make successful changes in faith communities

Making changes in religious communities is a challenging process. Generally speaking, progress is slow and hard-won. And sometimes it feels like two steps forward and one step back. But the work is well worth the effort because you are saving young people from real torment.

All over the country—and around the world—other religious people are struggling to improve life for the gay and lesbian people in their communities as well. So, if you feel discouraged, need ideas on how to proceed, or just want to increase your power through cooperation and collaboration, seek out other groups with similar goals.

◇ EDUCATE, EDUCATE, EDUCATE

The single most effective thing in helping people become more accepting, inclusive, and affirming is to provide education. As people know about—and get to know—gay, lesbian, and bisexual people, their stereotypes and prejudices break down. As one lesbian relates:

> Many of the congregation think they've never met a lesbian or gay person. This older woman said to me recently, "Have you always been this adorable? I thought lesbians were angry man-haters." As people have gotten to know me personally that has broken down their stereotypes about what lesbians are. Martha, my girlfriend, will come to services with me sometimes, and I always make a point of being particularly affectionate because I think it's important for people to see lesbians and gays being affectionate. I do feel that I've been under the microscope a little bit. A lot of people have watched me, but that's been OK.

◇ STRATEGIZE

The chance of making changes increases when you think through the best way to achieve your goals. *How* you go about making changes has a big impact on your success.

◇ DON'T EXPECT 100-PERCENT AGREEMENT

There will generally be some intense disagreement when you are trying to change long-standing practices and attitudes. Don't let that discourage you. Assume that it will occur. Actively enlist those who are supportive to your efforts. Don't give up on influencing everyone, but work your hardest to sway those who are not sure. Don't waste a lot of energy on those whose negative ideas seem set in cement. If a small portion of the congregation never feels comfortable welcoming bisexual, gay, and lesbian members, you can still create an affirming faith community.

◇ ENLIST THE SUPPORT OF RELIGIOUS LEADERS

The support of those in authority can do a great deal to move your plans forward. Take the time to talk to them, let them know what you want to do, ask for their backing. Don't assume that they will be in opposition. Sometimes people who seem like unlikely allies become staunch supporters.

◇ ALLOCATE STAFF TIME

It's important to have someone on the paid staff allocate time to work on these changes. It can be an assistant minister, a youth pastor, a cantor, a Sunday school teacher, a choir leader, or anyone else in a position of some authority. That person can play a helpful role in lending credibility to your efforts, sustaining continuity, and mediating, when necessary, between those with diverse viewpoints.

◇ TAKE ONE STEP AT A TIME

It may feel overwhelming to take on the responsibility of creating a church or temple that's wholly affirming of gay, lesbian, and bisexual people. But if you start with one thing you feel capable of doing, and do it, you'll have made a real contribution. Then if you decide to take another step, go ahead. If not, maybe someone else will lead the next effort.

◇ HAVE PASSION, PATIENCE, AND PERSISTENCE

It's a delicate balancing act between the sense of urgency that keeps us motivated to work for change and enough self-control to actually *build* the needed support among clergy and congregation members. You have to believe deeply in what you're doing, but if you try to change everything at once, it can backfire. When you face setbacks, analyze what went wrong, develop a different approach, and don't give up!

BOBBY GRIFFITHS

Bobby Griffiths killed himself on August 27, 1983, at the age of twenty. Since then, his mother, Mary Griffiths, has dedicated herself to speaking out about their family's experience so that, hopefully, other gay, lesbian, and bisexual youth and their families will be spared the anguish Bobby—and she— have gone through. This is her story:

> We could not accept Bobby as a homosexual person. We just felt he had to change. The bottom line was we thought that Bobby was going to go to hell. And we took Bobby to Christian counselors and prayed and prayed. And Bobby even prayed for God to heal him. Bobby said, "I want to be the kind of person God wants me to be." Looking back on that it's just very sick, because Bobby *was* the kind of person God wanted him to be.
>
> When the clergy condemns a homosexual person to hell and eternal damnation, we the congregation echo "Amen." When the clergy says "A homosexual person is sick, perverted, and a danger to our children," we again echo "Amen." I deeply regret my lack of knowledge concerning gay and lesbian people. Had I allowed myself to investigate what I now see as Bible bigotry and diabolical dehumanizing slander against our fellow human beings, I would not be looking back with regret.
>
> God did not heal or cure Bobby as he, our family, and clergy believed he should. It is obvious to us now why he did not. God has never been encumbered by His child's sexual orientation. God is pleased that Bobby had a kind and loving heart. In God's eyes, kindness and love are what life is about. I did not know that each time I echoed "Amen" to the eternal damnation, referring to Bobby as sick, perverted, and a danger to our children that his self-esteem and personal worth were being destroyed. Finally his spirit broke beyond repair, he could no longer rise above the injustice of it all. Bobby ended his life at age twenty.
>
> It was not God's will that Bobby jumped over the side of a

freeway overpass into the path of an eighteen-wheel truck, killing him instantly. Bobby's death was the direct result of his parent's ignorance and fear of the word "gay" and our trust in the clergy to provide guidance in our lives and the life of our gay son.

It's just been a real trauma to find out how wrong I was, and I always thought I was so right. I thought as long as you have the Bible you're always right. And that's not true. It has been such a traumatic thing to know that I made such a horrible mistake with an innocent child's life.

I feel like I was just indoctrinated, like I've come out of a cult, so to speak. It's taken this trauma for me to turn around and look at life the way it really is. During the time that we were dealing with Bobby's homosexuality, my beliefs formed my reality, and now it's shifted. Reality forms my beliefs.

There are no words to express the pain and emptiness remaining in the hearts of Bobby's family members, relatives, and friends. We miss his kind and gentle ways, his fun-loving spirit, his laughter. Bobby's hopes and dreams should not have been taken from him, but they were. We can't have Bobby back. Please don't let this happen again.

Grappling with the acknowledgment, tolerance, inclusion, and affirmation of gay people in your faith community propels you beyond your previous understandings—not only of people with different sexual orientations but of the very meaning of your religion itself. Although the task is definitely not easy, providing real and tangible support for lesbian, gay, and bisexual youth may well be one of the most gratifying ventures any church or temple can undertake.

community

◇ ◇ ◇ ◇ ◇ ◇ ◇ ◇ ◇ ◇

Joan Bobkoff © 1995

18
living in your community

Where, after all, do human rights begin? In small places, close to home—so small that they cannot be seen on any map of the world. Yet they are the world of the individual person: the neighborhood . . . the school or college . . . the factory, farm or office. Such are the places where every man, woman and child seeks equal justice, equal opportunity, equal dignity without discrimination. Unless these rights have meaning there, they have little meaning anywhere.

—*Eleanor Roosevelt*

Eleanor Roosevelt (1884–1962), wife of Franklin D. Roosevelt, President of the United States, was a powerful voice on behalf of a wide range of social causes, including youth employment and civil rights for African-Americans and women. Her relationship with Lorena Hickock is revealed through years of daily, and often passionate, correspondence.

Our planet seems to be growing smaller all the time as we become, increasingly, a "global village." Yet the immediate community in which we live day-to-day is still the place that has the most impact on us.

The communities in which we are raised influence us in ways that last a lifetime. We remember the smells, the sounds, and the feel of the place we grew up, whether it's kicking leaves in the fall or sitting on the steps eating an ice pop when the asphalt's too hot to walk on. The attitudes of the people around us, the understanding they offer or withhold, the opportunities extended or denied, all leave their mark on us. Our "home town," whether it's a suburb, rural community, or city neighborhood, is forever significant, even if we move away and put down roots in some other part of the world.

As a gay, lesbian, or bisexual person you will encounter in your general community the same range of attitudes that you face in your family, school, and place of worship. Some people will be accepting—even welcoming. Others may create a harmful atmosphere in which you are taunted, excluded, or simply invisible. In many communities, there's some of both.

The world at large does not usually affirm us as gay, lesbian, and bisexual people. When we walk down the street we may see insulting graffiti. When we turn on the radio, we hear heterosexual love songs. As we wait in line for the movies, we see straight couples holding hands and kissing. And when we look through magazines in the checkout line, the romance stories are always about women and men. In some places there is such hostility that we may even be afraid for our physical safety.

On the other hand, some communities are beginning to offer validation. Paintings by gay and lesbian artists have been hung in many city halls, and books with gay, lesbian, and bisexual themes are displayed at local bookstores. When you open the paper to the social pages, you may find an occasional announcement of a gay or lesbian commitment ceremony along with wedding announcements. And there may be a gay-positive editorial or letter to the editor. Your local radio station may have a program devoted to gay and lesbian music. Your community theater group may put on a play with lesbian or gay characters. And there are a number of thriving gay and lesbian communities where people are building neighborhoods, supporting local businesses, voicing their opinions, and generally taking an active role in their cities.

Although there's a long way to go, many people are already

working to create communities and community groups that are affirming of lesbian, gay, and bisexual youth. Making changes at the local level is a great place to start. As the saying goes, "Think globally. Act locally." If changes are made in enough neighborhoods, towns, and cities, the whole nation moves forward.

community involvement

There are many ways that we connect with our communities. We meet people who live on our block, shop at the same market, or play tennis in the neighborhood park. You may also seek out other means to become more actively involved in your community.

You can volunteer with local service groups, such as food delivery programs, shelters, hotlines, or programs providing care for the elderly. You can teach in literacy programs or work for NOW or Planned Parenthood.

You can join the Sierra Club or or other groups working to protect the environment. You might work in a community garden or radio station, join a theater group or chorus, or take part in a community conflict-resolution program.

Getting involved in electoral politics is another important way to make a difference. You could volunteer to work on the campaign of a gay or gay-friendly politician. In fact, quite a number of elected officials began their careers this way.

And work is, of course, one of the most common ways of taking part in your community. Whether you're working full-time or just after school or on weekends, a job can give you a chance to learn new skills, make a contribution, and meet a variety of people, as well as make money.

◇ RECREATIONAL GROUPS

Recreational groups are one of the most common ways that young people are active in their communities. You might play ball as part of an athletic league, take African drumming from the parks and recreation department, or hang out at the Boys and Girls Club playing pool.

For many people, such activities are a source of enrichment and positive self-esteem. As Dan relates:

During high school I swam for an athletic club team. It helped me become a national level swimmer. I got to travel to the junior nationals in different parts of the country. I made a lot of swimming friends. I became captain of the swim team at school, and I got respect because of what I could do.

One mother of a gay son describes the value of 4-H clubs:

My kids did everything. They took care of horses and sheep, goats, chickens, rabbits, and plants. 4-H was great because it allowed them to do what they wanted. They could take rock-etry or cooking—boys and girls. My son wasn't weird or odd when he cooked things to take to the fair. All the guys did.

Recreational groups are a place to develop your interests and skills, have fun, and socialize. If you are in a difficult living situation these groups can also provide a healthy place for escape and a much needed chance for caring connections to others.

Yet in most general community groups lesbian, bisexual, and gay youth are invisible, at best, and there is little sensitivity to gay issues. At worst there is formal rejection. The Boy Scouts are a notorious example. They have excluded gay men and boys from their ranks, solely on the basis of sexual orientation.

Quang describes the dilemma when you love the activity but not the atmosphere:

I played a lot of sports when I was growing up. But the cul-ture of a sports team can make it very hard to be gay. It's definitely hard for a gay person to be out, especially if there's a coach that is homophobic. Some people choose to stay hidden or just leave because they can't deal with it. Or they get drawn into acting homophobic themselves, and become part of it.

In situations like this, you have another one of those hard choices to make. You may love to sing so much that you stay in the chorus anyway. Or you may decide that it's not worth being in the ski club if you have to put up with the homophobic slurs that you hear on the bus. Situations like this are not fair. Whatever you want to do, you should be able to do it—and to do it *out*. But if that's not possible, you have to weigh the costs against the benefits and make the best decision for yourself.

As always, if you're in a strong enough place in your own coming out process, you can fight openly for equal rights and equal treatment. If you do, remember, you don't have to do it alone. Team up with allies and gather support around you. (For more ideas about this kind of teamwork, see Chapter 14, "Strategies for Building a Support Program," and Chapter 17, "Making Changes in Churches and Temples.")

getting help from your community

If you need emotional support, housing, health care, job counseling, or help with other basic needs, a community organization may be able to provide assistance.

If you are seeking counseling to support you in your coming out journey or because you are deeply depressed, you should insist upon a sensitive and affirming therapist. If you are looking for help to quit abusing drugs or alcohol you need a program that is affirming of your same-sex attractions. The same is true for family therapy or any other situation in which you are engaging the services of a counselor.

If you are having emotional problems or difficulties in your life, counseling can provide a safe and supportive environment to express your thoughts and feelings, clarify your needs, and learn the skills to help you grow emotionally and achieve your goals. Before you even begin—or at any point in the process—you can question the counselor about his or her attitudes regarding sexual orientation. You should be in a counseling relationship only with someone whose response is positive.

◇ COMMUNITY ORGANIZATIONS AT THEIR BEST

If you require housing and financial support because it's not possible for you to stay with your family, the agency that helps you should be compassionate and should advocate for you as a gay, lesbian, or bisexual person. If you get into trouble with the law, it's helpful if the probation department respects your sexual orientation. And if you need the help of the police, they should treat you fairly.

There are some social service agencies that are providing sensitive, knowledgeable, and respectful services to their lesbian, gay,
and bisexual clients. And sometimes there will be someone who can
truly help you through tough times. When Devan came to Project
Offstreets for homeless youth, they helped him find housing. But it's
his relationship with a counselor there, Mary Voit, that is most significant to him:

> Mary accepted me for all that I am and who I am. She was like
> a grandmother, a very loving role model. She gave me that
> love that has stayed with me and helped me make it through.

Jason had the terrifying experience of being followed, taunted,
and beaten by three young gay-bashers when he was returning
home one night from a date with his boyfriend. When he got home
his father convinced him to call the police:

> The policeman couldn't have been any nicer. He was very
> respectful and expressed real concern for how I was feeling.
> It was the scariest experience I've ever gone through, and I
> was hurting bad. He seemed to understand why I was so
> freaked. It would have been horrible if he'd just blown it off
> or acted like there was something wrong with me. The cop
> told me he had been through special training to deal with
> hate crimes. He referred me to county mental health, and my
> counselor there was terrific, though I still won't go back to
> that part of town.

After her mother told her to leave, Jessica wasn't able to make it
on her own. She finally went to an agency for runaway youth:

> I told them I wanted to find my dad who I hadn't seen in
> ten years. When they asked about my mom I didn't know
> what to say. I was afraid to tell them I'm a lesbian and that's
> why I couldn't go back there. But I took a chance and
> spilled the whole story. The counselor was cool and said
> she'd help me look for my father, but if it didn't work she'd
> have to call my mother. Thank God it worked.

Young gay people shouldn't have to have special worries about
telling the truth or about the treatment they'll receive when they

need help. But until everyone can be assured of getting the kind of response that Devan, Jessica, and Jason did, we all have our work cut out for us.

◇ ON THE STREETS

If you are kicked out of your home or if you run away from an abusive or violent home, you may think that being on the street is your only option. It may even look appealing at first. It may seem adventurous and exciting to be on your own with no rules, and there can be a feeling of camaraderie and a sense that people look after each other. But there will always be unscrupulous and desperate people who will take advantage of you and hurt you for their own survival. Jessica, who was kicked out of her home by her violent mother, relates:

> When I first left home, it was a relief. My friend let me stay with her, and no one was giving me a hard time. But then she lost her apartment and I had nowhere to go. I couch surfed. Sometimes I had sex with someone just to have a place to sleep. I thought I was making friends, but they were only my friends when I was getting them drugs or putting out.

Often, the way a teenager survives on the street is through survival sex or by getting involved in other dangerous activities—passing stolen goods, dealing drugs. A nineteen-year-old who has spent much painful time on the street offers this advice:

> You just have to be willing to ask for help, to make that first phone call or walk through that door. There are organizations that will help you. Take advantage of them. They take you off the street. They'll get you clean clothes, food in your stomach, a roof over your head. You may have to follow a rule or two, but it's worth it in the long run.
>
> There's rotten apples in every bunch, but on the streets it's all rotten. If it looks too good to be true, don't do it. Stay away from strangers who ask you, "You want to make a fast buck, kid?" It's all a game. It gets really old really fast. You get tired.
>
> Find someone you can trust. If not your high school counselor, just call a crisis line. I did. At first I didn't believe

them, but after a while I believed it would help. I got off the streets. I haven't prostituted for four months. I want something better.

Tangerine's Story: Being on the Streets

Tangerine was fifteen when he was beaten by his mother for being gay. He left home and lived with the first man he went out with, who was thirty-five. When that didn't last, he moved out, rented a room, got a job at Taco Bell, and tried to make it on his own. That only worked for a short time before he wound up in a number of group homes and then got involved with drugs, prostitution, and life on the streets.

I met this man Robert and I ended up living with him. We were hard-core lovers. I started go-go dancing at the local gay bar. They let me in the bar, paid me cash to dance on a little platform. People touched me all night and I couldn't do anything about it. It was degrading. But that's what Robert wanted me to do. So I did it. What was I supposed to do? I needed to make my share of the rent. I dropped out of school. I started doing a lot more drugs. It was hard.

Here I was a teenager and these guys were twenty-five, thirty years old. I thought that's what I was supposed to do. I was scared. I'm still scared today.

I can't remember if everything was safe. Sometimes I was so out of it because of the drugs. Then I started drinking. I was down to 125 pounds. I didn't know what to do. Robert passed me on to his friends as a toy. He would say, "Hey, this is my friend. Talk to him. Go to the room and talk to him." I knew what that meant already.

It hurt really bad. I would always wonder, does anyone love me out there? It felt so empty. You do it because you think someone loves you. You think that's what love's about. But all it does is scar you. It steals something from you that you can't get back. Suicide I attempted many times. Every form I could think of, I tried it.

What got stolen from me was my self-esteem, my dignity. It takes a lot of work to build back your self-esteem. I had my morals stolen from me. I didn't know what morals were. I don't think I had any. I'm pretty sure I have some now, but back then, all I knew was I have no say here.

If you're under eighteen and you live with someone, sex is the only thing you can give. That and being a little maid. You have to do it. What choice do you have? You thought you were loved, but you were never loved. You're just a toy object to be bought and sold and traded or thrown away any time. It's not a life at all.

Through a community organization Tangerine has found supportive gay foster parents and is joining the Job Corps.

THE JOB CORPS

The Job Corps is a national organization that offers both education and vocational skills to young people in need of career training and new opportunities. Because it provides housing, food, and other necessities, the Job Corps can be especially helpful for youth who are homeless or in abusive homes. You don't need to have finished high school to enter the Corps.

The Job Corps has centers throughout the country, and you can choose what vocation you want to study and at which center you want to work. Openly gay, lesbian, and bisexual youth find that their experience in the Corps reflects that of the larger society. Some people—and centers—are more accepting, some more homophobic. However, the Job Corps has a strict policy nationwide of "zero tolerance" for violence and sexual harassment, as well as drug and alcohol use, to make it a safe learning environment. And some centers have gay, lesbian, and bisexual support groups. (For more information, see p. 374 of the Resources).

◇ WHEN SOCIAL SERVICE AGENCIES ARE HOMOPHOBIC

There is no easy advice about what to do if you find yourself dealing, out of necessity, with a homophobic agency. If you are in urgent need of housing or health care or if you're in trouble with the law, you deserve sensitive treatment, but if you don't get it, you may not always be in a position to do much about it.

In these situations, you need to weigh the alternatives carefully. If coming out would put you in danger, you may need to stay closeted. Other times you can find one sympathetic staff person who will advocate for you. Or, in good circumstances, you may be able to help educate the agency about what's required to meet your needs.

One young lesbian, Tracy, was living in a group home while her county social worker searched for an appropriate foster family. Tracy told the social worker that she needed a home that would support her being out, proud, and politically active as a lesbian. The social worker realized that this was a legitimate request and Tracy went to live with a lesbian couple.

If your efforts to obtain respectful treatment within the agency aren't successful, check with the nearest gay community center to see if they can help or if they know of another organization that could.

PSYCHIATRIC ABUSE

Many people seek counseling at some time in their lives, and usually their experience is a positive one. A good counselor can provide understanding, support, and helpful insights.

However, some psychiatrists, psychologists, and other counselors are so ignorant about sexual orientation that they have tried to "cure" gay people by attempting to make them straight. One of the most barbaric ways that some of these misinformed mental health professionals—and some parents—harm gay, lesbian, and bisexual youth is by committing them, against their will, to a psychiatric hospital. During such institutionalization there may be efforts to change people's sexual orientation, and sometimes even their values and beliefs, under the guise of treating a psychiatric illness such as "gender identity disorder."

There are certainly some gay youth that have psychiatric problems serious enough to warrant hospitalization, but often when lesbian or gay youth are institutionalized it is simply because of their same-sex feelings, because they don't fit the accepted gender roles, or because their parents don't know how to cope with what is unfamiliar and frightening to them. In many situations parents have the power to commit their children to psychiatric hospitals until they reach legal adulthood. Even loving parents might subject their children to this torture because they believe the misinformation they have been told.

Alessandra was terrified when her parents sent her to therapy to cure her of bisexuality. When her girlfriend's family made it possible for Alessandra to move in with them, she left home immediately. As she explains:

> I was very scared of being taken to the hospital and not being able
> to express who I was. Running away was the way I felt I could pro-
> tect who I was from being damaged.

Misguided psychiatric treatment can include antipsychotic drugs, isolation rooms, or word association "therapy" where patients are trained to link words about sex with the same gender with "gutter" and "hell." Some people have even been shown pictures of people of the same gender, and if they became sexually aroused, they were given electric shocks on their genitals.

Although these atrocities may be happening less frequently than they used to, there is no question that these techniques are still in use, especially in some private hospitals for "troubled" youth.

If you are having severe emotional problems you deserve professional help and support. But you certainly don't need someone telling you not to be lesbian, gay, or bisexual. Just the opposite. You need people who will affirm your sexual orientation and help you to cope with any difficulties that you're facing because of it.

If you meet more subtle psychiatric abuse, such as a therapist who tells you that life would be easier if you were heterosexual, don't buy it! That's only true if you are straight! Life surely would be more comfortable if society accepted and respected who you are, but trying to have feelings that are not genuinely yours is enough to make you crazy—and that, after all, is *not* the point of mental health treatment.

◇ NCLR YOUTH PROJECT

If you are in danger or are dealing with issues of damaging psychiatric treatment, get help. The National Center for Lesbian Rights (NCLR) offers free and confidential legal and practical support to gay, lesbian, bisexual, and transgendered youth confronting problems in the mental health care system. Call toll-free 1–800–528-NCLR (6257).

groups for lesbian, gay, and bisexual youth

There are some community groups that have been established specifically for gay youth. These programs offer recreational activities, classes, and social events, as well as advocacy and help in troubled times.

There are well over two hundred support and social groups all over the country (and more around the world) especially for gay youth. Some are associated with schools, others with lesbian, gay, and bisexual community centers.

There are also a few organizations that have a special focus on serving the needs of gay youth. Hopefully, the day will come when there won't be a need for special programs because bisexual, gay, and lesbian youth won't face problems other than those common to young people in general. But in the meantime it's good to know that an increasing number of people are devoted to trying to make things better. Here are some examples of such organizations.

◇ THE HETRICK-MARTIN INSTITUTE

The premiere agency of this kind is the Hetrick-Martin Institute (HMI) in New York City. It was founded in 1979 by Emery Hetrick and Damien Martin, a psychiatrist and an educator, who were life partners. When they started the Institute they were outraged about violence and discrimination against lesbian and gay youth and wanted to create a "safety net" for those young people who couldn't get help other places. HMI has grown and expanded to include programs that enhance the life of all gay youth, as well as providing vital services for youth who are having troubles. One of their programs is an alternative high school, the Harvey Milk School. They also provide a variety of educational, recreational, and advocacy programs including an after-school drop-in center that offers a variety of classes, such as photography and computers. They have support groups, field trips, individual and family counseling, help for homeless youth, training for members of the general community, and national advocacy with professionals and elected officials.

HMI originally defined its mission in terms of the protection and care of youth. As HMI has matured, and been influenced by the youth movement, it has begun to develop more of a partnership with the young people in the organization. Youth now have seats on the board of directors and participate in a youth council where they articulate their needs and offer recommendations about how to serve them better.

Luna tells how his life improved after he found Hetrick-Martin:

> When I first came here I was amazed that there were so many other young gay people. I thought I was the only one. I started being friends with other guys in the group, and now I have too many friends. I came out about my HIV status and I wanted to educate young people. The people at Hetrick-Martin taught me public speaking and they did good. I started going to Harvey Milk because I was really messing up in regular high school. I graduated, so I'm set now. They helped me a lot.

◇ DISTRICT 202

In 1991 in Minneapolis, a group of gay, lesbian, and bisexual youth were determined to "open up a queer youth space, a place of our own to hang out," according to Michael Kaplan, twenty-six-year-old

Executive Director of District 202. With the help of a few adults they raised money, rented a storefront on a highly accessible main route, and remodeled it to meet their needs.

In the window is a neon sign, "District 202," a name chosen by members of the founding group. Inside is a cafe with tables and couches. You can get a cup of coffee and a snack, read, play cards, listen to music, and socialize with other gay young people under twenty-one. A computer and a resource library are also available. The lounge is furnished with comfortable seating, a TV and VCR, pool table, and pinball machine. At the back is a large room with black walls and a professional sound and light system where well-attended dances are held every weekend.

Other regular District 202 programs include a speaker's bureau and movie nights. Special events like dance lessons, art or theater opportunities, and holiday parties, including a prom at a downtown hotel, happen frequently.

District 202 is staffed by paid employees and trained volunteers, both young and old. There are common sense rules that ensure everyone's safety. Decisions are made at youth community meetings about day-to-day internal operating policies and programs. This advisory board is open to any interested youth, and there is also an adult board of directors that deals with legal issues, fund-raising, and public policies.

Carl, who attends regularly, says:

> District 202 gives youth a chance to worry about what we should be worrying about—school, friends, boyfriends, girl-friends—not whether someone will beat you up or call you faggot.[1]

◇ YOUTH SERVICES OF THE LOS ANGELES GAY AND LESBIAN COMMUNITY SERVICES CENTER

One entire floor of the Los Angeles Gay and Lesbian Community Services Center's four-story building is dedicated to providing youth services. Founded in 1968 (a year before Stonewall), the Center began addressing the needs of youth ten years later. Their extensive program serves people up to age twenty-three and includes a shelter for homeless youth. Other services include support groups,

[1] "After 1 Year, 202 a Success," *The Whittier Globe*, Dec., 1993, p. 1.

recreational activities, art and theater workshops, a phone talkline, a national and international pen pal service, a youth magazine (*Empowerment Times*), training in independent living skills, peer HIV education outreach, job referrals, and legal advice.

The Center is a large, well-established social service agency specially dedicated to providing for the needs of the gay community, including its youngest members.

AGENCIES ESPECIALLY FOR LESBIAN, BISEXUAL & GAY YOUTH

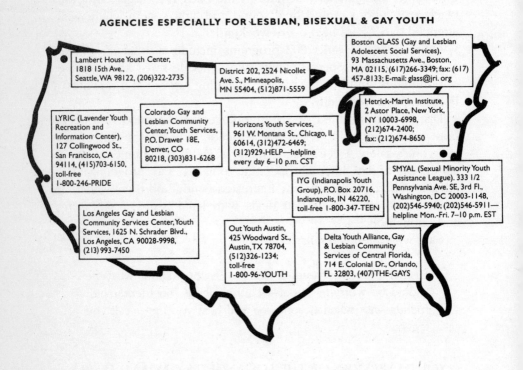

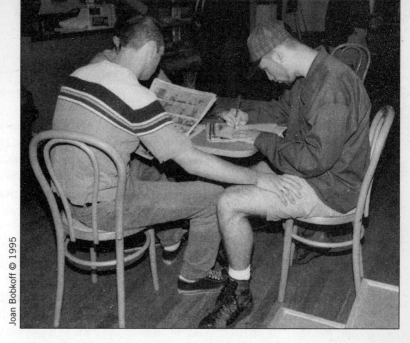

Joan Bobkoff © 1995

19
creating supportive community groups

For Service Providers and Allies

Spiders are patient weavers.
They never give up.
And who knows
What keeps them at it?
Hunger, no doubt,
And hope.

—*May Sarton*

May Sarton (1912–1995) was a poet, novelist, and journal writer. She explored themes of love and solitude, creativity, aging, and her passion for gardening. Her prolific work includes *A Reckoning, As We Are Now, The Education of Harriet Hatfield*, and *At Seventy*.

321

As a lesbian, bisexual, or gay youth, you have a right to feel welcome in your community. Reading this chapter will give you some ideas of what the staff of community groups can—and should—do to provide a supportive environment. You may also want to give it to social workers, counselors, and other professionals.

This chapter addresses everyone who provides services for young people through any kind of community group or government agency—including social service agencies, foster family programs, group homes drug and alcohol recovery programs, health clinics, police and juvenile justice departments, recreational groups, athletic groups, after-school activities, theater and art activities, and summer camps.

The kinds of things that are helpful in creating support and affirmation for gay, lesbian, and bisexual youth in community groups are, of course, similar to the things that are helpful in other institutions. Chapter 13, "Making Schools Safe for Gay, Lesbian, and Bisexual Students," Chapter 14, "Strategies for Building a Support Program," and Chapter 17, "Making Changes in Churches and Temples," as well as the section "How to Show You're Gay-Friendly" on p. 42, will be relevant as well.

As professionals, we have not succeeded in meeting the needs of gay youth. If each of us sat down with just one gay, lesbian, or bisexual young person and offered empathy and understanding, that would be a beginning. But although it's important to be individually affirming, the young people who reveal their same-sex orientation are just the tip of the iceberg. For each young person who shares enough for you to begin to talk, there are many others carrying their feelings in secrecy.

It takes enormous courage and determination, as well as a certain kind of personality, for a young person to be willing to be out as lesbian, gay, or bisexual. Young people who can do this are the exception, not the rule. Even the youth who is willing to come out to you in private is not typical. More commonly, young people conceal their same-sex feelings in order to be accepted.

Therefore, it's essential that affirming messages and inclusive policies be standard fare. In this way, everyone—gay and straight—learns that in your group all people will be respected and protected.

what you can do

Programs established specifically for gay youth are currently necessary and important, but ultimately we must transform *all* youth programs into affirming and supportive environments. Here are some ways that you can begin to make your group a welcoming and respectful place for gay youth.

◇ KNOW THAT THERE ARE LESBIAN, GAY, AND BISEXUAL YOUTH IN YOUR GROUP

Whether they are visible or not, every youth group includes gay youth. Some may identify themselves, but most won't tell you that they're gay. Additionally, it's highly probable that some young people in your group have gay and lesbian parents, relatives, and friends. Affirming messages will be extremely meaningful to these young people as well.

◇ CREATE A GAY-FRIENDLY SPACE

There are many easy and low-cost ways you can communicate that your organization is supportive of gay youth. You can put up gay-positive posters. You can set out pamphlets from local or national gay and lesbian organizations. As David Montgomery, a nurse in a community health center, explains:

> We try to make it as visible as possible. We keep information from the gay community center out and available. We keep their calendar around. We put out gay-positive books, magazines, and community newspapers.

◇ ESTABLISH ANTIDISCRIMINATION AND ANTISLUR POLICIES

Notice of antidiscrimination and antislur policies should be included in any advertising or promotional literature. The policies can also be publicly displayed and should be discussed with participants. And always, insults or slurs should be addressed and limits set. Jose Rodriquez, intake worker at a family services agency in the Southwest, describes how they establish the message that it's safe to be open about sexual orientation:

> I make a general statement about how we are an equal opportunity organization and that we welcome people from all backgrounds. We don't discriminate on race or religion or sexual orientation or culture—and I list them specifically.

Kirsten Gerber, counselor at The Bridge, a family reunification program for runaway youth and their families, describes how slurs and homophobic jokes are handled:

> In any residential setting, no matter what the counselors do, it's not always going to be respectful, so we have institutionalized rules that every insulting joke gets interrupted. Then a short educational statement follows so kids learn not only that you can't tell that joke here but why. We include the fact that there may be kids here now that are gay, lesbian, or bisexual, and staff people as well, and it's important to make it safe for everyone. That's standard procedure.

◇ USE INCLUSIVE LANGUAGE

Both in written materials and in interviews and conversation, inclusive language lets young people know that it's OK to be gay. Kirsten advises:

> When you're asking about family members, don't use the words "husband' and "wife" unless those words are used first by the kid. Instead you can ask, "Is there anyone else in your household?" "What is their relationship to you?" With kids we do the same thing: "Is there anyone special you're seeing?" On the forms it says, "Have you had sex with anyone?" There are boxes to check: female, male, both. It's amazing. The kids pick up on it like that—and they know.

◇ TRAIN YOUR STAFF, BOARD OF DIRECTORS, AND COMMUNITY ABOUT THE NEEDS OF GAY YOUTH

Training is absolutely necessary in any serious effort to improve services for gay youth. In a 1991 study only 25 percent of school counselors said that they felt very competent to counsel lesbian and gay youth.[1]

In many communities speakers are readily available through a gay speakers bureau, gay community center, or PFLAG (Parents, Family, and Friends of Lesbians and Gays). As a first step, education

[1] James H. Price and Susan K. Telljohann, "School Counselors' Perceptions of Adolescent Homosexuals," *Journal of School Health* (December 1991, vol. 61, no. 10), pp. 433–438.

and sensitization about the issues that gay youth face can take place in the context of a more general training on cultural diversity. As Kirsten describes it:

> We've found that it's more effective to look at issues in the context of multiculturalism than to simply focus on gay issues. This makes it clear that issues of concern for gay youth are comparable to other diversity issues, and it's easier to draw the parallels between oppressions of different cultures and ethnicity.

Irene van der Zande, Director of Kidpower and Teenpower, national self-defense programs for young people, relates this story about making their organization an affirming place both for gay staff and for young people:

> I show the *Gay Youth* video in the context of getting comfortable dealing with people from all walks of life and understanding what people have to deal with and what their issues are. Just bringing up the topic in this way lets everyone know that this is going to be an accepting place. One night I showed that movie and in the discussion afterward a new instructor said, "OK, Irene, you win." She meant that I'd done enough for her to feel safe to say that she was a lesbian.

◇ HIRE SOME OPENLY LESBIAN AND GAY STAFF PEOPLE

Having openly gay people on your staff is one of the most effective ways to create a safe environment for gay youth. The visible presence of openly gay staff provides healthy role models for gay, lesbian, and bisexual young people, whether they have revealed their same-sex feelings or not.

Ned Cost, Associate Director of an adolescent group home agency, relates:

> We fully support our lesbian and gay staff when they choose to be out. It's important for the kids to know that there are gay and lesbian people who are doing fine. It's critical for kids dealing with these feelings to have healthy role models. Secondarily, it's great for the other kids to lessen their prejudice, their homophobia.

I remember one fifteen-year-old girl who came out once she knew she had a lesbian therapist who it was safe to talk to. This kid had been holding onto a lot of feelings. She said she had been praying about this for three years and she felt that God had sent her to this particular therapist as an answer to her prayers.

◇ GET THE WORD OUT THAT YOU'RE GAY-FRIENDLY

You can advertize in gay and lesbian newspapers, take brochures to your nearest gay, lesbian, and bisexual community center, or give out literature about your organization at gay events. Concerts, conferences, and other gatherings often have tables or booths at which you can publicize your services.

◇ PLAN AN EDUCATIONAL FORUM FOR ALL YOUTH— GAY AND STRAIGHT

Again, this can—and should—be part of a larger diversity program. Since the peer environment may not be safe enough for gay youth to come out, it's important to provide opportunities that affirm them without pressuring them to identify themselves. And the concept of respect for diversity is basically the same whether we are talking about culture, race, religion, gender, or sexual orientation.

Even if not one gay young person reveals their sexual orientation, you can be certain that you've made a big difference for some kids—and possibly even a life-and-death difference for a few.

Andrew Schwartz, camp administrator, tells this story:

Some years ago we had a counselor at camp who was out with only a few people. He overheard some of the teenagers make hateful remarks about him. He told them directly that wouldn't be allowed, and he arranged for gay and lesbian speakers to come. Two years later I got a letter from one of our campers saying that the day the speakers came had changed his life and he wanted to thank us for doing that.

◇ PROVIDE A PROGRAM SPECIFICALLY FOR GAY, LESBIAN, AND BISEXUAL YOUTH

This isn't necessary for every kind of group. For example, a soccer team doesn't need to have a support group for its gay, lesbian, and bisexual members. But if your organization provides a wider variety of services, sponsoring a group for gay youth can be very helpful. Groups should be offered to all kids, not just to those who come out. As Kirsten Gerber explains:

> Our gay, lesbian, and bisexual support group is listed along with the other groups we have. I don't wait for someone to tell me they're gay. Every time I do an aftercare referral with a young person, I just read out the whole list and explain all the groups so that they know.

◇ COME OUT—AS GAY, LESBIAN, BISEXUAL, OR AS AN ALLY

If you are heterosexual, talk about the openly gay, lesbian, and bisexual people in your life. Talk about your lesbian sister, your gay son, your lesbian colleague or gay basketball buddy. As a straight person, you are in a unique position to affirm gay and lesbian people with very little risk of negative repercussions for yourself. Irene van der Zande describes one of the ways she does this:

> If anyone gives me any hint that they are testing the waters on our attitudes toward gay people—for example, among our staff or in instructor training—I'll mention something about the president of our board of directors. I'll tell how she and her partner, Janet, sent their son to Kidpower. They always come out to me later.

If you are gay, lesbian, or bisexual yourself, come out. (For a much longer version of this basic message, read "The Challenge of Coming Out" beginning on p. 231). It's impossible to overestimate the positive impact you have on gay youth when you come out as a proud, healthy, successful adult.

the positive effect on all youth

Creating an organization that is accepting and respectful of gay, lesbian, and bisexual young people will inevitably make your group a safer, more affirming place for *all* young people. A counselor in a Midwest family reunification program describes this:

I have only seen positive things come out of it. For instance, many kids who have been making hurtful jokes or comments might have a gay, lesbian, or bisexual aunt or uncle or family member or teacher that they really like but have been afraid to support until now. I've seen it happen. These kids are leaving here talking about what they've learned, and they're not laughing about it. They're teaching other kids.

Not only do young people learn sensitivity toward gay people, but those lessons extend to others as well. In groups where it's safe to reveal that you're gay, youth also reveal other sensitive information about themselves. The opportunity to share one's whole self and be affirmed is a cornerstone of self-esteem.

making changes isn't easy

Making changes isn't easy. When you begin to stand up for gay youth, there is, almost inevitably, some backlash. There will be people who get angry. There will be people who assert their belief that gay youth can—and should—be converted to heterosexuality. There will be people who question your motives, your competence, and your own sexual orientation.

Any program designed to meet the needs of gay youth will encounter some resistance if not outright opposition. As always, preparation is key, as Kirsten Gerber explains:

> Especially at the very beginning there were a lot of questions, classic questions I call them now, such as, "If we serve gay, lesbian, and bisexual clients too actively will our straight clientele drift away?" "Is this necessary? Why do we need to have a special group for these kids?" and "Where are these kids? I don't see them." And there were a lot of beliefs around "Kids can't know that they're gay so young, so there's no sense pushing them into this thing that they aren't ready to know."
>
> One of the most helpful things I did was to create an advisory committee—before we even started meeting with the kids. I pulled in well-known community people, both gay and straight, who were supportive of kids. Their backing was really important in those first months.

We also try to pull families in. Even as we continue to grow in providing services for youth, families are often left in the dust. There is a lot of hope for these families if they get support when the youth are coming out rather than waiting until the situation becomes unbearable. So we've included PFLAG as a visible referral, and we're trying to make parents' services more accessible.

◇ "BENIGN" NEGLECT

Even in organizations that make a conscious effort to serve gay youth and their families, there is sometimes less than wholehearted support for those programs. The coordinator of a gay and lesbian teen intervention program sponsored by a West Coast YMCA reports that "The Y has given a lot of silence to this program."

In one agency in the Midwest that serves youth who are living on the streets, a special group was started for the gay and lesbian kids. The counselor who was given responsibility for the group is passionate in her commitment to the youth with whom she works and considers it a great honor to be accepted and trusted by the members. But in spite of the fact that she was asked to start the group by the executive director of the agency, she reports:

> No one has asked me for a group mission statement. We made one, but nobody's ever asked for it. I was told to hold off. "You can't do this, you can't do that." The money's not there for brochures, T-shirts, or things to do street outreach with. When I read the annual report I was quite ticked. We weren't even mentioned as a project. Not even in small-case letters.

Most professionals who work in this field do so because they care about youth. Hopefully, as you work to increase their awareness of the needs of their young gay clients, they will work to make their organizations more responsive.

the need for supportive foster families

Too many gay, lesbian, and bisexual young people are rejected by their families—and sometimes they're kicked out of their homes.

Emotionally, they are abandoned and betrayed. Practically, they are in desperate need of a home. Because of this it's essential that foster family agencies recognize the particular needs of gay youth, create an environment in which it's safe for gay youth to be out, and provide foster parents capable of responding with sensitivity and validation.

When these things aren't offered, gay youth once again experience rejection and are left with urgent needs for basic housing and basic care. Verna Eggleston of Hetrick-Martin in New York City relates:

> In this city alone there's maybe fifty thousand kids in foster care. We don't know how many of those kids are gay and lesbian. But we know many gay kids run away from foster care beds where they don't feel accepted and come here to our clinical department, asking that they be rehoused. We get calls from clear down to Texas.

Renee describes coming out to her foster mother and being met with a total lack of response:

> All I heard was silence. When I looked in her eyes I didn't see anything. It was empty. I needed her to say something to me and she never did. So I walked around on pins and needles. These people meant a lot to me, but I made the decision that I had to leave. I realized she just could not support me.

Renee goes on to describe the response she wished she could have gotten:

> I wish she would have acknowledged the fact that that was the hardest thing I'd ever done in my life. If she could have acknowledged how hard it was and how much pain I went through, I think she would have been able to say something.
>
> I also wish that she would have said that she loved me before she knew and that she still continued to love me.
>
> And I wish she would have said, "I don't know a lot about this, but I'd be willing to learn, I'd be willing to come to a support group with you, I'd be willing to drive you to a meeting." Something.

Although Renee's story is painful, it has a much happier ending:

> My counselor said to me, "If you could have what you
> wanted, what would you want?" So I thought about it and I
> said, "I want to be somewhere I can live my life totally open
> and I can have total support. I want them to understand
> where I'm coming from." So a couple weeks later she called
> me and said, "We hit the jackpot. We found a foster home
> for you. There's two lesbians and two kids and they want
> you to come and live with them." I was so happy, I was just
> bouncing off the walls. I could not believe that after all these
> years and all the stuff I had to go through that finally, I'd
> have a home.

Renee's joy at finding a supportive foster family is echoed by
many other young gays and lesbians. After a number of agonizing
years living on the streets and being exploited by older men,
Tangerine also found foster parents who gave him genuine love and
protection. Even now that he's living on his own, he feels the power
of their love:

> My foster dads are still helping me. When I lived a hundred
> miles away, they came to visit me and to see the first play
> that I ever worked on. It's a great feeling to know that some-
> one cares. When someone believes in you, that helps you
> get up and go on.

Gay, lesbian, and bisexual people who want to become foster
parents should be encouraged and welcomed. Lamentably, this is
not always the case. New Hampshire, Florida, and most recently
Nebraska have all placed restrictions on foster parenting or adop-
tions by homosexuals. In spite of the fact that numerous psychological studies show that children of gay and lesbian parents grow up to
be just as well-adjusted as children of heterosexual parents,[2] young
people—both gay and straight—are being denied homes with capable gay and lesbian foster parents.

[2] Charlotte J. Patterson, "Chldren of Lesbian and Gay Parents," *Child
Development* (vol. 63, October 1992), pp. 1025–1042.

The impact of this kind of discrimination is all too clear in the tragic story of E. J. Byington of Omaha. E.J. had had a terribly painful life. He was HIV-positive, tormented by kids at school, never knew his father, and his mother had recently killed herself. But he regained hope when he was placed in a foster home with two gay parents. As he wrote in a school essay: "My new family is the one I have always wanted . . . things couldn't be better."

Just hours after the Nebraska Department of Social Services announced their new policy of banning gay people from being foster parents, E.J. hung himself.

Gay and lesbian youth need safe, supportive, and affirming homes. When their original families can't provide this, they need foster families who can. Foster parent agencies need to provide training to sensitize social workers to the issues involved in working with gay youth and to educate heterosexual foster parents so they can better meet their needs.

In addition, gay, lesbian, and bisexual people should be actively recruited to become foster parents. Foster placement agencies can indicate in their advertising that they welcome applications from single people, same-gender households, and people of all races, religions, and sexual orientations. Announcements in the gay press and notices sent to lesbian and gay parent organizations are also ways to find potential gay foster parents.

Although Craig didn't have an official foster family, his experience living with a gay couple in England as a foreign exchange student illustrates the power of an understanding and loving home:

> I just got such love, love and attention. I had somewhere to go home to, and that made all the difference. I am forever indebted to these guys. They're not politically active people. They never went to marches. But they were gay. Their friends were gay. And they were enjoying what they were doing.
>
> They're not psychologists. They don't know from nothing. But they loved me and supported me. They always seemed to genuinely listen to what I had to say, and they were on my side. The biggest blessing I ever had in my life probably was to move in with this gay couple.

CHECKLIST FOR ASSESSING HOMOPHOBIA/HETEROSEXISM IN YOUR AGENCY OR ORGANIZATION

1. We have special programs, as needed, for our bisexual, lesbian, and gay clients.

2. Gay, lesbian, and bisexual individuals are listed in our brochure of who we serve.

3. Gay, lesbian, and bisexual issues and policy are covered in staff orientation and volunteer training.

4. Our agency has periodic in-services on lesbian, gay, and bisexual issues, as part of a larger diversity training program.

5. When suicide, alcohol and drug abuse, or sexual risk behaviors are addressed in services provided or policy, the potential connection to sexual orientation issues is included.

6. Homophobic or heterosexist comments are not tolerated among staff or clients.

7. If I were a gay, lesbian, or bisexual client or staff person, I would choose to be open about my sexual orientation at this agency.

8. There have been openly lesbian, gay, and bisexual clients or families in our agency, as well as gay, lesbian, and bisexual people on our staff.

9. Forms for client and family completion take into account diversity of households, including homes with partners of the same gender.

10. Staff refer to "partners" or "someone special" rather than "husband," "wife," "spouse," "boyfriend," or "girlfriend" when speaking with clients or families.

11. We have contacts and make referrals within the bisexual, gay, and lesbian community.

12. We have gay and lesbian material such as magazines and newspapers in our waiting room and lesbian and gay pamphelets available in the area with other such informational brochures.

13. We advertize our services and job openings in the lesbian and gay media.

14.Sexual orientation is included in our antidiscrimination policy that relates to staff, clients, and families.

15.The personnel policy includes paid emergency leave for death or illness of significant others. Health benefits are available for domestic partners.

16.If this agency makes financial or in-kind donations, some of them are to gay, lesbian, and bisexual causes and organizations.

Adapted from materials written by Diane Benjamin and Beth Zemsky of the Gay and Lesbian Community Action Council, Minneapolis, Minnesota, 1990.

one step at a time

If you're in a position to institute sweeping changes immediately, that's great. But it's not necessary to do everything all at once. If the prospect of making your group a welcoming place for gay youth looks daunting, pick out one thing and start with that. Doing something is infinitely better than doing nothing. And even small things can be a lifeline to a despairing young person.

Cathy Cade © 1995

20
the gay, lesbian, and bisexual community

I did not know that organizing autonomously for their rights and history and cultural traditions and rightful place in society is all people ever have, that this is the weapon, territory, nation, power.

—Judy Grahn

Judy Grahn (b. 1940) has been a powerful voice of feminism and gay liberation. In 1970 she cofounded the first all-women's press. Her works incude *The Work of a Common Woman* and *Another Mother Tongue: Gay Words, Gay Worlds* in which she celebrates gay and lesbian history and culture.

In referring to her hometown of Oakland, California, the lesbian writer Gertrude Stein once said, "There is no there there." But there's a there there now. Oakland, like many other large cities throughout the United States, has developed a rich cultural life, which includes a strong gay, lesbian, and bisexual presence. In many metropolitan areas there are even gay neighborhoods where you can feel at ease holding hands with your boyfriend or girlfriend as you walk down the street.

Gertrude Stein (1874–1946) is best known for her innovative and abstract prose style. She and her lifetime companion, Alice B. Toklas, lived a legendary life which Stein chronicled in her popular book, *The Autobiography of Alice B. Toklas*.

The gay, lesbian, and bisexual community is rich and varied. So much so, that it may be more accurate to think of it as a variety of interlocking communities. Gay men, lesbians, people of color, and working-class people are a few of the broadest categories. And within each of those there are groups with their own distinct qualities and institutions. In the *San Francisco Bay Times* one week, there were over forty listings of various groups for gay people of color. They included an African-American young men's discussion group, a support group for Asian/Pacific Islander gay, lesbian, and bisexual young people, a Latina lesbians social group, and even a motorcycle club for Black gay women.

There are a million ways to take part in the gay, lesbian, and bisexual communities. Whatever it is that you're interested in, there's a gay version. For athletes, there are lesbian and gay softball, volleyball, basketball, track, swimming, skiing, and skating teams. And every four years the Gay Games provide an opportunity for athletes around the world to compete and celebrate. For computer buffs, there's Digital Queers, who introduce gay community groups to state-of-the-art technology.

There are community AIDS education and service groups like Gay Men's Health Crisis (GMHC) and political groups such as the National Gay and Lesbian Task Force (NGLTF), ACT UP, the National Center for Lesbian Rights (NCLR), and the Human Rights Campaign (HRC).

If you like to sing, there are gay and lesbian community choruses. If you write, there's the annual OutWrite conference for gay and lesbian writers. Even if you just like to watch movies, there are gay film festivals in large cities and on some college campuses. And gay and lesbian characters have appeared in popular films such as *Philadelphia,*

Desert Hearts, The Incredibly True Adventure of Two Girls in Love, and *The Bird Cage.*

Emerging groups often produce a vital culture as they recognize and document their experience. There is great energy and beauty in revealing the truth about lives that have been hidden or portrayed only in limited or distorted ways. Books, plays, music, and all the other arts—in which gay and lesbian people have always been prominent—are just now beginning to reflect our lives more honestly and fully. As we explore ourselves, our history, our struggles and triumphs, the cultural outcome will surely be exciting.

> Comedian Fran Lebowitz sums up the enormous artistic and cultural contributions of gay and lesbian people with this observation:
>
> If you removed all of the homosexuals and homosexual influence from what is generally regarded as American culture, you would pretty much be left with *Let's Make a Deal.*

we're not just like everyone else

Although gay, lesbian, bisexual, and heterosexual people are much more alike than they are different, there is, undeniably, a gay culture that's distinct from the mainstream. Gay and lesbian humor, art, music, language, and politics are all part of it. We see the world differently—and develop our sense of ourselves—based on our experience. As Kaleo Kaluhiwa, an HIV educator, says:

> I believe gay sexuality is more than just sex and body parts. The idea that "I'm just like everyone else except for what I do in bed"—I don't think that's true. We're confronted with the need to look deeper at ourselves at an earlier age, and I think that has a deep spiritual component.

Doe advises gay and lesbian youth to capitalize on those differences:

> Don't try to pretend that you're not different or you're just like everybody else when you're not. That's not going to get you very far as an individual. In the long run, you will suffer trying to downplay your identity rather than politicize it, make it more passsionate.

For any oppressed group, cultural identity is a survival skill, a way to maintain both unity and self-esteem. In the face of hatred and discrimination, gay people, like racial and religious minorities, preserve their integrity through shared commitments, rituals, humor, and common understanding. By joining together to deal with adversity, we sustain our strength and pride.

◇ CHALLENGING GENDER ROLES

Challenging gender roles is common in the gay community. Our very existence defies a traditional understanding of such roles. But confronting gender expectations is not limited to gays and lesbians. Feminism, with its insistence that our gender not thwart our aspirations or achievements, has led us to acknowledge the limitations and injustice of rigid roles. The women's liberation movement created space for women—and girls—to be recognized as strong, smart, and independent and for men—and boys—to be sensitive, nurturing, and receptive. Most profoundly, absolute sex roles are part of the foundation of the inequalities of power in all areas of life, from domestic violence to war, from the work world to family life.

Inevitably, relationships between people of the same sex necessitate a redefinition of gender expectations. Since it's impossible to divide responsibilities by gender, each person has to carve out his or her own niche according to personal temperament, strengths, and preferences. Decisions about who will earn the money, keep communication going, decorate the apartment, reach out for intimacy, do the dishes, nurture, drive the car, or take out the trash can't be made according to whether you're a man or a woman. This is one of the delightful opportunities—and challenges—of gay and lesbian relationships.

And there is definitely more permission to act in ways that don't comply with gender regulations in the gay and lesbian community. For example, some gay men use drag as a way to cut through rigid gender conformity. And some lesbians like to put on a tie for panache. This is sometimes misinterpreted to mean that gay men want to be women or that lesbians want to be men, but in reality we are often simply rejecting—or making fun of—the sanctity of roles.

The arbitrariness of gender rules can be remarkable. One lesbian in Hawaii was looking at a rack of Aloha shirts when a saleswoman rushed over to inform her that she was in the men's section. "What's the difference?" she asked, noting that the shirts looked identical. "Oh no," the saleswoman explained, "The men's shirts button from left to right. Women's button right to left."

Interestingly, what starts out as nonconformity is often picked up by the commercial fashion industry and sold to the mainstream. Whether this is because many fashion designers are gay or because gays just have irresistible style we'll never know.

More Dykes to Watch Out For. Alison Bechdel, Firebrand Books, Ithaca, N.Y., ©1986

not just one way to be gay

There can be a feeling of solidarity and comaraderie in being part of a group that's set apart from the mainstream. You share a common experience and a sense of belonging. But being lesbian, gay, or bisexual doesn't mean that you'll automatically share all the values of other gay people—or even enjoy their company. When Richard was a senior in high school, he told his friend that he was gay and she responded, "Oh, so is Derek." As Richard explained, "That didn't do me any good. I disliked Derek—a very obnoxious person."

Although there are commonalities in the gay community, there are many differences too. We are enormously diverse, with differences in class, race, gender, religion, politics, and education. Beyond that, there's also just personal preference. There will be people you like and respect—and those you don't. Richard goes on to relate:

> The group I'd been in at the university was very elitist, Caucasian people whose parents probably made over a hundred thousand dollars a year. And I didn't relate to that. It's like, "Oh yeah, come over my house. We'll have espresso and eat brie." Pleeeze! So I found a community group with people a little more mature, a little more diverse.

When Richard first came out, he found himself trying to dress and act a certain way:

> When I came out, I came out with a bang. It was a very embarrassing experience actually. I was conforming to the group. That's when I shaved my head. That's when I started being a Madonna fan when I never cared about Madonna before. Then I realized very quickly that I was sickening myself. And so I changed it. I realized there were lots of different types of people and I didn't have to act any one particular way to fit into the gay community.

There can be pressure from both the straight and gay worlds to act, talk, or dress a certain way. But ultimately, people have the right to be themselves—whether that fits someone else's expectations or not. As Stone says:

> I really shook up their reality because I walk around in flats and nylons and frilly dresses and all kinds of things that they

did not consider dyke stuff. This one guy told me, "You're not a dyke. They wear pants and flannels and Doc Martens." I just looked at him and laughed and laughed and laughed.

More Dykes to Watch Out For. Alison Bechdel, Firebrand Books, Ithaca, N.Y., © 1986

No one has the last word on what it means to be gay. As Dan says:

> I'm barely through the process of healing, of melding my two identities—gay and athlete—together. So if there's some gay boy out there who's playing baseball and thinking, "I'm all alone. I'm the only gay man in sports," I want him to know that he's not. Don't let anyone tell you there's only one way to be gay.

There's a lot of room to be yourself in this world. You can be quirky or conventional, radical or conservative. If you're a person who hasn't fit in elsewhere, you may be surprised to find you feel at home here.

we are family

It's important for all of us to have people who know, love, and accept us over time. Ideally, our original families will fit this description, and as we mature, other special people will become part of our lives in lasting ways. But when our families are unsupportive or rejecting, it is even more important to build nurturing bonds with loyal and loving friends. In this way, we create alternative families, families of choice. As Kaleo Kaluhiwa says:

> The most important thing is creating a community, a process where people can get together and experience themselves and grow and share and help each other.

Some young people don't have to go far to find the gay, lesbian, and bisexual community. As Stone relates:

> I was raised with many, many lesbians. I always knew there was a strong community out there and that I would belong to it no matter how I turned out because my parents had basically birthed me there. All these people had changed my diapers and seen me take my first couple of steps. I was one of the community children.

For Amy, being closely connected with the gay community feels healing:

I find it very important that I work with a lot of gay people, that I live in a house with gay people, that most of my social activities are with gay people. I don't go into all-straight situations anymore unless I have to. I spent so many years not being around any gay people that I choose now to separate myself and just be with people who are going to understand, nurture, support, and completely accept me for who I am.

And for Chris, it's a profound experience of coming home:

I'd heard all this stuff about Pride Day and I thought, what is it? I had no idea. When we started marching, I thought, every gay person in the world must be here, because they lined the street. They were on top of buildings. And someone said, "This isn't even all the gay people in Boston."

I honestly understand Pride. There is nothing in the world better than this. I felt as if everyone was family, like I could just run up to anyone and give them a hug and they would understand. I just felt, I never want to go home. I am home.

How involved you become in the gay community is up to you. It's OK to be immersed—even exclusively—if that's what you really want. But you also have every right to feel comfortable in the straight world. Most gay people live their lives partly within and partly outside of the gay community. And the proportion varies from person to person. You get to choose what's best for you—and that may be different at different times.

the history of the gay and lesbian community[1]

It's important to know that we have a history. A sense of our roots gives us feelings of belonging, continuity, and pride. It helps us gain perspective on ourselves as part of a larger journey. We realize that we're not the first and we won't be the last. Yet we can do our part, make our contribution.

[1]Much of this history is based upon Kevin Jennings's clear and well-documented book, *Becoming Visible: A Reader in Gay and Lesbian History for High School and College Students* (Boston: Alyson Publications, 1994).

By understanding our history, we can learn from the past so that we're not fated to repeat mistakes over and over. Especially now, when the progress that we've made toward equal rights and respect is met with growing opposition, it's essential that we have the knowledge of our history to inform us and guide our way.

◇ THE ORIGINS OF THE U.S. LESBIAN AND GAY MOVEMENT

The modern gay movement was enabled by changing social conditions. In the eighteenth and nineteenth centuries, both Europe and America were dramatically affected by the Industrial Revolution. People began to move to cities where it was possible to find work and to live independently. Living away from one's family allowed a degree of privacy and autonomy that hadn't been possible before. Also, because there were so many people in the cities, it was easier for those who were attracted to members of the same sex to meet and form relationships.

Although this liberation was welcome to people with same-sex attractions, those who wanted to control the sexual behavior of others needed an effective way to do so. As science began to take precedence over religion in the understanding of human nature, psychiatry offered a justification for condemning same-sex attraction. Now people could be labeled "psychologically sick" rather than "sinners."

In 1869 the Hungarian psychiatrist Karl Maria Kertbeny coined the term "homosexual." Before then, the idea of identifying people by their sexual attraction was unknown. Naming the person homosexual rather than labeling the same-sex behavior was a shift with far-reaching implications. Now people with same-sex attraction were classified into a group based on their sexual orientation. This categorization furthered the persecution of gay people, but it also led them to begin to see themselves as a group with the potential to organize and achieve their rights.

◇ EARLY DEFENDERS

The first person in modern times known to have spoken out on behalf of gay people is Karl Heinrich Ulrichs. In 1867, even before the word "homosexual" was invented, Ulrichs gave a speech at the Congress of German Jurists, in which he pleaded for a revision of the laws that persecuted people with same-sex attractions. He tried to persuade the group that same-sex attraction was a natural and innate quality.

Although Ulrichs did not succeed in convincing the jurists, his legacy lives on. His concept that gay people have a separate and unique group identity—and that same-sex attraction is natural to them—has become a foundation of the gay liberation movement.

Following Ulrichs, another German, Magnus Hirschfeld, took up the struggle and fought for legal and social reform. He worked to establish the World League for Sexual Reform, which by the late 1920s had gained a membership of 130,000 worldwide and looked as though it would be successful in repealing the laws against homosexuality.

During this time, there were strong, though largely invisible, gay and lesbian enclaves in urban areas such as New York, Berlin, London, and Paris. However, in this increasingly liberal environment, a crisis was brewing. Germany had serious economic problems and the Nazi Party was on the rise.

Throughout history—and still today—a common stratgegy used by those in power to maintain their control is to generate anger toward a scapegoat group. This is the tactic the Nazis employed. And as they took over, homosexuals were inlcuded among those targeted. Along with the millions of Jews who were killed in the Holocaust, thousands of gays were killed as well. And tens of thousands more suffered in concentration camps.

◇ WORLD WAR II AND ITS AFTERMATH

World War II was a turning point for gays and lesbians in the United States. The number of people—both men and women—who served in the military expanded dramatically. As so many people went into the service, others, including women and African-American and Latino men, flocked to the cities to work in jobs that previously had been closed to them. Gays and lesbians found each other in the quickly growing cities as well as within the military itself. And the emergence of homosexuals as a social group and as a political movement accelerated.

The military was not, however, an institution that accepted gay and lesbian people. Before the war, only people who were actually "caught in the act" could be tried and punished. But with the increasing influence of psychiatry, new policies were established that made homosexuality itself into a disqualifying "illness." The numbers of gays who were discharged because of their sexual orientation skyrocketed.

Again, this discrimination was two-edged. While it victimized gay and lesbian individuals, it also encouraged gays to see themselves as an oppressed group that deserved equal rights. And after the war, some gays and lesbians were no longer content to be second-class citizens. The experience of fighting for their country, as well as the companionship of other gay and lesbian people in the military and abroad, gave veterans a new sense of entitlement. As gay people compared their minority status with that of Jews and African-Americans, a clearly political perspective was formed. The first gay political group in the United States, the Society for Human Rights, had been founded in 1924, but it wasn't until 1945 that a major organization, the Veterans' Benevolent Association, emerged.

In the years following World War II, gays and lesbians experienced some formidable setbacks. Though the war was over, the cold war between the United States and the Soviet Union replaced it. The fear of Communism swelled into a national hysteria, and once again scapegoats were needed to take the blame.

Senator Joseph McCarthy, the ringleader of this era, proposed that "subversives" within the government were leaking confidential information to the Communists and thus were undermining our country. Hundreds of thousands of Americans were quickly targeted as traitors. Along with people who had an association with the Communist Party, and Jews—who through the centuries have always been vulnerable to attack—a full-scale campaign was waged against gay people, who were labeled as subversive by their very nature. Large numbers of gays and lesbians lost their jobs.

Although McCarthy was discredited in 1954 when it was exposed that most of his accusations were outright lies made up to gain political power, his legacy lived on. Until 1975 gays were banned from federal civil jobs, and it was only in 1995 that President Clinton finally repealed the disqualification of gay people from receiving security clearance. In most states we still do not have legislation that protects gays and lesbians from discrimination in their work, as well as in housing and other basic areas of life.

◇ EARLY GROUPS WORKING FOR HUMAN RIGHTS

Once again, these assaults led gays and lesbians to an increased awareness of their identity as an oppressed minority. In 1950 Harry

Hay and several other gay men in Los Angeles organized the first successful group to fight for civil rights for gay people, the Mattachine Society.

Harry Hay had been active in the labor union movement, from which he gained a strong belief in the power of organizing, as well as the skills to go about it. Although the progressive movement was generally silent and occasionally hostile about gay issues, their ideals and tactics sparked many social justice movements that followed, including the struggle for the rights of of lesbians and gay men.

The Mattachine Society put forth concepts that were strikingly progressive. They proposed that homosexuals had to undergo a shift in consciousness, that they had to become unified as a group and come to an understanding of their identity and their relationship to society in order to achieve power. They proclaimed that "homosexuals can lead well-adjusted, wholesome, and socially productive lives once ignorance and prejudice against them are successfully combatted, and once homosexuals themselves feel they have a dignified and useful role to play in society."[2]

In 1955 the first organization to work for the recognition and rights of lesbians, the Daughters of Bilitis, was founded by Del Martin and Phyllis Lyon. Their magazine, *The Ladder*, was the first publication to give voice to the experience of lesbians.

◇ STONEWALL

The most dramatic event in gay history—and a pivotal moment in the emergence of the modern gay community—is Stonewall. The Stonewall riots in Greenwich Village, New York, mark the point at which gays and lesbians stopped apologizing and started demanding. Although the existing organizations working to improve life for gay people had originally proposed some astoundingly radical ideas, they had generally grown cautious, advocating "fitting in" rather than fighting back. Stonewall changed all that.

Yet Stonewall did not occur in a vacuum. The gay and lesbian struggle for liberation was rooted in the movements for peace and justice that preceded it. And resistance was brewing. The first

[2] Stuart Timmons, *The Trouble with Harry Hay* (Boston: Alyson Publications, 1990). Cited by Jennings in *Becoming Visible*, p. 171.

demonstrations for an end to discrimination against lesbians and gay men began in 1965, with gay people picketing outside the White House, and in 1967 at Independence Hall in Philadelphia. In 1965 there were militant protests when police raided a fund-raising ball in San Francisco sponsored by the Council on Religion and the Homosexual, and in 1967 when the Black Cat, a gay bar in Los Angeles, was raided on New Year's Eve.

There was a long and ugly tradition of police raiding gay bars. They would barge in, insult patrons, push them around, and arrest anyone who didn't have an ID, anyone in drag, and some employees. Afterward, the bar would reopen. And the drinking and dancing continued.

But on June 27, 1969, at the Stonewall Inn, things didn't go according to plan. The police had thrown everyone out of the bar and were rounding them up and pushing them into a paddy wagon. But instead of going along with the abuse as usual, this time the crowd fought back.

It was the night of Judy Garland's funeral, and as Sylvia Rivera, an eighteen-year-old drag queen who joined in the riot, summed up: "I was just not in the mood."

Feisty drag queens, gays, hippies, and radical political activists joined together to fight back. They began to boo, yell, throw coins, beer bottles, and bricks. Alarmed by the mob on the streets, the police retreated into the bar and locked themselves in. The crowd outside went wild, battering the door with an uprooted parking meter, then breaking a window and setting the bar on fire.

> Although **Judy Garland** wasn't lesbian, she was a beloved idol of the gay community. As Dorothy in *The Wizard of Oz*, she searched for a more loving world. "Somewhere Over the Rainbow," and as a singer who shared an intensity of both love and pain, she touched the gay community. In fact, "Friends of Dorothy" became a code name for gay people.

The Tactical Police Force was called in, but undaunted, the crowd dispersed only to reform again and again. In the midst of this melee, a chorus line of queens, kicking their legs up like the Rockettes, confronted the police, singing:

We are the Stonewall girls
We wear our hair in curls
We wear no underwear
We show our pubic hair . . .

Although police finally cleared the streets, it was only temporarily. The next night the crowd gathered again, swelling into the thousands. Though the riots eventually subsided, the gay community would never be the same again. Immediately, meetings and rallies were organized and new gay liberation groups were formed.

The following year, the Stonewall uprising was commemorated with Christopher Street Liberation Day. A parade of two thousand in New York, and simultaneous parades in Los Angeles, Chicago, and Boston, started the first of what would become known as Gay Pride Day. Since then, annual June parades are held in both large and small cities across the country and abroad, with the Stonewall 25 Commemorative March drawing a million people to New York in 1994.

where we are now

Since the Stonewall riots, the gay and lesbian movement has expanded at an astounding rate. Informed and enriched by the liberation movements that preceded it, it has drawn upon their beliefs, as well as their strategies. The civil rights movement of the fifties and sixties, with its fundamental principle that African-Americans and all people deserve—and must have—equal rights, provided an inspiration and a model of grassroots organizing. The antiwar movement of the sixties and seventies called into question the policies and practices of government and for many young people was the catalyst for them to think critically. The women's liberation movement of the seventies and eighties created a huge shift in consciousness, with its assertion that women have the right to full equality—in both the personal and the public sphere. Much of the leadership, energy, and philosophy of gay, lesbian, and bisexual organizations comes directly from the feminist movement.

For both people of color and women, we're a long way from justice in terms of real opportunity and attitudes—and some of the gains we've made are now under attack. Yet in these struggles, as in the fight for full equality for lesbian, gay, and bisexual people, progress continues. And some of our gains are remarkable.

In 1969 there were fifty gay and lesbian organizations in the United States. Now there are thousands. A multitude of lesbian journals and books have taken up where *The Ladder* left off. There are gay and lesbian publishing companies and bookstores, gay film festivals, women's music festivals, and even gay and lesbian cruises.

There are health clinics, realtors, lawyers, and financial planners specifically serving the gay and lesbian population.

A number of labor unions have gone on record in support of lesbian and gay civil rights, as have many national professional organizations. And some government agencies have specifically invited gay people to join. For example, the Los Angeles Police Department recruits at the annual Los Angeles Gay Pride Parade.

In 1973 the American Psychiatric Association removed homosexuality from its list of illnesses, doing away with a label that had stigmatized gays for a century. In 1974 Elaine Noble became the first openly gay person to be elected to public office when she became a Massachusetts state representative. And since then the numbers are growing. Over one hundred openly gay and lesbian people now hold elective office in the United States.

In 1978 the Briggs Initiative, a proposition on the California ballot that would have banned gay people from working with children, was defeated by a massive grassroots effort organized by lesbians and gays across the state. By coming out to small groups of friends and neighbors to counteract homophobic stereotypes, they steadily eroded support for the initiative and showed how individuals can make a decisive difference.

In 1983 Wisconsin became the first state to forbid discrimination on the basis of sexual orientation, and as of 1995 eight more states, along with many municipalities, had followed. Many cities and corporations have recognized domestic partnerships, granting gay couples the same benefits married heterosexual couples receive. And in 1993 over a million gay people marched on Washington for justice and equal rights in what is believed to be the largest demonstration in American history.

There have been some stunning gains in recent years in the struggle for lesbian and gay equality around the world. Gays can now legally marry in Holland, Denmark, Norway, and Sweden. They can serve openly in the military in many countries, including France, Germany, Japan, and Israel. In 1994 the European Parliament passed a resolution to establish guidelines for member nations to prohibit discrimination against gays and lesbians. South Africa, so long a stronghold of oppression, has become the first country to forbid discrimination based on sexual orientation in its new interim constitution. And Amnesty International has recognized gay oppression as a human rights issue.

At the same time, we are living in an era of tragedy, struggle, and fierce opposition. The AIDS crisis, while not unique to the gay community, has killed more than a hundred thousand gay men since the outbreak of the disease in 1981, and it is likely that it will kill hundreds of thousands more. It is certain that homophobia contributed to the lack of a swift response in the early years when its spread might have been arrested.

Antigay violence is so prevalent that a report comissioned by the United States Department of Justice stated that "a wave of homophobic violence seems to be sweeping the nation."[3] Suicide is the leading cause of death among gay, lesbian, bisexual, and transgendered youth, according to the United States Department of Health and Human Services.[4] And in 1992 voters in Colorado passed a ballot question that would prevent local governments from creating laws to protect gay people from discrimination. The question of whether it is constitutional for a state to pass such a law is now before the U.S. Supreme Court.

Clearly we have made important strides toward achieving civil rights for gay, lesbian, and bisexual people. Yet as we have seen throughout history, when oppressed people become empowered, those who want to maintain their domination inevitably fight back. Visible progress in human rights gives rise to reactionary backlash. It is foolish to think that progress is inevitable. In reality, we must work to achieve it—and to keep it!

When our efforts to create a more just world are met with retaliation, we shouldn't be surprised. Instead, we must recognize this reaction—even anticipate it—and develop strategies for dealing with the backlash set off by our progress.

youth activism

Young people are often at the forefront of movements for social change. Youth have the idealism, energy, and boldness to do what

[3]Peter Finn and Taylor McNeil, "Bias Crime and the Criminal Justice Response" (Cambridge: Abt Associates for the National Institute of Justice, May 1988), p. 3.

[4]Paul Gibson, "Gay Male and Lesbian Youth Suicide," in *Report of the Secretary's Task Force on Youth Suicide,* Publication No. ADM 89-1623, vol. 3 (Washington, D.C.: U.S. Department of Health and Human Services, 1989), p. 110.

older people think can't be done. And youth are an important part of the struggle for equal rights for lesbian, bisexual, and gay people.

As a young person, there are many ways that you can contribute: from volunteering at gay and lesbian community centers, youth groups, and AIDS organizations to demonstrating with ACT UP, marching in Pride parades, putting buttons on your backpack, and—when it's safe—demanding that the adults in your life respect you as a bisexual, gay, or lesbian person. Stone is a speaker at her local gay speakers bureau:

> It's been wonderful to be a speaker. I've gotten a lot of really positive responses from people who say, "My brother—mother, sister, uncle—is gay and this really helped me understand." Some people have come up and said, "I could never tell anybody, but I guess I can tell you that I'm questioning." A lot of people talk to me because I'm around the same age as they are.

Christopher describes some original consciousness-raising actions he and some friends did at his college in Iowa:

> We wanted to show how many gay students were at our school—what 10 percent really looks like. So we decided to label all the fixtures in the bathroom, all the sinks, the mirrors, the showers. We did it proportionately, so one in ten of those showers had a gay label, and in the girl's bathroom there was a lesbian label, and every once in a while we'd just stick in a transgender or transsexual. We canvassed the whole campus at three in the morning. We just wanted to make people aware.
>
> We also put a half-page ad in the school paper—a day in the life of the gay student. And a lot of it was, "Wake up, take a shower, do your homework," but then it got into, "Go to class, refrain from talking about what you did with your partner over the weekend, listen to homophobic jokes, go to English, discuss straight authors, discuss gay authors as though they were straight," things like that.

Nancy, from New York, shares:

> I volunteer at the Neutral Zone, the gay and lesbian youth center. Just helping out. They have a juice bar. Sometimes

there's a person who's crying. Her girlfriend left her or he's just been through the mill because he's gay. I'm there if they want. I hug them. They can cry on my shoulder. It comes naturally to me. I come from such a loving family. It makes me feel great. It makes me feel like I've accomplished something, little as it may be.

Activism can be personally rewarding, as well as a way to make a meaningful contribution toward creating a better, safer world for gay, lesbian, and bisexual youth—and everyone else. Manny has this perspective:

I work to improve myself. And if I improve myself, my image, I'm going to improve the image of the Hispanic community and the image of the gay community. I think we all work for ourselves. Because when we help others, we help ourselves.

Stacey describes her commitment to activism:

For me, it is less about being an activist and more about having a responsibility because I went through something. If I can help one kid now, I think that's what it's about. If I am talking to a schoolroom of teachers and one of them changes, that's what it is about. And for me, it's also a healing process. Speaking has helped me—even more than therapy—to realize that I had nothing wrong with me. Activism is why I'm here.

Activism can also be an effective response to harassment. As Stacey goes on to say:

I've learned that I don't have to argue everything one-to-one with people who harass me. It's less important to put everything into one person who might not change than to affect all the people who will. I can do other things instead. For example, I invited two gay judges and two gay attorneys to come to my law school to give a panel.

And sometimes, as with Stonewall, it's just being plain fed up that leads people into action. Daphne relates the following incident during her senior year in high school:

There was a big blowup at the school board meeting with some parents protesting because the number of the Billie De Frank Gay and Lesbian Community Center was put on the back of student ID cards along with other community organizations. Two or three people came out that night and said, "I'm who you're talking about. I'm a straight A student. I'm on the school paper. And you're putting me down." They hadn't come out to anyone before, except maybe a few close friends. So they had to go home that night and explain to their parents. And it wasn't so much courageous. They were just so mad that they couldn't hold back any longer.

Many of the other young people you've met in this book have also found activism to be rewarding. Chris has helped to enact an antidiscrimination law in Massachusetts. Alessandra is an openly lesbian role model in her job as Resident Assistant in her dorm at the University of Memphis. Beth was out on MTV's *Real Life*. Rick is the publisher and Arwyn the editor of the gay youth zine *InsideOUT*. And Renee, Matt, Sara, Luna, and Yevette are HIV educators.

These creative and commited young people, and so many others, are leading us toward a future in which we can all enjoy the equal rights and full justice to which we are entitled.

Symbols of Pride

◇ **Rainbow flag**

Designed for the 1978 Gay Pride celebration in San Francisco, the rainbow colored stripes symbolize the diversity within our community. The flags have became an international symbol of lesbian, gay, and bisexual freedom and pride.

◇ **Freedom rings**

In the early 1990s people started to wear necklaces with six metallic rings in the same rainbow colors as the flag. It is a fun play on words from the patriotic phrase "let freedom ring" and signifies the determination to be free from prejudice and discrimination.

◇ **Triangles—pink, black, pink/blue**

In the Nazi death camps of World War II, the prisoners were forced to wear colored symbols on their clothes to mark them as members of particular groups. Jews had to wear yellow stars. Gay men had to wear pink triangles and lesbians, as well as prostitutes and other "asocial" women, black triangles. At the end of the war most people in the concentration camps were liberated, but those with pink triangles were considered to be criminals and were transferred to prisons.

In the early 1970s gay people began wearing these triangles as a statement of pride in their identity and a refusal to be oppressed any longer. The triangles serve to remind us all, "Never Forget/Never Again." The triangles always point down, the way they were worn during the Holocaust.

Bisexual people have adopted two overlapping triangles—one pink, one blue—that create a lavender triangle in the middle.

◇ Lambda–λ

In 1970 the Gay Activists Alliance of New York designated the lambda—the letter L in the Greek alphabet—as a symbol of our liberation.

◇ Lesbian symbol–

◇ Gay men's symbol–

◇ Bisexual symbol–

The astrological symbol for the planet Mars signifies men, and the symbol for Venus signifies women. Two intersecting women's or men's symbols, then, mean gay or lesbian. And combining them all means bisexual.

◇ Lavender

There are various theories about how the color lavender came to be associated with gay men and lesbians. One favorite is the custom in sixteenth century England in which both men and women indicated that they did not intend to marry by wearing violets. However it began, the link between lavender and gayness has been passed on throughout the generations.

Joan Bobkoff © 1995

21
standing up for lesbian, gay, and bisexual youth

For the Adult Gay Community

Without community there is no liberation.

—Audre Lorde[1]

This chapter is addressed to the adults in the gay, lesbian, and bisexual community.

As a young person, it will give you an idea about the kind of support that could—and should—be offered to you. You may also want to give it to gay adults to encourage them to advocate for youth. When adults and young people work together, the results are much greater than either group could achieve on its own.

[1]A note about Audre Lorde appears in Chapter 3, "Reaching Out."

> And don't forget—it won't be too long until you'll be in a position to be helping those younger than you. Even if adults didn't extend enough of this support to you, you can be the one who helps to make it happen for future youth.

It's crucial that lesbian, gay, and bisexual adults fight for the rights of gay youth. We need to speak out in support of their concerns. We need to stand up for them—and with them.

As Patrick said when he was interviewed by *OUT* magazine:

> Whenever you read gay magazines, there are always articles about domestic partnership. And domestic partnership is not nearly as important an issue as queer youth. People don't kill themselves over domestic partnership. If someone could pick up a gay magazine and read a column by a gay kid, it might save someone's life.[2]

making youth issues a priority

Some gay and lesbian adults have made significant contributions to youth, and the focus on youth issues is definitely increasing, but on the whole our community has been slow to take up the concerns that are most urgent for young people.

There are a number of reasons why it's taken so long for youth issues to become a priority. David LaFontaine, Chairperson of the Massachusetts Governor's Commission on Gay and Lesbian Youth, explains:

> Working on this issue has brought back a lot of memories from my own adolescence. And it's very painful. I think the major reason we haven't reached out to gay youth is not that we don't care, but we don't want to remember what we went through ourselves. And we need to remember, so that we can make sure that it doesn't happen anymore. Those of us who have lived through the persecution, hate crimes, sui-

[2]Michelangelo Signorile, "The Post-Stonewall Generation," *OUT Magazine* (July/August 1994), p. 89.

cide attempts—we need to confront our own past. As a community, we need to confront just how much we have suffered from oppression.

Another reason why gay, lesbian, and bisexual adults have not helped gay youth is the fear of being accused of recruitment or exploitation. Child sexual abuse is a grave problem in our society, but the stereotype that gay people are more likely to molest children than straight people are is simply not true. However, an accusation of abuse can be so devastating that the threat of it has kept gay people from supporting youth. As Curt Shepard, campus organizer for the National Gay and Lesbian Task Force, says:

> Why have our organizations been so slow on the uptake on youth issues? One word: pedophilia. I'm sure that's why we've been very reluctant, as a community, to take on anything that could be used to reinforce—or even hint at—the false stereotype that we're abusing young people sexually. It's fear-based.

Yet in spite of these fears, gay and lesbian adults are increasingly reaching out to support young people. Leo Treadway, consultant for the Minneapolis Public Schools in their newly created support program for gay, lesbian, bisexual, and transgender students and teachers, notes:

> Finally, the community has moved from a period in which they were terribly afraid to work with gay and lesbian youth, for all the obvious reasons, to a mind-set where it is now crucial to their thinking that no other kid would have to go through what they went through. They see themselves investing in the community's future. And suddenly all the things that we say about youth in general—how they're the next generation of leaders—now makes sense just in terms of queer youth.
>
> Primarily what we did was to stop living in fear. We began to see that none of the horrible things which we all thought were going to happen to us as adults who were working with the kids happened. We didn't have irate parents coming in and threatening to smash our faces in or sue us or any of these things we dreaded. We'd scared ourselves to death, and finally we had to just bite the bullet and say,

"Look, we can't protect ourselves from everything. So let's just do what makes sense and what's right."

I don't date these kids. I'm certainly not about to be sexual with them. But they don't have a lot of adults in their lives who are close and supportive and willing to go to the mat for them. Or willing to hug them. I take reasonable precautions, but if a kid needs something legitimate I'm not willing to protect myself at their expense.

More and more gay and lesbian adults are committing themselves to work with and for gay youth in spite of the possibility that they may be accused of exploitation.

Chris Kryzan, Executive Director of !OutProud!, has done a great deal of work helping gay and lesbian youth connect with each other on-line, and he's also the foster parent of a gay teenager:

People raise their eyebrows whenever you say you want to work on issues of gay teens. There is an assumption of pederasty. There is an assumption of evil intent. And you've got to get past that.

Part of how Chris—and others who are dedicated to making the world a safer place for gay youth—"get past that" is to act in ways that are consistently responsible and nonexploitive toward young people. When Chris first met the young man who became his foster child, he was vigilant about protecting both this young man and his own reputation. And he got licensed as a foster home by the county children's services department.

In order for us to be able to support gay, lesbian, and bisexual youth, we need, as a community, to take a clear stand against sexual exploitation and to be healthy role models for safe and appropriate boundaries. Mary Voit, who facilitates a support group for gay, lesbian, bisexual, and transgender homeless youth, says:

I work with kids who have been exploited by every adult they have ever met, so it's extremely important to have good clear boundaries. For example, one night I was out very late with a kid. It was nine-thirty or ten o'clock. This kid just got his own apartment, brand new. We drive up and he said, "Oh, come in and see my apartment." I said, "No, this isn't an appropriate time for me to be in your apartment." Things like that, where the welfare and the safety of the youth come first. And you explain it and it gives them that secure feeling that they know that you know what's going on, what's appropriate. They come to count on it, to rely on it, that you're not going to exploit them.

Gay youth need an environment that's supportive, nurturing, and safe. Although it's important that *all* adults provide this, we, as gay, lesbian, and bisexual adults, have a special responsibility to these young people. After all, they're *our* kids.

what you can do

There are a multitude of ways that gay, lesbian, and bisexual adults can offer tangible support, opportunities, guidance, and inspiration to gay youth.

◇ START A SUPPORT GROUP

If your town or city doesn't have its own support group for gay, lesbian, and bisexual youth, you could begin one. Network with PFLAG and the closest gay and lesbian community center to determine what's already available and to collaborate on assessing the needs. You will have to secure space for weekly meetings in a social service agency, church or temple, school, or other safe and public place. Then find a skilled and responsible group facilitator. You may also need to raise money to cover costs such as publicity, rent, or facilitator's salary.

◇ SPONSOR EVENTS—OR ONGOING EXPENSES— FOR THE YOUTH GROUP

If there's already an ongoing lesbian, gay, and bisexual youth group, you could raise money for a recreation fund. You could sponsor a pizza night, bowling afternoon, or camping trip. If the group's funding isn't stable, you could contribute to rent, underwrite the costs of a newsletter, or pay for group T-shirts.

◇ SPONSOR SCHOLARSHIPS

Getting an education is important for young people, but it can be a real challenge to finance a college education. If you have the resources to sponsor a scholarship—or if you can raise funds—this is a great way to help. Even small scholarships can be very meaningful. And some colleges and universities now have gay and lesbian alumni groups that can offer scholarships.

In New Orleans, gay, lesbian, and bisexual community members and their PFLAG chapter have awarded $62,000 in college scholarships for gay, lesbian, and bisexual students! When they began five years ago, they had no fund-raising history, but they've awarded twenty $1,000 scholarships each of the last two years.

BACK-TO-SCHOOL CAMPAIGN

The Gay, Lesbian, and Straight Teachers Network (GLSTN), a national organization working to end homophobia in the schools, invites you to join an historic educational effort—the Back-to-School Campaign.

Because many teachers, administrators, and community members believe homophobia is someone else's problem and that it doesn't happen in their community, they need to learn that it does. And you can tell them.

To participate in the Back-to-School Campaign, just follow these simple steps:

1. Choose a teacher or administrator from a school you attended.

2. Write him or her a detailed personal letter that uses your experiences at that school to illustrate what homophobia does to young people.

3. Ask for a reply that specifies what they will do this year to end homophobia in their school or classroom.

4. Send along a copy of GLSTN's packet, "What You Can Do: Ideas and Resources for Educators Working to End Homophobia in Schools," available free of charge.

5. Copy your letter to GLSTN so they can use it to raise awareness among other educators.

6. Get involved! Membership in GLSTN and its local chapters is open to all who want to end homophobia in education: gay or straight, teacher or community member, we all have a role to play in this struggle.

Contact GLSTN at 122 West 26th Street, #1100, New York, NY 10001, (212)727–0135.

◇ BE A MENTOR

Gay, lesbian, and bisexual youth need adults in their lives who are truly concerned with their well-being. Especially if gay youth are rejected by their families—or when there's serious conflict about their sexual orientation—they need responsible adults who care about them.

As a mentor to gay youth, you spend time with them on a regular basis, and, depending on their needs, you may take an interest in their school work, offer guidance about possible careers, help them to achieve their educational goals, encourage healthy peer relationships, and introduce them to cultural events.

It's important that your involvement as a mentor not be in conflict with gay youth's relationships with their families. If at all possible, meet with the gay youth's parents and join with them in defining your goals. Under no circumstances do you want to put young people in a position where they have to choose between their attachments to their families and to you.

◇ HIRE A BISEXUAL, LESBIAN, OR GAY YOUTH

If you own a bicycle repair shop or a bakery, if you're a lawyer or general contractor, if you have any kind of business where you can create a trainee or entry-level position, hire a gay youth. Publicize this opportunity through your local gay youth group or in the gay press.

◇ COUNSEL GAY YOUTH

If you're a psychologist, psychiatrist, social worker, marriage, family, and child counselor, or any other kind of mental health professional, offer free or low-fee services to gay youth and their families.

◇ START A SPEAKERS BUREAU

If your community doesn't already have one, a gay, lesbian, and bisexual speakers bureau is an effective way of educating your community. Schools, churches, agencies, and other community groups are beginning to recognize the need to become more aware of the concerns of gay youth. The most successful speakers panels include young people who tell their stories.

TRIANGLE SPEAKERS

Triangle Speakers is a speakers bureau in Santa Cruz, California, begun by a group of lesbian, gay, and bisexual community members, along with parents of gay children, who wanted to support youth. Their goal is to dispel myths and stereotypes about gay people so that a healthy and safe environment can exist for everyone, so that gay youth can feel affirmed and supported, and so the schools and the community at large can become more respectful of bisexual, gay, and lesbian people.

Triangle's basic philosophy is that speakers share from their own experience rather than engaging in debate. To that effect, they use a format in which a panel of gay, lesbian, and bisexual people, as well as a parent, introduce themselves with short autobiographical statements and then answer questions. Speakers respond to questions by sharing their personal life stories and experiences rather than attempting to represent the views of the entire community.

Triangle Speakers has become an important element in a team approach. Teachers, principals, and religious or community leaders concerned about the needs of gay youth don't need to devise programs or locate appropriate speakers themselves. Instead, they can call Triangle Speakers and a trained panel is provided.

Although Triangle began quietly, it became a lightning rod for protest and opposition. There were a number of ugly incidents, a great deal of press coverage, and a difficult struggle. But the leadership of Triangle Speakers was well organized, thoughtful, and prepared. Although some educators hesitated to invite Triangle back into their schools, many others came forward with new support, as did the community at large, so that Triangle continues to thrive and to serve the community.

◇ MAKE FINANCIAL CONTRIBUTIONS

If you have money and no time, make regular contributions to people who are engaging in these efforts—and to the organizations listed throughout this book.

◇ BECOME A FOSTER PARENT

There is an urgent need for responsible adults to be foster parents for gay, lesbian, and bisexual youth who are rejected by their families or in such conflict with them that they cannot live at home. If every gay, lesbian, and bisexual adult who was able to would offer a safe and caring home to one young person with no place to live, our community would be transformed.

CHRIS AND TOMMY'S STORY: FOSTER PARENT AND CHILD

Tommy is a gay teenager who was suffering with depression and suicidal feelings. His parents, though well intentioned, didn't understand what he was going through and considered hospitalizing him. After Tommy left home, several agencies worked together to help convince Tommy's mother that it was in his best interests to live with a foster dad, Chris.

Learning to live together and be a family has required adjustments for both Chris and Tommy. Chris was astonished by the new demands on his time:

> It took the first month just to get Tommy into school. I made six trips to the enrollment office and five trips to the school to get him registered. Nobody in any of these administrative capacities has any understanding of what it means to be a single parent.

And Tommy describes the process of getting to know each other:

> It took getting used to because it's a different type of parent situation. I got upset with him because he was spending so much time with his business. But I adjusted and he realized what was bothering me and made an extra effort. It's basically a learning process.

Both Tommy and Chris describe the outcome as unequivocally positive. Tommy is doing well and has started college. He has reconciled with his parents, they talk on the phone regularly, and he's spent time with them on short visits. And most important, Tommy has become comfortable with himself:

> As time has gone on, I've become more and more accepting of myself. I've become more confident in everything I do. I got a job at the mall, and after a month and a half I got promoted to be assistant manager. I'm making A's and B's in school. I was able to completely start from scratch, rebuild things, get my life back together.

Chris shares the rewards he's experienced:

The biggest reward for me is seeing Tommy take control of his life and become the person that he wants to be. I've seen him do well in school and in his job, and he has a very loving and caring relationship with his boyfriend. I get a lot of satisfaction and emotional fulfillment out of seeing that.

There's a new kind of love I found in me—the love of a parent for a child—that's a very profound experience. And it really has helped me grow as a person. I liked myself before, but there's a new aspect to me that has been very meaningful.

At Christmas something happened which meant more than any other gift. He told me he loved me. I'd told him that probably every other day, but that was the first time he said it back. That really meant a lot to me.

◇ BE AN OUT VISIBLE ROLE MODEL IN YOUR COMMUNITY

We say this over and over again—and it can't be said too many times: gay, lesbian, and bisexual young people need to see gay, lesbian, and bisexual adults living healthy, successful, satisfying lives so they can be reminded—over and over again—that this is possible for them too.

"powerful beyond measure"

No one can do all the things suggested, or even most of them. But everyone can do something—at least one thing. Supporting gay youth, and working in collaboration with them, is a mutually rewarding endeavor.

These *brilliant, gorgeous, talented,* and *fabulous* young people inspire us all to make manifest our full potential. They dare us to imagine—and to have faith in our dreams.

resources

youth resources

GENERAL HELPLINES

LYRIC Gay Youth Talkline—San Francisco
1-800-246-PRIDE
Mon, Wed, Fri 6:30–9 pm PST, Tues, Thurs 4–9 pm PST

National Gay/Lesbian/Bisexual Youth Hotline—Indianapolis
1-800-347-TEEN
Thurs through Sun, 7–9:45 pm EST, Fri–Sat, 7–11:45 EST

The Out Youth Austin Helpline
1-800-96-YOUTH
Every day 5:30–9:30 pm CST

**TO LOCATE GAY, LESBIAN, AND BISEXUAL
RESOURCES IN YOUR AREA**

Lambda Youth Network
P.O. Box 7911
Culver City, CA 90233
E-mail: lambdayn@aol.com

To receive a customized listing of lesbian, gay, and bisexual youth groups, gay community centers, and PFLAG chapters in your area, send a large self-addressed envelope along with $2 and include your city, state, zip code, and area code.

!OutProud!
P.O. Box 24589
San Jose, CA 95154-4589
E-mail: info@outproud.org

To receive a customized listing—for your area—of lesbian, gay, and bisexual youth groups, gay community centers, and PFLAG chapters through E-mail, send an E-mail with your city, state, zip code, and area code.

AGENCIES ESPECIALLY FOR LESBIAN, GAY, AND BISEXUAL YOUTH

Boston GLASS (Gay and Lesbian Adolescent Social Services)
93 Massachusetts Ave.
Boston, MA 02115
(617)266-3349; fax: (617)457-8133; E-mail: glass@jri.org

Delta Youth Alliance
Gay and Lesbian Community Services of Central Florida
714 East Colonial Dr.
Orlando, FL 32803
(407)THE-GAYS

District 202
2524 Nicollet Ave. S.
Minneapolis, MN 55404
(612)871-5559

Hetrick-Martin Institute
2 Astor Place
New York, NY 10003-6998
(212)674-2400; fax: (212)674-8650

Horizons Youth Services
961 W. Montana St.
Chicago, IL 60614
(312)472-6469; helpline every day 6–10 pm CST: (312)929-HELP

IYG (Indianapolis Youth Group)
P.O. Box 20716
Indianapolis, IN 46220
(317)541-8726

Lambert House Youth Center
1818–15th Ave.
Seattle, WA 98122
(206)322-2735

LYRIC (Lavender Youth Recreation and Information Center)
127 Collingwood St.
San Francisco, CA 94114
(415)703-6150; toll-free: 1-800-246-PRIDE

Out Youth Austin
425 Woodward St.
Austin, TX 78704
(512)326-1234; toll-free: 1-800-96-YOUTH

SMYAL (Sexual Minority Youth Assistance League)
333½ Pennsylvania Ave. SE, 3rd fl
Washington, DC 20003-1148
(202)546-5940; helpline Mon–Fri 7–10 pm EST: (202)546-5911

Youth Services
Colorado Gay and Lesbian Community Center
P.O. Drawer 18E
Denver, CO 80218
(303)831-6268

Youth Services
Los Angeles Gay and Lesbian Community Services Center
1625 N. Schrader Blvd.
Los Angeles, CA 90028-9998
(213)993-7450

PEN-PAL SERVICES

Lesbian and Gay Youth Network [under the age of 21]
IGY (Indianapolis Youth Group)
P.O. Box 20716
Indianapolis, IN 46220
(317)541-8726; fax: (317)545-8594

International Pen-Pal Program [under the age of 24]
Youth Outreach
Los Angeles Gay and Lesbian Community Services Center
1625 N. Schrader St.
Los Angeles, CA 90028
(213)993-7451

ON-LINE/INTERNET ADDRESSES

AMERICA ONLINE

Gay and Lesbian Community Forum: keyword GAY. Then the Gay Message Board-Teens Issues, Lesbian Message Board-Baby Dykes, and Bisexual Message Board-Bisexual Teens

Planet Out: keyword PNO. Then Civic Center-!OutProud! and Youth Assistance Organization

InsideOUT is a magazine by, for, and about lesbian, gay, and bisexual youth: InsideOUT2@aol.com

WORLD WIDE WEB

!OutProud! home page: go to URL http://www.outproud.org/outproud/

QueerAmerica database: go to URL http.//www.youth.org/outproud/

Planet Out: go to URL http://www.planetout.com/

Youth Assistance Organization home page: go to URL http://www.youth.org./

FOR PEOPLE OF COLOR

Black Gay and Lesbian Leadership Forum
1219 S. La Brea
Los Angeles, CA 90019
(213)964-7820; fax: (213)964-7830

LLEGO (National Latino/a Lesbian and Gay Organization)
703 G Street SE
Washington, D. C. 20003
(202)454-0092

Trikone
P.O. Box 21354
San Jose, CA 95151-1354
(408)270-8776; fax: (408)274-2733; E-mail: trikone@rahul.net

An organization of gay and lesbian South Asians. Publishes a quarterly magazine.

TRANSGENDER

AEGIS (American Education Gender Information Service)
P.O. Box 33724
Decatur, GA 30033-0724
(404)939-2122 (business); (404)939-0244 (information and referral); fax: (404)939-1770; E-mail: aegis@mindspring.com

Transexual/trangender information, referrals, and publications available.

IFGE (International Foundation for Gender Education)
P.O. Box 229
Waltham, MA 02254-0229
(617)894-8340; fax: (617)899-5703; E-mail: IFGE@world.std.com
  An education and service organization for the transsexual/trangender community. Publishes a magazine. Book catalog free on request.

AIDS

National AIDS Hotline
1-800-342-AIDS
  24 hours with HIV/AIDS information

Project Inform Hotline
1-800-822-7422 (U.S.)
1-800-334-7422 (Calif.)
  HIV/AIDS information Mon–Fri 10 am–4 pm PST and Sat 10 am–1 pm PST

ACT UP San Francisco (AIDS Coalition to Unleash Power)
1388 Haight St. #218
San Francisco, CA 94117
(415)522-2907; fax: (415)834-0243; E-mail: actupsf@aol.com
  A direct political action group fighting to end the AIDS crisis. Has many chapters across the country. Call to find one near you.

Gay Men's Health Crisis (GMHC)
129 W. 20th St. 4th fl
New York, NY 10011
(212)807-6655 (information line)
  Has a young adult project, will send written materials and provide information and referrals.

Lesbian AIDS Project
129 W. 20th St. 4th fl
New York, NY 10011
(212)337-3532 (information line)
  Will provide information, referrals, and written materials.

The NAMES Project
310 Townsend St. #310
San Francisco, CA 94107
(415)882-5500
  Sponsors the AIDS Memorial Quilt, which is made up of thousands of individual three-by-six-foot cloth panels that commemorate the lives of people who have died of AIDS. Contact them to bring the Quilt to your community.

BOOKS

Hein, Karen, and Theresa Foy DiGeronimo. *AIDS: Trading Fears for Facts: A Guide for Young People*. Yonkers: Consumer Reports Books, 1991.

A readable, well-illustrated, informative book intended for a high school audience.

RUNAWAY HELP

National Runaway Switchboard
1-800-621-4000
If you've left home, are thinking of leaving, or if your parents are threatening to throw you out, this helpline can tell you about resources near you.

PSYCHIATRIC ABUSE HELP

The National Center for Lesbian Rights
870 Market St. Suite 570
San Francisco, CA 94102
(415)392-6257; toll-free: 1-800-528-6257
Has a special project to stop the mental health abuse of lesbian, gay, bisexual, and transgender youth. Provides free legal and practical support.

ANTIVIOLENCE

Gay and Lesbian Anti-Violence Project
647 Hudson St.
New York, NY 10014
(212)807-0197
Call if you are afraid or have been the victim of antigay violence. They give referrals and are collecting national data.

HEALING FROM CHILD SEXUAL ABUSE

National Child Abuse Hotline
1-800-4-A-CHILD
This 24-hour child abuse hotline provides crisis intervention, information, and referrals.

Survivors of Incest Anonymous (SIA)
P.O. Box 21817
Baltimore, MD 21222-6817
(410)282-3400

A national twelve-step self-help program for incest survivors that will help you locate programs in your area.

BOOKS

Bass, Ellen, and Laura Davis. *The Courage to Heal: A Guide for Women Survivors of Child Sexual Abuse.* New York: HarperCollins, 1988.

Informative, encouraging, practical, and inspiring. Written for women but helpful to men as well.

Lew, Mike. *Victims No Longer: Men Recovering from Incest and Other Sexual Child Abuse.* New York: HarperCollins, 1988.

Clear, warm information and encouragement.

Loiselle, Mindy B., and Leslie Bailey Wright. *Shining Through: Pulling It Together after Sexual Abuse.* Brandon, VT: The Safer Society Press, 1992.

Excellent for adolescents and teens.

ALCOHOLISM AND DRUG ABUSE

Alcoholics Anonymous (AA) and Narcotics Anonymous (NA)
AA and NA are usually listed in the white pages alphabetically. Often they have a 24-hour number. If you call the number in the phone book, someone will give you information about when and where there are meetings. If you are interested, be sure to ask about gay and/or lesbian meetings.

Harm Reduction Coalition (HRC)
3223 Lakeshore Ave.
Oakland, CA 94610
(510)444-6969; fax: (510)444-6977; E-mail: kershnar@well.com
HRC will provide education, resources, and local referrals for those actively using drugs and alcohol and for people who are providing services to active users.

Pride Institute
14400 Martin Dr.
Eden Prairie, MN 55344
(612)934-7554; toll-free: 1-800-54-PRIDE
A private drug and alcohol treatment organization especially for lesbian, gay, and bisexual people. Program is for those 18 and older, but if you have your guardian's consent they can make exceptions. They make national referrals to other programs and professionals.

ABUSIVE RELATIONSHIPS

BOOKS

Island, David, and Patrick Letellier. *Men Who Beat the Men That Love Them*. New York: Haworth Press, 1991.

Useful survival guide with good information. Has one of the author's personal story woven throughout the text.

Lobel, Kerry. *Naming the Violence: Speaking Out about Lesbian Battering*. Seattle: Seal Press, 1986.

Essays and poetry about the personal experience and politics of lesbian domestic violence.

NiCarthy, Ginny. *Getting Free: A Handbook for Women in Abusive Relationships*. Seattle: Seal Press, 1986.

Valuable information on both practical and emotional issues. Sections on lesbian abuse, teen abuse, and emotional abuse.

JOB TRAINING PROGRAM FOR ALL YOUTH

The Job Corps
1-800-733-JOBS
A federal program for youth ages 16–24, provides full-time educational and vocational skills training, as well as meals, dormitory housing, medical care, spending money, and a savings account. Has 125 different training programs all around the country, most of which take about a year to complete.

BOOKS OF INTEREST TO LESBIAN, GAY, AND BISEXUAL YOUTH

WHERE TO GET BOOKS

Lambda Rising Bookstores
1625 Connecticut Ave., NW
Washington, DC
(202)462-6969; toll-free: 1-800-621-6969; fax:(202)462 7257; E-mail: lambdarising@his.com (via Internet) and keyword GAYBOOKS (via America Online)
Lambda Rising stocks virtually every gay and lesbian book in print, as well as magazines, music, videos, T-shirts, and gay gifts. They have a catalog and will mail in plain wrapping if you wish.

FICTION

Andersen, Hans Christian. *Michael Hague's Favorite Hans Christian Andersen Fairy Tales*. New York: Holt, Rinehart & Winston, 1981.

Once you know that Andersen was gay, you'll never read "The Ugly Duckling" the same way again.

Bauer, Marion Dane, ed. *Am I Blue: Coming Out from the Silence*. New York: HarperCollins, 1994.

Heartwarming short stories that explore growing up lesbian or gay or with lesbian or gay parents. Title story is terrific.

Brett, Catherine. *S.P. Likes A.D.* Toronto: The Women's Press, 1989.

The central character comes to the realization that she is a lesbian and has friends that accept it comfortably.

Brown, Rita Mae. *RubyFruit Jungle*. New York: Bantam Books, 1973.

The classic lesbian coming out novel. Hilarious and enduring.

Garden, Nancy. *Annie on My Mind*. New York: Farrar, Strauss & Giroux, 1982.

A tender romance about two young women in high school.

Guy, Rosa. *Ruby*. New York: Viking, 1976.

The story of a love affair between two high school young women, one West Indian and the other African-American.

Miller, Isabel. *Patience and Sarah*. New York: Fawcett Crest, 1983.

A wonderful story of two women falling in love in nineteenth-century New England.

Mosca, Frank. *All American Boys*. Boston: Alyson Publications, 1983.

The love story of two young men who face homophobia and fag-bashing but prevail.

Walker, Kate. *Peter*. Boston: Houghton Mifflin, 1993.

An ordinary fifteen-year-old struggles with sexual identity issues when he feels attracted to his brother's gay friend.

Winterson, Jeannette. *Oranges Are Not the Only Fruit*. New York: Atlantic Monthly Press, 1985.

A young woman—and her fundamentalist Christian family—must come to terms with her emerging lesbian identity. Intense and well done.

Nonfiction/Biography

Beam, Joseph, ed. *In the Life: A Black Gay Anthology*. Boston: Alyson Publications, 1986.

A collection by African-American authors who explore what it means to be doubly different in modern America.

Chandler, Kurt. *Passages of Pride: Lesbian and Gay Youth Come of Age.* New York: Random House, 1995.

Well-written in-depth journalistic studies of six teenagers moving through their coming out process. Also included are briefer profiles of dozens of other teens, some parents, and insights from experts.

Fricke, Aaron. *Reflections of a Rock Lobster: A Story about Growing Up Gay.* Boston: Alyson Publications, 1981.

Aaron's own story of growing up and winning a court case in order to bring his boyfriend to the senior prom.

Harris, Robie H. *It's Perfectly Normal: A Book about Changing Bodies, Growing Up, Sex, and Sexual Health.* Cambridge, MA: Candlewick Press, 1994.

Excellent book that presents ethnic and sexual diversity, including affirming information about being gay and lesbian. Engaging illustrations that are both informative and funny. Especially useful as a teaching tool for younger teens.

Heron, Ann, ed. *Two Teenagers in Twenty: Writings by Gay and Lesbian Youth.* Boston: Alyson Publications, 1994.

First-person stories that combine new voices with many from the earlier *One Teenager in Ten.*

Hutchins, Loraine, and Lani Kaahumanu. *Bi Any Other Name: Bisexual People Speak Out.* Boston: Alyson Publications, 1991.

A ground-breaking anthology in which over seventy women and men share their stories in prose, poetry, art and essays.

Mishima, Ykio. *Confessions of a Mask.* New York: New Directions, 1988.

Autobiography that details growing up gay in Japan after World War II.

Monette, Paul. *Becoming a Man: Half a Life Story.* New York: Harcourt Brace Jovanovich, 1992.

An honest, funny, and unsparing account of one man's struggle to come out. Award winning.

Pollack, Rachel, and Cheryl Schwartz. *The Journey Out: A Guide For and About Lesbian, Gay, and Bisexual Teens.* New York, Penguin Books, 1995.

A great book to help younger teens through the coming out process. Positive, friendly, and useful.

Reid, John. *The Best Little Boy in the World.* New York: Ballantine, 1976.

A poignant and humorous autobiographical coming out story.

Singer, Bennett L., ed. *Growing Up Gay/Growing Up Lesbian: A Literary Anthology*. New York: New Press, 1994.

A collection of fiction, poetry, and testimony from prominent writers, celebrities, and gay youth.

MUSIC

Ladyslipper
P.O. Box 3124
Durham, NC 27715
(919)683-1570; toll-free: 1-800-634-6044; fax: (919)682-5601

Ladyslipper's catalog offers a rich selection of music by women, including many lesbians, as well as a small but terrific selection of "men's" music. They also have videos, T-shirts, songbooks, and sheet music.

VIDEOS

Homoteens. Joan Jubela. 1994. Frameline, 346 Ninth St., San Francisco, CA 94103, (415)703-8650

Portraits of five diverse New York City teens. Well done and engaging, with much of the filming done by the youth. 58 minutes.

Out: Stories of Lesbian and Gay Youth. David Adkin. 1993. National Film Board of Canada, 1251 Ave. of the Americas, 16th fl, New York, NY 10020, (212)596-1770

A sensitive look at the lives of a rich cross-section of young gays and lesbians and some of their families. Filmed mostly in the Toronto area. 79 minutes.

POSTERS

"What Can You Do . . . ," poster on p. 70, is available from:

Wingspan Ministry
Saint Paul-Reformation Lutheran Church
100 N. Oxford St.
Saint Paul, MN 55104
(612)224-3371

"When I Told My Mum. . . ," poster on p. 168, is available from:

Victorian AIDS Council/Gay Men's Health Centre
6 Claremont St.
South Yarra 3141
Australia
(011)(039)865-6700

◇   ◇   ◇

family resources

Parents, Family, and Friends of Lesbians and Gays (PFLAG)
1101 14th St. NW, Suite 1030
Washington, DC 20005
(202)638-4200; fax: (202)638-0243; E-mail: pflagntl@aol.com
  PFLAG is a national organization devoted to support, education, and advocacy with over 340 local chapters.

BOOKS/PAMPHLETS

Bernstein, Robert. *Straight Parents, Gay Children: Keeping Families Together.* New York: Thunder's Mouth Press, 1995.

The story of a father's coming to terms with his daughter's lesbianism. A call to action to speak out on behalf of gay relatives.

Clark, Don. *Loving Someone Gay.* Berkeley: Celestial Arts, 1990.

A sensitive, intelligent guide for all who care about gay people.

Dew, Robb Forman. *The Family Heart: A Memoir of When Our Son Came Out.* New York: Ballantine, 1995.

A moving account of one loving family's emotional journey from fear and confusion to acceptance and activism.

Fairchild, Betty, and Nancy Hayward. *Now That You Know: What Every Parent Should Know about Homosexuality.* San Diego: Harcourt Brace, 1989.

The classic for parents that have just been told. Deals with stereotypes, myths, and misconceptions.

Griffin, Carolyn Welch, and Marian and Arthur Wirth. *Beyond Acceptance.* New York: Saint Martin's Press, 1986.

Many parents share their experiences coming to a place of special appreciation for their lesbian and gay children.

Parents, Families, and Friends of Lesbians and Gays. *Our Daughters and Sons: Questions and Answers for Parents of Gay, Lesbian and Bisexual People.* Washington, D.C.: PFLAG, 1995.

An easy-to-read 20-page booklet that provides information about the most common parental concerns.

VIDEOS

Straight from the Heart: Stories of Parents' Journeys to a New
  Understanding of Their Gay and Lesbian Children. Dee Mosbacher.
  1994. Motivational Media, 8430 Santa Monica Blvd., Los Angeles, CA
  90069, (800)848-2707

Nominated for a documentary Academy Award, this touching video
examines the issues parents face in coming to terms with having a gay or
lesbian child. Especially useful in regard to religious concerns. 24 minutes.

Queer Son: Family Journeys to Understanding and Love. Vickie Seitchik. 1994.
  Vickie Seitchik, 19 Jackson St., Cape May, NJ 08204, (212)929-4199

An excellent personal documentary with interviews of families from
diverse racial, ethnic, and social backgrounds. Compelling. 48 minutes.

school resources

EAGLES Center
7051 Santa Monica Blvd.
Hollywood, CA 90038
(213)957-0348
  A Los Angeles Unified School District High School Options Program:
Emphasizing Adolescent Gay and Lesbian Education Services.

Harvard Gay and Lesbian School Issues Project
Harvard Graduate School of Education
Longfellow Hall 210
Cambridge MA 02138
(617)491-5301; fax: (617)495-8510
  An excellent source of curriculum and staff development materials.

Human Sexuality Program
Toronto Board of Education
Student Support Services
155 College St.
Toronto, Ontario
Canada M5T 1P6
(416)397-3755; fax: (416)397-3758
  A comprehensive program of services to students, teachers, families,
and the community.

The Gay, Lesbian and Straight Teachers Network (GLSTN)
122 W. 26th St. Suite 1100
New York, NY 10001
(212)727-0135; fax: (212)727-0254; E-mail: GLSTN@glstn.org
Teachers and community members work together to help make schools places where all people are valued, regardless of sexual orientation. GLSTN has over twenty-five chapters and administers the National Lesbian, Gay, and Bisexual History Month Project.

The Harvey Milk School
2 Astor Place
New York, NY 10003-6998
(212)674-2400; fax: (212)674-8650
An alternative high school for gay, lesbian, and bisexual students sponsored by the Hetrick-Martin Institute and the New York City Board of Education.

Out for Equity
Saint Paul Public School
1930 Como Ave.
Saint Paul, MN 55108
(612)293-8757; fax: (612)293-8769
Creates supportive school environments for lesbian, gay, and bisexual students, staff, and families.

PROJECT 10
7850 Melrose Ave.
Los Angeles, CA 90046
(818)577-4553
The first school support program, which has become the model for others. Services include counseling and education. Handbook and video available.

PROJECT 10 East
Cambridge Public Schools
459 Broadway
Cambridge, MA 02138
(617)349-6486; fax: (617)349-6897
Pre-K through 12th grade support services and resource information on creating safe schools.

PROJECT 21
1360 Mission St. Suite 200
San Francisco, CA 94103
(415)861-2244; fax: (415)861-4893
Project 21 is a campaign for educational equity sponsored by the Gay and Lesbian Alliance against Defamation of the San Francisco Bay Area

(GLAAD/SFBA). They work for textbook and curriculum reform and have published a poster depicting famous lesbian, gay, and bisexual people.

Support Services for Gay, Lesbian, and Bisexual Youth
San Francisco Unified School District
Health Programs Department
1512 Golden Gate Avenue
San Francisco, CA 94115
(415)749-3400 or 749-3424; fax: (415)749-3420
Provides educational, counseling, and training services. A resource curriculum guide and ten-minute video available.

Teaching Tolerance
400 Washington Ave.
Montgomery, AL 36104
(334)264-0286; fax: (334)264-3121
Provides teachers with materials, ideas, and strategies for teaching about how to accept those who are different. Their magazine, *Teaching Tolerance,* is available free to any educator involved in human rights work. Their curriculum kit, *The Shadow of Hate,* covers the history of intolerance in America from colonial times and includes a lesson about a young gay man killed in New York. Available free upon request of the principal.

BOOKS/PAMPHLETS

Harbeck, Karen, ed. *Coming Out of the Classroom Closet: Gay and Lesbian Students, Teachers, and Curricula.* Binghamton, NY: Haworth Press, 1992.

A highly worthwhile collection of scholarly articles and papers.

Jennings, Kevin, ed. *Becoming Visible: A Reader in Gay and Lesbian History for High School and College Students.* Boston: Alyson Publications, 1994.

Excellent reader covering over two thousand years of history and a diverse range of cultures. It includes primary and secondary sources and suggested study questions and classroom activities. Enormously valuable.

Marshall, David, Robert Kaplan, and Jessea Greenman. *The P.E.R.S.O.N. Organizing Manual: Public Education Regarding Sexual Orientation Nationally.* Oakland: The P.E.R.S.O.N. Project, 1995. Available from: The P.E.R.S.O.N. Project, 586 62nd St., Oakland, CA 94609-1245, fax: (510)601-8883; E-mail: jessea@uclink2.berkeley.edu

Includes general and state-by-state information to help in the effort to make curricular and textbook policies more fair and accurate about sexual orientation and lesbian, gay, bisexual, and transgender people.

Massachusetts Governor's Commission on Gay and Lesbian Youth. *Making Schools Safe for Gay and Lesbian Youth: Breaking the Silence in Schools and Families*. Boston: The Commission, 1993. Available from: Massachusetts Governor's Commission on Gay and Lesbian Youth, State House, Room 111, Boston, MA 02133, (617)828-3039

Includes useful general information about the need and specific recommendations for a school support program.

Minnesota Department of Education. *Alone No More: Developing a School Support System for Gay, Lesbian and Bisexual Youth*. Saint Paul: The Department, 1994. Available from: District 202, 2524 Nicollet Ave S., Minneapolis, MN 55404, (612)871-5559; fax: (612)871-1445

A practical and readable 60-page booklet. Excellent ideas about implementation of a student support program.

Sherrill, Jan-Mitchell, and Craig A. Hardesty. *The Gay, Lesbian and Bisexual Students' Guide to Colleges, Universities and Graduate Schools*. New York: New York University Press, 1994.

Useful information that is seldom available in college catalogs.

Unks, Gerald, ed. *The Gay Teen: Educational Practice and Theory for Lesbian, Gay, and Bisexual Adolescents*. New York: Routledge, 1995.

Academic collection of essays to equip gay and straight educators in meeting the needs of their gay students.

Woog, Dan. *School's Out: The Impact of Gay and Lesbian Issues on America's Schools*. Boston: Alyson Publications, 1995.

Filled with true stories from gay and lesbian students, teachers, principals, coaches, counselors, and their straight allies.

VIDEOS

Both of My Moms' Names Are Judy. Lesbian and Gay Parents Association (LGPA). 1994. GLPCI, P.O. Box 43206, Montclair, NJ 07043, (202)583-8029

The video presents a racially diverse group of children (ages seven to ten) talking about the love they feel for their gay and lesbian families. Powerful. Excellent tool for sensitizing elementary school educators and parents. Comes with training materials. 10 minutes.

Gay Youth: An Educational Video for the Nineties. Pam Walton. 1992. Wolfe Video, Box 64, New Almaden, CA 95042, (408)268-6782

Excellent, award-winning documentary highlighting two powerful stories, one with a positive outcome, one with a tragic suicide. Comes with study guide. Appropriate for youth and adult audiences. 40 minutes.

Just for Fun. Gordon Seaman. 1994. Direct Cinema Limited, P.O. Box
10003, Santa Monica, CA 90410-1003, 1-800-525-0000

Well-acted, well-written drama that examines the issues surrounding
homophobia and gay-bashing. Excellent for high school or college use.
Will stimulate meaningful classroom discussion. 24 minutes.

Sticks, Stones, and Stereotypes. Cindy Marshall, Equity Institute. 1988.
ETR Associates, P.O. Box 1830, Santa Cruz, CA 95061-1830, 1-800-
321-4407

Excellent video and curriculum module about name-calling, appropriate
for high school or first-year college. Homophobia is the focus. Extensive
guide available in English and Spanish. 26 minutes.

Too Close . . . for Comfort. Wild Ginger Productions. 1990. ETR Associates,
P.O. Box 1830, Santa Cruz, CA 95061-1830, 1-800-321-4407

Well-done video with excellent study and discussion guide. Deals with
fear of AIDS, homophobia, and discrimination. Appropriate for high
school and first-year college classrooms. 27 minutes.

Who's Afraid of Project 10. University of Southern California. 1989.
Friends of Project 10, 7850 Melrose Ave., Los Angeles, CA 90046,
(818)577-4553

Well-edited interviews with supporters and opponents of Project 10.
Especially good for audiences of educators. Virginia Uribe is featured. 23
minutes.

spirituality resources

All of these organizations can help you find local groups.

Affirmation (Mormon)
P.O. Box 46022
Los Angeles, CA 90046
(213)255-7251

American Baptists Concerned
P.O. Box 16128
Oakland, CA 94610
(510)530-6562; fax: (510)530-6501

Dignity/USA (Roman Catholic)
1500 Massachusetts Ave. NW Suite 11
Washington, DC 20005
(202)861-0017; toll-free: 1-800-877-8797; fax: (202)429-9808

Evangelicals Concerned
311 E. 72nd St. Suite 1-G
New York, NY 10021
(212)517-3171

Friends for Lesbian and Gay Concerns (Quakers)
143 Campbell Ave.
Ithaca, NY 14850
(607)272-1024; fax: (607)272-0801

Integrity, Inc. (Episcopal)
P.O. Box 19561
Washington, DC 20036
(718)720-3054

Presbyterians for Lesbian/Gay Concerns
P.O. Box 38
New Brunswick, NJ 08903-0038
(908)249-1016; fax: (908)932-6916; E-mail: jda@mariner.rutgers.edu

San Francisco Zen Center
300 Page St.
San Francisco,CA 94102
(415)863-3136

Unitarian Universalist Office for Lesbian, Bisexual and Gay Concerns
25 Beacon St.
Boston, MA 02108
(617)742-2100 ext.470; fax: (617)523-4123; E-mail: bgreve@uua.org

United Church of Religious Science
3251 W. Sixth St.
Los Angeles, CA 90020
(213)338-2181

Universal Fellowship of Metropolitan Community Churches (MCC)
5300 Santa Monica Blvd. Suite 304
Los Angeles, CA 90029
(213)464-5100; fax: (213)464-2123; E-mail: UFMCCHQ@aol.com

World Congress of Gay and Lesbian Jewish Organizations
P.O. Box 3345
New York, NY 10008-3345

BOOKS/PAMPHLETS

Aarons, Leroy. *Prayers for Bobby: A Mother's Coming to Terms with the Suicide of Her Gay Son*. San Francisco: Harper San Francisco, 1995.

When her gay son committed suicide at the age of twenty, Mary Griffith embarked on her own personal journey of growth from Fundamentalist Christian toward enlightenment and advocacy for gay and lesbian youth. This is her powerful story.

Anderson, Sherry Ruth, and Patricia Hopkins. *The Feminine Face of God: The Unfolding of the Sacred in Women*. New York: Bantam, 1991.

Through interviews with more than a hundred women, the authors share a rich and diverse array of spiritual journeys that are distinctively female.

Angel, Camille, and Shifra Teitelbaum. *Intimate Connections: Integrating Human Love with God's Love*. 1995. Shifra Teitelbaum, 1800 S. Robertson Blvd., #408, Los Angeles, CA 90035, (310)985-4609.

A ten-lesson curriculum and resource packet addressing the parallels between Jewish and lesbian and gay identity, visibility, community, and culture. Good for high school and adult groups.

Balka, Christie, and Andy Rose, eds. *Twice Blessed: On Being Gay and Jewish*. Boston: Beacon Press, 1989.

This is the first anthology by and about lesbian and gay Jews who are maintaining their ties to Jewish tradition. Inspiring.

Bess, Howard. *Pastor, I Am Gay*. Palmer, Alaska: Palmer Publishing Co., 1995.

In an easy-to-read storytelling style, Pastor Bess issues a plea for the dignity and sanctity of gay and lesbian people.

Boswell, John. *Christianity, Social Tolerance, and Homosexuality*. Chicago: University of Chicago Press, 1980.

This is considered by many to be the definitive scholary work regarding gay issues and Christianity.

Cherry, Kittredge, and Zalmon Sherwood, eds. *Equal Rites: Lesbian and Gay Worship, Ceremonies, and Celebrations*. Louisville, KY: Westminster John Knox Press, 1995.

A collection of Christian liturgy, prayers, and rituals to address spiritual beginnings, healing, blessings, holy unions, and communions.

Helminiak, Daniel. *What the Bible Really Says about Homosexuality*. San Francisco: Alamo Square Press, 1994.

Helminiak explains in a clear, accessible fashion recent insights by top scholars. Very useful.

Parents, Families, and Friends of Lesbians and Gays. *Is Homosexuality A Sin?* Washington, D.C.: PFLAG, 1992.

A useful 24-page booklet where various religious leaders answer some of the most basic questions.

Spong, John. *Living in Sin? A Bishop Rethinks Human Sexuality.* New York: Harper & Row, 1988.

Bishop Spong calls for inclusive church teachings about loving, nonexploitative relationships between all people.

Thompson, Mark. *Gay Soul: Finding the Heart of Gay Spirit and Nature: With Sixteen Writers, Healers, Teachers, and Visionaries.* San Francisco: Harper San Francisco, 1994.

Interviews illuminate the spiritual dimension of gay lives.

Women of Reform Judaism. *Covenant of the Heart.* 1995. Women of Reform Judaism, 838 Fifth Ave., New York, NY 10021, (212)249-0100 ext: 352

Jewish liturgy collection with prayers, poetry, and meditations for study and worship.

VIDEO

Always My Kid: A Family Guide to Understanding Homosexuality. Steve Baker and Russell Byrd. 1994. TriAngle Video Productions, 550 Westcott, #400, Houston, TX 77007, (713)869-4477

A collection of interviews that provides answers to the negative myths and stereotypes. Interviews of religious leaders are especially useful. 74 minutes.

community resources

CIVIL RIGHTS

Gay and Lesbian Alliance Against Defamation (GLAAD)
150 W. 26th St. #503
New York, NY 10001
(212)807-1700; fax: (212)807-1805; E-mail: GLAADNY@aol.com

Devoted to identifying and responding to public expressions of homophobia, particularly in the media. Offices in many large U.S. cities.

Human Rights Campaign (HRC)
1101 14th St. NW #200
Washington, DC 20005
(202)628-4160; fax: (202)347-5323

The nation's largest gay and lesbian political organization. Works to secure full civil rights for lesbians and gay men and responsible federal policies on AIDS.

Lambda Legal Defense and Education Fund
666 Broadway 12th fl.
New York, NY 10012-2317
(212)995-8585

The nation's oldest and largest lesbian and gay legal organization. Works to achieve full recognition of the civil rights of lesbians, gay men, and people with HIV/AIDS, through impact litigation, education, and public policy work. Call if you feel you've been discriminated against or need legal advice or representation.

The National Gay and Lesbian Task Force (NGLTF)
6030 Wilshire Blvd. Suite 200
Los Angeles, CA 90036
(213)934-9030

The oldest national lesbian and gay civil rights advocacy group. The Los Angeles office is responsible for the NGLTF campus organizing project and annual youth organizing institute.

SPECIAL INTEREST

Camp It Up!
4000 Waterhouse Rd.
Oakland, CA 94602
(510)530-0107; (510)524-6945

Sponsors a series of family recreation programs, including two weeks at a family camp near Yosemite. Has a Counselor in Training/Leadership Development program for youth.

Digital Queers (DQ)
584 Castro St. Suite 150
San Francisco, CA 94114
(415)252-6282

Promotes equal rights through the effective use of digital technology and communications.

Gay and Lesbian Association of Choruses (GALA)
P.O. Box 65084
Washington, DC 20035

(202)467-5830; fax: (202)467-5831; E-mail: galachorus@aol.com

An alliance of over a hundred men's, women's, and mixed choruses in the United States, Canada, and Europe.

Lesbian Herstory Archives
P.O. Box 1258
New York, NY 10116
(718)768-3953; fax: (718)768-4663

Founded in 1973, this is a fabulous collection of lesbian memorabilia through the ages. Available for research or browsing by appointment.

BOOKS/PAMPHLETS

Berube, Alan. *Coming Out under Fire: The History of Gay Men and Women in World War II.* New York: Free Press, 1990.

Drawing on extensive interviews with veterans, wartime letters, and declassified governemnt documents, this book provides a new perspective on military history. Powerful, sensitive, and memorable.

Community United Against Violence (CUAV). *Lesbian/Gay Speakers Bureau Training Manual.* San Francisco: CUAV, 1993. CUAV, 973 Market St. #500, San Francisco, CA 94103, (415)777-5500; fax: (415)777-5565.

Very useful. Includes information on what you need to know to be a speaker, how to deal with hostile audience participants, typically asked questions, sample evaluation, and other forms.

Cowan, Thomas. *Gay Men and Women Who Enriched the World.* Boston: Alyson Publications, 1992.

Forty easy-to-read biographies of people from a variety of fields.

DeCrescenzo, Teresa, ed. *Helping Gay and Lesbian Youth: New Policies, New Programs, New Practice.* Binghamton, NY: Haworth Press, 1994.

A collection of essays by practitioners. Especially informative about community-based programs.

Deitcher, David, ed. *The Question of Equality: Lesbian and Gay Politics in America Since Stonewall.* New York: Scribner, 1995.

Very readable, with great photos. Inclusive of women and people of color. Companion piece to PBS documentary of the same name.

Duberman, Martin, ed. *Lives of Notable Gay Men and Lesbians.* New York: Chelsea House Publishers, starting in 1994.

A few books a year are being published in this series of informative and readable biographies, including works about James Baldwin and Martina Navratilova.

Duberman, Martin. *Stonewall.* New York: Penguin, 1993.

Highly readable account of the life stories of six diverse lesbian and gay men who were politically active in the Stonewall era.

Grahn, Judy. *Another Mother Tongue.* Boston: Beacon Press, 1990.

A beautiful blending of history and autobiography that reveals and celebrates gay culture. Fascinating, funny, and intelligent.

Hall, Marny. *The Lavender Couch: A Consumer's Guide to Psychotherapy for Lesbians and Gay Men.* Boston: Alyson Publications, 1985.

Helps you evaluate and choose a therapist.

Herdt, Gilbert, ed. *Gay and Lesbian Youth.* New York: Harrington Park Press, 1989.

An academic book that includes studies exploring adolescent homosexuality around the world.

Herdt, Gilbert, and Andrew Boxer, eds. *Children of Horizons: How Gay and Lesbian Teens Are Leading a New Way Out of the Closet.* Boston: Beacon Press, 1993.

A scholarly work of passion and conviction. It follows a diverse group of lesbian and gay youth through their coming out process.

Parents, Families, and Friends of Lesbians and Gays. *Be Yourself: Questions and Answers for Gay, Lesbian, and Bisexual Youth.* Washington, DC: PFLAG, 1994.

This excellent, easy-to-read 22-page booklet should be prominently displayed in every place that any youth receive services!

Remafedi, Gary, ed. *Death by Denial: Studies of Suicide in Gay and Lesbian Teenagers.* Boston: Alyson Publications, 1994.

This research collection includes the 1989 federal study and others documenting the difficulties faced by teenagers who are coming out.

VIDEO

From a Secret Place. Karin Heller and Bill Domonkos. 1994. Fanlight Productions, 47 Halifax St., Boston, MA 02130, (617)524-0980

Six gay and lesbian young people and three supportive parents are interviewed, with on-going commentary from a psychotherapist. Good tool for sensitizing counselors and other adults. 40 minutes.

◇   ◇   ◇

state-by-state resources[1]

There are *many* more resources than we have space to list. We trust this sample will get you started.

ALABAMA

PFLAG Auburn – 230 East Samford, Apt. 107, Auburn, AL 36830, (334) 317-2509

PFLAG Mobile – 957 Church Street, Mobile, AL 36604, (334)438-9381

ALASKA

PFLAG Fairbanks – P.O. Box 72376, Fairbanks, AK 99707, (907) 457-FLAG

PFLAG Southcentral Alaska – P. O. Box 203231, Anchorage, AK 99520-3231, (907)562-4992 or (907)562-7161

ARIZONA

Gay & Lesbian Tucson Community Center – 422 North 4th Avenue, Tucson, AZ 85705, (520)624-1779

PFLAG Valley of the Sun – P. O. Box 37525, Phoenix, AZ 85069, (602)843-1404

ARKANSAS

PFLAG Little Rock – PO Box 251191, Little Rock, AR 72225, (501)663-5233

PFLAG Northwest Arkansas – P. O. Box 2897, Fayetteville, AR 72702, (501)756-8444

CALIFORNIA

Billy DeFrank Lesbian & Gay Community Center – 175 Stockton Avenue, San Jose, CA 95126-2760, (408)293-4525

Gay Youth Alliance/San Diego – P. O. Box 83022, San Diego, CA 92138-3022, (619)233-9309

[1]Resource information was provided by !OutProud!, the National Coalition for Gay, Lesbian and Bisexual Youth, publishers of QueerAmerica™, the national database of lesbigay resources.

© Copyright 1995 !OutProud! Reprinted with permission. Although !OutProud! attempts to verify all information, it is subject to change and !OutProud! makes no claim to accuracy nor accepts any liability for incorrect information.

PFLAG San Francisco – P. O. Box 640223, San Francisco, CA 94164-0223, (415)921-8850

COLORADO

Aspen Gay and Lesbian Community – P. O. Box 3143, Aspen, CO 81612-3143, (970)925-9249

PFLAG Boulder – P. O. Box 19696, Boulder, CO 80308-2696, (303)444-8164

PFLAG Denver – P. O. Box 18901, Denver, CO 80218-0901, (303)333-0286

CONNECTICUT

Bisexual Gay Lesbian Active Dialogue for Youth (BGLAD4YOUTH) – c/o AIDS Project New Haven, P. O. Box 636, New Haven, CT 06503, (203)624-0114

Gay, Lesbian & Bisexual Community Center – 1841 Broad Street, Hartford, CT 06114-1780, (860)724-5542

PFLAG Norwich Area – Norwich, CT 06365-8604, (203)886-6784

DELAWARE

PFLAG of Northern Delaware – P. O. Box 26049, Wilmington, DE 19899, (302)654-2995

DISTRICT OF COLUMBIA

PFLAG Washington DC Metro Area – P. O. Box 28009, Washington, DC 20038, (301)439-FLAG

FLORIDA

Lesbian, Gay & Bisexual Community Center - 1335 Alton Road, Miami Beach, FL 33139-3811, (305)531-3666

PFLAG Jacksonville – 3820 La Vista Circle #116, Jacksonville, FL 32217-4316, (904)737-3329

True Expressions – 6085 Park Blvd., Pinellas Park, FL 34665, (813)344-6555

GEORGIA

Atlanta Gay and Lesbian Community Center – 63 Twelfth Street, Atlanta, GA 30309, (404)876-5372

Atlanta Lambda Community Center – P. O. Box 15180, Atlanta, GA 30333, (770)662-9010

PFLAG Atlanta, Inc. – P. O. Box 8482, Atlanta, GA 31106-0482, (404)875-9440

HAWAII

Gay & Lesbian Community Services Center – 1820 University Avenue, 2nd Floor, Honolulu, HI 96822, (808)951-7000

Lesbian, Gay, Bisexual and Transexual Teen Support Group – Wailuku, HI, (808)575-2681

PFLAG Kailua-Kona – 74–5615 Luhia Street, D–2, Kailua-Kona, HI 96740, (808)329-1116

IDAHO

PFLAG Eastern Idaho – P. O. Box 50191, Idaho Falls, ID 83405-0191, (208)522-3228

PFLAG Twin Falls – 1434 Pole Line Road East, Twin Falls, ID 83301, (208)733-2578

The Bisexual, Gay and Lesbian Community Center – P. O. Box 323, Boise, ID 83701, (208)336-3870

ILLINOIS

Gay and Lesbian Youth Education/Supp. o.rt Group (GALES) – Urbana, IL, (217)328-6068

Oak Park Lesbian & Gay Association (OPLGA) – P. O. Box 0784, Oak Park, IL 60303, (708)848-0273

PFLAG of Southern Illinois – 505 Orchard Drive, Carbondale, IL 62901, (618)457-5479

INDIANA

IYG (Youth Group)-Evansville – P. O. Box 2901, Evansville, IN 47728, (812)474-5870

PFLAG South Bend – P. O. Box 4195, South Bend, IN 46634, (219)277-2684

PFLAG Terre Haute – 135 Aikman Place, Terre Haute, IN 47803, (812)232-5188

IOWA

Gay and Lesbian Resource Center of Cedar Rapids – P. O. Box 1643, Cedar Rapids, IA 52406-1643, (319)366-2055

Gay & Lesbian Resource Center Youth Group – 522 11th Street, Des Moines, IA 50309, (515)281-0634

PFLAG Waterloo – 317 Hartman Avenue, Waterloo, IA 50701, (319)234-6531

KANSAS

PFLAG Hays – 2910 Country Lane, Hays, KS 67601-1710, (913)625-6937

PFLAG Lawrence-Topeka – P. O. Box 1284, Lawrence, KS 66044-8284, (913)842-0225

PFLAG Wichita – P. O. Box 686, Wichita, KS 67201-0686, (316)687-3524

KENTUCKY

Louisville Youth Group – P. O. Box 4664, Louisville, KY 40204, (502)894-9787

PFLAG Lexington – P. O. Box 55484, Lexington, KY 40555-5484, (606)272-7075

PFLAG Paducah – 2942 Clay Street, Paducah, KY 42001-4133, (502)442-7972

LOUISIANA

Lesbian & Gay Community Center of New Orleans – 816 North Rampart Street, New Orleans, LA 70116, (504)522-1103

PFLAG Lafayette – P. O. Box 31078, Lafayette, LA 70593, (318)984-2216

PFLAG New Orleans – P. O. Box 15515, New Orleans, LA 70175, (504)895-3936

MAINE

Outright (Portland) – P. O. Box 5077, Portland, ME 04101, (207)774-HELP

PFLAG Augusta – 23 Winthrop Street, Hallowell, ME 04347, (207)623-2349

MARYLAND

Frostburg Gay, Lesbian & Bisexual Students – 32 Mill Street, Suite 3, Frostburg, MD 21532, (301)689-0362

Gay & Lesbian Community Center of Baltimore – 241 West Chase Street, Baltimore, MD 21201, (410)837-5445

PFLAG of Maryland's Eastern Shore – P. O. Box 171, Stevensville, MD 21666, (410)643-3235

MASSACHUSETTS

Gay, Lesbian And Straight Society (GLASS) – FCAC Youth Program, 86 Washington Street, Greenfield, MA 01060, (413)774-7028

PFLAG Williamstown/Berkshire – 29 Stringer Avenue, Lee, MA 01238-9569, (413)243-2382

Supporters of Worcester Area Gay and Lesbian Youth – P. O. Box 592, Westside Station, Worcester, MA 01602, (508)755-0005

MICHIGAN

Kalamazoo Gay & Lesbian Resource Center – P. O. Box 51532, Kalamazoo, MI 49005-1532, (616)345-7878

Michigan Alliance for Lesbian and Gay Youth Services (MALGYS) – 617 North Jenison, Lansing, MI 48915, (517)484-0946

PFLAG Traverse City Area – P. O Box 1705, Acme, MI 49610, (616)271-5045

MINNESOTA

Minnesota Gay, Lesbian, Bisexual Transgender Educational Fund – P. O. Box 7275, Minneapolis, MN 55403, (612)220-4888

PFLAG Alexandria – 12556 East Lake Miltona Dr. NE, Miltona, MN 56354, (218)943-1431

Rochester Gay and Lesbian Youth Services – P. O. Box 91, Rochester, MN 55903, (507) 289-6329

MISSISSIPPI

PFLAG Walls – Walls, Ms., (601) 781-2295

PFLAG Jackson – Jackson, MS 39211, (601)956-4953

MISSOURI

Growing American Youth (G.A.Y.) – c/o Our World Too, Inc., 11 South Vandeventer, St. Louis, MO 63108, (314)533-5322

PFLAG Kansas City – P. O. Box 414101, Kansas City, MO 64141-4101, (816)765-9818

St. Louis Gay & Lesbian Community Center – P. O. Box 4589, St. Louis, MO 63108, (314)997-9897

MONTANA

PFLAG Montana – 38 Sloway West, St. Regis, MT 59866 – 406-822-3352

PRIDE – P. O. Box 4815, Butte, MT 59702-4815, (406)723-3339

NEBRASKA

Gay and Lesbian Youth Talkline – 726 ½ S. 18th St., Lincoln, NE 68508, (402)473-7932.

PFLAG Holdrege/Kearney – 1320 8th Avenue, Holdrege, NE 68949, (308)995-5490

Support Group for Lesbigay Youth – c/o Omaha PFLAG Chapter, 2912 Lynwood Drive, Omaha, NE 68123-1957, (402)291-6781

NEVADA

Gay & Lesbian Community Center of Las Vegas – P. O. Box 70481, Las Vegas, NV 89170, (702)733-9800

Gay Youth Outreach Program – University of Nevada (Reno), Mailstop 058, Reno, NV 89557, (702)784-1944

PFLAG Las Vegas – P. O. Box 20145, Las Vegas, NV 89112-0145, (702)438-7838

NEW HAMPSHIRE

PFLAG Concord – P. O. Box 386, Manchester, NH 03105, (603)472-4944

PFLAG in the Upper Valley of Vermont & New Hampshire – P. O. Box 981, Lebanon, NH 03766, (603)448-1982

Seacoast Outright – P. O. Box 842, Portsmouth, NH 03802, (603)431-1013

NEW JERSEY

Gay and Lesbian Youth in New Jersey (GALY-NJ) – P. O. Box 137, Convent Station, NJ 07961-0137, (201)285-1595

PFLAG Bergen County – P. O. Box 1330, Ridgewood, NJ 07450, (201)652-2287

PFLAG Mays Landing – 103 Dover Avenue, Mays Landing, NJ 08330, (609)653-6337

NEW MEXICO

PFLAG Albuquerque – 1907 Buena Vista SE #75, Albuquerque, NM 87106-4178, (505)842-5281

PFLAG Santa Fe – P. O. Box 16498, Santa Fe, NM 87506, (505)988-9708

PFLAG Taos – P. O. Box 3550, Taos, NM 87571, (505)758-8133

NEW YORK

Bisexual, Gay and Lesbian Youth of New York (BiGLYNY) – Lesbian and Gay Community Services Center, 208 West 13th Street, New York, NY 10011-7799, (212)620-7310

Capital District Gay and Lesbian Community Center – P. O. Box 131, Albany, NY 12201-0131, (518)462-6138

PFLAG Buffalo/Niagara Area – P. O. Box 861, Buffalo, NY 14225, (716)883-0384

NORTH CAROLINA

PFLAG Western North Carolina – P. O. Box 5978, Asheville, NC 28813, (704)277-7815

PFLAG Raleigh/Durham – P. O. Box 10844, Raleigh, NC 27605-0844, (919)380-9325

Time Out Youth – 1431 Armory Drive, Charlotte, NC 28204, (704)537-5050

NORTH DAKOTA

PFLAG Central Dakota – P. O. Box 2491, Bismarck, ND 58502-2491, (701)223-7773

PFLAG Fargo/Moorhead – P. O. Box 10625, Fargo, ND 58106, (701)235-SEEK

PFLAG Grand Forks – 3210 Cherry, #24, Grand Forks, ND 58201, (701)775-4447

OHIO

Greater Cincinnati Gay/Lesbian Center – P. O. Box 19158, Cincinnati, OH 45219, (513)651-0040

PFLAG Columbus – P. O. Box 340101, Columbus, OH 43234, (614)227-9355

Youth Rap Group – The Center, 1432 West 29th Street, Cleveland, OH, (216)522-1999

OKLAHOMA

Lesbian, Gay & Bisexual Youth Support Program – Youth Services of Tulsa, 302 South Cheyenne, Tulsa, OK 74103, (918)582-0061

Oasis Community Center – 2135 NW 39th Street, Oklahoma City, OK 73112, (405)525-2437

PFLAG Tulsa – P. O. Box 52800, Tulsa, OK 74152, (918)749-4901

OREGON

PFLAG Portland – P.O. Box 8944, Portland, OR 97207, (503)232-7676

PFLAG Ontario – 450 Bar-O Drive, Ontario, OR 97914, (503)889-5774

Roseburg Gay & Lesbian Community Center – P. O. Box 813, Roseburg, OR 97470-0166, (503)672-4126

PENNSYLVANIA

Bi, Gay, Lesbian Youth Association of Harrisburg (BI-GLYAH) – P. O. Box 872, Harrisburg, PA 17108

Gay & Lesbian Community Center (GLCC) – P. O. Box 5441, Pittsburgh, PA 15206-5441, (412)422-0114

PFLAG Philadelphia – P. O. Box 15711, Philadelphia, PA 19103, (215)572-1833

PUERTO RICO

PFLAG Santurce, Puerto Rico – P. O. Box 116, Calle Loiza 1505, Santurce, PR 00911, (809)726-2888

RHODE ISLAND

PFLAG East Bay Rhode Island – 85 Roseland Terrace, Tiverton, RI 02878, (401)624-6944

PFLAG Narragansett – Narragansett, RI 02882, (401)789-5705

Youth Pride, Inc. – P. O. Box 603017, Providence, RI 02906, (401)421-5626

SOUTH CAROLINA

Gay/Lesbian/Bisexual Youth Circle – 141 South Shandon Street, Suite A, Columbia, SC 29205, (803)771-7713

PFLAG Greenville – 801 Butler Springs Road, Greenville, SC 29615, (803)244-6675

South Carolina Gay and Lesbian Community Center – P. O. Box 12648, Columbia, SC 29211, (803)771-7713

SOUTH DAKOTA

PFLAG Custer – Route 3, Box 94, Custer, SD 57730, (605)673-4182

PFLAG Sioux Falls – 300 North Duluth, Sioux Falls, SD 57104, (605)334-5508

TENNESSEE

Memphis Gay & Lesbian Community Center (MGLCC) – P. O. Box 41074, Memphis, TN 38174-1074, (901)726-5790

One in Teen Youth Services – c/o The Center for Lesbian & Gay Community Services, 703 Berry Road, Nashville, TN 37204-2803, (615)297-0008

PFLAG Greater Chattanooga – P. O. Box 17252, Chattanooga, TN 37415, (423)875-5750

TEXAS

Gay and Lesbian Community Center – P. O. Box 190869, Dallas, TX 75219-0869, (214)528-4233

Houston Area Teenage Coalition of Homosexuals (HATCH) – P. O. Box 667053, Houston, TX 77266-7053, (713)942-7002

PFLAG Austin – P. O. Box 9151, Austin, TX 78766, (512)302-FLAG

UTAH

Cache Valley Gay and Lesbian Youth – 395 West 200 North, Logan, UT

PFLAG Salt Lake City – 3363 Enchanted Hills Drive, Salt Lake City, UT 84121-5465, (801)942-0157

Utah Stonewall Center – 770 South, 300 West, Salt Lake City, UT 84101, (801)539-8800

VERMONT

PFLAG Barre/Montpelier – 15 Vine Street, Northfield, VT 05663, (802)479-9246

PFLAG Brattleboro – 409 Hillwinds, Brattleboro, VT 05301, (802)257-5409

PFLAG Burlington – 23 Birchwood Lane, Burlington, VT 05401, (802)863-4285

VIRGINIA

PFLAG Roanoke and Western VA – 12 Lakeshore Terrace, Hardy, VA 24101-3501, (540)890-3957

Richmond Organization for Sexual Minority Youth (ROSMY) – P. O. Box 5542, Richmond, VA 23220, (804)353-2077

PFLAG Tidewater – 2 Liberty Circle, Newport News, VA 23602, (804)881-9221

WASHINGTON

PFLAG Spokane – P. O. Box 40122, Spokane, WA 99202-0901, (509)489-2266

PFLAG Yakima Valley – 732 Summitview #584, Yakima, WA 98902, (509)576-9625

Stonewall Youth – P. O. Box 7383, Olympia, WA 98507, (360)705-2738

WEST VIRGINIA

PFLAG Parkersburg – 1610 Park Street, Parkersburg, WV 26101, (304)422-5528

PFLAG Wheeling – 115 18th Street, Wheeling, WV 26003, (304)232-8743

PFLAG Huntington – P.O. Box 921, Huntington WV 25712, (304)522-3328

WISCONSIN

PFLAG Galesville/Western Wisconsin – Box 399, Galesville, WI 54630, (608)582-2114

PFLAG Milwaukee – c/o Lutheran Campus Ministries, 3074 North Maryland, Milwaukee, WI 53211, (414)962-9320

Teens Like Us – 512 East Washington, Madison, WI 53703, (608)251-6211

WYOMING

PFLAG Casper – 404 South McKinley Street, Casper, WY 82601-2916, (307)265-6569

PFLAG Jackson – P. O. Box 2704, Jackson, WY 83001, (307)733-0584

canada

ALBERTA

PFLAG Calgary Alberta – 20 Hendon Drive NW, Calgary, AB T2K 1Y5, (403)246-3686, (403)282-6592

PFLAG Edmonton – 51 Beacon Cres., St. Albert, AB, T8N 0A2, (403)462-5958

BRITISH COLUMBIA

PFLAG Oliver BC – P. O. Box 1477, Oliver, BC, V0H 1T0, (604)498-6520

PFLAG Prince George BC – 5635 Moriarty Cresent, Prince George, BC V2N 3P7, (604)964-6753

PFLAG Vancouver British Columbia – P.O. Box 30502 Brentwood Post, 201-4567 Lougheed Hwy, Burnaby, BC, (604)255-4429

MANITOBA

PFLAG Winnipeg Manitoba – 2900 Pembina Hwy, #401, Winnipeg, MB R3T 3Z3, (204)275-0799

NEW BRUNSWICK

PFLAG Sackville New Brunswick – P.O. Box 249, Sackville, NB, E0A 3C0, (506)364-2556

ONTARIO

PFLAG Kingston Ontario – P.O. Box 1751, Kingston, Ontario, K7L 5J6, (613)546-0267

PFLAG North Toronto Ontario – 3266 Yonge Street, P.O. Box 2020, Toronto, Ontario, M4N 3P6, (416)351-1384

PFLAG Toronto-Mississauga-Brampton – 35 Willis Drive, Brampton, Ontario, L6W 1B2, (905)457-4570

QUEBEC

PFLAG Montreal West Quebec – 12 A Radcliffe Road, Montreal West P.Q., PQ H4X 1B9, (514)488-4608

index

LIBRARY OF CONGRESS